"These well-respected authors have given Christian therapists a useful example of how to integrate faith and work in the clinic office. Their model is especially valuable because it reflects an appreciation for the different levels on which human struggles occur and for the need to adapt our interventions accordingly. McMinn and Campbell have produced a good integration of good psychology and good theology."

JAMES R. BECK, PH.D., SENIOR PROFESSOR OF COUNSELING, DENVER SEMINARY

"*Integrative Psychotherapy* is an extraordinary book. Grounded in a thoroughly biblical understanding of the human condition and of God's grace in Christ and calling on his people, McMinn and Campbell critically and thoughtfully mine the cognitive and relational clinical traditions for wisdom to guide psychotherapeutic conceptualization and intervention with hurting people. This work reflects the years of friendship and the differing perspectives of the authors, and shows each to be an outstanding scholar and clinician. This book can deepen the reader's understanding of what is possible through deep integrative reflection, and should serve to enrich the understanding of all about what it means to be a Christian psychotherapist."

STANTON L. JONES, PROVOST AND PROFESSOR OF PSYCHOLOGY, WHEATON COLLEGE

"Christian counselors and psychologists have been talking about integration for years; McMinn and Campbell give us a model for how to do it. *Integrative Psychotherapy* is theologically sound, relationally sensitive and empirically sophisticated. It will prove to be among the most important and widely used books in our discipline."

C. JEFFREY TERREL, PH.D., PRESIDENT, PSYCHOLOGICAL STUDIES INSTITUTE

"This is a most important contribution to the literature on the integration of Christianity and psychology. Such a book could not be more timely!"

RICHARD E. BUTMAN, PH.D., PROFESSOR OF PSYCHOLOGY, WHEATON COLLEGE, AND COAUTHOR OF *MODERN PSYCHOTHERAPIES* AND *MODERN PSYCHOPATHOLOGIES*

"McMinn and Campbell bring over fifty collective years of psychological, psychotherapeutic and Christian experience to bear on Christian psychotherapy. It was worth the wait! Drawing on the best clinical science, *Integrative Psychotherapy* is perhaps the closest to a comprehensive Christian approach that has yet been written. This compassionate psychotherapy will surely become a classic."

EVERETT L. WORTHINGTON JR., AUTHOR OF *FORGIVING AND RECONCILING*

"While everyone talks about integration, McMinn and Campbell actually do it. Their book is easy to read and practical without sacrificing a more nuanced understanding of the complex relationship between Christianity and psychology. *Integrative Psychotherapy* is an example of integration at its finest.

McMinn and Campbell demonstrate how thinking and relating are reflections of God's love for his creation. They incorporate traditional treatments offered by cognitive and interpersonal therapy yet go beyond by emphasizing the redemptive quality of a therapeutic relationship. If you're looking for a model of counseling informed by advances in modern psychology while honoring the rich tradition of the Christian faith—this is it!"

BRANDY LIEBSCHER, PSY.D., ASSISTANT PROFESSOR OF PSYCHOLOGY, SIMPSON UNIVERSITY

"*Integrative Psychotherapy* by McMinn and Campbell is a substantial work that integrates behavioral, cognitive and interpersonal models of therapy within a Christian theological framework. While I do not agree with some of its conclusions (e.g., not integrating spiritual direction with integrative psychotherapy), I highly recommend it as essential reading."

SIANG-YANG TAN, PH.D., PROFESSOR OF PSYCHOLOGY, FULLER THEOLOGICAL SEMINARY

"Inviting and inspiring, *Integrative Psychotherapy* is a must-read for thoughtful Christian therapists. McMinn and Campbell offer a theoretically rich and theologically grounded model. It reflects the combined wisdom of their decades of listening to real people, digesting psychological science, studying theology and living out the Christian faith. Rich in theory and practice, this book will positively and powerfully reshape our approach to integrative psychotherapy."

CHARLOTTE vanOYEN WITVLIET, PH.D., ASSOCIATE PROFESSOR OF PSYCHOLOGY, HOPE COLLEGE

"As a professional association, CAPS has spent over fifty years deeply invested in seeing the highest quality work in the field of integration brought to light. Not only do McMinn and Campbell integrate Christian faith and spirituality with the latest thinking in behavioral science at a theoretical level, they also integrate the theoretical and academic with the pastoral and clinical. The publication of *Integrative Psychotherapy* as the lead volume in partnership with IVP demonstrates our mutual commitment to producing leading-edge integration work that advances theory and application to a broad intellectual audience."

PAUL S. REGAN, EXECUTIVE DIRECTOR, CHRISTIAN ASSOCIATION FOR PSYCHOLOGICAL STUDIES, INC.

Integrative Psychotherapy

TOWARD A COMPREHENSIVE

CHRISTIAN APPROACH

Mark R. McMinn
and Clark D. Campbell

IVP Academic

An imprint of InterVarsity Press
Downers Grove, Illinois

InterVarsity Press
P.O. Box 1400, Downers Grove, IL 60515-1426
World Wide Web: www.ivpress.com
E-mail: email@ivpress.com

InterVarsity Press® is the book-publishing division of InterVarsity Christian Fellowship/USA®, a student movement active on campus at hundreds of universities, colleges and schools of nursing in the United States of America, and a member movement of the International Fellowship of Evangelical Students. For information about local and regional activities, write Public Relations Dept., InterVarsity Christian Fellowship/USA, 6400 Schroeder Rd., P.O. Box 7895, Madison, WI 53707-7895, or visit the IVCF website at <www.ivcf.org>.

Design: Cindy Kiple
Images: istockphoto.com

ISBN 978-0-8308-2830-2

Printed in Canada ∞

Library of Congress Cataloging-in-Publication Data

McMinn, Mark R.
  Integrative psychotherapy: toward a comprehensive Christian
  approach / Mark R. McMinn and Clark D. Campbell.
      p. ; cm.
  Includes bibliographical references and index.
  ISBN 978-0-8308-2830-2 (cloth (casebound) : alk. paper)
  1. Psychotherapy—Religious aspects—Christianity. 2. Eclectic
  psychotherapy. I. Campbell, Clark D., 1956- II. Title.
  [DNLM: 1. Psychotherapy—methods. 2. Christianity. 3. Religion
  and Psychology. WM 420 M4795i 2007] RC489.S676M46 2007
  616.89'14—dc22

                                                                    2006101567

P	18	17	16	15	14	13	12	11	10	9	8	7	6	5	4	3	2	1
Y	21	20	19	18	17	16	15	14	13	12	11	10	09	08	07			

To our doctoral students—

> *courageous women and men*
>
> *who make enormous sacrifices*
>
> *to become Christian psychologists.*

And to Lisa and Donell, always.

Contents

Acknowledgments

THE JOURNEY OF LIFE HAS TWISTS AND TURNS, some of which are reflected in our friendship and in this book. Our paths first crossed when our young families settled in a small, rural community in northwest Oregon. We both taught on the faculty at George Fox College and worked in the clinical practice Clark established—Valley Psychological Associates (at the time, we were the only psychologists in Yamhill County). Collegiality grew into a warm and secure friendship that is now entering its third decade. At some point Mark left for a thirteen-year stint at Wheaton College in Illinois, but will be returning to Oregon shortly before this book appears in print. George Fox College is now George Fox University, Valley Psychological Associates is now a thriving practice involving many psychologists, and the small rural community of Newberg is feeling more and more like a suburb of Portland. Our friendship has stood the tests of time and change.

Our colleagues have helped shape our thinking about integration and psychotherapy. While at Wheaton College, Mark had opportunity to work alongside many gifted scholars and clinicians: Stanton Jones, Richard Butman, Robert Gregory, Francis White, Robert Roberts, Barrett McRay, James Wilhoit, Katheryn Meek, Amy Dominguez, Helen DeVries, Natalia Yangarber-Hicks, Michael Mangis, Elizabeth Hillstrom, Robert Vautin, Joan Laidig Brady, J. Derek McNeil, Sally Schwer Canning, Terri Watson, Robert Watson, Carlos Pozzi, Donald Preussler, Cynthia Neal Kimball, Kelly Flanagan, Trey Buchanan, William Struthers, Darlene Hannah, John Vessey, Raymond Phinney, James Rogers and others. Clark has benefited from numerous interactions with his colleagues as well: Wayne Adams, Rodger Bufford, Nancy Thurston, Mary Peterson, Kathleen Gathercoal, Bob Buckler, Brad Johnson, Carol Dell Oliver, Katherine Ecklund, Leo Marmol, Sally Hopkins, Jim Foster and Claire Russunen to name a few.

This book is an effort to bring psychology and Christian doctrine together into a coherent psychotherapy model. Such an endeavor is only possible because of the role that biblical scholars and theologians have played in our lives. Though we do not wish to implicate any of these individuals in whatever theological blunders may appear in the following pages, we are grateful for the friendship, teaching, writing and tutelage of Timothy Phillips, Walter Elwell, Gary Burge, Dennis Okholm, Paul Anderson, Tim Tsohantaridis, Gerald Wilson, Daniel Treier, Mark Husbands, Larry Shelton, Robert Webber, Carl Laney, Robert Hughes, Ronald Allen and Robert Cook. It is a male-dominated list, which says something disappointing about evangelical theological scholarship as well as the homogeneity of the company we keep. But still, we are grateful for the wisdom and preparation of these fine men. They have helped us think beyond what our psychology training provided.

Ask a college educator what the best thing about his or her work is, and you will probably hear something about students. It is an incredible honor and privilege to work with tomorrow's leaders. Many of our students have read drafts of this book in various stages and offered both words of encouragement and suggestions for improvement. We are grateful for them and their ideas.

We have met with many psychotherapy clients over the past twenty-five years—enough to fill numerous file cabinets with aging clinical records. Many of these clients have been people with remarkable courage, wisdom, insight, resilience and tenacity. Whatever useful clinical advice is found in this book is due in large part to what we have learned from the people we have been privileged to serve in our role as clinical psychologists.

Like us, the Christian Association for Psychological Studies (CAPS) is about to turn fifty years old. Paul Regan, executive director of CAPS, and Jeffrey Terrell, current chair of the board, have encouraged us with their friendship and willingness to pursue a marketing partnership between CAPS and InterVarsity Press (IVP). CAPS is a steady organization—more solid than flashy, and more rooted than faddish. We commend the organization to those involved in psychology and Christianity as a good professional home. It is a privilege and honor to lead off the IVP/CAPS book series with this book.

IVP Academic has its reputation as an excellent evangelical press for good reason. We found out through back channels that our editor, Gary Deddo, has a Ph.D. in systematic theology. At first that was a bit daunting, but we learned quickly that Gary balances his knowledge with patience and kindness. He has been a joy to work with. Jeff Crosby, Mark's good friend and director of marketing at IVP, has been both a personal encourager and a major reason that the IVP/CAPS book series has come to fruition. It is hard to understand how someone who gets three hundred e-mails a day, as Jeff does, can respond so promptly to our questions, which have been plentiful. We are also grateful for the two anonymous reviewers who read an early draft of this manuscript and made helpful recommendations.

Finally, our friends and families have been a tremendous source of satisfaction and support for us. We are two blessed men, grateful every day for the relationships God has brought into our lives. Mark is enlivened and supported by Lisa, his wife of twenty-eight years and an author in her own right (most recently, *The Contented Soul,* InterVarsity Press, 2006). Their grown children—Rae, Sarah and Megan—are a great joy. Over the years Clark has benefited from discussing several integrative ideas with his brother, Mark, who is a chaplain in the Air Force. He also appreciates the prayer group that has supported him through this project—Joe and Jamie O'Halloran, Steve and Glenda Gilroy, Tom and Dorie Byrd, and Hugh and Sue Anderson. Clark is encouraged, challenged and stretched by the love of his life, Donell. She has been a true partner in their journey of married life for twenty-eight years. Their children—Erin, Bryce and Alex—have enriched their lives and are further evidence of God's blessing.

Introduction

GOOD COUNSELORS LISTEN MORE THAN THEY SPEAK. Believing writers should do the same, we have been listening for many years, trying to understand the opportunities and challenges of an integrative approach to psychotherapy.

We have listened to our colleagues. An ambitious book such as this may have two author names on the front cover, but it reflects the wisdom and work of numerous others who have taught, mentored, encouraged, critiqued and inspired us over the years. The contemporary movement to integrate psychology and Christianity has been championed by various godly men and women; we have been influenced by them and are privileged to call many our friends. Scholars have been doing important integration work over the past several decades, credible graduate programs have been developed, thoughtful Christian clinicians provide therapy that is sensitive to both psychology and faith, church communities have been helped by psychological principles, useful books have been written and scientific journals established, and the Christian Association for Psychological Studies has grown in depth and number. Indeed, psychology as a discipline has done well in considering integration, perhaps better than other academic disciplines. It is upon this foundation—formed by the insights and hard work of many dedicated scholars, clinicians, pastors, authors and educators—that we have developed *Integrative Psychotherapy*.

We have listened to our students. The integration of psychology and Christianity has become an important force in higher education—Christian colleges educate undergraduates in models of integration and theories of personality, most seminaries offer counseling courses and degree programs, countless masters programs offer degrees in Christian counseling or psychology, and various integration-based doctoral programs prepare students to become licensed psychologists. Students often make enormous sacrifices to study integration. They come to their training with a passion to learn an integrative approach to psychotherapy—one built on a Christian worldview—and too often they are offered only a variety of psychological models derived from nonreligious worldviews, a smattering of theology courses, and a charge to go out into the world and do good integration with what we have taught them. It need not surprise us that most students do very little integrative work after graduating. They have learned important information about psychology and Christianity, but they have not been taught what they came to study: the integration of psychology and Christianity as it relates to counseling and psychotherapy.

We have listened to pastors and others committed to church ministries. From storefront churches in crowded urban areas to sprawling suburban megachurch campuses to rural community chapels, pastors and church leaders face the same challenge of finding help for hurting parishioners. Everywhere Christian leaders are asking the same question: "Who can I trust to help care for the souls in my congregation?" Too often the Christian psychologist or Christian counselor across town turns out to be untrustworthy—a wolf in sheep's clothing, someone who has bought into a nonreligious psychological worldview and yet attempts to build a practice by soliciting referrals from pastors. Perhaps the problem is not malice on the part of the therapists; often these are graduates of our integration-based graduate programs and seminaries just doing what they have been trained to do.

We have listened to our clients. People in pain take enormous risks to overcome inhibitions and admit their problems to a stranger. Some potential clients may still let their fingers do the walking through the Yellow Pages, or their mouse do the clicking through superpages.com, but most clients choose more carefully. They talk to a friend, a pastor, a physician, asking particular questions so they can find a trustworthy helper in a time of need: "I'm looking for a good counselor—do you know of any?" Often they add a coda, "It needs to be a Christian," because the general public is more attuned to religious matters than the psychological community (Shafranske, 1996). When clients come for help they are sometimes surprised by how little faith is considered in therapy, even by therapists who promote themselves as Christian therapists.

We have listened to our critics. Biblical counselors argue that integrationists do not take Scripture and Christian doctrine seriously enough. Most of us in the integration movement respond by calling biblical counselors naive and uninformed, and sadly, we often do it without even reading their books or articles or developing relationships with biblical counselors. One might question who is really naive and uninformed under these circumstances. We Christian psychologists have too often maligned these critics without hearing their arguments, and so we have forgone the possibility of transformation and growth.

We have both spent many years in church-related service, clinical practice, reading and studying psychology and theology, and teaching doctoral students in clinical psychology. *Integrative Psychotherapy* represents our effort to articulate a model of psychotherapy that is faithful to both Christianity and psychology. It took almost three years to write, and the ideas behind it took almost three decades of listening, study and experience to develop.

An Integrative Model

Integration is a controversial notion. Some prefer to reject psychology altogether and look for a Christian model of helping that is completely scriptural. This is an ambitious endeavor, and one that we admire, but it seems to overlook the possibility of finding truth through created order as well as in Scripture. By looking only to Scripture, these counselors foreclose the possibility of learning through contemporary science. As a result, stunning scientific advances in treating many conditions are overlooked in deference to approaches deemed to be more consistent with Scripture (for a fascinating discussion on this, see Jones, 2001, and Powlison, 2001). Others reject integration by minimizing the importance of faith. Indeed, it seems that some come dangerously close to deeming their Christian faith irrelevant as they acculturate into their roles as mental health professionals. Preliminary evidence suggests graduates of Christian doctoral programs are less likely to use spiritual interventions in their clinical work than Christian graduates of secular programs (Sorenson & Hales, 2002). This could be good news—if graduates of Christian programs are more aware of the subtle ways spiritual interventions can be misused with vulnerable clients. But it could also be bad news if graduates of Christian programs are somehow abandoning the spiritual worldview that drew them to graduate school in the first place. Much of today's Christian psychology is imbalanced in its integrative focus (Beck, 2003), failing to draw on both psychology and Christian thought.

Integrative Psychotherapy (IP) is integrative in two dimensions: theologically and theoretically. By theological integration we mean that a Christian psychotherapy must begin with a Christian view of persons. Christianity is the starting point—the fundamental worldview on which a Christian psychotherapy is based. Psychology provides a great deal of help once an adequate Christian foundation is established. By theoretical integration we refer to the general trend in the psychotherapy literature to find value in various theoretical approaches. Rarely does one find a purist cognitive therapist, for example. It is much more common to find a cognitive therapist who also values attachment theory, or a psychodynamic therapist who draws on various cognitive and behavior techniques for initial symptom relief. Integrative models are becoming increasingly popular among professionals as they realize the limitations of any single theory. In IP we integrate behavioral, cognitive and relational models of therapy.

It would be grossly overstated to say that ours is the first integrative understanding of psychotherapy in either of these two dimensions. Many have developed models of theoretical integration (Norcross & Goldfried, 2005). Others have developed models for Christian counseling and psychotherapy, and some with distinction. Counselors and pastors and scholars have developed helpful and innovative approaches to healing prayer and Christian counseling, or offered Christian appraisals of secular models, or provided models of biblical counseling that include occasional insights from psychology. But none of these models has gained prominence in integrative training programs, sometimes because they skim the surface of Christian doctrine—sprinkling Bible verses atop secular theories—or because they overlook advances of contemporary psychological theory and science. IP is unique in that it provides both a theoretical and a theological dimension of integration.

Avoiding Extremes

Whoever wrote that "every road has two ditches" must have lived before modern highway and drainage systems. Updating the adage to "every street has two curbs" would never work. But even in the suburbs and cities, where we have no ditches, the metaphor has lasting value. Much of life involves navigating between the boundaries on the right and the left, avoiding the extremes that render us irrelevant, fanatical or irresponsible. The task of this book—constructing a model of Christian psychotherapy—is, among other things, a task of avoiding two ditches.

At one extreme is the risk of implying that we have developed the only correct model for Christian counseling, psychotherapy and pastoral counseling. Though we believe the approach to therapy presented in this book to be theologically—and psychologically—sound and effective, we have no aspirations of joining the ranks of those who claim to have discovered the *one true approach* to Christian counseling. There is no single system of Christian psychology or psychotherapy and, it seems to us, there never will be. The Bible does not teach a single, unifying theory of personality that accounts for individual differences; that is simply not the purpose of Scripture (Jones & Butman, 1991). And any authority other than Scripture cannot possibly provide a foundation for counseling that will be agreeable to all Christians. History has proven how difficult it is for Christians to agree with one another. A parallel argument can be made on the basis of science: there are many psychotherapeutic paradigms available, but research evidence to date does not support claims of vast superiority for any one approach (Nathan, Stuart & Dolan, 2000). Thus, one of our navigational challenges in crafting this book is to avoid communicating that IP is *the* Christian approach to psychotherapy. It is not. IP is simply *one* approach to psychotherapy, informed by Christian theology and spirituality as well as contemporary psychology.

We have already mentioned the other extreme—one that ultimately disappoints our students, churches, clients and critics. Some Christian therapists and biblical counselors seem content to abandon the possibility of a truly integrative psychotherapy. They may wonder how such a task could ever be accomplished when there are so many incompatible theories and ideas swirling about us in both the realms of psychology and Christian thought. They become segregationists rather than integrationists.

We have tried to avoid these two extremes—the one that tickles our grandiosity by suggesting we are unveiling the long-awaited answer to how all Christians should do psychotherapy, and the one that segregates faith from psychology—and in the midst of these extremes to construct a responsible and helpful approach to psychotherapy. This, of course, is no easy task. We advocate IP because it is built on two foundations we value: Christian faith and science. Christian doctrine provides the ideological structure for IP while the methods of psychotherapy, with their weighty scientific support, provide a means for identifying and modifying emotions, cognitions, behaviors and relational patterns.

Responding to the Challenge

Adages abound, so we conclude this introduction by plundering two more for our purposes. The first likens a good book to a good friend. If so, *Modern Psychotherapies: A Comprehensive Christian Appraisal* (Jones & Butman, 1991) has become a good friend to many Christian psychologists and their students. Stanton L. Jones and Richard E. Butman provide an incisive Christian evaluation of the contemporary psychotherapies. Near the beginning of their book they describe two stages of constructive integration. The first, accomplished admirably with their volume, is critical appraisal—looking intently at various psychotherapies from a Christian vantage point. The second is to build a new theory of psychotherapy based on a Christian foundation. The authors issue a challenge of sorts:

> We anticipate that a thoughtful reader will find this book inadequate, in that we will end with finding none of the approaches adequate for understanding human nature, while pointing out many benefits of most of the approaches. We challenge such a thoughtful reader to join in the dialog of developing the comprehensive Christian approach that we all so need! (p. 23)

Here is where the second adage comes to mind: it is about fools rushing in where angels (and other wise creatures) fear to tread. Our combined forty-five years of teaching psychology and fifty years of clinical practice have either rendered us fools or given us enough confidence to enter the dialogue that Jones and Butman suggest, or perhaps it is some of both. This book is an effort to articulate a Christian psychotherapy—one that takes both Christianity and psychology seriously, and that helps to serve hurting people through the ministries of Christian counselors, psychologists, social workers and pastors.

The first four chapters establish a theoretical frame for IP. Chapter one provides an overview of Christian doctrine, viewed from an evangelical Protestant perspective, with special attention given to three theological views of what it means to be made in the image of God *(imago Dei)*. These three views of the *imago Dei* correspond with the three domains of IP: functional, structural and relational. Chapter two gives an overview of scientific findings regarding psychotherapy. This chapter will humble theoretical purists because it demonstrates that no single therapeutic approach can claim vast superiority over any other. The so-called cognitive revolution is described in chapter three, along with an overview and Christian critique of cognitive therapy—an important task because the first two domains of IP are closely related to contemporary cognitive therapy. Chapter four is where we provide a theoretical overview of IP, drawing on the doctrinal, scientific and theoretical perspectives developed in the first three chapters.

Once a theoretical foundation is established, we consider the practice of IP in the next seven chapters. Chapter five is a brief survey of assessment and case conceptualization. Chapters six and seven describe symptom-focused interventions, known as the functional domain. We pay special attention to treating anxiety disorders because they are well suited for functional-domain interventions. The structural, or schema-focused, domain of IP is the focus of chapters eight and nine. We discuss the treatment of depression in the context of describing schema-focused interventions. In chapters ten and eleven, we look at the relational domain of IP, concentrating on the importance of the therapeutic relationship in promoting change. Although relationship-focused interventions have many applications, we devote special attention to the treatment of personality disorders.

The final chapter summarizes and reiterates the integrative focus that we emphasize throughout the book while identifying various challenges and limitations to our integrative approach to psychotherapy. We intend this book to reflect both ambition and modesty, so we propose an integrative model of psychotherapy with confidence and hopefulness even as we acknowledge that there is more work to do.

References

Beck, J. R. (2003). The integration of psychology and theology: An enterprise out of balance. *Journal of Psychology & Christianity, 22,* 20-29.

Jones, S. L. (2001). An apologetic apologia for the integration of psychology and theology. In M. R. McMinn & T. R. Phillips (Eds.), *Care for the soul: Exploring the intersection of psychology and theology* (pp. 62-77). Downers Grove, IL: InterVarsity Press.

Jones, S. L., & Butman, R. E. (1991). *Modern psychotherapies: A comprehensive Christian appraisal.* Downers Grove, IL: InterVarsity Press.

Nathan, P. E., Stuart, S. P., & Dolan, S. L. (2000). Research on psychotherapy efficacy and effectiveness: Between Scylla and Charybdis? *Psychological Bulletin, 126,* 964-81.

Norcross, J. C., & Goldfried, M. R. (2005). *Handbook of psychotherapy integration* (2nd ed.). New York: Oxford University Press.

Powlison, D. (2001). Questions at the crossroads: The care of souls and modern psychotherapies. In M. R. McMinn & T. R. Phillips (Eds.), *Care for the soul: Exploring the intersection of psychology & theology* (pp. 23-61). Downers Grove, IL: InterVarsity Press.

Shafranske, E. P. (1996). Religious beliefs, affiliations, and practices of clinical psychologists. In E. P. Shafranske (Ed.), *Religion and the clinical practice of psychology* (pp. 149-62). Washington, DC: American Psychological Association.

Sorenson, R. L., & Hales, S. (2002). Comparing evangelical Protestant psychologists trained at secular versus religiously affiliated programs. *Psychotherapy: Theory, Research, Practice, Training, 39,* 163-70.

1

Christian Foundations

PSYCHOLOGY AND COUNSELING HAVE ATTRACTED ENORMOUS attention in recent decades. Graduate programs in psychology and counseling have proliferated, both in mainstream universities and in distinctively Christian settings. In 1973 the American Psychological Association (APA) accredited 118 doctoral programs; by 2001 the number swelled to 346 programs (Peterson, 2003). Today's membership in the APA is approximately one thousand times greater than its membership in the early twentieth century. Both the APA and the National Association of Social Workers now have more than 100,000 members, and the American Counseling Association's membership exceeds 50,000. Numerous books authored by psychologists and counselors have caught the public's attention, psychologists' opinions ride radio and television waves into our living rooms, and we can even purchase Freudian slippers on the Internet to keep our feet warm at night.

Of course these changes have affected Christianity. Many churches have psychological counseling centers or extensive referral networks of mental health professionals in the community. Models of pastoral care have changed dramatically; most seminaries now teach courses in pastoral care that are heavily steeped in psychological theories and practices. Teaching within the church has been affected too—we hear more about personal stories, emotions, developmental processes and childhood experiences than in the past. Lay counseling ministries and support groups are being established in many churches, and small groups do more than study the Bible these days. Some have lamented psychology's influence on the church (Bulkley, 1994) while others have embraced it cautiously (Collins, 1988; McMinn & Dominguez, 2005).

At least to some small degree, Christianity has also influenced psychology. There are now seven doctoral programs in clinical psychology at distinctively Christian institutions, most of them accredited by the APA. The APA has published various books on spirituality in recent years, many of them with chapters by Christian psychologists (Miller, 1999; Miller & Delaney, 2005; Richards & Bergin, 2000, 2004, 2005; Shafranske, 1996; Sperry & Shafranske, 2005), and the APA has even published a psychotherapy video demonstrating the Christian approach to psychotherapy that we describe in this book (McMinn, 2006). Religion is now considered an important form of diversity within APA, and a number of committed Christian psychologists have served in key leadership roles in the APA's Psychology of Religion division and in related organizations, such as the National Council of Schools and Programs of Professional Psychology (NCSPP).

With all the interplay between psychology and religion, it seems regrettable that prevailing personality and counseling theories have not been influenced much by the Christian faith. Ask a new Christian psychologist about his or her theoretical orientation, and you will probably hear something about cognitive-behavioral therapy, object-relations theory or family systems, and it is likely that these theoretical viewpoints will be quite pristine—relatively untouched by the influence of Christian doctrine.

Some have responded by developing distinctly Christian alternatives to counseling. We respect these alternatives, but they can easily move to the other extreme—relying so heavily on Christian resources for counseling that they overlook the scientific and theoretical advances of contemporary psychology.

We write this book on integrative psychotherapy because we believe it is possible to provide therapy that is informed by *both* Christian theology and psychological science. Rather than viewing these two realms of knowledge as competitors, we begin with the assumption that both have important perspectives to offer.

Integration as Reciprocal Interaction

Though the integration of psychology and Christianity has deep historical roots that go back many centuries, contemporary integration began in the mid-1800s in reaction to those trying to extricate psychology from its theological and philosophical roots. By the late 1900s the movement had "coalesced into a distinct psychological and interdisciplinary specialty" (Vande Kemp, 1996, p. 77). Today's proliferation of integrative writings and training programs is truly phenomenal—influencing the academy, the church, and the practice of clinical and counseling psychology.

But not everyone who works in counseling or psychology is interested in doing integration. There are various ways to construe the relationship between faith and psychology, some of them integrative and some not. The litmus test is the extent to which reciprocal interaction is perceived as desirable and possible—what Jones (1994) refers to as a "constructive relationship" between psychology and religion. To what extent should counseling and our view of persons be influenced by both the Christian faith and contemporary psychology? Some believe that faith is enough, that psychology is irrelevant and perhaps dangerous. Others believe that psychology is enough, that faith ought to be left outside the counseling office. Integrationists believe that some sort of reciprocal interaction between faith and psychology is the best way to gain a comprehensive understanding of personality and counseling. This is not to say that psychology carries the same authority as the Christian faith, but that understanding and wisdom can be discovered in both.

By way of analogy, consider the temperature system in an automobile (see figure 1.1). On one end of the continuum is hot air and on the other end is cool air. Often a person selects a temperature in the middle, mixing the hot and cool air for the desired effect. The climate is more desirable and adaptable by combining both sources of air than it could be if only one source of air were available. Though some Christians would be quick to say that psychology is a bunch of hot air, and some scientists would say the same about religion, this is not the point of the analogy. In this analogy we are considering two sources of information: psychology and Christian faith. To what extent do we let the "air" from both systems mix in order to achieve an optimal balance? Or should we trust only one source of information and not the other? Reciprocal interaction involves the assumption that caring for people's souls is best done by bringing together truth from both sources.

Different approaches to soul care can be viewed along the continuum of figure 1.1. At one end of the continuum are those who trust Christian faith exclusively for the care of souls. Many biblical counselors would position themselves near this end of the continuum, and indeed they provide an important corrective

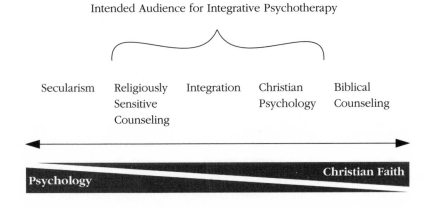

Figure 1.1. Integrative psychotherapy in relation to psychology and Christianity

for those who have embraced the naturalistic worldview assumptions offered by many contemporary psychologists. At the other end of the continuum are the secularists who view religion as unimportant and irrelevant to the psychological services they provide. Though some secularists and biblical counselors may find parts of this book on IP interesting, most will find our desire to mix Christianity and psychology frustrating. It is for the people in the middle of the continuum that we write this book.

Squarely in the middle of figure 1.1 is an integration perspective, which we hold as the most tenable position. Integrationists attempt to find truth from both sources—Christian faith and psychology. Christian psychology is a relatively new movement that views psychology through the lens of historic Christianity (Johnson, 2007). Though advocates of Christian psychology may question our affinity for psychological theory and science, they are likely to find IP interesting and useful in various ways as well. The remaining category in figure 1.1 is religiously sensitive counseling. Many counselors and psychotherapists today are trained primarily in the mainstream theories and methods of counseling, but have become attuned to the religious issues of their clients and want to consider these issues in the process of counseling. Religiously sensitive counselors may find some of our assumptions about Christianity and the authority of Scripture troubling, but will probably find the principles of IP useful in working with Christian clients.

Beginning with a Christian Worldview

An integrative endeavor such as this—constructing a Christian approach to psychotherapy—must have a beginning point. Some integrationists would argue that we should build this model atop two equally authoritative pillars: special revelation and general revelation. (Special revelation is God's truth revealed through Scripture and seen in the life of Jesus, and general revelation is God's truth revealed throughout creation.) After all, we are told, all truth is God's truth. This adage has caused a good deal of mischief and misunderstanding.

Whereas it is undoubtedly true that God ordained all truth that exists—and that truth can be discovered in creation as well as Scripture—it does not necessarily follow that both sources of truth are equally authoritative throughout all of life. General revelation is more authoritative on issues left unaddressed in the Bible. For example, when it comes to constructing microprocessors or treating bacterial pneumonia, general revelation is the place to look. But many issues in life, including matters of great importance, are addressed in the Bible. Here the wise Christian places more confidence in special revelation than general revelation. Thus, when it comes to matters of understanding human nature—motivation, spiritual yearnings, relational needs, repentance, forgiveness and so on—the truths of the Christian faith form the foundation of our understanding. General revelation may also be useful, but should not be deemed an equivalent form of truth because all of creation, including all the data of general revelation, is fallen and is tainted by the effects of sin. Jones and Butman (1991) write: "The claims of Christian truth should fundamentally transform, at a basic and profound level, the ways we conceptualize and understand our human subject matter, as well as our problems, our goals and the processes of change" (p. 403).

As the contemporary integration movement was being established several decades ago, it was not uncommon to read that psychology and theology should both have an equal footing for true integration to occur. If this is meant to say that both fields should be open to the influence of the other then we agree, but if it is meant to be an assertion of equal authority we cannot agree. For responsible Christian psychotherapy to occur, a Christian worldview must provide the foundational bedrock upon which an integrative system is built. There may be great benefit to understanding family systems and psychodynamics and information processing, but none of these will provide the necessary anthropological foundation for a responsible Christian psychology. For matters of understanding the human condition, Christianity—informed by Scripture and responsible theological appraisal—is trump.

An influential article in the psychology literature was titled "In the final analysis, it's the data that count" (Nathan, 1997). Such an assertion is simplistic and potentially misleading. In the final analysis, no data can be viewed apart from underlying presuppositions and worldview assumptions. The final analyses are often not much different than the beginning assumptions because both are founded on particular beliefs about how the world works. If we are to construct a Christian psychotherapy, it behooves us to pay close attention to the beginning assumptions because those presuppositions will have a profound impact on whatever final analyses we may produce.

This first chapter provides a brief overview of a Christian anthropology based on three core Christian themes: creation, fall and redemption. Here we establish a foundation on which we will build our model of integrative psychotherapy. It is no perfunctory task to begin this book with a discussion of Christian doctrine. Indeed, it would be difficult for us to imagine any understanding of human nature or psychology apart from the Christian foundations that we outline here. J. I. Packer (1973) puts it well:

> Knowing about God is crucially important for the living of our lives. As it would
> be cruel to an Amazonian tribesman to fly him to London, put him down without

explanation in Trafalgar Square and leave him, as one who knew nothing of English or England, to fend for himself, so we are cruel to ourselves if we try to live in this world without knowing about the God whose world it is and who runs it. The world becomes a strange, mad, painful place, and life in it a disappointing and unpleasant business, for those who do not know about God. Disregard the study of God, and you sentence yourself to stumble and blunder through life blindfolded, as it were, with no sense of direction and no understanding of what surrounds you. (p. 19)

Creation

Discussions of creation sometimes lead to squabbles about how old the earth is, whether or not the creation occurred in seven literal days, and to what extent creation has adapted to earth's changing environment since the beginning of time. But if we back up a few steps to look at the majesty of material creation, the significance of these questions fades. God, the eternal one, made something from nothing (Sproul, 1992). Notice the grass and sky, crocodiles and cocker spaniels, the wind and the sea, cardinals and cockroaches, the soil and everything produced in the soil. Everything we see, touch, smell, hear and taste exists because of what we read in the Bible's first verse: "God created the heavens and the earth" (Gen 1:1).

Creation has profound implications. It means we are the creatures and God the Creator. We are not offshoots of God's spiritual essence, as pantheists might assert, but finite material creatures crafted by God, on whom we are utterly dependent: "The human person does not exist autonomously or independently, but as a creature of God" (Hoekema, 1986, p. 5). A theology of creation means there is goodness and order around us. We can learn something about God by studying general revelation because everything around us has a sacred beginning: the periodic table, harmonics, art, vision, trigonometry, photosynthesis, food, light and so on. Creation means we reject the gnosticism that has fueled various heresies throughout many centuries. God, a spiritual being, created materiality and called it good. Our bodies and the physical world around us cannot be inherently bad because they were created by One who is purely good. The doctrine of creation also reveals that God is surely glorious. The stunning magnificence of nature, including human nature, reflects God's majesty and splendor: "He is to be the object of worship, praise, and obedience" (Erickson, 1985, p. 378).

Made in God's image. Perhaps the most exceptional thing about creation is the biblical assertion that humans are created in the image of God (or, *imago Dei*). This means that humans reflect something about God that is not revealed in the rest of creation, and that we represent God and are called to be ambassadors of God's interests for the world (Hoekema, 1986). This has profound implications for psychotherapists. Any competent therapist is likely to treat a client as a person of dignity. The therapist will listen to the client's story, validate emotions and genuinely care about the client's losses. We do this because we believe humans have intrinsic dignity and are worthy of respect and care. But why? What gives our clients dignity and makes it important for us to respect them? What makes each of us valuable? In a Christian worldview, the basis for human dignity comes from being created in God's image. Every human being is more than a survivor-of-the-fittest, more than a complex system of neurons evolved through natural selection. Each person is a created one, made in the image of a loving God. And Christian therapists are called a step beyond recognizing God's dignity in other humans; we are to be ambassadors of God's character in our dealings with others.

The image of God has captured the attention of theologians throughout the centuries. Erickson (1985) divides the various views of God's image into three categories: functional, structural and relational views. It is striking to see the parallel between these views of the image of God and major systems within the history of psychology. Psychology also has functional, structural and relational perspectives, and although these terms do not mean exactly the same thing to psychologists as they do to theologians, there is substantial overlap. It seems reasonable that psychologists and theologians—both of whom engage in systematic efforts to understand the human person—have created similar categories.

Functional. Functional views consider God's image as revealed in human behavior, specifically behaviors related to managing creation. We see this in the creation story and again in Psalm 8:

> So God created people in his own image;
>> God patterned them after himself;
>> male and female he created them.
> God blessed them and told them, "Multiply and fill the earth and subdue it. Be masters over the fish and birds and all the animals. (Gen 1:27-28)

> For you made us only a little lower than God,
>> and you crowned us with glory and honor.
> You put us in charge of everything you made,
>> giving us authority over all things—
> the sheep and the cattle
>> and all the wild animals,
> the birds in the sky, the fish in the sea,
>> and everything that swims the ocean currents. (Ps 8:5-8)

IN THE OFFICE 1.1: God's Image and a Stance of Acceptance

If we want to know about being made in God's image, the best place to look is the life of Christ. Jesus is the perfect image of God, revealed in human form (Col 1:15).

In Romans 15:7, the apostle Paul instructs believers to "accept each other just as Christ has accepted you; then God will be glorified." Christ, the flawless image of God, accepts us in the midst of our greatest weaknesses and struggles, and so we are called to accept others in the same spirit of love and compassion.

James: I feel so ashamed. Online gambling has taken over my life, and I couldn't even see it until a few weeks ago when I got an $18,000 Visa bill. And the worst part is that I had kept it a secret from Cheryl. She has always trusted me with our finances, and now she doesn't know what to do. We have hit bottom. We're arguing and crying and struggling every day. I have never felt so empty and broken and lost.

Mark: It sounds like a crisis for both of you; a time of facing painful emotions and some difficult realities.

James: I just can't believe I got involved in this. It started out just being fun—just sort of online recreation. But somehow I kept getting in deeper and deeper, then it wasn't fun any more but I had to keep going to make up for all I had lost. I keep asking myself how this could have happened.

Mark: It's like the person you have been is not the person you truly are.

James: Definitely. I desperately want to change. I need to change. And I want to earn back Cheryl's trust and love. I can't imagine how awful this must be for her.

Mark: Yes, I'm sure this is a huge shock for Cheryl. It must hurt so much to see the pain in her eyes.

James: Oh, that's the worst part of all, to see how deeply I have wounded her.

This is not a time to confront James about his selfishness and impulsiveness; he is already broken by the weight of his transgressions. James needs care and acceptance, someone who will try to understand the depth of his pain. Notice that I can accept and care for James without condoning or excusing his behavior.

Functional views emphasize that we are to behave as stewards or managers, functioning as God's representatives in watching over a good creation. Some emphasize dominion—that humans are to exert mastery over creation—and we certainly see human capacity for dominion in magnificent architectural feats that defy gravity and withstand nature's elements, in cultivating the soil to produce the foods we desire, and in subduing wild animals that might otherwise lower us several notches in the food chain. Others emphasize stewardship—that we are to manage the earth well on God's behalf—which we see in efforts to preserve and conserve the environment, in rotating crops so as to keep the soil vibrant and productive, in loving and caring for animals, and so on. Whether we think of dominion or stewardship, being managers of creation requires self-control. If a dog is left alone with a freshly baked pie, it is unlikely the pie will survive. But given sufficient rationale, a human will be able to leave the pie alone because humans have a capacity to control and discipline their own behaviors. Managing creation involves controlling personal urges and creating social structures that help others control their urges too. And so we till the soil, sow the crop, reap the harvest, feast on the earth's bounty, create social mores and governments to keep one person from feasting at another person's expense, and care for the land so that it will continue to produce. In all these ways we function in God's image.

Psychology also has a functional emphasis, including (but not limited to) the functionalist school of thought that was popularized at the turn of the twentieth century with the work of William James and his contemporaries. (The philosophical foundations of functionalism go back much further, at least to Aristotle.) Functionalists in psychology were interested in looking at mental activities in relation to how they help humans function and adapt. This stood in contrast to the structuralism practiced in early psychology laboratories where psychologists attempted to break down complex experiences into smaller elements that could be studied systematically. One might imagine a structuralist such as Wilhelm Wundt stubbing his toe and then sitting down to contemplate exactly what the pain was like. What sensations were occurring in his toe, his stomach, his head? In contrast, William James would have looked at the function of pain after stubbing his toe. What sort of perceptions, motivations, emotions and behaviors were associated with the pain? Did the pain make him want to scream and hit something, or to curl up in a corner and cry? To a functionalist, an internal state is always viewed in relation to human functioning. Functionalism is pragmatic, always considering the experiential "cash value" of one's ideas or beliefs. Psychology's functionalist school and behaviorist school gradually merged over the twentieth century, and today both are being incorporated into the rapidly growing area of evolutionary psychology.

At first glance these theological and psychological views of functionalism may appear to be quite different, but they share important similarities. Both are more interested in how humans function than in exploring the substance or structure of being human; both consider how humans relate and adapt to their environment; and both look closely at human behavior.

Clinical psychologists and other mental health therapists often help people gain dominion over their lives and their environment. A young businesswoman finds that she gets intensely anxious and stammers over her words when pre-

---

COUNSELING TIP 1.1: Remember the Practical Concerns

Functional views of human behavior are important to remember when dealing with a person in pain. For adults coming to therapy to get help with a stifling depression or a debilitating anxiety problem, they may not want to start by talking about their childhood memories or peer relationships in elementary school. They want help functioning now! It is usually best to address these functional concerns early in therapy. This helps build rapport, eases the immediate crisis and gives the client a sense of competency. If the client chooses, there will be time later to explore underlying personality and developmental factors.

---

senting reports in staff meetings. A therapist helps her overcome her anxiety disorder through a combination of breathing and relaxation training, interoceptive exposure, and *in vivo* exposure (see chap. 7). Even for psychologists who do not think of this as a theological task, it bears similarity to functional views of the *imago Dei.*

Structural. Structural perspectives on the image of God have a long and important theological history, and many contemporary evangelical theologians continue to hold to a structural view of the *imago Dei* (e.g., Erickson, 1985). The idea is that human nature reflects something of the nature of God. There is something majestic and noble built into our character. We see it every time we cry out for justice, when we think reasonably, when we feel deeply, when we extend mercy, when we long for relationship.

> The swift and versatile movements of the soul in glancing from heaven to earth, connecting the future with the past, retaining the remembrance of former years,

nay, forming creations of its own—its skill, moreover, in making astonishing dis-
coveries, and inventing so many wonderful arts, are sure indications of the agency
of God in man. . . . What shall we say but that man *[sic]* bears about with him a
stamp of immortality which can never be effaced? (Calvin, 1559/1997, p. 54)

Structural views of the *imago Dei* typically emphasize the moral or rational
capacity of humans. One's ability to study, analyze, ponder, choose, speak,
value and discern reflect many qualities of our omniscient God. Look at creation
and marvel at the regulated harmony. Notice the order of physics, the predict-
ability of astronomy, the precision of chemistry, the interconnections of biology.
The rational and moral genius of God is evident all around. And we humans are
made in the image of this mastermind creator. Think of our capacity to learn,
how we move from helpless infants to language-bearing toddlers to literate
grade-schoolers all in a period of a few years. We are wondrously made!

The rational capacities of humans as a reflection of God's image have been
both overstated and hotly debated throughout history. In the second century
Irenaeus distinguished between the *image* and *likeness* of God (see Gen 1:26-
27), describing the image as humans' natural capacity to reason and choose and
the likeness as a supernatural maturity into which Adam and Eve could have
grown. When Adam and Eve sinned, they lost the likeness and retained the image. Thus, the only way to see the likeness of God is to look at Christ, who
possessed both the image (being fully human) and the likeness (being fully divine). This notion of Irenaeus's, which is quite appealing in its Christology, was
exaggerated by medieval scholastic theologians to suggest that human reasoning (the image of God) remains relatively untainted by sin, whereas our innate
capacity for goodness was damaged by original sin. The problem with this view
is its optimism regarding human reason. It suggests that we may struggle in various ways because we have lost the likeness—the moral capacity that Christ
had—but at least we have a reasoning capacity similar to Adam, Eve and Christ.
Do we really?

Things changed with the Reformation. Luther, Calvin and other Reformers
helped dismantle the distinction between God's image and likeness, arguing that
these are simply parallel words describing the same notion. Various facets of
God's image—rational, moral, volitional, social and so on—were built into
Adam's and Eve's character, and every aspect was damaged by sin. Now only a
remnant remains. Thus the Reformers provided a more sobering look at human
rationality. It is not so close to divine reason as their predecessors thought.

Psychologists have also developed structural views of human nature, ranging
from the late-nineteenth-century school of thought known as structuralism to to-

day's fascination with cognitive science, information processing and cognitive therapy. Just as some theologians have attempted to dissect the human psyche in order to isolate the substance of God's image, so some psychologists have attempted to investigate particular structures of human experience. And just as theologians settled on rationality as an important area of study, so also psychologists have honed in on the topic of human rationality.

Contemporary cognitive therapy, which is based largely on information processing models coming out of cognitive science (Safran & Segal, 1990), assumes that people become healthier as they learn to think more rationally. In the grip of depression or anxiety or relational conflicts, thinking becomes compromised.

COUNSELING TIP 1.2: Rationality in the Therapy Office

Helping people think more rationally is an important goal of therapy. Psychological troubles get worse as people are swept away by extreme and irrational thinking. A depressed client may see herself as worthless and unlovable. An addicted client may say that he can stop any time he wants. A husband and wife in crisis may each believe it is the other person's fault. Therapists help clients see things more rationally.

But just as medieval theologians may have overestimated human rationality, so also some therapists seem to elevate rationality too high and fail to give enough attention to relational, emotional and cultural issues. And sometimes therapists forget that they themselves are prone to faulty thinking. What seems rational to one therapist may seem quite irrational to another. One famous cognitive therapist once promoted adultery, arguing that it helps bring sexual energy into the marriage relationship. His advice seemed rational to him at the time, but to most other therapists—and virtually all Christian therapists—it seems irrational.

The depressed person looks at the world through a dark rain cloud. The anxious person evaluates the future based on feelings of dread or apprehension. The couple in distress sees the negative in one another but has misplaced the positive. Effective cognitive therapy—whether it is considered Christian or not—frequently involves helping people salvage their rational abilities and think more clearly about the circumstances they face.

Mirroring the historical arguments about the image of God, we see that contemporary cognitive therapy began with a very optimistic view of human rationality. Indeed, when reading the earliest books on cognitive therapy one gets the sense that learning to think correctly is the solution to all mental health problems. But time has eroded this sort of optimism, at least for many cognitive therapists. Rationality is still considered important, but it is not the only factor to consider for providing effective therapy.

Relational. Many contemporary theologians have shifted away from structural views of the *imago Dei* toward relational views. Emil Brunner, Karl Barth, Stanley Grenz and others have emphasized the relational nature of humans as reflective of God's relational character. The *imago Dei* is verb rather than noun; it is not so much that each individual human contains the image of God—as is postulated in structural views—but that we collectively image God as we engage in loving relationships with God and one another. "As is evident throughout Scripture, the divine image is not primarily individual, but is shared or relational" (Grenz, 2000, p. 213).

The relational view of the *imago Dei* is argued by emphasizing communication within the Trinity as evidence of God's relational character (Balswick, King & Reimer, 2005; Barth, 1945/1958; Grenz, 2000). "Then God said, 'Let us make people in our image, to be like ourselves'" (Gen 1:26). Barth (1945/1958) refers to this as a "divine conversation" (p. 183) that illustrates a prototype within the Godhead that will be reflected in the creation of humans. As God is three persons in one, so humans are created male and female and are whole by being together in relationship. "God patterned them after himself; male and female he created them" (Gen 1:27). The very nature of God is seen in what Barth considered an I-Thou relationship; neither the male nor the female contain the image in themselves, but rather in their relating to one another. In the same way, humans are created to be in a covenant relationship with God. Further and foremost, the relational view of the *imago Dei* is argued by looking at Christ. If we want to understand the image of God in humanity, the best way is to look at Jesus, who is the only human image of God that has not been tainted by sin. "Christ is the visible image of the invisible God" (Col 1: 15). In Jesus we see one who loves his neighbor and God perfectly, even to the point of sacrificing his own life on a cross (see Rom 5:6-8). Jesus revealed God's relational image in human form.

Relational (interpersonal) views have also been prominent in psychology, especially in the psychodynamic tradition (Sullivan, 1953). Recent adaptations of psychodynamic theory, including object-relations theory, are almost purely relational in their understanding of human pathology and treatment (Kernberg, 1976; Benjamin, 1996). Relational views of human nature are also evident in theories of human development, such as attachment theory (Bowlby, 1990). Some psychologists have introduced interpersonal dimensions into cognitive therapy (e.g., Safran, 1998; Safran & Segal, 1990). We applaud this trend toward relational forms of cognitive therapy; IP is a Christian adaptation and further development of ideas that have been emerging over the past two decades.

Whereas psychotherapists of various persuasions emphasize the importance of therapeutic relationships (e.g., Norcross, 2002), Christian psychotherapists take this a step further, recognizing our God-given call to relationships. We are made to relate, and so we look to Christ as our exemplar—the One who loves perfectly. Christian psychotherapy is motivated by and centered in an amazing and magnificent truth claim: God loves us more than we can imagine and created us to be relational. We experience some semblance of God's image in re-

---

COUNSELING TIP 1.3: The Rate-Limiting Step

Chemists speak of the "rate-limiting step"—the slowest chemical reaction in a series of cascading reactions. The entire chemical process can never go any faster than the rate-limiting step.

Establishing a good therapeutic relationship is like a rate-limiting step. No matter how technically expert a therapist may be, he or she also needs to relate well with others. Once trust and rapport are established in a warm and accepting therapeutic relationship, then the client is more likely to progress in therapy. Some would argue that the relationship itself is the healing ingredient in therapy.

---

lating to one another—love that forgives and endures and persists through the clamor of life (Tjeltveit, 2006). A yearning to connect is knitted into our souls.

Functional, structural and relational. The image of God is complex, defying simple explanation or categorization. Rather than choosing one of the three views just described, perhaps value can be found in all three. Jones and Butman (1991) suggest the same: "it seems judicious at this time to not fight for an exclusive meaning of the image, but rather to conclude that being created in the image of God means all this and more" (p. 44). The thoughtful Christian theologian is likely to have a primary allegiance to one view of the *imago Dei,* just as the thoughtful therapist will have a primary allegiance to one particular theoretical orientation in psychology, but still it is reasonable to find value in all three perspectives.

Hoekema's (1986) helpful treatise on the *imago Dei* lends credence to each of the major views. Hoekema demonstrates that function and structure are closely related:

> Must we think of the image of God in man *[sic]* as involving only what man is and not what he does, or only what he does and not what he is, or both what he is and what he does? . . . It is my conviction that we need to maintain both aspects. Since the image of God includes the whole person, it must include both man's structure and man's functioning. One cannot function without a certain structure. An eagle, for example, propels itself through the air by flying—this is one of its functions. The eagle would be unable to fly, however, unless it had wings—one of its structures. (p. 69)

Similarly, one need not reject the functional or structural aspects of human character in favor of relational aspects. Hoekema points out that Christ was directed toward God and neighbor while also demonstrating his mastery over creation. The one who rose early in the morning to pray (relationship with God) was also the one who befriended the needy and downtrodden (relationship with neighbor) and healed the sick and walked on water and fed the masses and calmed the storm (mastery over creation). Here Hoekema connects relational and functional aspects of the *imago Dei*.

IP draws on all three perspectives, shown as concentric circles in figure 1.2. The outer circle, and the first domain of intervention in IP, pertains to how a person functions in relation to a complex environment. In a sense, every person is faced with the managerial challenge posed to Adam and Eve—we are all called to function properly in relation to the creation around us. A person who experiences extreme terror when speaking in public is not functioning well in relation to the demands of the environment and may come to a psychotherapist for help. The therapist will focus on thoughts and behaviors, and rightly so because this is a functional problem.

But human thoughts and behaviors always exist in the context of structural capacities—the second circle in figure 1.2 and the second domain of intervention in IP. Functioning well requires rational and moral abilities that reflect the ontological nature of God's image. For example, the client who feels terror about speaking in public still has the rational and moral sensibility not to run out of the room. This demonstrates something unique about humans not seen in the rest of the animal kingdom. Humans have the cognitive capacity to see a bigger story, to transcend impulses of seeking pleasure and avoiding pain, to find meaning in life circumstances even when it involves tolerating discomfort. Some people come for therapy when their efforts to find meaning in life are falling short.

The inner circle in figure 1.2, and the third domain of intervention in IP, is relational. The moral and rational structures of life—how we find meaning—are always embedded in the context of relationships with God and others. Brunner,

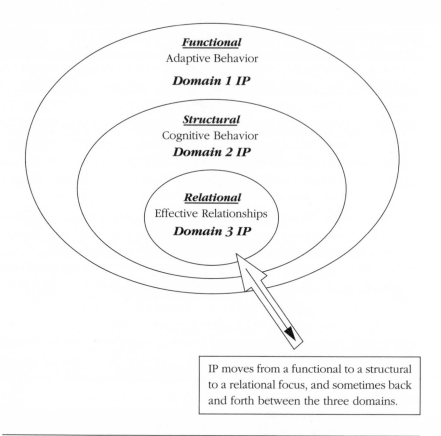

Figure 1.2. Integrative psychotherapy and three views of the *imago Dei*

Barth, Grenz and others argue this theologically, but social science brings us to
the same conclusion (Andersen & Chen, 2002). Even the human capacity to think
rationally—which is viewed as paramount in structural views of the *imago Dei*—
is shaped by relationships. Culture, social mores, family background and close
friendships all influence what we deem to be rational and irrational. One person
considers it rational to eat dog for dinner while another person takes a dog to be
groomed and bathed each week, or even to a pet therapist if the dog seems particularly subdued. These widely disparate views of rationality are shaped by a
complex network of present and past relationships that we call culture.

The human capacities for functional behavior, cognitive appraisal and rela-
tionality are evident throughout IP—not just because this makes for effective
therapy, but because these qualities reflect important realities about how we are

created by God. In the earliest stage of treatment, IP draws most heavily on functional views. As therapy progresses the functional interventions become less important as structural and relational views gain prominence, though there is typically movement back and forth between the three domains of intervention.

Fall

The great tragedy of human history, according to Christian theology, is humanity's fall into sin. Figure 1.2 ought to have crayon scribbles all over it, because the beauty of God's image has been vandalized, marred by the effects of human rebellion. Many volumes have been written on the problem of sin (e.g., Berkouwer, 1971; McMinn, in press; Moroney, 2000; Taylor, 2000), though space allows only a few observations here.

Beyond denial, beyond Pelagianism. One approach to the problem of sin is denial. Sin is a concept that has fallen out of favor in contemporary mental health professions, so many psychotherapists function with an "I'm okay, you're okay" assumption (Harris, 1973). But denying a problem does not make it go away, and sometimes it makes it worse. Augustine (398/1986) reflected, "[My] sin was all the more incurable because I did not judge myself to be a sinner" (p. 80). As Powlison (2001), Monroe (2001) and others have noted, Christian psychologists have often emphasized psychological theory and technique to the exclusion of biblical concepts such as sin—a warning that occasionally echoes within the ranks of psychology (e.g., Menninger, 1973; Mowrer, 1960). In IP we take the human propensity to sin seriously. Taking sin seriously does not mean that therapy becomes a place for harsh judgment and condescension. To the contrary, it is a place to honestly explore all the contours of sin and brokenness in life and to extend mercy and understanding in the midst of life's messes. Therapists do not stand above their clients, but with them.

Another approach is to view sin solely as a violation of particular behavioral standards. This approach leads to list-building, a careful articulation of how people should and should not behave. Gossip, adultery, idolatry, murder, theft and many more items are on the "Don't" side of the ledger. Kindness, generosity, forgiveness, compassion, tithing and similar things are on the "Do" side. Though this view is partly consistent with a Christian way of thinking, it falls short insofar as it suggests that sin is only a matter of willpower and choice. Pelagius championed the fifth-century viewpoint that humans have the capacity to live without sin. This view, known as Pelagianism, suggests that each person faces the same choice Adam and Eve faced, and each has the same free will and moral capacity to say yes or no to the lure of sin. Augustine disagreed, arguing instead that something happened when creation fell so that now humanity lives in a state of original sin.

IN THE OFFICE 1.2: Watching What We Say

Though Christian therapists think about the problem of sin when working with clients, it is rarely wise to use the word *sin* in the session itself. It is a word that has been tarnished by coercive efforts to manipulate people or trivialized as a synonym for pleasure.

But even without using the word *sin,* therapists can use words that challenge a client, leaving room for the conviction of the Holy Spirit.

Melinda: She got all preachy with me, like somehow I'm not supposed to be sleeping with anyone at all. She's really stuffy about that stuff. My dad is too. I mean, it's like they don't realize I'm twenty-two years old and making my own decisions. It's not like they've been perfect parents all their lives. They've done their share of stupid things.

Clark: It seems like it hits a nerve when your parents challenge your sexual choices.

Melinda: Yeah, I mean I don't even live with them now. It's none of their business what I do or don't do any more.

Clark: I'm wondering if their words hurt so much because they resonate with some questions you're asking about yourself.

Melinda: What do you mean?

Clark: Well, a minute ago you seemed displeased with your choice to sleep with Michael on your second date. And then you mentioned your Mom's reaction. I'm just wondering if you might have been feeling some of the same things even before she spoke them.

Melinda: [tears welling] Maybe. I don't know.

According to Augustine, sin is no longer limited to a choice of free will; it is also a general state of corruption. Augustine (398/1986) confesses, "For in your sight, no one is free from sin, not even the infant whose life is but a day upon the earth" (p. 7). Though Pelagianism was renounced as heresy sixteen centuries ago, Pelagian perspectives still lurk in the corridors of the Christian faith.

Neither denial of sin nor a Pelagian view is ultimately satisfying, and both lie outside of Christian orthodoxy. IP is based on the larger Augustinian perspective, where sin is viewed as both a state and an act.

Sin as state. The state of sin—sometimes called original sin by theologians—

precedes personal sinful choices. Sin is not just a set of behaviors, but a condition—a state—that influences the very fabric of creation and touches every aspect of human existence. Humans are inevitably sinners, contaminated by sin's corruption even before we make sinful choices (Bloesch, 1978; Erickson, 1985; Packer, 1993; Sproul, 1992). Something went terribly wrong with creation, and now every part of creation is tainted, infected by the curse of sin in our world. Shalom—a Hebrew greeting meaning peace, wholeness and completeness—has been broken (C. Plantinga, 1995).

This means free will and personal resolve are not enough. Everyone is prone to turn the Great Commandment upside down and love self above God and neighbor (A. Plantinga, 2000). Because of original sin, our passions are distorted and self-serving, our thinking is skewed, our bodies are prone to disease and decay, and we live among damage caused by others who are also prone to sin (McMinn, 2004).

Living in a state of sin also means the proper relationship between Creator and creature is broken. The idea of conversing with God in the Garden of Eden is so far from our experience that we can barely even comprehend such a thing. Our communication with God is so badly broken that we are powerless to make it right no matter how we may try. Our only hope to know God is found in God's desire to reach out in grace and restore our broken relationship.

There is little reason to feel guilty about original sinfulness because this sad state of affairs is simply the way things are. Guilt is quite reasonable in response to sinful actions (discussed below), but it is an unhelpful and potentially destructive response to the state of sin. No amount of willpower or spiritual maturity or genetic engineering can ever take away our sin nature. Augustine's phrase *non posse non peccare* means that it is not possible for us not to sin. We are born twisted, inclined to rebel and to put our own desires above the needs of others. If our hope is in achieving a state of sinlessness or restoring a relationship with God by our good intentions and deeds, then each of us is doomed and lost. Thankfully, our hope is in God's grace.

Sin as act. Sin is also seen in human action. Because all creation exists in a sinful state, we are prone to selfish choices, putting personal interests above God and neighbor. Sometimes sin comes from impulses of passion—what C. S. Lewis (1952) has described as animalistic impulses to sin. Other sin is more calculated, where pride is fostered and evil plotted in order to achieve personal gain at the expense of another. Lewis calls this diabolical sin and considers it worse than sins emerging from our animal nature, though he is quick to note that it is best to avoid both forms of sin.

Christian theology teaches that everyone has sinned: "For all have sinned; all fall short of God's glorious standard" (Rom 3:23). The church has emphasized various sets of guidelines to keep followers of Christ from sinning, such as the Ten Commandments of the Old Testament (Ex 20), the Seven Deadly Sins of the ancient church or the famous sermon that Jesus preached on a mountainside (Mt 5–7). These are important and good, setting boundaries for how we should live, yet still we fall.

It is not only that we ourselves sin, but also that we are sinned against. Sin moves in two directions—emerging out of Person A to hurt Person B, and emerging out of Person B to hurt Person A—and both can have devastating consequences on mental health and on the relationships we were created to enjoy. It is also important to acknowledge that Person A and Person B and several billions of other persons live in collective cultures and societies that are capable of collective evil. This reminds us that sin is not confined to a list of individual actions; groups are also capable of sinful actions that hurt individuals and other groups. Some of the most powerful litanies in liturgical worship confess our corporate sin, acknowledging our collective capacity to hurt others just by taking part in the shared assumptions and daily activities of oppressive social structures.

Whereas there is little point to feeling guilty for our sinful state, guilt is the expected and proper response to acts of sin. When we violate God's moral will we sense a relational distance from God and others and an inner contrition that returns us to God in a state of humble remorse. As we confess our sins to God and admit our sinfulness we receive God's forgiveness and hope of healing and transformation in our very being and relationship with God. Israel's King David wrote of this in one of his psalms:

> When I refused to confess my sin,
>> I was weak and miserable,
>> and I groaned all day long.
> Day and night your hand of discipline was heavy on me.
>> My strength evaporated like water in the summer heat.
>
> Finally, I confessed all my sins to you
>> and stopped trying to hide them.
> I said to myself, "I will confess my rebellion to the LORD."
>> And you forgave me! All my guilt is gone.
>
> Therefore, let all the godly confess their rebellion to you while there is time,
>> that they may not drown in the floodwaters of judgment.
> For you are my hiding place;
>> you protect me from trouble.
>> You surround me with songs of victory. (Ps 32:3-7)

Psychologists have sometimes labeled guilt as neurotic and unhealthy, and this is certainly true of excessive and unrealistic guilt. But labeling all guilt as destructive is both bad theology and, according to recent scientific evidence, bad psychology (Tangney & Dearing, 2002). Guilt can play a constructive role in human functioning when it leads to remorse and sorrow for the pain inflicted on another. Indeed, contemporary psychologists become concerned when people seem incapable of remorse, as is often the case with antisocial personality disorder.

Why sin matters. An Augustinian view of sin is important to Christian therapists for several reasons. First, it helps us understand our human tendency to deny and distort our shortcomings and to deceive ourselves and others. Because we exist in a sinful state, it is difficult to see our sin. Theologians refer to this as

---

COUNSELING TIP 1.4: Shame and Guilt

After they sinned, Adam and Eve hid their nakedness with fig leaves, and shame has been part of human life ever since. In our sin-stained world, we will never completely free ourselves and others from shame, but we can help people become less bound by their shame. Sometimes we can help people replace a self-oriented sense of shame with an other-oriented experience of guilt. Shame tends to be self-focused and psychologically destructive. Guilt is other-focused and can be psychologically useful. The husband who has offended his wife may be thinking, *I'm such a terrible person, so insensitive and selfish.* This sort of shame-based thinking is not helpful because it is self-focused and damaging, and may paradoxically increase the likelihood of reoffense.

It will be more helpful if the client can think of his wife's experience, *She was expecting me to show up for lunch when and where we agreed, and when I didn't come she probably felt unimportant and abandoned.* Now the client is experiencing guilt, which can help him build empathy for his wife and lead to more thoughtful behavior in the future. A key emotion in guilt is sorrow—sorrow for the other, not for the self.

---

the noetic effects of sin (Moroney, 2000), meaning that sin blinds us to all sorts of things but especially to our fallen condition and our need for God. It is easier to blame others than to acknowledge we are sinners, and sometimes psychotherapists unwittingly contribute to this.

Second, it means that sin contaminates far more than just human functioning.

Our structural capacities and relationships are also damaged and misaligned. Whereas Pelagianism suggests that humans have the capacity to choose good or evil, Augustinianism holds that sin changes everything: relationships, biological factors, emotions, cognitions, rationality, the capacity for willful change and so much more. This makes change and growth difficult, and it makes therapy complicated. One cannot simply instruct someone how to function better and assume it will have a curative effect because in our sinful state we resist self-awareness and change. We even resist good changes; in our sinful state of pride we would rather be self-sufficient and miserable than confess our weaknesses, receive help and change.

Third, an Augustinian view reminds us that no one escapes the damage of living in a sin-stained world. Picture a demolition derby. Dozens of battered cars are scurrying around, backing into other cars inflicting damage as they themselves are damaged. One by one the cars die as the battle rages on. Though we may not be trying deliberately to inflict damage as those demolition derby drivers are, we keep running into people, wounding them with our pride and selfishness and self-sufficiency. With each collision we do almost as much damage to ourselves as we do to others. And, of course, we are not the only drivers in this derby. Others are bouncing around too, damaging themselves and others with each ricochet.

Sin has consequences. Psychotherapists see this every day. The first client of the day is struggling with a chronic depression that has its origin in years of childhood sexual abuse. She has been hurt by another person's sin. The next client is clinging to years of bitterness and unforgiveness toward his ex-spouse. He was wounded by her sin, and now he is complicating the wound by nursing his sinful desires for retribution. The third client of the afternoon screams at her children in anger before becoming overwhelmed with shame and guilt. She seeks help to control her sinful rage. The fourth client is a man whose mother never got control of her screaming. He was hurt by his mother's sin, and now he feels intermittently anxious and angry around women. Psychotherapists see the consequences of sin day after day, session after session.

Fourth, an Augustinian view of sin prevents simplistic connections between sin and psychological problems. Imagine being asked if depression is the result of sin. If the person asking the question has a simplistic understanding of sin, the question being asked is, "Are people depressed as a direct result of their personal acts of sin?" The answer to this question may be quite different than a question based on an Augustinian view: "Are people depressed as a result of our human state of sin, sinful actions and the consequences of living in a sinful world?" A Christian's answer to the latter question must be yes, of course. Without the sinfulness of our world, without the realities of war, abuse, divorce, oppression, defiance of God, bad parenting, physical illness, rebellious choices and all other forms of brokenness, then shalom would never have been shattered. No one would be depressed or anxious, there would be no neurotransmitter deficits or other chemical imbalances, no one would die of leukemia or AIDS, and lions and lambs would tumble playfully on verdant hillsides. But in answering yes to the Augustinian question some folks wrongly assume simplistic connections between personal choices and psychological problems. This inadequate view of sin has sometimes been quite harmful to those seeking help from Christian pastors, counselors and psychotherapists. (Some Christian psychologists have accused biblical counselors of this simplistic approach to therapy, but in doing so they have often failed to appreciate the depth, wisdom and theological sophistication that characterize most biblical counselors.)

Ideally Christian psychotherapists acknowledge the brokenness of our world and are bold enough to assert that something is terribly wrong, but remember that the sin problem is complex. Sin is a state as well as an act, and sin has long-term consequences that ripple along the surface of life for generations. Jesus had an opportunity to condemn a woman caught in adultery, but instead he knelt and wrote in the sand, perhaps reflecting in sadness on the profound brokenness of the world. When he stood, he communicated the complexity of the sin problem with a simple directive, "All right, stone her. But let those who have never sinned throw the first stones!" (Jn 8:7). One by one her accusers slinked away.

Jesus calls his followers to a place of understanding, compassion and hope

---

COUNSELING TIP 1.5: Truth and Grace

One of the most remarkable things about Jesus was his capacity to be a person of both truth and grace (Jn 1:14). In our fallen state we tend to veer one direction or the other. Some therapists are very direct and confrontational about sinful choices in their clients' lives, but often they fail to demonstrate the grace and acceptance of Christ. Others are gracious and kind, but they sometimes fail to speak the truth when moral questions arise.

Jesus, who provides us the perfect picture of God's image, should be the exemplar for every Christian's work, including those who do psychotherapy. Try praying this simple prayer at the beginning of each therapy session: "Lord, you have shown such grace to me, a sinner. I ask that you allow me to minister both grace and truth to your beloved child in this upcoming appointment."

for transformation more than to a place of judgment and condemnation. When the woman told Jesus that none of her accusers remained to condemn her, he looked at her, felt compassion for her broken state, and probably experienced deep sadness over the legalistic, self-righteous Pharisees who preferred stoning to transformation. Then Jesus said, "Neither do I [condemn you]. Go and sin no more" (Jn 8:11). Jesus' compassion moved him to acknowledge the sins of adultery and self-righteousness and call both the woman and religious leaders to live lives that better reflect the love of God.

Redemption

Some have critiqued a Christian understanding of sin by pointing out how dismal the Christian life must be: always looking at the problems of existence and dwelling on the evil in the world. Though some Christians have slipped into this trap, nothing should be further from the truth. A sound doctrine of sin paves the way for a solid understanding of grace—God's unmerited favor offered to those who could never earn it by their own efforts. Those first six words that Sunday school children commit to memory, "For God so loved the world," affirm the foundation of the Christian faith. The first and last truth of the cosmos is that God loves humanity.

A doctrine of sin, viewed in the context of a God who loves humanity, is the Christian's great hope because it opens the possibility of redemption—God buying us back from the bondage of sin through the atoning work of Jesus Christ, restoring a right relationship with those who were lost in their sin. And so we learn more than six words: "For God so loved the world that he gave his only Son, so that everyone who believes in him will not perish but have eternal life. God did not send his Son into the world to condemn it, but to save it" (Jn 3:16-17). The Christian story is not dismal, but is filled with hope and life and possibility. When the apostle Paul decries his sinful state, "Oh, what a miserable person I am! Who will free me from this life that is dominated by sin?" (Rom 7:24), it sounds dismal enough, but then Paul goes on to answer his own question. "So now there is no condemnation for those who belong to Christ Jesus. For the power of the life-giving Spirit has freed you through Christ Jesus from the power of sin that leads to death" (Rom 8:1-2).

There is a rhythm of hope here for those who are transformed by the grace and truth of God, revealed in Christ: we become aware of our sinful condition, acknowledge it and remember that our sins are forgiven because of the work of Jesus Christ, which we receive by faith. It is a grand salvific rhythm that for some has a dramatic beginning and echoes time and time again throughout our lives. We stray from God over and over, and in grace God calls us back to restored relationship. Even those who do not follow Christ benefit from the relational rhythm embedded in the story of salvation—human relationships are broken by sin and selfishness and renewed by confession, forgiveness and reconciliation. One person hurts another, then confesses the wrong and seeks forgiveness, and

COUNSELING TIP 1.6: The Hope of Redemption

God is actively involved in redeeming us, in restoring us to complete relationship with him. God pursues us in the most loving yet unrelenting fashion. The thought of this gives the therapist great hope. In the midst of a busy day of seeing clients whose lives are torn by the effects of sin—despair, chaos and confusion—it is hopeful to think of God's active redemptive pursuit of those clients. When the client seems unlovable, strongly defensive, actively psychotic or in some other way distant, reflecting on God's active pursuit of that person in the process of redemption brings hope and a renewed sense of empathy. In a real sense redemption is restorative, and reflecting on God's redemptive work can bring a restorative pause to a draining day.

the relationship is restored. Largely unaware, the world revolves to this rhythm, reflecting the common grace of its Creator.

For centuries Roman Catholics have practiced the sacrament of reconciliation, where sin is confessed, forgiveness granted and hope renewed. Christian leaders recognize that people want to confess their weaknesses and misdeeds, to name the ways they have been sinned against, to be forgiven and to grant forgiveness to their offenders, and perhaps even to be reconciled to them. In our sinful state, we may cloak our longings for redemption beneath layers of anger and blame and resentment, but underneath we desire to be healed in the midst of life's dis-ease. Sometimes psychotherapists, who tend to be less religious than the general public (Shafranske, 1996), fail to see the power of this simple rhythm of confession and forgiveness. Those who disallow the language of sin and wrongdoing also inhibit the possibility of forgiveness, grace and reconciliation. Over twenty years ago Stanley Graham, a leading psychologist, had this to say to counseling and clinical psychologists:

> Quite early in the treatment process, the patient begins to use words like good and bad, and it is our tendency as therapists to diminish the intensity of these words since they relate to a value system within the individual which has led to the cur-

rent state of stress. . . . We have collectively done an excellent job of diminishing the demonstration of good and bad and a very poor job of replacing these concepts with acceptable definitions which allow the individual self-acceptance and peace. (Graham, 1980, pp. 370-71)

A Christian view of psychotherapy makes room for concepts such as right and wrong, good and bad, sin and forgiveness, brokenness and redemption. Humans live each day as sinners in relationship with other sinners, so there are always wounds and struggles and misunderstandings. But this mire of sin need not shackle a person with fear and self-doubt, because it gives opportunity to glimpse grace and forgiveness.

A Christocentric view. A Christian view of redemption, informed by special revelation, is Christ-centered. Such a statement seems, at first glance, to be tautological and redundant. It is, nonetheless, an important point to emphasize in our contemporary world where spirituality often seems vague and poorly defined. Many psychologists and counselors are interested in spirituality these days, but few are interested in making any particular truth claims about the precise nature of our spiritual quest or where we can find hope and redemption. The Christian faith is distinct in its particularity. The climax of God's redemptive work occurred in the atoning work of Jesus Christ.

Over the centuries, various Christian viewpoints on the nature of Christ's atoning work have been articulated—some emphasize the love of Christ, some the incarnation, some the sacrificial death. The common theme in all Christian theories of atonement is that they focus on Jesus. The apostle Paul, writing to the Colossians, is clearly Christ-centered in his view of redemption:

> For God in all his fullness was pleased to live in Christ, and by him God reconciled everything to himself. He made peace with everything in heaven and on earth by means of his blood on the cross. This includes you who were once so far away from God. You were his enemies, separated from him by your evil thoughts and actions, yet now he has brought you back as his friends. He has done this through his death on the cross in his own human body. As a result, he has brought you into the very presence of God, and you are holy and blameless as you stand before him without a single fault. (Col 1:19-22)

This Christ who redeems is God incarnate, the eternal Word who existed in the beginning with God (Jn 1:1-4), through whom everything was created and is sustained (Col 1:17).

If God is dead or merely watching from a distance and does not care much about our daily affairs, then therapists might help people feel better and develop a more cheerful disposition to enjoy their few remaining years or decades of life—but the ultimate end of every life is tragedy. In contrast, if Christ is active in sustaining a world broken by sin, then the goal is not merely surviving as long and happily as we can but actively participating in and celebrating God's work of renewal. Beauty can be discovered and celebrated even in the midst of suffering, mourning can give way to laughter, sinners can be forgiven, and the grip of shame can be exchanged for the joy of mercy. Hope abounds within a Christocentric worldview.

God revealed in Christ. Biblical Christianity, articulated and affirmed throughout the centuries, views God as both transcendent and immanent. God exists above and beyond creation, but also chooses to remain connected with creation and in relationship with humanity. God chooses to be known and so is revealed through both Scripture (special revelation) and nature (general revelation). The greatest revelation of all is found in the incarnation: "The Word became human and lived here on earth among us" (Jn 1:14). Jesus, fully God and fully human, came to live in our midst. He suffered real pain, perspired real sweat (and eventually blood) and died a real death. He proved his victory over death through his bodily resurrection and ascension, and now he continues to be involved in the material world, remaining one with our humanity, continuing his ministry of mediation and holding all creation together (Col 1:17).

God's incarnation has implications for psychotherapy. Because God remains connected with creation, we can be assured that God knows and cares about human suffering. It means that God still loves creation and desires to see healing and wholeness. We can celebrate food and art and dance and sport and sexuality and so much more because all good things are created and sustained by a benevolent, loving God. It means that God's redemptive care is not limited to ephemeral, spiritual realities; God loves materiality, and longs to see it healed wherever it may be broken. God is pleased when medication relieves pain, hungry children are fed, Habitat for Humanity builds houses for the indigent, exercise prolongs life and psychotherapy relieves anxiety symptoms. Because God is revealed through general revelation, we can engage fearlessly in studying the world around us. Therapists can embrace science wholeheartedly and can use the findings of science to enhance their work with troubled individuals and families. God loves the material world and calls us to be good stewards of it.

But God also transcends the material world, so God's desire is not merely for our comfort but also for our hearts to be made right. In this, God's law is higher than natural law. It is not enough to determine what comes naturally and then do it. One must also consider what God deems proper. Christians are called to be holy, set apart from others who live their lives as if God does not exist. Furthermore, though general revelation is one way to understand God, it is not self-

IN THE OFFICE 1.3: God Is Working

A therapist must be prudent with spiritual advice, especially when it might be perceived as insensitive or as minimizing the pain the client is experiencing. But still, there are many opportunities to remind clients that God is working. Therapy is different than teaching or preaching, so it is important to keep these reminders centered on the client's story.

Pam: I just feel lost right now. After all these months of depression, it's like I don't know who I am any longer. I don't find that much pleasure in my job. Things at home are tough, so I don't really think of myself as a good wife or mother. I'm just sort of no one.

Mark: It's like you're floundering at sea, without any anchors to define who you are.

Pam: Yeah, that's exactly it. I'm just drifting.

Mark: Or at least it feels that way.

Pam: Right. I mean, it feels that way. But I think it really is that way. I have no roots, no identity, no moorings to make sense of my life.

Mark: We've talked before about the power of emotional reasoning when you're feeling depressed. If a thing *feels* a certain way, then it's natural to assume it *is* that way. Are there any firm anchors in your life?

Pam: Well, my faith, I guess. But I feel like I'm a long way from God right now too.

Mark: That also sounds like emotional reasoning. Let's dig beneath that if we can. You feel far from God. What would God have to say about that?

Pam: It's funny, as you say that I remember a line from *The Count of Monte Cristo* when Edmond says, "I don't believe in God," and the old priest answers back, "That doesn't matter. He believes in you."

Mark: What a great thought.

Pam: Yeah, I remember tears coming to my eyes when I watched that movie.

explanatory. General revelation is enough to let us know that God exists and that there is something majestic and beautiful about nature and humanity, but it is not enough to teach us about the nature of God. General revelation is tainted with brokenness, so we can never conclude that some finding of science is the way God intends for things to be. God's intention is for creation to become more than it could ever become on its own, to move back toward the glory of Eden through redeemed relationship with God (1 Cor 15). This *telos* (i.e., ultimate end) cannot be found in creation itself but only in the intentions of God revealed in special revelation.

And so a Christian approach to psychotherapy calls us to consider more than general revelation. Special revelation addresses bigger issues of truth beyond the findings of contemporary science and psychological theory. Helping a client to feel and function well is a good goal, but it is often not the only goal that Christian psychotherapists have for their work. We must also take seriously issues of moral choices, spiritual yearnings and character formation. In short, Christian psychotherapy involves an awareness of sanctification as we all seek to be transformed by the divine life revealed in and mediated to us by Christ.

Redemption and hope. In the beginning, God created a perfect home for humans. It was to be a place of joy and beauty and goodness. In many ways, today's world is still like that world—there is delight to be found in good food and good company, in memories of yesterday and hopes for tomorrow, in children and spouses and parents, in planting flowers and watching them bloom, in waking to the sound of birds singing, in visual art and dance and music, in reading and writing. Joy abounds and life is abundant. But the world is also tainted by sin, so joy is marred by struggle and pain. For some, the pain is overwhelming. Some are treated so unjustly that it is hard to imagine how the joy of living can survive the trauma. Instinctively we yearn for things to be set right, the way they were in the beginning.

As Christians, we have at least three proper responses. The first is to see the world as a good place worth being restored and sustained. We ought to celebrate life however we can, and invite others to be part of the celebration. God loves the material world, and we should too. Christian therapists demonstrate good stewardship by helping restore wholeness to individuals, families and communities.

Second, we cling by faith to the belief that God works redemptively in this broken world. God works everywhere, even in pain and silence, and certainly in therapy offices. When a person is brought back from the stifling confines of a panic disorder with the help of a therapist, God is at work. When a wounded adult recognizes an alcohol problem and staggers in the door of a treatment center, God is working. When couples reconcile and depressed clients feel better and social anxiety problems wane, God is working, whether we know it or not, whether or not we acknowledge God's presence. Take this a step further: God is also working when our treatments are not effective. God is at work in the midst of panic attacks just as surely as in their healing. God is present in our sufferings as well as in our healing.

> Look now; I myself am he!
>> There is no god other than me!
> I am the one who kills and gives life;
>> I am the one who wounds and heals;
>>> no one delivers from my power! (Deut 32:39)

God is working everywhere and always, in wounds and in healing, and often in ways we in our finiteness cannot comprehend.

Third, we see ourselves as "no more than foreigners and nomads here on earth" (Heb 11:13) because our destination is ultimately a new heaven and a new earth—an "immeasurably great glory that will last forever!" (2 Cor 4:17). Though we cannot fully understand what heaven is like (Roberts, 2003), all of our inner instincts call us there. Knitted into the essence of our souls is a yearning to be home where there will be no more injustice, where we will no longer struggle against disease and death, where relationships will never be broken by

---

COUNSELING TIP 1.7: A Redemptive Response

In graduate school we are trained to have a repertoire of responses to clients—paraphrases, reflections, interpretations, summaries, and so on. Rarely is a redemptive response described in the professional literature. A redemptive response could include any of the responses just mentioned, but what makes it redemptive is the response of the client. A redemptive response moves clients toward wholeness—having a more complete view of themselves in relation to their problems. When a client is mired in her own guilt and shame, a redemptive response would be one that moves her toward grace and a more complete picture of God's view of her and her problems. When a client is completely full of himself and seems to have no recognition of the effects of his behavior on others, a redemptive response would be one that brings about this insight.

Perhaps this kind of response can't be taught, but it can be revealed as one prayerfully contemplates God throughout the therapy session. Sometimes a momentary silent prayer in the midst of a session, asking God to reveal a redemptive response, can bring about a new response for the therapist to provide to the client. Sometimes the redemptive response is silence where the therapist just remains in thoughtful connection with the client.

strife and misunderstanding, and—most of all—where we will fully experience the love of God (McMinn, 2005). To the Christian this is not just a neurotic wish or a meaningful delusion; it is the great hope of the Christian faith.

Because Christian therapists help clients tell their life stories as they find meaning in the present and past, it is important to consider the future also. Heaven is the Christian's *telos*—an anchor that grants renewed perspective on the present. The promise of heaven allows Christians to live lightly, not clinging so tightly to possessions, accomplishments and agendas. The best is yet to come.

Conclusion

Integrative psychotherapy is rooted in theology and psychology. In this chapter we have provided a brief overview of the theological assumptions of IP. Humans are created in the image of a loving God—an image that has been viewed in various ways by Christian theologians. Some have emphasized God's mandate to manage creation and so describe the *imago Dei* as functional. Others have identified a particular quality or substance of God's character that is evident in humans, most often rational and moral capacities. Still others have argued that the image is not contained within an individual per se, but is seen in relationships. IP draws on all three of these views, beginning with a functional view of change, then moving to structural interventions as needed and finally to relational interventions. Rather than denying sin or settling for an oversimplified view of sin, IP is based on the Augustinian view that sin is both a state and an act. This calls Christian psychotherapists to a place of understanding, mercy and acceptance rather than harsh criticism because sin taints all of creation and affects every person. But things are not ruined—God still loves, restores and sustains creation. So we live in a state of paradox as broken image-bearers, sinners in the hands of a loving God who is present in our wounds and in our healing and provides us with hope.

References

Andersen, S. M., & Chen, S. (2002). The relational self: An interpersonal social-cognitive theory. *Psychological Review, 109,* 619-45.

Augustine. (398/1986). *The confessions of St. Augustine* (H. M. Helms, Trans.). Brewster, MA: Paraclete.

Balswick, J. O., King, P. E., & Reimer, K. S. (2005). *The reciprocating self: Human development in theological perspective.* Downers Grove, IL: InterVarsity Press.

Barth, K. (1945/1958). *Church dogmatics* (Vol. 3, Part 1) (J. W. Edwards, O. Bussey & H. Knight, Trans.). Edinburgh: T & T Clark.

Benjamin, L. S. (1996). *Interpersonal diagnosis and treatment of personality disorders.* New York: Guilford.

Berkouwer, G. C. (1971). *Studies in dogmatics: Sin.* Grand Rapids, MI: Eerdmans.

Bloesch, D. G. (1978). *Essentials of evangelical theology: God, authority, & salvation* (Vol. 1). Peabody, MA: Prince.

Bowlby, J. (1990). *A secure base: Parent-child attachment and healthy human development.* New York: Basic Books.

Bulkley, E. (1994). *Why Christians can't trust psychology.* Eugene, OR: Harvest House.

Calvin, J. (1559/1997). *Institutes of the Christian religion* (H. Beveridge, Trans.). Grand Rapids, MI: Eerdmans.

Collins, G. R. (1988). *Can you trust psychology? Exposing the facts & the fictions.* Downers Grove, IL: InterVarsity Press.

Erickson, M. J. (1985). *Christian theology.* Grand Rapids, MI: Baker.

Graham, S. R. (1980). Desire, belief, and grace: A psychotherapeutic paradigm. *Psychotherapy: Theory, Research and Practice, 17,* 370-71.

Grenz, S. J. (2000). *Renewing the center: Evangelical theology in a post-theological era.* Grand Rapids, MI: Baker Academic.

Harris, T. A. (1973). *I'm OK—you're OK.* New York: Avon.

Hoekema, A. A. (1986). *Created in God's image.* Grand Rapids, MI: Eerdmans.

Johnson, E. L. (2007). *Foundations for Soul Care.* Downers Grove, IL: IVP Academic.

Jones, S. L. (1994). A constructive relationship for religion within the science and profession of psychology: Perhaps the boldest model yet. *American Psychologist, 49,* 184-99.

Jones, S. L., & Butman, R. E. (1991). *Modern psychotherapies: A comprehensive Christian appraisal.* Downers Grove, IL: InterVarsity Press.

Kernberg, O. (1976). *Object-relations theory and clinical psychoanalysis.* New York: Jason Aronson.

Lewis, C. S. (1952). *Mere Christianity.* New York: Macmillan.

McMinn, M. R. (2004). *Why sin matters: The surprising relationship between our sin and God's grace.* Wheaton, IL: Tyndale House.

McMinn, M. R. (2005). *Finding our way home: Turning back to what matters most.* San Francisco: Jossey-Bass.

McMinn, M. R. (2006). *Christian counseling* [video in APA Psychotherapy Series]. Washington, DC: American Psychological Association.

McMinn, M. R. (in press). *Sin and grace in Christian counseling.* Downers Grove, IL: InterVarsity Press.

McMinn, M. R., & Dominguez, A. D. (Eds.) (2005). *Psychology and the church.* Huntington, NY: Nova Science Publishers.

Menninger, K. (1973). *Whatever became of sin?* New York: Hawthorn Books.

Miller, W. R. (Ed.) (1999). *Integrating spirituality into treatment: Resources for practitioners.* Washington, DC: American Psychological Association.

Miller, W. R., & Delaney, H. D. (Eds.) (2005). *Judeo-Christian perspectives on psychology: Human nature, motivation, and change.* Washington, DC: American Psychological Association.

Monroe, P. G. (2001). Exploring clients' personal sin in the therapeutic context: Theological perspectives on a case study of self-deceit. In M. R. McMinn & T. R. Phillips (Eds.), *Care for the soul: Exploring the intersection of psychology & theology* (pp. 202-17). Downers Grove, IL: InterVarsity Press.

Moroney, S. K. (2000). *The noetic effects of sin.* Lanham, MA: Lexington Books.

Mowrer, O. H. (1960). "Sin": The lesser of two evils. *American Psychologist, 15,* 301-4.

Nathan, P. E. (1997). In the final analysis, it's the data that count. *Clinical Psychology: Science & Practice, 4,* 281-84.

Norcross, J. C. (Ed.) (2002). *Psychotherapy relationships that work: Therapist contributions and responsiveness to patients.* New York: Oxford University Press.

Packer, J. I. (1973). *Knowing God.* Downers Grove, IL: InterVarsity Press.

Peterson, D. R. (2003). Unintended consequences: Ventures and misadventures in the education of professional psychologists. *American Psychologist, 58,* 791-800.

Plantinga, A. (2000). *Warranted Christian belief.* New York: Oxford University Press.

Plantinga, C., Jr. (1995). *Not the way it's supposed to be: A breviary of sin.* Grand Rapids, MI: Eerdmans.

Powlison, D. (2001). Questions at the crossroads: The care of souls and modern psychotherapies. In M. R. McMinn & T. R. Phillips (Eds.), *Care for the soul: Exploring the intersection of psychology & theology* (pp. 23-61). Downers Grove, IL: InterVarsity Press.

Richards, P. S., & Bergin, A. E. (Eds.) (2000). *Handbook of psychotherapy and religious diversity.* Washington, DC: American Psychological Association.

Richards, P. S., & Bergin, A. E. (Eds.) (2004). *Casebook for a spiritual strategy for counseling and psychotherapy.* Washington, DC: American Psychological Association.

Richards, P. S., & Bergin, A. E. (2005). *A spiritual strategy for counseling and psychotherapy* (2nd ed.). Washington, DC: American Psychological Association.

Roberts, R. O. (2003). *Exploring heaven: What great Christian thinkers tell us about our afterlife with God*. San Francisco: HarperSanFrancisco.

Safran, J. D. (1998). *Widening the scope of cognitive therapy: The therapeutic relationship, emotion, and the process of change*. Northvale, NJ: Aronson.

Safran, J. D., & Segal, Z. V. (1990). *Interpersonal process in cognitive therapy*. New York: Basic Books.

Shafranske, E. P. (Ed.) (1996). *Religion and the clinical practice of psychology*. Washington, DC: American Psychological Association.

Sperry, L., & Shafranske, E. P. (Eds.) (2005). *Spiritually oriented psychotherapy*. Washington, DC: American Psychological Association.

Sproul, R. C. (1992). *Essentials of the Christian faith*. Wheaton, IL: Tyndale House.

Sullivan, H. S. (1953). *The interpersonal theory of psychiatry*. New York: W. W. Norton.

Tangney, J. P., & Dearing, R. L. (2002). *Shame and guilt*. New York: Guilford.

Taylor, B. B. (2000). *Speaking of sin: The lost language of salvation*. Boston: Cowley.

Tjeltveit, A. C. (Ed.). (2006). Love, psychology and theology [special issue]. *Journal of Psychology and Theology, 34*(1).

Vande Kemp, H. (1996). Historical perspective: Religion and clinical psychology in America. In E. P. Shafranske (Ed.), *Religion and the clinical practice of psychology* (pp. 71-112). Washington, DC: American Psychological Association.

2

Scientific Foundations

THERE IS AN OLD JOKE AMONG PSYCHOLOGISTS that you can ask three psychologists their views on how to treat a particular client, and you will get four opinions. There is a kernel of truth in this. Psychologists have offered many ideas, models, techniques and theories all of which were thought to help people. The bad news is that many of these techniques and theories lack scientific support for their claims (e.g., primal scream therapy or neurolinguistic programming); the good news is that psychologists keep testing new treatments in order to discover which treatments work best. Various approaches to psychological treatment are effective, which sometimes makes it difficult for students, therapists and clients to choose which approach they want to pursue.

Consider how widely accepted yet different theories can be applied to a case. Jim has grown increasingly impatient with his position as a warehouse supervisor. He has been in this position for eight years and sees it as a dead-end job. Particularly frustrating to him is his demanding and nonsupportive boss, who seems committed to making sure that Jim's job is unrewarding. Seeking to resolve his frustration, Jim consults with various counselors on ways to deal with his mounting anxiety and depression. He consults one therapist who focuses on the similarities between Jim's demanding boss and his unsupportive father; the therapist hopes Jim will benefit by gaining insight into his displaced reactions to his boss. Another therapist offers a structured eight-session program that focuses on the self-defeating thoughts that seem to predispose Jim to looking at the pessimistic and unrewarding aspects of his work. This therapist hopes that alterations in Jim's thinking will lead to changed feelings and behaviors. A third therapist advocates that Jim confront his boss and assertively insist on some major changes in his job assignment. This therapist believes that behavioral changes will promote changes in Jim's work environment and positively alter his feelings.

Which of these approaches will most help Jim? Will any of them help him? Or should he avoid counseling or psychotherapy altogether and focus on spiritual means of dealing with his situation—growing in prayer, seeking guidance, fasting in order to experience the sufficiency of Christ, fostering an attitude of self-sacrifice and service?

In chapter one, we argued that doctrine provides an essential backdrop for understanding any Christian approach to psychotherapy. As clinical psychologists, we are also trained and committed to investigate and evaluate psychotherapy with scientific methods. Sometimes scientifically trained psychologists make disparaging comments about spiritual ways of knowing, as if science has deemed Scripture irrelevant. Conversely, Christian counselors sometimes devalue the importance of scientific investigation, as if the Bible answers every question so thoroughly that we no longer need to observe the world around us. We believe that both science and Scripture are important in establishing a credible Christian approach to counseling and psychotherapy. Christian faith provides an essential worldview for the Christian therapist, and scientific research on psychotherapy has the potential to tell us what works, when and why. Quantitative and qualitative research methodologies have been developed that can provide useful insights into the seemingly opaque world of psychotherapy.

Psychological scientists tend not to talk much about the integration of Christianity and psychology, and those interested in integration tend not to talk much about science. This is an unfortunate divide insofar as both science and Christian faith ought to have shared roots in the virtue of humility. Ironically, most people may not think of either scientists or Christian theologians as particularly humble, but both approaches are based on an intrinsically humble worldview. Christianity, as outlined in chapter one, assumes a pervasive state of human brokenness. The noetic effects of sin mean that we are naturally blinded, that we cannot trust our own inclinations in determining what is true. In humility we must test our frail human reasoning by comparing our beliefs and assumptions against the standard of special revelation. And this cannot be an individual enterprise because our personal interpretations of Scripture are easily distorted. So throughout history we see Christians coming together for dialogue so that a collective understanding of revealed truth can be established. The historic church councils (e.g., Nicea, Chalcedon, Trent and many more) illustrate this sort of collective process of identifying and affirming truth. The councils are born out of a theological humility—recognizing that none of us is holy or wise enough to discern truth correctly on our own. Similarly, science is based on the assumption that human ideas cannot be fully trusted unless they gain empirical validation. Ideas are tested under well-defined conditions, and conclusions derived based on statistical probabilities. As with theology, science is more than an individual endeavor. Ideally, scientific findings are replicated in more than one laboratory and evaluated within a scientific community. There is humility built into the process of science, because the scientific method presumes individuals will come to faulty conclusions if not held to some external standards. Theologians assume the same.

Though both Christian theology and science call for humility, they rely on different external standards: special revelation for the theologian and general revelation for the scientist. But to the Christian, both are legitimate forms of revelation so we need not fear either the methods or findings of science.

Psychotherapy Effectiveness

The effectiveness of psychotherapy has been an object of attack by Christians who oppose psychological interventions. Sadly, much of this has been based on outdated and incorrect information. One of the first studies on the effectiveness of psychotherapy was conducted by Hans Eysenck in 1952. He published a review of twenty-four studies on psychotherapy and concluded that there was no research evidence to support the effectiveness of psychotherapy compared to no-treatment control groups. His conclusion was both provocative and controversial in the research community, and subsequently his findings were soundly criticized by numerous researchers on methodological grounds (see Bergin, 1971; Lambert, 1976). However questionable Eysenck's research may have been, a report by a respected psychologist on the ineffectiveness of psychotherapy was all the evidence some Christian writers needed to support their preconceived opinion that psychotherapy doesn't work. (See Bobgan & Bobgan [1987] for their perspective on Eysenck's [1952] study. Also see McMinn & Foster [1990] for a response.)

Following Eysenck's report, hundreds of outcome studies were conducted on psychotherapy in the ensuing decades. The application of a statistical procedure known as meta-analysis allowed findings of large numbers of studies to be analyzed together. In a landmark meta-analysis, Smith, Glass and Miller (1980) scoured the scientific literature—including journals, books, unpublished dissertations and other sources—to find and analyze 475 psychotherapy outcome studies. They concluded that psychotherapy is effective. It is not perfectly effective for everyone who seeks help, but the authors conclude that psychotherapy works at least as well as education works for our children, medicine works on our ailments or business turns a profit.

The beauty of meta-analysis is that it simultaneously evaluates the effects of many studies. In a large body of literature, there may be a few studies that do not support the effectiveness of psychotherapy and several others that provide outlandish success rates that are bigger than real life. Looking at studies from either extreme could easily skew our understanding of psychotherapy effectiveness.

This is what some Christian authors have done when they handpick a few studies and then conclude that psychotherapy never works. Meta-analysis controls our impulse to find only what we are looking for by comparing treatment groups from a large number of studies with the control groups from those same studies. The

---

COUNSELING TIP 2.1: A Confident Optimism

What should a therapist say if a client asks, "Are you sure this will help me?"

In most cases the proper answer is an optimistic one. Research strongly suggests effectiveness, but one cannot be absolutely sure that psychotherapy will help because therapy is not effective for every person or every problem. But still, there is good reason to be hopeful. Both efficacy and effectiveness studies suggest that psychotherapy is effective for most people and for a variety of problems.

---

results are reported as an effect size, which, roughly speaking, is the distance between the average of the treatment groups and the average of the control groups, expressed in a standard unit that is analogous to a standard deviation.

Accumulating research over sixty years involving hundreds of controlled studies, thousands of patients and therapists using various therapeutic approaches with many presenting problems has shown that psychotherapy is effective (Asay & Lambert, 1999). Meta-analytic reviews of numerous psychotherapy outcome studies have shown that the average effect size for psychotherapy is .82, indicating that the average treated person is less symptomatic than 80 percent of untreated persons.

The effect size for psychotherapy becomes more meaningful when compared to the effect size of commonly prescribed medications for psychological disorders. Faraone (2003) reported the following common effect sizes for these medications (the greater the number, the larger the effect): Immediate-release stimulants (e.g., Ritalin) for attention deficit hyperactivity disorder = .91; serotonin specific reuptake inhibitors (e.g., Prozac) for depression and obsessive-compulsive disorder = .50; atypical antipsychotic medications (e.g., Risperiodone) for schizophrenia = .25. Within this context, the average effect size for psychotherapy appears quite respectable.

Most research studies that evaluate psychotherapy outcomes are known as efficacy studies. These studies carefully control various factors such as client demographics, client diagnoses, therapist variables and intervention protocols so that the outcomes can be attributed to the interventions only. Additionally, control and comparison groups are used to further substantiate the effect of the interventions. This model of evaluating psychotherapy outcome is the same model used in evaluating the effectiveness of medications. The strength of efficacy studies lies in their carefully controlled laboratory qualities. The weakness of this approach is that it may lack a "real world" quality. For example, few clients in the real world of psychotherapy practice are so carefully screened that they have only one diagnosis, have no previous history of psychological problems or have no history of abuse.

Another approach to measuring psychotherapy outcomes has been accomplished by surveying consumers of psychotherapy. These surveys are known as effectiveness studies. Although they lack the careful controls of efficacy studies, they do have the power of showing how typical clients respond to psychotherapy. Seligman (1995) described a *Consumer Reports* survey on the perceived effects of psychotherapy as reported by those who received the services. Patients

---

COUNSELING TIP 2.2: Collecting Data

Some therapists find it useful to keep track of their own therapy outcomes. By giving an anxiety, depression, spiritual well-being or relationship questionnaire at the beginning and end of treatment, or by administering a satisfaction survey during the final session, therapists can keep track of their success rate. This can sometimes be useful in negotiating contracts with health insurers or in obtaining other mental health credentials. For therapists who collect their own outcome data, it is important to get information from *every* client—not just those who do well in therapy. Otherwise, the integrity of the research is questionable. For more about keeping outcome records in clinical practice, see Paul W. Clement's (1999) book *Outcomes and Incomes.*

---

indicated that they "benefited very substantially from psychotherapy, that long-term treatment did considerably better than short-term treatment, and that psychotherapy alone did not differ in effectiveness from medication plus psychotherapy. Furthermore, no specific modality of psychotherapy did better than any other for any disorder" (p. 965). Thus, various research methods point to the clear effectiveness of psychotherapy as a way to relieve the suffering of psychological disorders.

With strong support from the research literature, professionals no longer question whether or not psychotherapy is an effective way to treat psychological disorders. Contemporary researchers are seeking answers to different questions now. For example, what kinds of psychotherapy are most effective with which disorders? How much psychotherapy is needed for positive results to be obtained? How long do the positive results last? What are the effective components of psychotherapy?

Psychotherapy Models

Traditionally graduate education in psychotherapy has revolved around various schools of thought. Students learn early that major systems of psychotherapy grew from grand theories of personality. Thus students are pushed to survey these theories, such as psychodynamic, client-centered, cognitive and behavioral models, and endorse one of these theoretical orientations prior to graduation. Students are asked to describe their theoretical orientation in internship interviews and later in state licensure evaluations. Most states require ongoing postdoctoral education for psychologists, and it is common for these continuing education workshops to focus on specific therapy models or techniques. Attending one of these workshops gives the impression that you have just learned the best (and perhaps the one and only) way to treat a specific disorder.

Some people become such ardent proponents of a particular psychological theory that they cling to it as a worldview. One of us was recently at a meeting of psychologists where an enthusiastic attendee proclaimed, "Psychoanalysis is my political party." Sometimes one gets the sense that a particular theory takes on such importance to some psychologists that it replaces political ideology, historical wisdom and spiritual understanding. As we argued in chapter one, sound doctrine provides a better center for one's worldview, not one's theoretical persuasions in psychology.

Interestingly, there is little evidence that one model or kind of psychotherapy is superior to another. Despite the zeal and fervor with which various psychologists promote their theoretical models, most approaches to therapy fare about the same in large meta-analytic studies (Wampold, Mondin, Moody, Stich, Benson & Ahn, 1997). Psychoanalytic, object-relations, behavioral, cognitive and family therapists may be ardent believers in their models and techniques, but none of these models has been shown to be more effective than another as a global model of psychotherapy. The finding of similar outcomes among psychotherapies was long ago dubbed the "dodo bird verdict" by Rozenzweig (1936) and elaborated upon by Luborsky, Singer and Luborsky (1975). This comes from Alice in Wonderland who proclaimed, "Everyone has won, and all must have prizes."

Despite the dodo bird verdict—which is held to be true by most psychotherapy researchers—cognitive and cognitive-behavioral therapies have gained momentum in recent years. Some of these therapies had only recently been developed when Smith, Glass and Miller reported their meta-analysis in 1980. Their analyses included Albert Ellis's Rational Emotive Therapy, now known as Rational-Emotive Behavior Therapy (REBT), but did not include the more recent developments of Aaron Beck, Judith Beck, Arthur Freeman, Jacqueline Persons, David Barlow, Donald Meichenbaum, Samuel Turner, Mark Reinecke, Christine Padesky, Michael Mahoney and others. There are several reasons for the rising prominence of the cognitive and cognitive-behavioral therapies: it is easier to research short-term treatments such as cognitive therapy than longer-term treatments; cognitive and behavior therapies lend themselves well to the symptom-based outcome measures used in research studies; and they have been shown to be effective with particular disorders such as depression, anxiety disorders, borderline personality disorder and a variety of other problems (Chambless et al., 1998).

Given the research evidence, it does not seem reasonable to proclaim superiority of one particular theoretical paradigm over any other. Recent developments within the field of psychotherapy support integration of psychotherapy models (Norcross & Goldfried, 2005), and IP demonstrates a similar integrative attempt. Integrative psychotherapy is integrative in two dimensions. First and foremost, it integrates Christian thought with psychological theory and practice. Second, it integrates various theoretical perspectives within psychology. IP draws heavily on cognitive therapy perspectives but also relies on the more relational theories in psychology, including interpersonal psychotherapy and family therapy.

Length of Psychotherapy

At the beginning of the animated movie *Antz,* a neurotic ant named Z who sounds just like Woody Allen is lying down exploring the various traumas of life: how he feels physically inadequate because he has never been able to lift more than ten times his body weight, how he struggles with abandonment issues because his father flew away when he was only a larva, and how he longs for attention because he was the middle child in a family of five million. One gets the sense that Z will be lying in the therapist's office for a very long time dealing with a long list of issues ranging from body image to birth order. How realistic is this portrayal of therapy?

Traditionally, psychotherapy has been conceptualized as a long-term process that can last for years. Although some forms of psychotherapy (e.g., psychoanal-

---

IN THE OFFICE 2.1: Setting a Time Limit

Some clients may be concerned that the therapist will recommend several years of intensive therapy. These fears are fueled by inaccurate media portrayals of therapy and stories the client may have heard from others. It is often wise to respond by suggesting a specific length for the therapy relationship.

Bill: How long is this going to take? I've heard of people going to a therapist for years, and I'm just not interested in that sort of thing.

Mark: Yes, that's an important question. Most often therapy lasts a matter of weeks or months rather than years, though there are times when therapy can last longer.

Bill: I don't want something that goes on forever.

Mark: Right. We agree on that. Perhaps it would be good for us to agree on a particular time frame—say eight sessions—and then at the end of the eight sessions we will have this conversation again. We may agree that it is time to stop, or perhaps we will still have some things to work on. In either case, it keeps us focused on making progress and it keeps us talking about how long you want to invest in this process.

Bill: That sounds like a good plan. I just don't want eight weeks to turn into eight years.

Mark: Yes, I hear your concern and I think you are wise to be asking these questions. We are talking about eight sessions, not eight years.

---

ysis) may require several years, the time frame of psychotherapy has been greatly reduced over the last twenty years. There are several reasons for the reduction in time to months or weeks, including the advent of managed health care; a better-informed, health-consuming public; development of short-term psychotherapy models; the development of more effective psychotropic medications and a focus on symptom relief rather than personality change. Regardless of the cause, most psychotherapy practiced today tends to be brief.

Lambert (2004) reports that most research on psychotherapy examines therapy that is conducted once per week for no more than fourteen weeks. Psychotherapy as practiced in actual treatment settings may average closer to five sessions. Among clients who persist beyond the first few sessions, approximately half show significant improvement by eight to ten sessions, and 75 percent improve within twenty-six sessions (Kadera, Lambert & Andrews, 1996). Thus accumulating research indicates that most psychotherapy lasts for weeks or months rather than years.

IP is well suited for the relatively brief treatments that occur in the real world of psychotherapy practice, but it can also function as a longer-term therapy for clients who are seeking more extensive personal insight and change. The length of treatment is related to the domains-of-intervention approach we describe in chapter four.

Lasting Effects of Psychotherapy

Although psychotherapy should not be conceptualized as forever curing someone of emotional troubles, the effects of psychotherapy, in general, are long lasting. Follow-up studies indicate that most clients tend to maintain therapy gains for significant periods of time, especially if clients attribute changes to their own efforts (Lambert & Bergin, 1994). Additionally, clients tend to have more lasting gains when their problems are related to situational causes rather than long-standing difficulties and when they have substantial social support.

Of course there are particular conditions that are prone to relapse—substance abuse, eating disorders, some forms of depression, and personality disorders. Typically these disorders have multiple causes and may involve biochemical or neurological determinants. Although psychotherapy effects appear to be long lasting for many clients, some clients are prone to relapse and will require either ongoing care or subsequent episodes of psychotherapy treatment.

A caveat is in order. The long-term effectiveness of psychotherapy should not be determined by whether or not a therapist ever sees a client again after a course of therapy has been completed. This can be illustrated by considering two hypothetical therapists, both caricatures. Dr. Grossman is an obnoxious, in-your-face therapist who does not like his clients very much. He criticizes them, gives advice prematurely and has bad breath. He sees clients for an average of five sessions each and then they rarely return. Dr. Goodheart is a kind, sensitive therapist who listens well to her clients, offers them coffee at the beginning of each session, remembers the details of their lives and cares deeply about their healing. She sees clients for an average of fourteen sessions each, and they often return again at a later time in life for more therapy. From a pure research perspective, one could argue that Dr. Grossman is a better therapist than Dr. Goodheart because he requires fewer sessions with his clients, and once they improve they never again need his help. Of course we know better. Dr. Goodheart is a better therapist, which is why her clients stay in therapy longer and come back again when the need arises.

IN THE OFFICE 2.2: Back to Square One?

Therapy is usually effective and typically brings sustained, long-term benefits. But this doesn't mean that people never take steps backwards. Oftentimes therapists schedule booster sessions in order to check in with clients to see if they are maintaining their progress. Other times clients will call for some additional appointments after completing therapy. It is good to reassure a client at times such as these. Just because a person has taken a step backwards, it does not mean that all the previous work was for naught.

Consider the following telephone conversation.

Clark: Hello, Jean.

Jean: Hello. Thanks for calling me back. I'm not sure what happened. I was doing just great until a couple weeks ago, and then these feelings of depression just started up again. I thought I was all over this.

Clark: It can be so discouraging to have those feelings of depression come back. You're depressed, which is bad enough, and then you're also feeling depressed about being depressed.

Jean: Exactly. I feel like I'm back at square one, like I didn't really learn anything after six months of therapy.

Clark: It's natural for it to feel that way. Depression can be a very persistent thing. But this time you already know some of the tools to fight against it. Maybe we should plan to meet for a few more sessions, and we can also talk about whether it would be good to get you back in to see your physician.

Jean: That's encouraging to hear. I'm glad to know you are willing to see me again.

Clark: Oh, of course. I look forward to helping you figure this out.

Notice that a reassuring, matter-of-fact tone is calming and helpful in this situation.

IP represents an effort to balance relational and technical skills. If done properly, many clients will respond quickly to therapy and will make long-term changes. However, it is also important to realize that some clients will come back later for additional care. This should not be seen as a failure, but as a relational success.

Change Processes and Stages

Although psychotherapy models may use different terminology, there is mounting evidence that various models encourage similar change processes. Prochaska and DiClemente (1983) described some of the common psychotherapy change processes as consciousness raising, catharsis, self-reevaluation, counterconditioning and stimulus control. These processes may be implemented in different ways in various therapies, but all are quite likely to be facilitated in one way or another. For example, virtually all psychotherapies help clients become more aware of themselves (self-reevaluation) and specific foci of change (consciousness raising). Prochaska and Norcross (1994) indicated that psychotherapies differ more in the content of change rather than the change processes.

Prochaska and DiClemente (1983) further identified stages involved in personal changes. They presented some evidence indicating that stages of change are likely involved whether the change occurs in one's natural environment, a specific program designed for personal change or in individual psychotherapy. The stages identified include Precontemplation (no intention to change), Contemplation (intention to take action), Preparation (intention to take immediate action), Action (implementing specific modifications in behavior) and Maintenance (steps to avoid relapse).

Some enhanced successes in therapeutic interventions have been obtained when client stage level has been assessed prior to therapy beginning (Prochaska and DiClemente, 1983, 1984, 1985; Prochaska, DiClemente, Velicer & Rossi, 1993). Appropriate therapeutic strategies are then aimed at addressing client problems according to their stage of change. For example, it would not make sense to promote active implementation of new behaviors with a client who is in the Precontemplation stage. This client may benefit most from considering the negative consequences to self and family by remaining at the present status. Overall, the empirical evidence on this matching approach is encouraging, but it seems to be most useful for clients with various substance disorders such as smoking addiction.

Common Factors in Psychotherapy

Researchers are particularly interested in determining which components of psychotherapy are most effective. The results are humbling to ardent advocates of a specific theoretical approach because over the last couple of decades it has become increasingly clear that there are certain common elements in all psychotherapies that appear to be the primary components of change. We now know

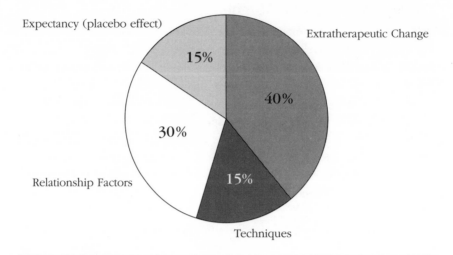

Figure 2.1. Psychotherapy outcome research

that the specific techniques or models of psychotherapy generally have a modest impact on the outcome. Although proponents continue to voice their convictions that psychodynamic, cognitive-behavioral, family and many other models are the source of psychotherapy outcome, the research indicates a different perspective.

What has emerged from the research literature is known as common factors. These are the factors present in all psychotherapies that seem to account for outcomes regardless of model or technique. Lambert (1992) persuasively described four common factors which have been elaborated by various authors (see Hubble, Duncan & Miller, 1999; Duncan, Hubble & Miller, 1997; Miller, Duncan & Hubble, 1997; Lambert, 2004). The four common factors are (1) client/extratherapeutic, (2) relationship, (3) hope/expectancy and (4) model/technique. Figure 2.1 shows these factors and Lambert's estimates of the degree to which each factor contributes to the outcome of psychotherapy.

Client/extratherapeutic factors. A recurring observation by supervisors in training beginning graduate students involves the attributions students make in their early clinical training. Trainees often feel like failures when clients do not make giant strides toward psychological health: progress is slow, symptoms intensify, or the client may drop out of treatment. It is quite natural for students to attribute these "failures" to a lack of counseling knowledge, skill or experience. While knowledge, skill and experience are all important, these client "failures" are often due to client factors rather than therapist factors.

Client/extratherapeutic factors involve both internal and external features that affect the client. Internal factors include strengths such as intelligence, motivation, persistence, faith, emotional management and so on. External factors include social, financial and community support. This includes involvement and support from a religious community, which appears to play a helpful role in providing clients with ongoing emotional and spiritual sustenance.

Some clients come to counseling having just faced a severe loss or transition, while others have dealt with multiple stressful issues for years. Some come from abusive families, while others were provided consistent love and security at home. Some believe they have emotional issues they need assistance in changing, and others see no problems in themselves and simply arrive at the psychologist's doorstep at the demand of a weary spouse. Traditionally psychologists have been aware of these significant client factors, but the magnitude of their effect on psychotherapy outcome has been underestimated. Lambert (1992) estimates these factors account for 40 percent of psychotherapy outcomes.

COUNSELING TIP 2.3: Church Is Good for Body and Soul

Social scientists are discovering various ways that church involvement promotes physical and mental health and protects people from premature death (Koenig, McCullough & Larson, 2001; Powell, Shahabi & Thoresen, 2003). In addition, church communities often promote spiritual hope and meaning in life, and provide social support in times of isolation and loss. For all these reasons, church involvement should be considered a significant client/extratherapeutic factor. It is not appropriate to coerce a client into attending church, but it is worth asking about church attendance and gently encouraging clients who are not currently involved in a church to consider the possibility.

The power of client factors, such as personal resiliency and social support to name a couple, is a likely reason why some people improve without psychotherapy. Asay and Lambert (1999) reported several studies indicating that on average 43 percent of people improved with little or no treatment. It is unclear how rapidly they improved or how long the improvement lasted, but it appears that people can recover from emotional difficulties through many of their own resources. The last couple decades have witnessed a huge rise in the availability of self-help literature and support groups, which provide needed help for clients apart from formal psychotherapy. This also helps explain the powerful role of the church in helping people heal from emotional struggles. Not only does the church provide spiritual resources for help, it also provides a social support network and helps individuals gain a meaning or purpose for living. All of these factors bode well in recovering from psychological problems.

The importance of a client's diagnosis in determining the type of therapy is a research question that has garnered a good deal of attention. Many psychotherapists rely on an accurate diagnosis to assist in determining the nature of psychological treatment and the potential for improvement in psychotherapy. Although diagnosis is a client factor and is related to improvement, it appears to have relatively little impact on psychotherapy outcome. Thus, diagnosis is important for a variety of reasons (see chapter five), but of relatively little significance in determining psychotherapy outcome.

Relationship factors. Graduate students sometimes express disappointment at the start of clinical training when the focus is on developing basic relationship skills. Listening, empathy, reflection and self-awareness are common foundational relationship skills that psychotherapists use. Some students express concerns that these skills are elementary and that they need to focus on learning techniques such as *in vivo* exposure or cognitive restructuring. These same students may hold strong beliefs that psychotherapy is very complex and that they must adopt a specific theoretical orientation and master the related therapy techniques. The temptation is to see the therapeutic relationship as elementary.

Regardless of the therapist's theoretical orientation, the therapeutic relationship is an important factor in the success of the therapy. Although some models may place relatively less emphasis on the relationship (e.g., Rational-Emotive Behavior Therapy), most models emphasize the prominence of the alliance between therapist and client. Relationship factors include caring, empathy and emotional support to name a few. These factors account for 30 percent of the success in psychotherapy outcome research.

In 1957 Carl Rogers posited several necessary and sufficient conditions for change in psychotherapy. Among them were acceptance, empathy and genuineness. Acceptance promotes the feeling of being heard, respected and valued by another. Empathy facilitates the sense of being understood by the therapist—not just the words that are spoken but the underlying emotions and conflicts. Finally, genuineness or congruence on the part of the therapist communicates honesty and consistency. The client can then trust the therapist and discuss painful issues openly. Rogers believed these therapeutic attitudes were so powerful that they were the sufficient causes of therapeutic change. Decades of research and reflection seem to support the necessity of these attitudes, but not the sufficiency of them. In other words, these therapist relational qualities are essential to successful psychotherapy, but in and of themselves they are not always enough to bring about change and growth.

Significantly, these factors need to be detected by the client to be effective. It is not enough for the therapist to believe that the attitudes have been present and communicated to the client. Rather, the client has to experience these qualities—to feel accepted, understood and safe.

Expectancy/hope factors. People do not come to a therapist's office expecting to spend an hour and a good deal of discretionary income each week to no avail. Fortunately, they come with hopes of feeling and functioning better. Their expectations of getting better are one of the reasons they do get better.

The expectancy effect—sometimes called the placebo effect—comes from the belief clients have that their condition is being treated effectively. People typically downplay the significance of the placebo effect, but it plays a substantial role in all kinds of change, including response to medications. Expectancy and hope factors include the belief that one is going to get better, that the therapist has the knowledge and skill to help, that there is hope in a brighter future. Lambert (1992) summarized these factors as accounting for 15

COUNSELING TIP 2.4: Beyond Technique

Many counseling texts give specific tips for how to express therapeutic warmth and compassion. A therapist may learn to lean forward when a client is encountering particularly troubling memories or to use a softer voice when a client is weeping. All these tips may be useful but they are no substitute for a caring and compassionate heart. Effective therapists do not simply learn tricks to express care—they truly care. Clients can tell the difference between genuine care and technique-based care.

If sincere compassion does not come naturally, it may be a reminder to listen more intently to the client's story, to consider the developmental and environmental factors that have contributed to the client's current difficulties, and to pray more fervently for the client outside of therapy sessions.

Therapists facing excessive stress and burn-out may find they are relying more on technique than genuine compassion day after day. In times such as these, it is important for therapists to seek spiritual and emotional support, to get the help of a supervisor and to consider taking a break from clinical work.

percent of the outcome variance in psychotherapy.

In 1973 Jerome Frank published a seminal book titled *Persuasion and Healing: A Comparative Study of Psychotherapy*. In this book Frank described a broad range of healing practices across various cultures, including religious practices, faith healings, shaman rituals and psychotherapy. He showed that many of these practices had common elements, including a healing ritual, an expert who provided some kind of treatment, a willing and hopeful person in need of treatment, and the expectation by all involved that healing would occur. These factors are common to a variety of healing practices and exert a powerful effect on the success of treatment.

Expectation, hope and belief are so powerful that these effects have been measured in improvement rates. Lambert, Weber and Sykes (1993) summarized findings of placebo effects in terms of effect size and showed that the average client receiving placebo treatment improved more than 66 percent of no-treatment control participants. This improvement rate should be viewed in the context of a variety of psychotherapy outcome studies which show that the average client receiving psychotherapy improves more than 80 percent of no-treatment control subjects. These reports point to the strong impact that hope, expectation and belief have on therapeutic outcomes.

COUNSELING TIP 2.5: Measuring Hope

For years psychologists have measured hopelessness. Now there are ways to measure hope. For a brief scale measuring one's current state of hope, C. R. Synder and colleagues' State Hope Scale is worthwhile (Snyder, Sympsom, Ybasco, Borders, Babyak & Higgins, 1996). The scale is available online at <http://www.psych.ku.edu/faculty/rsnyder/state.htm#State%20Hope>.

Snyder and his colleagues have also developed a dispositional hope scale for children (Snyder et al., 1997). The Children's Dispositional Hope Scale is also available online at <http://www.psych.ku.edu/faculty/rsnyder/child.htm#Child%20Scale>.

Model/technique factors. Like expectation/hope effects, Lambert (1992) reported that model and technique factors account for 15 percent of the outcome in psychotherapy. These factors include specific procedures used in various psychotherapies. Examples include progressive relaxation, hypnosis, biofeedback, transference interpretation, dream analysis, behavioral contingency arrangements, thought stopping, tracking dysfunctional thinking, assertiveness training and so on. These factors may also include the rationale, explanation or structure that specific therapies provide. It is these factors that psychotherapists have traditionally emphasized in training programs with the notion that the accurate application of techniques in a manner congruent with a particular therapy model would lead to behavior change.

It is sometimes discouraging to students to realize that they go through undergraduate training, then another five years of doctoral training, then a year or two of postdoctoral training, and much of their training pertains to something that accounts for only 15 percent of therapy outcome. But this may not be as dismal as it sounds at first. Although 15 percent of the change in psychotherapy may be seen as a modest contribution to the overall effectiveness of change, it is still a substantial contribution. Also, some specific techniques have been shown to be effective with particular disorders, so it is not as though the techniques are equally important. An example of an effective technique is exposure in the treatment of specific phobias (discussed in chapter seven). With this technique phobic clients are slowly and systematically exposed to the feared object or situation while maintaining minimal levels of anxiety. This procedure has been shown to be more effective than other techniques in the treatment of these sometimes debilitating disorders.

The nature of common factors that account for change in psychotherapy should not be too surprising to Christians. Scripture and Christian tradition seem to support a common-factors approach to understanding change. Change does not simply occur by understanding proper doctrine (though this is important), but also by a variety of factors that shape the direction and quality of one's life. For example, hope through re-interpretation of current circumstances was frequently taught by the apostles. Christ taught in the Sermon on the Mount that various personal spiritual qualities were important in leading a fulfilling life. Similarly, Christian community—filled with meaningful relationships—is necessary for support, encouragement and admonishment. Specific techniques such as prayer, confession, meditation and service are also described as necessary for growth. These common elements of life, available to everyone, are seen as helpful in withstanding the negative events we encounter and in promoting godly character.

Empirically Supported Treatments

Over the last two decades there has been a strong movement in health care to demonstrate the effectiveness of various interventions (Deegear & Lawson, 2003). Variously referred to as evidence-based or empirically supported treatments (ESTs), these are medical or mental health interventions that have demonstrated effectiveness (Nathan & Gorman, 2002). A task force created by Division 12 (Society of Clinical Psychology) of the American Psychological Association (APA) has been documenting mental health interventions that have empirical support for their effectiveness in treating specific disorders. A specific intervention must meet relatively strict criteria to be included on the list of effective treatments. Of these empirically supported treatments, most are cognitive-behavioral in nature. "The vast majority of ESTs identified to date—60% to 90% depending on the list—are cognitive-behavioral treatments" (Norcross, 2004, p. 13). Although techniques make only a modest contribution to the overall outcome of psychotherapy, the cognitive-behavioral techniques have the most research support.

Determining the effective components of all psychotherapies is different than determining the most effective treatments for a specific disorder. That is, showing that common factors in psychotherapy matter a great deal is not synonymous with showing that specific factors (techniques) don't matter. The Dodo Bird finding by Rozenzweig (1936)—that all psychotherapies are similarly effective—may be analogous to stating that medications are effective in treating illnesses. However, it is apparent that some medications are designed to specifically treat certain illnesses, and when we probe at this level it is evident that some medications are more effective than others for specified illnesses.

Various cognitive therapy interventions have been shown to be helpful with particular disorders (Butler & Beck, 2001), and several meta-analytic studies have shown that cognitive-behavioral methods yield slightly more favorable outcomes than other psychotherapy methods (cf. Shapiro & Shapiro, 1982; Robinson, Berman & Neimeyer, 1990). Admittedly, this finding may be partially due to the relative ease with which cognitive-behavioral treatments can be translated into research protocols, but it is unlikely that this can fully account for the magnitude of cognitive therapy's success in the research literature. Recent studies demonstrate that cognitive-behavioral therapy is more effective than supportive counseling for anxiety symptoms in older adults (Barrowclough et al., 2001), more effective than emotion-focused psychotherapy for patients with panic disorder (Shear, Houck, Greeno & Masters, 2001), more effective than supportive counseling for adult survivors of trauma (Ehlers & Clark, 2003), and more effective than medication for relapse prevention in depression (Butler & Beck, 2001). Christian approaches to cognitive therapy have not been proven superior to other nonreligious cognitive therapy approaches (Johnson, 1993; McCullough, 1999; Worthington & Sandage, 2001).

Cognitive-behavioral therapy has been studied extensively, and many meta-analyses have been conducted on the effectiveness of this form of psychotherapy. Butler, Chapman, Forman and Beck (2006) recently reviewed sixteen meta-analyses that demonstrated methodological rigor. Their findings show that cognitive therapy is highly effective for adult and adolescent unipolar depression, generalized anxiety disorder, panic disorder, social phobia, posttraumatic stress disorder, and childhood depressive and anxiety disorders (grand mean effect size = .95). Additionally, cognitive-behavioral therapy is effective for bulimia (average effect size = 1.27) and as an adjunct to medication in treating schizophrenia (average effect size = 1.23). Cognitive therapy was moderately effective for marital distress, anger, childhood somatic disorders and symptoms of chronic pain (average effect size = .62). Cognitive therapy is relatively ineffective in treating sexual offenders (average effect size = .35).

Conclusion

At the beginning of this chapter we considered the situation of Jim who experienced anxiety and depression in the midst of a frustrating job. Which conceptualization of his problems is most appropriate? Although there is no formula to address such complex human problems, there is some guidance available from the psychological research literature. A careful assessment of Jim's background, resources and traits would likely yield information that would help a therapist identify Jim's expectations, hopes and beliefs about himself, the world and change processes. A wise therapist would use this information to facilitate a sound therapeutic relationship designed to further enhance Jim's personal resources at an appropriate change stage.

Regardless of the specific techniques used in therapy, Jim will probably improve. Factors that will increase his chances of a successful outcome include his psychological resources and social support system, a positive and trusting relationship with his therapist, his positive expectations for successful therapy, and the specific techniques used by his therapist. A cognitive-behavioral approach to Jim's anxiety and depression might be most helpful in alleviating his specific symptoms, though many other approaches to therapy could also be helpful. In the process of therapy, Jim may request further assistance with understanding how his distress is related to his job, family or faith—topics that go beyond the realm of standard cognitive therapy.

The integrative psychotherapy that we describe in this book is rooted in cognitive therapy techniques, but not exclusively so. The research literature allows us to be confident in cognitive therapy interventions, but it also requires humility because many different approaches to therapy are also effective. The domains-of-intervention approach described in chapter four integrates various theoretical approaches to psychotherapy, emphasizes the importance of a healthy psychotherapy relationship, and requires therapists to be familiar with the various stages of change and to work collaboratively with clients in determining how much change is being requested.

References

Asay, T. P., & Lambert, M. J. (1999). The empirical case for the common factors in therapy: Quantitative findings. In M. A. Hubble, B. L. Duncan & S. D. Miller (Eds.), *The heart and soul of change: What works in therapy.* Washington, DC: American Psychological Association.

Barrowclough, C., King, P., Colville, J., Russell, E., Burns, A., & Tarrier, N. (2001). A randomized trial of the effectiveness of cognitive-behavioral therapy and supportive counseling for anxiety symptoms in older adults. *Journal of Consulting and Clinical Psychology, 69,* 756-62.

Bergin, A. E. (1971). The evaluation of therapeutic outcomes. In A. E. Bergin & S. L. Garfield (Eds.), *Handbook of psychotherapy and behavior change: An empirical analysis* (pp. 217-70). New York: John Wiley & Sons.

Bobgan, M., & Bobgan, D. (1987). *Psychoheresy.* Santa Barbara, CA: Eastgate Publishers.

Butler, A. C., & Beck, J. S. (2001). Cognitive therapy outcomes: A review of meta-analyses. *Tidsskrift for Norsk Psykologforening, 38,* 698-706.

Butler, A. C., Chapman, J. E., Forman, E. M., & Beck, A. T. (2006). The empirical status of cognitive-behavioral therapy: A review of meta-analyses. *Clinical Psychology Review, 26,* 17-31.

Chambless, D. L., Baker, M. J., Baucom, D. H., Beutler, L. E., Calhoun, K. S., Crits-Christoph, P., Daiuto, A., DeRubeis, R., Detweiler, J., Haaga, D. A. F., Johnson, S. B., McCurry, S., Mueser, K. T., Pope, K. S., Sanderson, W. C., Shoham, V., Stickle, T., Williams, D. A., & Woody, S. R. (1998). Update on empirically validated therapies, II. *The Clinical Psychologist, 51,* 3-16.

Clement, P. W. (1999). *Outcomes and incomes: How to evaluate, improve, and market your psychotherapy practice by measuring outcomes.* New York: Guilford.

Deegear, J., & Lawson, D. M. (2003). The utility of empirically supported treatments. *Professional Psychology: Research & Practice, 34,* 271-77.

Duncan, B. L., Hubble, M. A., & Miller, S. D. (1997). Stepping off the throne. *The Family Therapy Networker, 21,* 22-31.

Ehlers, A., & Clark, D. M. (2003). Early psychological interventions for adult survivors of trauma: A review. *Biological Psychiatry, 53,* 817-26.

Eysenck, H. F. (1952). The effects of psychotherapy: An evaluation. *Journal of Consulting Psychology, 15,* 319-24.

Faraone, S. V. (2003). Understanding the effect size of ADHD medications: Implications for clinical care. *Medscape Psychiatry & Mental Health 8*(2). www.medscape.com/viewarticle/461543.

Frank, J. (1973). *Persuasion and Healing* (rev. ed.). Baltimore: Johns Hopkins University Press.

Hubble, M. A., Duncan, B. L., & Miller, S. D. (1999). *The heart and soul of change: What works in therapy.* Washington, DC: American Psychological Association.

Johnson, W. B. (1993). Outcome research and religious psychotherapies: Where are we and where are we going? *Journal of Psychology and Theology, 21,* 297-308.

Kadera, S. W., Lambert, M. J., & Andrews, A. A. (1996). How much therapy is really enough?: A session-by-session analysis of the psychotherapy dose-effect relationship. *Journal of Psychotherapy: Practice and Research, 5,* 1-22.

Koenig, H. G., McCullough, M. E., & Larson, D. B. (2001). *Handbook of religion and health.* New York: Oxford.

Lambert, M. J. (1976). Spontaneous remission in adult neurotic disorders: A revision and summary. *Psychological Bulletin, 83*(1), 107-19.

Lambert, M. J. (1992). Implications of outcome research for psychotherapy integration. In J. C. Norcross & M. R. Goldfried (Eds.), *Handbook of psychotherapy integration* (pp. 94-129). New York: Basic Books.

Lambert, M. J. (Ed). (2004). *Bergin & Garfield's handbook of psychotherapy and behavior change* (5th ed.). New York: Wiley.

Lambert, M. J., & Bergin, A. E. (1994). The effectiveness of psychotherapy. In A. E. Bergin & S. L. Garfield (Eds.), *Handbook of psychotherapy and behavior change: An empirical analysis* (4th ed.) (pp. 143-89). New York: John Wiley & Sons.

Lambert, M. J., Weber, R. D., & Sykes, J. D. (1993, April). Psychotherapy versus placebo. Poster presented at the annual meetings of the Western Psychological Association, Phoenix, AZ.

Luborsky, L., Singer, B., & Luborsky, L. (1975). Comparative studies of psychotherapies: Is it true that "everybody has won and all must have prizes"? *Archives of General Psychiatry, 32,* 995-1008.

McCullough, M. E. (1999). Research on religion-accommodation counseling: Review and meta-analysis. *Journal of Counseling Psychology, 46,* 92-98.

McMinn, M., & Foster, J. (1990). *Christians in the crossfire.* Newberg, OR: Barclay Press.

Miller, S. D., Duncan, B. L., & Hubble, M. A. (1997). *Escape from Babel: Toward a unifying language for psychotherapy practice.* New York: Norton.

Nathan, P. E., & Gorman, J. M. (2002). *A guide to treatments that work* (2nd ed.). New York: Oxford University Press.

Norcross, J. C. (2004). Empirically supported treatments (ESTs): Context, consensus, and controversy. *The Register Report, 30*, 12-14.

Norcross, J. C., & Goldfried, M. R. (2005). *Handbook of psychotherapy integration* (2nd ed.). New York: Oxford University Press.

Powell, L. H., Shahabi, L., & Thoresen, C. E. (2003). Religion and spirituality: Linkages to physical health. *American Psychologist, 58*, 36-52.

Prochaska, J. H., & DiClemente, C. C. (1983). Stages and process of self-change of smoking: Toward an integrative model of change. *Journal of Consulting and Clinical Psychology, 51*, 390-95.

Prochaska, J. H., & DiClemente, C. C. (1984). *The transtheoretical approach: Crossing traditional boundaries of change.* Homewood, IL: DowJones/Irwin.

Prochaska, J. H., & DiClemente, C. C. (1985). Common processes of change in smoking, weight control, and psychological distress. In S. Shiffman & T. Wills (Eds.), *Coping and substance abuse.* New York: Academic Press.

Prochaska, J. H., & Norcross, J. C. (1994). *Systems of psychotherapy: A transtheoretical analysis* (3rd. ed.). Pacific Grove, CA: Brooks/Cole.

Prochaska, J. H., DiClemente, C. C., Velicer, W. F., & Rossi, J. S. (1993). Standardized, individualized, interactive and personalized self-help programs for smoking cessation. *Health Psychology, 12*, 399-405.

Robinson, L. A., Berman, J. S., & Neimeyer, R. A. (1990). Psychotherapy for the treatment of depression: A comprehensive review of controlled outcome resources. *Psychological Bulletin, 108*, 30-49.

Rogers, C. R. (1957). The necessary and sufficient conditions of therapeutic personality change. *Journal of Consulting Psychology, 21*, 95-103.

Rozenzweig, S. (1936). Some implicit common factors in diverse methods of psychotherapy. *American Journal of Orthopsychiatry, 6*, 412-15.

Seligman, M. E. P. (1995). The effectiveness of psychotherapy. *American Psychologist, 50*, 965-74.

Shapiro, D. A., & Shapiro, D. (1982). Meta-analysis of comparative therapy outcome studies: A republication and refinement. *Psychological Bulletin, 92*, 581-604.

Shear, M. K., Houck, P., Greeno, C., & Masters, S. (2001). Emotion-focused psychotherapy for patients with panic disorder. *American Journal of Psychiatry, 158*, 1993-98.

Smith, M. L., Glass, G. V., & Miller, T. I. (1980). *The benefits of psychotherapy.* Baltimore: Johns Hopkins University Press.

Snyder, C. R., Hoza, B., Pelham, W. E., Rapoff, M., Ware, L., Danovsky, M., Highberger, L., Rubinstein, H., & Stahl, K. (1997). The development and validation of the Children's Hope Scale. *Journal of Pediatric Psychology, 22,* 399-421.

Snyder, C. R., Sympson, S. C., Ybasco, F. C., Borders, T. F., Babyak, M. A., & Higgins, R. L. (1996). Development and validation of the State Hope Scale. *Journal of Personality and Social Psychology, 70,* 321-35.

Wampold, B. E., Mondin, G. W., Moody, M., Stich, F., Benson, K., & Ahn, H. (1997). A meta-analysis of outcome studies comparing bona fide psychotherapies: Empirically "all must have prizes." *Psychological Bulletin, 122,* 203-15.

Worthington, E. L., Jr., & Sandage, S. J. (2001). Religion and spirituality. *Psychotherapy: Theory, Research, Practice, Training, 38,* 473-78.

3

Psychology's Revolution

In 1968, as the Beatles were singing "You say you want a revolution," psychology was engaging in a quiet revolution of its own. The radical behaviorism of B. F. Skinner and his predecessors waned after its apex in the 1960s. Psychoanalysis enjoyed a surge of interest in the 1950s, but its influence atrophied throughout the '60s and '70s. A new school of cognitive psychology started revolutionizing research and clinical practice as old schools lost momentum (R. W. Robins, Gosling & Craik, 1999). The transition became known as the cognitive revolution.

Researchers began investigating cognitive phenomena such as causal attributions, social constructions, helplessness, optimism, information processing, heuristics, social cognitions and attitude change. Clinical practice also changed. Behavior therapists pried open the black box and begin looking at the vast domain of thought, beliefs and values residing between stimulus and response. Some psychoanalytic therapists became disenchanted with the years of intensive therapy required for personality change and began exploring the new, faster cognitive paradigm of change. Clinical scientists began studying the effects of the new cognitive therapies, and results were encouraging. Centers for cognitive therapy appeared in major cities throughout the United States.

Today we live in a postrevolution state where cognitive interventions are assumed, and even preeminent. Psychiatric hospital treatment programs routinely include cognitive therapy groups to help patients realign their thinking; university training programs in psychology must teach the scientifically based cognitive interventions in order to be accredited; self-help books based on principles of cognitive therapy flourish; and insurance companies sometimes mandate short-term cognitive approaches be used.

Integrative Psychotherapy (IP) begins with a Christian worldview, calling for three different domains of intervention corresponding with three views of the *imago Dei*. The first two domains of intervention are closely tied to cognitive therapy, so it is important to carefully review and critique cognitive therapy from a Christian perspective. In this chapter we first overview and then critique the basic assumptions of the cognitive therapies that emerged from the cognitive revolution.

AN OVERVIEW OF THE COGNITIVE THERAPIES

Cognitive therapies are typically divided into two broad categories. *Semantic cognitive therapies* focus on the words we use to talk to ourselves and on how we can change our self-talk to feel better. *Constructivist cognitive therapies* look beyond our self-talk and consider the ways we construct our experience of reality—how we shape the direction of our lives with values, assumptions and beliefs, and actively interpret life's events.

Semantic Cognitive Therapies

It is quite natural to link feelings with the events of life. A person gets a speeding ticket and then feels annoyed and disappointed for the rest of the day, assuming the speeding ticket caused the feelings. Another person receives a gift from a spouse and spends the evening feeling content, happy and loved, again assum-

Figure 3.1. Our normal assumption about the cause of feelings

ing the gift caused the good evening. People often attribute moods to the circumstances of life rather than exercising some control over their feelings (see figure 3.1).

The premise of the semantic cognitive therapies is that this simplistic connection between events and feelings overlooks an essential part of the process. Humans are not just logical machines that assess accurately and then respond predictably to the events of the world, but are active interpreters. Two inexperienced

Figure 3.2. The fundamental premise of cognitive therapy

skiers stand atop a hill; one feels anxious and the other thrilled. Both encounter the same event, but their feelings are quite distinct because they are interpreting their situation differently. One is thinking, *This will be so much fun.* The other is thinking, *Isn't this how Sonny Bono died?* The first person's evaluation leads to an emotion of euphoria, the other's to panic. These two skiers' appraisals of an identical situation reflects the fundamental premise of the semantic cognitive therapies: thoughts intervene between events and feelings (see figure 3.2).

Cognitive therapists help their clients consider and evaluate thinking patterns which, in turn, gives them greater control over their emotions. Returning to the previous example, it may well be that the second skier can learn to love skiing after adjusting some of the anxiety-provoking cognitions.

Albert Ellis, the founder of Rational-Emotive Behavior Therapy (REBT) and one of the pioneers of the cognitive revolution, uses ABCs to articulate this

---

IN THE OFFICE 3.1: Reflection with Direction

Most therapists use reflection and restatement to communicate active listening and care for their clients. For example:

Joyce: My car died yesterday, right in the middle of the expressway. I couldn't believe it! How could the timing have been any worse?

Mark: Oh my, how challenging. And it was right in the midst of traffic too.

In cognitive therapy, the therapist still reflects back the content of what the client is saying, but does it in a way to draw attention to the underlying thought processes.

Joyce: My car died yesterday, right in the middle of the expressway. I couldn't believe it! How could the timing have been any worse?

Mark: Oh my, how challenging. So there you were, stuck in the midst of traffic with a dead car, and all these emotions and thoughts start bombarding you.

Joyce: Yes, exactly. I mean I was able to get my car to the shoulder, and then I just curled up in a heap over the steering wheel and started sobbing uncontrollably. I mean how will I ever afford this, for one thing? And why did it have to happen now, right in the midst of these other problems in my life?

Mark: That's quite a picture. You're in this heap, feeling terrible and saying something like, "I just can't possibly handle one more thing right now."

Notice that the therapist can use reflections to communicate empathy while still nudging the conversation toward the thoughts that contribute to the negative feelings.

premise: A stands for *activating event,* B for *belief,* and C for *cons̶*
emotion (Ellis & Harper, 1997). Ellis's model corresponds to the ␣␣␣␣␣-
thoughts-feeling formulation that is common to all semantic cognitive therapies. A person gets a speeding ticket (A) and then upsets himself unnecessarily
with beliefs (B) such as, *These police officers are idiots. Why don't they spend
their time catching the real bad guys?* or, *I am so stupid to drive so fast. What
was I thinking? I can never afford to pay this ticket!* And so he spends the rest
of his day in an unhappy state (C), with his sour thoughts infesting various interactions and activities. Another person gets a speeding ticket (A), but with a
different outcome. She feels an immediate surge of disappointment and then
reminds herself that things will work out fine (B): *It's too bad I got this ticket,
and it is a nuisance, but I guess this stuff happens when I drive too fast. Oh well,
it's not the end of the world.* After fifteen minutes she feels fairly normal again
and moves ahead with a relatively normal day (C). One person gets a gift from
her spouse (A) and tells herself that it is a waste of money and just a cover-up
for the lousy way he treats her (B). She ends up feeling resentful (C). Another
person gets a similar gift (A) then spends the evening reflecting on what a generous and kind woman he married (B). He feels content and joyful (C). The
same event can lead to wildly disparate emotions, depending on what beliefs
a person uses to interpret the event.

Ellis does not stop with A-B-C. He adds D for *disputing* irrational beliefs and
E for the revised cognitive *effect.* Driving down the road after the speeding
ticket, the healthy person knows to dispute (D) the out-of-control catastrophic
thinking with calm, rational thoughts. The effect (E) is a better mood and a better day.

A similar premise is seen in Aaron Beck's cognitive learning therapy (Beck,
Rush, Shaw & Emery, 1979). Beck suggests that we are plagued with dysfunctional automatic thoughts (DATs) in response to life situations. These DATs
cause us to feel worse than necessary: more depressed, stressed, anxious, angry,
guilty and so on. The therapist helps the client build skills to fight against the
irrational and dysfunctional thoughts that arise throughout the day, using what
David Burns calls "mental judo" (Burns, 1999). By replacing DATs with rational
responses, the client gains control over unwanted emotional states.

The similarities between Ellis's approach and Beck's are striking: both assume
that life situations trigger automatic appraisal processes and that these appraisals
determine emotional responses. They also assume that these appraisals are plas-
tic: they can be molded and shaped to give individuals greater control over their
feelings. In this sense cognitive therapy puts each person in a position of control. People who learn to alter their beliefs—as Ellis and Beck suggest they

can—can also change the emotions they carry around from hour to hour. Feelings can be controlled by managing thoughts. Rather than telling oneself that things are terrible and awful, a person can learn to say they are unfortunate. Instead of believing that one cannot tolerate the bad things in life, inconve-

---

COUNSELING TIP 3.1: Practicing What We Preach

The principles of cognitive therapy are not only useful to clients; therapists can find them useful as well. Try monitoring your thoughts for several hours, looking for ways that exaggerated thoughts lead to unpleasant feelings. For example:

1. Do things ever seem more awful than they really are? Spilling a cup of coffee is embarrassing and inconvenient, but is it really as terrible as it seems at the time?

2. Do you ever imagine that you know what others are thinking? Perhaps someone looks at you a bit longer than usual and you assume that your clothes clash or you have something in your teeth. There are many other possible explanations.

3. Do you ever anticipate some bad event in the future? Perhaps you assume that it will rain just because you washed your car, or you feel convinced that you will fail an upcoming exam. Anticipating negative outcomes only increases anxiety; none of us can know what will happen in the future.

---

niences can be viewed as inevitable and manageable. Rather than living life with an arbitrary list of musts and shoulds, one can think flexibly about obligations. Instead of yelling at oneself or others for mistakes of the past, a person can learn to smile at human folly and move ahead with life.

Though Beck's approach shares many similarities with Ellis's, Beck and others (e.g., Beck, Freeman & Davis, 2003; Young, 1999) also added a vertical dimension to understanding faulty thinking (see figure 3.3). It seems reasonable enough to assert that people have automatic thoughts that contribute to unpleasant feelings, but where do these thoughts come from? What makes them automatic? Why do they hold so much power in determining emotions? To answer these questions, Beck and many other cognitive therapists believe that we have foundational beliefs operating beneath our full conscious awareness that predispose us to particular automatic thoughts.

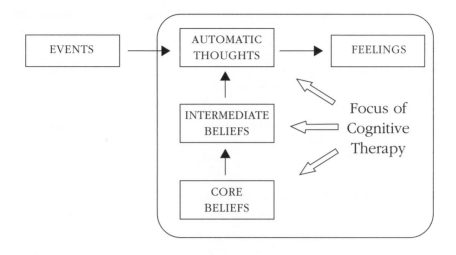

Figure 3.3. Cognitive therapy with a vertical dimension added

These foundational beliefs can be distinguished from automatic thoughts because the latter reside at the surface of consciousness, are relatively easily refuted by evidence and are situationally specific. For example, if a student believes she is bound to fail an upcoming final exam, this thought is specific to one situation (the exam), it is easily accessed (she may spontaneously tell her friends, even without prompting), and it can be refuted quickly once this student remembers that she has rarely failed exams and that she is studying quite diligently for this one. In contrast to DATs, deeper beliefs apply to more than one specific situation, are less accessible to consciousness and are not easily refuted with contrary evidence. Perhaps the anxious student is prone to anxiety about tests because she believes—consciously or not—that she must always be highly successful in all aspects of life. This general belief will be more resistant to change than her concerns about the particular test ahead of her.

Beck conceptualizes these deeper levels of thought in layers (see Needleman, 1999). Beneath automatic thoughts are intermediate beliefs. These intermediate beliefs might take the form of implicit rules (e.g., "I should be successful at everything I try"), if-then statements (e.g., "If I accomplish a great deal, then people will admire and love me"), or central goals (e.g., "I must become a successful professional"). The deepest beliefs—those that function at the most general level and are almost completely buried in the unconscious—are called core beliefs, or maladaptive underlying assumptions, and are extremely difficult to refute with evidence. Often these deepest beliefs have to do with self-image and a sense of trust or mistrust in the world around us. For example, the person who sees himself as fundamentally flawed and unlovable is prone to depression because his core belief will generate distressing intermediate beliefs and dysfunctional automatic thoughts. A friend or a therapist may try to bolster this person, telling him that he is lovable and good, but such reassurances are unlikely to help. Change will not be so easy because core beliefs are highly resistant to change.

Beck postulates that core beliefs are embedded in cognitive structures known as schemas. Schemas are activated or deactivated depending on the circumstances of life. Returning to the student with test anxiety, she does not feel particularly concerned until three days before the exam. Then the schema gets activated. She begins having DATs that flow from her core and intermediate beliefs, and certain predictable emotions result (e.g., anxiety, fear). These emotions and thoughts motivate her to study, and she develops conscious mechanisms to manage her upset feelings by focusing on behavior change (e.g., "I will study until midnight each night, then sleep until 5:00 a.m., then study until class time"). Once the final exam week is over, her schema is deactivated and she experiences peace and relaxation during her semester break.

This illustrates a relatively normal process of schema activation and deactivation, but what if the schema is activated at random times or is not easily deactivated once the crisis is over? Most students want their "alarm-and-mobilization" schema to be activated if a major exam is approaching because it motivates them to prepare for the exam. Similarly, we would want a "get-out-of-Dodge" schema to be activated if we were to encounter a hungry bear in the woods

---

COUNSELING TIP 3.2: Looking Beneath

Look for themes in a client's thoughts, because the themes often reflect some deeper value or assumption that is causing the client turmoil. For example, in the third session your client Justin discusses how much he has disappointed God. In the fifth session Justin describes how he has messed up his marriage and how every time he sees his wife he is reminded of what a bad husband he has been to her. In the sixth session he describes his anger toward his boss—how he never notices the good things Justin does and always criticizes him for his mistakes.

An astute therapist will notice that approval is a big theme for Justin and that he becomes rather self-focused in his yearning for approval. The deeper themes beneath his immediate situations will be productive to explore.

because it allows us to mobilize our resources and cope with the situation. But we would not want the same alarm-and-mobilization or get-out-of-Dodge schemas to suddenly appear as we are driving down the expressway or enjoying a quiet lunch with a friend. Those with panic attacks have unwanted schemas activated at seemingly random moments. Similarly, most of us value a remorse schema when we have done something that harms or violates another person, but we would not want our remorse schema activated arbitrarily. Those suffering from clinical depression often experience profound shame without cause. One goal of psychotherapy, then, is to help individuals gain more conscious control over schema deactivation.

The semantic cognitive therapies are simple to understand and, in a sense, have always been plagued by their simplicity. If a computer algorithm can replicate an approach to psychotherapy—as has been done with the cognitive therapies (Bloom, 1992; Kenardy & Adams, 1993)—then the complexities of human change have probably been oversimplified.

Constructivist Cognitive Therapies

In the late 1980s and early 1990s a refreshing alternative emerged, known as constructivist cognitive therapy (see the April 1993 issue of *Journal of Consulting and Clinical Psychology* for more information). The older semantic cognitive therapies are linear (see figure 3.2), assuming that reality is fixed and that our perceptions of reality determine how we feel and behave. But what if the relationships between external realities and our perceptions are actually dynamic and bidirectional? Perhaps the assumption that our thoughts affect our feelings is only half of the story; maybe feelings affect our thoughts also. What if reality itself is sometimes shaped by our thoughts and feelings (see figure 3.4)?

Imagine, for example, that a client named Jared has the belief that others are bound to reject him. A semantic cognitive therapy will consider this an errant

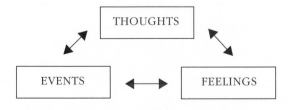

Figure 3.4. Constructivist cognitive therapies postulate bidirectional interactions between events, thoughts and feelings.

belief and help Jared conduct personal experiments to test out the validity of his belief. Eventually Jared will see the truth and realize that though some people might reject him it is simply not true that everyone rejects him. As a result, Jared will begin to feel better and will gain confidence in his social interactions with others. A constructivist cognitive therapist will do many of these same things, but will also consider the bidirectional relationship between beliefs and reality. In other words, the semantic and constructivist therapist will both be interested in how Jared interprets the events of his life, but the constructivist will also be interested in how Jared is understanding his developing life in relation to others and how his interpretations alter the events themselves. Jared's anticipation of rejection might actually be changing his experiences.

Jared has a new friend Jon. Jared calls Jon late one afternoon and says, "You know, Jon, it's been a while since I have heard from you and I just want to be sure that things are all right between us. I haven't offended you or anything, have I?" Jon reassures Jared that everything is fine, and Jared feels better, until the next day when Jared again begins questioning Jon's commitment to the friendship. So Jared picks up the phone again and phones Jon for reassurance. Jon reassures Jared, but privately feels annoyed by his insecurity. This happens day after day, week after week, until Jon is annoyed and stops answering when the caller ID has Jared's name. Soon they lose touch with one another and Jared concludes that his belief is correct: people are bound to reject him. Notice that Jared is not just an interpreter of reality; he is a constructor of reality. It is not just that his self-talk needs to be changed, but rather that he needs to see how he is sabotaging his desires for relationship by clinging to others so tightly.

The constructivist cognitive therapies emphasize the active nature of knowing: "A constructive view of human experience is one that emphasizes *meaningful action by a developing self in relationship*" (Mahoney, 2003, p. 5, italics his). Our beliefs do not simply reflect a passive understanding or misunderstanding of reality; they actually change reality, and they are formed in and changed by relationships with others in the context of a cultural milieu. This is closely tied to the field of hermeneutics—a field of study that emerged from biblical scholarship—which considers how every reader brings an interpretive strategy (and perhaps a bias) to a text. Hermeneutists have a familiar adage: "The reader is in the text and the text is in the reader." So when we approach a passage of Scripture, for example, we cannot help but bring our own experiences, preconceptions and biases to the passage we are interpreting. The reader is in the text. And, of course, the text will also influence our experiences, preconceptions and biases. The text is in the reader. In the same way, each of us is an active participant in our world—always shaping and changing things by our interpretations, beliefs and behaviors, and always being shaped by events around us.

The most extreme constructivists argue that *all* knowledge and reality are constructed through human processes such as social mores, cultural values, personal experiences, thinking patterns and so on. This leaves no room for objective reality outside of a human perceiver. For this reason, many Christians have looked skeptically at extreme expressions of postmodernism and constructivism. But not all constructivism is so radical and extreme. One can still believe in external authority and truth while acknowledging that human processes influence the actual events of everyday life. Indeed, the New Testament Epistles assume that we Christians can change ourselves and, at least to some extent, the world around us by holding fast to beliefs about our identity in Christ. For example, Peter helps his readers shape their thoughts by establishing their identity in Christ: "Once you were not a people; now you are the people of God. Once you received none of God's mercy; now you have received his mercy. Dear brothers and sisters, you are foreigners and aliens here. So I warn you to keep away from evil desires because they fight against your very souls" (1 Pet 2:10-11). But then Peter goes on to suggest that this sort of identity in Christ has an external effect on the world in which Christians live—helping others to "give honor to God" (1 Pet 2:12) and to "silence those who make foolish accusations against you" (1 Pet 2:15). Many more examples could be drawn from Scripture; the point is that Christians can and should accept the premise that personal values and perceptions of reality end up changing reality itself. Yet we cannot go so far as the radical constructivists who suggest that all reality is shaped by human processes, because Christians believe in a transcendent God who exists objectively and immutably beyond our thoughts and perceptions. Hip, hip, but no hurray for postmodernism and constructivism: they provide a helpful corrective to the simplistic linearity of semantic cognitive therapy, but they can easily become too extreme and lead to a denial of transcendent truth.

The constructivist cognitive therapies added new dimensions to cognitive therapy with in-depth consideration of developmental histories, emotions, culture, motivation and the social construction of reality. The constructivists reached their heyday in the early 1990s (Beck, 1993; Ellis, 1993; Haaga & Davison, 1993; Mahoney, 1993; Martin & Sugarman, 1993; Meichenbaum, 1993; Neimeyer, 1993; C. J. Robins & Hayes, 1993), and around the same time psychotherapy researchers presented compelling evidence that should humble semantic cognitive therapists for their oversimplified views of human experience (e.g., Jones & Pulos, 1993).

Constructivist cognitive therapy was heartening for many of us in the field, but it soon began to sputter because of health care's faltering economic engine. As managed care gained a stranglehold on health care, including mental health care, increasing emphasis was placed on short-term interventions. Of course it is much quicker to conduct psychotherapy with an advanced set of right and wrong beliefs than it is to take the time to learn the client's story in context. Constructivist cognitive therapy lost momentum in the face of these economic challenges.

In the early 1990s, the Society of Clinical Psychology—a division of the American Psychological Association—commissioned the task force we described briefly in chapter two. The task force was charged with the monumental task of

---

COUNSELING TIP 3.3: Treatment Manuals and You

Only therapies with treatment manuals can be included in the Division 12 list of empirically validated treatment procedures. A treatment manual is a step-by-step guide to help a therapist navigate the process of delivering a psychological treatment.

Many experienced therapists resist the idea of using treatment manuals in their work, because manuals stifle creativity and make the human change process seem formulaic and mechanical. Paint-by-numbers meets psychotherapy.

We concur that the routine use of treatment manuals can become onerous and stifling, but there are also times when manuals can be helpful. When learning a new therapy approach, a good manual and a good supervisor can both be useful. Sometimes treatment manuals come with client workbooks that are helpful even for clients working with experienced therapists.

Keep open to the possibility of using treatment manuals, at least during training and then perhaps from time to time throughout your psychotherapy career.

---

identifying empirically validated treatment procedures—therapy methods that had clear empirical support for their effectiveness (see Chambless et al., 1996; Chambless & Hollon, 1998; Crits-Christoph, Chambless, Frank, Brody, & Karp, 1995; Task Force, 1995). The task force hoped to preempt managed care companies, reasoning that it would be better for the profession to regulate itself rather than having outside insurance companies determine which therapies would be reimbursed and which would not. The result was a list of treatment procedures that are documented to be effective. Most of the therapies on the list are behavioral and cognitive interventions for various problems, but because the newer constructivist therapies are too young to have the solid research support that the earlier semantic therapies enjoyed, they are not included on the list. The task force's list has had a powerful effect on the practice of psychology, and as a result we rarely hear about constructivist cognitive therapies today. Despite cautions raised by respected professionals and researchers (e.g., Garfield, 1996; Havik & VandenBos, 1996; Messer, 2004; Silverman, 1996; Wampold & Bhati, 2004), the momentum has returned to the semantic cognitive therapies because they can be easily manualized and studied in laboratory settings.

We acknowledge that histories are constructed too, and this account of the rise and fall of constructivist cognitive therapy might be told differently by others in the field. Whatever the full story, we do not hear much about constructivist cognitive therapies these days, and we find the loss regrettable.

CRITIQUING COGNITIVE THERAPY

The cognitive revolution leaves lingering questions, especially for Christians. Which premises of cognitive therapy can be embraced, and which should be viewed skeptically? We begin with a brief discussion of the strengths of cognitive therapy, followed by concerns. Some of the concerns we identify should be considered by all psychotherapists, and others are specific to those endorsing a Christian view of persons.

Strengths of the Cognitive Therapy Premise

Chief among the various strengths of cognitive therapy is its commonsense appeal. A distressed person seeking help from a psychologist may resist approaches that are difficult to understand and those that seem unnecessarily circuitous. Cognitive therapy is refreshing because it is sensible and easy to explain and understand. The most basic premise of cognitive therapy—that the words we use to understand the world shape our feelings and behaviors—is so much a part of mainstream culture that it simply seems like common sense.

For example, the following sign appeared in front of an old house in an otherwise upscale suburban neighborhood. The new owners planned to tear down the house and build a new one in its place.

> This building is subject to demolition. Should there be any questions, contact the Suburban Building Department at 555-2050.

At first glance there is nothing particularly surprising or unusual about this sign, but if one looks more closely we see the premises of cognitive therapy at work. It's difficult to imagine any of us saying at the end of a workday, "Well, I'm going to call it a day and head to my building now." Or if we were visiting friends it would be unlikely to say, "What a beautiful building you have." Calling it a building helps us cope with the fact that it is about to be torn down. It is more difficult to destroy a home than to demolish a building.

Marketers have taken the premise of cognitive therapy to the bank. When a major ice cream maker changed their packaging from a 2-quart size to a 1.75-quart size—still charging the same price—they marketed the smaller size as the "New Spacesaver Size." Consumers bought the more expensive ice cream and felt fine about it because they could fit more in their freezers. Similarly, a restaurant offers two sizes of orange juice: big and really big. Calling the small orange juice big changes the way customers perceive the price of orange juice. The same is true of a popular coffee shop that sells tall, grande and venti drinks rather than small, medium and large.

In all these examples, and many more that can be observed in daily life, we see the fundamental premise of cognitive therapy at work. By changing words, and thereby changing thoughts, one's experience of reality is shifted. The ubiquity of this premise in daily life makes the concepts of cognitive therapy simple to describe and comprehend.

Also, cognitive therapy is appealing because it is goal-focused. If a client has a bridge phobia that keeps her from driving to work on the east side of the city from her house on the west side of the city, she may not welcome a therapist who begins the first session with, "So, tell me about your early life experiences." It is common for clients to come to therapy hoping for a focused, goal-oriented approach to help relieve their symptoms of distress; they may find it frustrating if their therapist spends excessive time focusing on personal growth, emotional exploration or childhood experiences.

Cognitive therapy is time-limited. Sometimes people resist getting help because they fear the open-ended nature of a psychotherapy relationship. Will a first visit to the therapist's office cascade into the expectation of weekly visits for several years? Many have heard stories of those who stay in therapy through most of their adult lives, and they naturally resist this idea. Cognitive therapy typically requires twelve to twenty sessions for most presenting problems, which is reassuring for those who resist long-term commitments to the therapy process.

Jones and Butman (1991) articulate several ways that cognitive-behavioral therapy is consistent with a Christian worldview. Cognitive therapy and Christianity both assume a limited freedom and a partial determinism. They reside between the complete freedom and autonomy assumed in humanistic theories and the hard determinism found in radical behaviorism. Also, both Christianity and cognitive therapy assume some degree of human agency over one's thoughts. We are responsible creatures with the capacity to exert some control over what and how we think. But neither Christianity nor cognitive therapy go so far as to suggest that materiality is unimportant or irrelevant. Humans are biologically bound, so our capacity to think is affected by neurophysiology, neuroanatomy, previous learning history and so on. The cognitive processes involved in sanctification provide another area of compatibility between cognitive therapy and Christianity. Of course, therapy is not sanctification, but growth in both systems assumes that one exerts personal control over thoughts and behaviors that promote change in a healthy direction.

COUNSELING TIP 3.4: Human Agency

Some models of psychotherapy are so heavily deterministic that they leave little room for personal choice. Therapists sometimes fall into the trap of assuming their clients are so affected by early childhood or previous learning patterns that they can no longer exercise choice over their behaviors, thoughts and feelings. Cognitive therapy is refreshing in its assumptions of human agency. No matter how difficult past circumstances, clients can choose to think and behave in new ways.

Christianity also assumes humans have agency to choose. The goals of cognitive therapy and Christian sanctification are not the same, so one should not be confused with the other. But still, it is important to recognize the common assumption—both cognitive therapy and Christianity assume a person has choice and that choices have consequences. Over and over in Scripture, humans are called to choose.

> Today I have given you the choice between life and death, between blessings and curses. I call on heaven and earth to witness the choice you make. Oh, that you would chose life, that you and your descendents might live! (Deut 30:19)

> Choose a good reputation over great riches, for being held in high esteem is better than having silver or gold. (Prov 22:1)

> Don't you realize that whatever you choose to obey becomes your master? You can choose sin, which leads to death, or you can choose to obey God and receive his approval. (Rom 6:16)

It is good for psychotherapists to experience empathy for their clients, to realize that wounds from the past often make current circumstances painful and difficult, but we should never forget that humans have the capacity to make healthy, godly choices even in the midst of terrible circumstances.

Another strength of cognitive therapy is found in the scientific evidence for its effectiveness, as discussed in chapter two. Cognitive therapy interventions have been successfully applied to depression, panic disorder, generalized anxiety disorder, social phobia, irritable bowel syndrome, chronic pain, bulimia, posttraumatic stress disorder, obsessive-compulsive disorder, substance abuse and dependence, borderline personality disorder, and more (Chambless et al., 1998). Psychology is a discipline consisting of scholars and professionals who place a good deal of confidence in scientific methods and conclusions, and the mounting scientific support for cognitive therapy is both substantial and compelling. The cognitive revolution is strongly rooted in scientific inquiry, so when it comes to the things that can be measured in the research laboratory (i.e., self-reported reduction of symptoms), cognitive therapy can be endorsed with enthusiasm. But some are quick to add that not everything important in psychotherapy is easily measured in the research laboratory.

Concerns with the Cognitive Therapy Premise

All psychotherapies are built on ideological and theoretical foundations (Jones & Butman, 1991). Psychodynamic therapy is based on the premises of Freud's psychoanalytic theory and the more contemporary modifications of neo-Freudians and object-relations theorists. Behavior therapy comes from classical and operant learning theory. Humanistic therapy was crafted to fit the ideologies of contemporary humanist psychologists such as Carl Rogers and Abraham Maslow. Much of contemporary family therapy is based on family systems theory and systems science.

Beck's and Ellis's cognitive therapy emerged out of clinical pragmatism; both were trained in insight-oriented psychotherapy but became disenchanted with the slow rate of progress observed in their patients. So Beck and Ellis, working independently of one another, found a quicker way to relieve symptoms by teaching people to think in new and different ways. As a result, there is somewhat of a theoretical void with the practice of cognitive therapy. Ideally, psychotherapies would emerge from carefully developed personality theories, but the process has been backward for cognitive therapy. The therapies came first, emerging out of clinical pragmatism, and now we are left to sort out what theoretical underpinnings fit best with the practice of cognitive therapy (see figure 3.5). Of course, no therapy can function with a true theoretical void because theoretical assumptions are eventually developed to match the therapy. What theoretical foundations have been developed to explain cognitive therapy? There are at least three possible ways to answer this question: social learning theory, information processing theory and pragmatic rationalism.

Ideally, interventions emerge out of personality theories.

Cognitive therapy interventions came first, developed out of clinical pragmatism, and now we are left with the task of identifying the underlying personality theory.

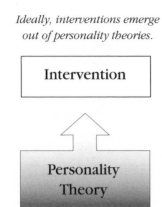

Figure 3.5. The relationship of theory and practice

Social learning theory and cognitive therapy. Some suggest that cognitive therapy is based on the social learning theory of Bandura (1986), Mischel (1973) and others. Social learning theory emerged out of behavioral theory, but with a softer form of determinism (known as reciprocal determinism) and more room for human agency. When Jones and Butman (1991) evaluated cognitive therapy from a Christian perspective, they did so with the assumption that cognitive therapy is closely related to social learning theory. This assumption makes sense for various reasons: cognitive therapy and social learning theory share similar philosophical assumptions, they emerged at similar times in the last half of the twentieth century, and both are gentler adaptations of radical behaviorism. But even with these commonalities, we are not so confident in the connection between cognitive therapy and social learning theory because most social learning theorists do not seem particularly interested in the clinical applications developed by the primary figures in cognitive therapy, and most cognitive therapists do not identify social learning theory as the theoretical basis of their work. There are strands of connection, of course—both social learning theory and cognitive therapy emerged during the cognitive revolution, both emphasize the reciprocal relationship between human choice and environmental contingencies, and some psychologists (e.g., Donald Meichenbaum, in his earlier work) were influential in both movements. But for today's most prolific and influential cognitive therapists—Aaron Beck, Albert Ellis and even Donald Meichenbaum in his recent work—there is relatively little connection with social learning theory.

In perusing the pages of Aaron Beck's or Albert Ellis's books, one does not get the sense that these authors are particularly interested in the work of the social learning theorists. Likewise, social learning theorists do not seem highly invested in the contemporary practice of cognitive therapy. The connection between social learning theory and cognitive therapy seems to be based on historical and ideological coincidence more than a mutual collaboration between theory and practice.

Information processing theory and cognitive therapy. A second way to conceptualize the theoretical base of cognitive therapy is to look to cognitive science, especially early forms of information processing theory. Safran and Segal (1990) suggest that the practice of cognitive therapy is based on information processing theory, though they are quick to point out the inadequacies of the connection. Information processing theory is represented in its simplest form in figure 3.6.

Figure 3.6. Information processing theory

Information is retrieved from the environment, filtered through a cognitive processing system, and then certain emotions and behaviors are emitted as a result. The connections with Beck's and Ellis's system are obvious—clear, rational processing leads to a more favorable outcome than irrational, dysfunctional processing.

A quick glance at the books written by today's cognitive therapists—or even scanning the diagrams in their books—reveals the connection between today's practice of cognitive therapy and this simple version of information processing theory. The assumption is that rational thinking leads to a good outcome and irrational thinking leads to a bad outcome. (Here we ought to distinguish between the detailed, sophisticated forms of information processing theory that have been developed in cognitive science—i.e., the scientific study of memory, thinking processes, language, intelligence and so on—and the simple, linear version that forms the basis of cognitive therapy.)

In the spirit of good cognitive therapy, let us test out the premises that un-

derlie this connection between cognitive interventions and information processing theory. Each of the premises described below ultimately fails to stand up to
social science and/or Christian theology.

False premise #1: Healthy people think rationally. If it is true that health is
found in rational information processing, then it follows that healthy people
should be quite rational. This is not the case. Even healthy, highly functioning
humans are prone to great irrationality. Psychologist Daniel Kahneman won the
Nobel Prize in 2002 for his research on human irrationality. People will drive
across town to save five dollars on a fifteen-dollar coffee maker, but they will
not make the same trip to save five dollars on a seventy-five-dollar sweater. Either way the result is a five-dollar savings, but we tend not to think rationally
about such decisions. Kahneman's earlier work with Amos Tversky demonstrates all sorts of human irrationalities among otherwise healthy individuals.
Imagine the following situation, which is adapted from one of Tversky and Kahneman's (1982) scenarios:

> An eyewitness sees a pedestrian hit by a checkered cab in a hit-and-run accident.
> It turns out that the checkered cab company owns and operates 10% of the cabs
> in the city and the yellow cab company owns and operates the other 90% of the
> cabs. When tested under conditions similar to the night of the accident, the eye-
> witness correctly identifies the color of the cab 80% of the time. Can this witness
> be trusted?

Tversky and Kahneman found that many people will say that there is an 80
percent chance that a checkered cab was involved in the accident, when actually it is most likely to be a yellow cab. Here is the logical analysis:

1. If there were 100 such accidents, 90 of them would involve yellow cabs and
   10 checkered cabs.

2. When yellow cabs were involved, this witness would correctly identify the
   color of the cab 72 times (80% of 90) and would incorrectly say it was a
   checkered cab 18 times (20% of 90).

3. When checkered cabs were involved, the witness would correctly identify
   the color of the cab 8 times (80% of 10) and would incorrectly say it was a
   yellow cab 2 times (20% of 10).

4. Thus, if there were 100 accidents, the witness would say it was a checkered
   cab 26 times (18 + 8), and would be correct only 8 times. The chance it was
   actually a checkered cab for this particular accident is only 31% (8/26).

Many, perhaps most, healthy people avoid these sorts of logical, analytical
solutions to problems, and may even find this paragraph quite uninteresting. In-

deed, those of us who enjoy this sort of analysis are likely to be deemed less than fully healthy by large sectors of society!

A person might hear a scenario such as the one just described, come to the last question (can this witness be trusted?), and immediately ask whether the witness was a man or a woman, a young person or an old person. Many people would be more inclined to trust a woman over a man, or vice versa, not because of logic but because of previous experiences. Whereas information processing theory assumes we live well by thinking analytically and logically, most of us are less inclined toward logical calculations than making relational connections and associations. If God's image is relational, rational and functional, then it seems reasonable that all three are interconnected in human nature. Thinking is more likely to be clear for people whose lives are filled with meaningful, rich relationships. When relationships are absent, isolated people often drift off into the world of unusual and unrealistic thoughts, and rationality suffers. Conversely, relationships work best when both people bring balanced and wise perspectives into discussions.

Health is not as connected to rationality as information processing theory implies; healthy people are not particularly rational, and there are many nonrational facets of human experience that bring health, wisdom and goodness.

False premise #2: Cognitive errors tend to be in a negative direction. When information processing theory is linked with cognitive therapy, the underlying assumption is that the cognitive errors tend to be negative. That is, people have a sort of negative filter toward themselves and others, and this negative way of thinking needs to be corrected in order for the person to see things more clearly.

Research in human cognition suggests otherwise. If we have negative filters, they tend to be directed toward others but not toward ourselves. Social scientists have reported ample evidence showing that most people overestimate their abilities, take credit for their successes while blaming others for their failures, and perceive themselves to be holier than others (McMinn, 2004; Moroney, 2000). One polling expert noted: "It's the great contradiction: the average person believes he is a better person than the average person" (Berke, cited in Epley & Dunning, 2000, p. 861). The *fundamental attribution error*—also known as *correspondence bias* in the social psychology literature—suggests that most of us explain our bad fortune by looking to external circumstances and our good fortune by looking to character qualities. But things are reversed when explaining other people's bad fortune. That is, most of us assume the bad events we observe in others' lives are due to their character qualities. "If something goes wrong in your life, then it's your fault. If something goes wrong in my life, it's still your fault." Contrary to the assumptions of standard cognitive therapy, the most common cognitive errors appear to be self-serving rather than self-deprecating.

Psychodynamic therapists have long recognized the tendency for people to protect themselves by construing reality in defensive ways. Defense mechanisms such as denial, projection, repression and idealization protect people from the harsh edge of truth. Even therapists outside the psychodynamic tradition find defensive styles essential to understand when doing therapy. Paradoxically, cognitive therapists seem to assume that clients naturally distort reality in ways that exaggerate their faults and overlook their strengths whereas most other therapists see client distortions as being self-protective. Social science seems to support the psychodynamic position on this point—people tend to cushion themselves from their faults and overestimate their strengths.

Cognitive therapists are correct that we are prone to cognitive errors, but most often we do not evaluate ourselves too negatively. Rather, we have self-enhancing perceptions that make us think we are better than we truly are. The apostle Paul seemed aware of self-enhancing perceptions when he instructed his readers to "be honest in your estimate of yourselves" (Rom 12:3), and to "be humble, thinking of others as better than yourself" (Phil 2:3).

False premise #3: Healthy, rational people eliminate negative emotions. A third assumption of a cognitive therapy based on information processing theory is that healthy, rational people are known by a relative absence of negative emotions. Emotional output becomes the test of good cognitive processing: a healthy thinker produces positive feelings and an irrational thinker produces negative feelings. In reading cognitive therapists one sometimes gets the sense that the best life would be a life without negative emotions and that the way to accomplish this is to gain full control over one's thought life. Negative emotions are seen as little more than a postcognitive nuisance.

There are at least two problems with this. First, emotions are an essential part of our identity; they are far more than a postcognitive nuisance. We seek out emotions, even negative emotions. Each summer people stand in long lines all over the world to climb aboard roller coasters and feel scared to death. People pay money to watch movies that terrify them or make them well up with sadness. Others jump out of airplanes and leap from bridges with elastic cords tied around their ankles and fly down mountain slopes standing on one or two narrow boards. Emotions engage us. We are created in God's image, with the capacity to experience a wide variety of emotions. Indeed, we see in Scripture that God experiences emotions, positive and negative.

We are relational beings, created by a relational God, and emotions are an important part of what makes relationships work. Those who have difficulty ex-

periencing and expressing emotions—for example those who meet criteria for
obsessive-compulsive personality disorder—tend not to have good relationships. We need emotions—all sorts of emotions—to connect well with one another and to add variety and interest to life. Emotions allow us to experience
and express empathy for others, to weep when they weep and rejoice when
they rejoice (Rom 12:15). We see others through our own emotions, and we
learn about ourselves through their emotions.

Second, a Christian perspective causes us to remember that negative emotions are often used by God to produce growth and good things in our lives.
Most of the heroes of Scripture encountered difficult times with various negative
emotions, and they grew to know God better because of their pain. Think of
Abraham venturing out from his hometown to live as a nomad, Moses begging
God to choose someone else to lead the Hebrew people, Joseph being forgotten
in prison, Ezekiel lying on his left side for 390 days, Mary enduring the shame
of being pregnant before marriage, Jesus sweating drops of blood in anticipation of his arrest and crucifixion, Peter weeping after denying Jesus, or Paul
struggling with his thorn in the flesh. The Bible is not a book of G-rated fairy
tales; it speaks of arduous struggle and toil, suffering and pain, temptation and
trial, defeat and discouragement. But ultimately it shows that God is at work in
all creation, always bringing hope and restoration in the midst of life's challenges. This is not to suggest that we should go out of our way to experience
suffering and struggle, but when life brings difficult times and painful emotions,
it is important to remember that God is still working. Ours is a God who loves
to bring hope and restoration in the midst of life's most difficult circumstances.
If asked to identify their time of greatest growth, many people would point to
an emotionally painful season. If given a choice, they probably would never
choose to go through the same pain again, but still they recognize that their pain
was a catalyst for growth and maturation. Information processing theory fails to
value the redemptive possibilities found in negative emotions and difficult life
circumstances.

False premise #4: Thoughts come before feelings. Like the early semantic cognitive therapies, information processing theory is wrapped up in the tidy assumption that thoughts come before feelings. Some therapists still practice cognitive therapy with this naive linear assumption. After some initial debate in the
scientific literature near the beginning of the cognitive revolution (e.g., Lazarus,
1984; Zajonc, 1984), most scholars now acknowledge that the A-B-C formula is
simplistic and unrealistic. Some emotions are not preceded by thoughts. Think
of infants, for example, who experience powerful emotions but do not yet have
language to formulate specific thoughts about life's experiences. Or consider re-

search findings that show people report feeling happier after they smile for a while (Laird, 1974). People randomly assigned to a smiling condition while reading cartoons find the cartoons funnier than those assigned to a frowning condition (Strack, Martin & Stepper, 1988). A great deal of research evidence suggests that some feelings occur before or without specific thoughts. Even the neural pathways in our brain are quite separate, with emotions being largely regulated by the limbic system and thoughts by the cortical regions. Of course there are many points of neurological connection, but they are much more complex than the A-B-C model of cognitive therapy or the linearity of information processing theory imply.

False premise #5: We are motivated to become more rational. Personality theories, like theologies, must include an explanation for human motivation. According to Freudian psychoanalysis, we are propelled through life by forces of energy—a psychosexual life energy and a death energy. Managing these forces becomes the great challenge of living well. Behavioral theory suggests we are motivated by rewards and punishments. We naturally seek rewards and avoid punishment, so good therapy involves manipulating the conditions and contingencies that maintain destructive behaviors. Humanistic theorists such as Carl Rogers suggest we are motivated by an actualizing tendency—a natural inclination to get better and better over time. Humanistic therapists try to remove the psychological barriers to actualization so that the client can do what comes naturally: grow. The Christian narrative assumes there is a compelling inner desire to seek God, what Pascal called a "God-shaped vacuum" and what Augustine (398/1986) described in the now-familiar words of his Confessions: "You awake us to delight in your praise . . . and our hearts are restless until they rest in you" (p. 1).

So what is the motivating force according to information processing theory? Is it logic, the desire to be rational thinkers? As good as logic may be, it is difficult to conceive of this as a primary motivator in life (see Safran & Segal, 1990, for an excellent discussion of motivation and cognitive therapy). Imagine being asked to put the following motives in order, from most significant to least significant.

Sex

Seeking rewards and avoiding punishment

Drawing close to others

Thinking accurately

Personal growth

Seeking God

Most of us would put thinking accurately dead last. The other motivations on the list are simply more powerful, more compelling and more relevant to daily life.

In all five of these premises, information processing theory fails to serve as an adequate foundation for cognitive therapy. Ultimately, a thoughtful Christian needs to keep looking for an adequate theoretical foundation—neither social learning theory nor information processing theory seems to capture the essence of cognitive therapy.

Pragmatic rationalism and cognitive therapy. A third alternative, which we call pragmatic rationalism, is perhaps the most honest look at how cognitive therapy is actually practiced, but is ultimately the least satisfying from a Christian perspective. The philosophy of rationalism suggests that truth is best discovered through careful reason and analysis; it has a rich philosophical foundation going back many centuries and gaining momentum through the work of René Descartes in the seventeenth century. In and of itself, rationalism is not all bad; Christian scholarship certainly calls us to thoughtful reason, exegesis of Scripture, comparative analyses and so on. But because rationalism attempts to discover truth without relying on personal experience, most rationalists are opposed to religious ways of knowing. This in itself makes rationalism suspect as a foundation for Christian therapy, but it is further complicated by the odd mix of rationalism and empiricism that one finds with cognitive therapy.

In its purest form, rationalism is distinct from empiricism, which suggests we discover truth through the senses. But cognitive therapists speak of both by helping their clients think as clearly as possible (rationalism) yet defining the outcome of clear thinking by the extent to which it makes the client feel better (empiricism). The notion of collaborative empiricism—common in cognitive therapy—is that a client and therapist set up experiments to test out a client's thinking. The empirical observations help reshape faulty beliefs and assumptions. So rational thought is a means to an empirical end; "clear" thinking is defined as that which produces more positive feelings.

At first glance, it seems unarguable for cognitive therapists to assert that health is found through rationality. Of course we function best when we think clearly. We are made in God's image as rational, relational and functional beings, so the more rational we become, the better we function. But the rationality of cognitive therapy is a biased sort of rationality that is both shaped and measured by empirical events; good thoughts are those that make the client feel better, and bad thoughts are those that lead to distress. The reasoning is circular: the client evaluates empirical events to become more rational, but the ultimate arbiter of rationality is an empirical outcome. Thus, we use the term "pragmatic rationalism," realizing it is somewhat of an oxymoron insofar as it mixes empirical and rational ways of knowing. Cognitive therapists seem primarily interested in rational thoughts that are pragmatic, as defined by enhancing a person's subjective sense of well-being.

There are numerous problems with using pragmatic rationalism as a foundation for psychotherapy.

Problem #1: The goal of rationality is disingenuous. Some describe cognitive therapy as a method of helping clients see the world clearly and accurately, but the roots of pragmatic rationalism suggest it may be more complex than this. Does a depressed person lie awake in the early morning hours wishing to become a more accurate thinker? No, the depressed person longs to feel better. Becoming a better thinker is not sufficiently motivating to cause a person to spend the time, energy and money required in cognitive therapy. To the extent that clients are motivated to engage in cognitive therapy, it is because they are learning new thinking skills that help them feel better. Good thinking is not the ultimate goal—feeling better is. Similarly, those with relationship problems are not seeking therapy in order to think more clearly, but to strengthen their attachment to another person. They may be motivated to change their thinking if they are convinced it will help the relationship, but here the motive is not so much rationality for its own sake but as a means to another more motivating end. This renders the philosophical basis for cognitive therapy quite similar to behaviorism. Both emphasize changing behaviors in order to minimize punishment and maximize rewards, but with cognitive therapy the "behaviors" in question are mental behaviors, or thoughts. By altering these mental behaviors, we can reconstruct a person's perception of the world and produce happier humans.

We are not disparaging the goal of feeling better; we are merely trying to expose the underlying motive of cognitive therapy for what it is. People don't care nearly as much about thinking correctly as they do about feeling good, so it is not surprising that therapists adapt their views of rationality to help people feel better. Rationalism becomes pragmatic rationalism.

Still, it is a noble thing to help others feel better. Remembering the views of redemption described in chapter one is essential here; God loves this broken world and the people in it, and wants us to experience joy and goodness during our years on earth. But feeling good is not the only desire God has for us. Though happiness is a noble goal, it seems contrived, disingenuous and misleading to construct our views of reality based on the extent to which they produce happiness. Such a view of motivation is troubling to the astute Christian, who sees truth as being larger than the social construction of reality.

Imagine a client, Denise, who feels discouraged with her marriage, and yet she stays in the marriage because of the vow she made on her wedding day (we will follow Denise's story further in several later chapters). After a disap-

pointing meeting with an elder in her church, Denise comes to a psychotherapist to help her sort out her depression and uncertainty about her eighteen-
month marriage to Don. The marriage has been troubled from the beginning.
A cognitive therapist might help Denise change her thoughts by pointing out
how her notions of commitment have led her to feel unhappy, stuck and resentful of her husband. Over time, Denise may come to think differently about
her situation. Soon she may begin to see that many people make marriage
promises that are impossible to keep and that she can experience freedom and
hope by extricating herself from an unwise vow. She is motivated to change
her thinking because her new construction of reality brings relief and hope. As
a result, Denise learns to write a new script for her life—one that she and her
therapist believe will bring her freedom, happiness and hope. It is easy to see
why Denise might be motivated to think differently about her situation and to
let the cognitive therapist guide her in new directions. The motivation does not
come from enhanced logic, but from her natural human desire to seek pleasure
and avoid discomfort. (This notion, which we call functional relativism, is explored further in chapter six.)

To the thoughtful Christian therapist, this scenario causes discomfort. Though
there are times when divorce is inevitable, and perhaps even advisable, the historic witness of the church and the teachings of Scripture clearly discourage divorce. The new socially constructed "truth" that Denise and her therapist create
may provide her with a surge of hope and happiness, but it contradicts a transcendent truth that God ordained and revealed. Of course it must be said that
all truth is understood through social constructions such as gender and race and
culture, so we can rarely know God's truth with absolute certainty, but Christians believe that God ordained certain standards that hold true across all times
and cultures. Even if we cannot know these truths with perfect clarity we are
called to discern them as well as possible and to walk faithfully in them. It may
seem to Denise that divorce will set her free, but Jesus taught that we are free
if we obey his teachings. "And you will know the truth, and the truth will set
you free" (Jn 8:32). So the Christian therapist will affirm the virtue of commitment more than personal happiness, which may not be particularly motivating
to the client looking for relief from a troubled marriage.

Here we see the problem of motivation in traditional cognitive therapy. Pursuing truthful, clear thinking is not nearly as compelling as pursuing thinking that
causes a person to feel better. Pragmatic rationalism is disingenuous in its claim
to promote clear thinking, because so-called clear thinking is often clouded by
vested interests in seeking pleasurable emotions and avoiding painful ones. Thus,
the cognitive therapist's pursuit of logic can devolve into a pursuit of ease and can

---

COUNSELING TIP 3-5: Drop-Out Blues

Therapists often find it discouraging how many clients stop coming as soon as they start feeling better. Symptom improvement often happens quickly—perhaps because of the hope instilled by the therapist, the warmth of the therapeutic relationship or the pragmatic form of rationalism that often results from cognitive methods. Even if the therapist does not intend to promote pragmatic rationalism, many clients naturally gravitate toward ways of thinking that help them feel better. "There is more work to do," the therapist says, but the client has lost motivation and drops out of therapy.

Misery is one of the strongest motivations for seeking help, so it need not be surprising that people sometimes drop out of therapy once they start feeling better. It is good to keep in mind that many clients come back later for additional help, as the need arises.

---

easily undermine the truth claims inherent in a Christian worldview.

Problem #2: Pragmatic rationalism minimizes the importance of relationships. Pragmatic rationalism can easily elevate effective reasoning above good relationships. Recall the common factors discussed in chapter two. Extratherapeutic factors include the client's quality of relationships outside the therapy sessions, and relationship factors pertain to the relationship between the therapist and client. Both extratherapeutic and relational factors are relatively more influential than the therapy techniques being used (see figure 2.1). When one watches cognitive therapists do their work, there is often a sense that the relational dimensions of the client's life are being overlooked. Even cognitive therapists with relatively good relational skills can seem insensitive to relational realities by focusing too much on thought patterns. Imagine the following interaction between a cognitive therapist and a client:

Marla: The evening times are the worst. I often feel so lonely ever since my husband left me. I just sit around and think about how utterly alone I am.

Therapist: Is that true? Are you really all alone in the world?

Marla: Well, I suppose not. I get along okay with the people at work, but in the evenings it's so quiet and I feel so sad.

Therapist: So the thought you have in the evenings, that you are utterly alone, is actually not correct.

Marla: No, I suppose not.

Therapist: Let's try a roleplay here. I'll be you as you're sitting alone at home in the evening, and you tell me how you might answer back some of these thoughts. "Okay, here I am, all alone in the world, there's no one to talk with. No one cares about me."

Marla: Well, you're alone now, but you weren't alone all day long.

Therapist: Yes, but now I am. I am all alone in the world.

Marla: People care about you. You're not all alone.

Here the therapist has helped Marla think more rationally about being alone in the evening, and this might help with feelings of depression, but it seems a deeper, more painful reality is lurking beneath the conversation. In some ways the client really is alone. She has lost a marriage, and though she has casual friends at work, they are apparently not the sort of friends that help her feel connected outside of work. There is something superficial and unsatisfying about this cognitive intervention, as if the client has a more legitimate concern than the therapist has acknowledged. Here is a wounded soul, not just an illogical brain.

Relationships seem to be devalued in both the theory and the practice of cognitive therapy. Some cognitive therapists also lack practical skills of relational engagement that have been an important part of helping relationships for many centuries. Many of the leading cognitive therapy texts—and the demonstration videos that teach students how to do cognitive therapy—seem dry, prescriptive and nonrelational. It is as if the client and therapist are playing a chess game, trying to align thoughts to capture and destroy unwanted emotions. In contrast, IP places relationships at the heart of the change process. Because relationships are part of the problem that has caused pain in the first place, they must also be part of the solution.

Problem #3: Culture and context. Pragmatic rationalism easily becomes ethnocentric and oppressive. Imagine the position that either of us, both European American males, put ourselves in when working with a female client or one of a different ethnic origin. We discuss the client's life situation, listen for what seems rational and what does not, and then get the person to change the irrational thoughts to be more rational. In other words, we cause our clients to think more like we think, presuming it will help the person feel better. But what if our standards of thinking are not culturally relevant for this particular client?

Early in my career, I (Mark) worked with a woman of an ethnic origin different than my own who came for therapy because her sexual drive was decreased after having a hysterectomy. As we talked, we uncovered the irrational belief that she was less than a complete woman now that her uterus had been removed. I worked with her over several weeks to help disabuse her of this silly belief. Then a colleague of mine attended a workshop to learn more about the particular ethnic enclave where many of our clients lived, including my client. My colleague learned that in this enclave a hysterectomy is indeed believed to take away from one's status as a woman. So there I was, a white male spending an hour a week trying to convince my client that her deeply held beliefs were wrong, and then she went back and spent the other 167 hours each week in a cultural context that told her she had been diminished by her hysterectomy. Of course my therapy was not helpful. I was being ethnocentric to superimpose my values over her cultural milieu, and utterly unrealistic to assume that I could change those beliefs. She needed someone to help her identify her losses—as defined by her cultural context—and to grieve. Instead she got a young pragmatic rationalist therapist who was mostly oblivious to cultural differences. Midway through therapy, after my colleague informed me of my error, I apologized to my client and we tried a different approach with much greater cultural relevance, and ultimately greater success. From that point forward I stopped trying to convince her how she should think, and instead we began constructing her story together: I learned the meanings she associated with various life events, and together we began to consider alternative meanings and to craft her story into one with hope for the future.

With all the different ways of thinking that swirl around in our diverse cultures, how do we determine which ways of thinking are rational and which are not? Who distinguishes sound, reasonable thoughts from irrational, dysfunctional ones? Does a degree in psychology or counseling automatically qualify a person to make distinctions between clear and murky thinking? These questions point to a significant problem with the way cognitive therapy is too often practiced. Elevating the therapist to the omniscient arbiter of rationality and irrationality places unrealistic confidence in the personal qualities and training of the therapist. Thoughts deemed to be rational need to be rooted horizontally (in community and culture) and vertically (in history) rather than just in the whims of a convincing therapist.

Problem #4: What goes wrong with the human condition? Another flaw of pragmatic rationalism is seen in how we account for problems in our world. Pragmatic rationalism assumes that carefully crafted thinking leads to positive outcomes whereas sloppy thinking leads to problems. To some extent this is undeniable, but how central is rationality to our human problems? Ask one hundred people what the most basic problems with human nature are, and very few (probably none) will say that we are just not logical enough. People will articulate problems of selfishness, conflict, abuse, arrogance, broken relationships,

COUNSELING TIP 3.6: Alpha and Beta Error

Experts in cultural diversity talk about alpha and beta error—terms borrowed from statistics and research methods. Alpha error, or Type I error, is falsely concluding there is a difference when in reality there is not. With human diversity, this occurs when something is improperly attributed to culture. For example, a solemn, withdrawn, hopeless client should be assessed for suicidal risk regardless of the client's culture. The therapist who assumes these symptoms are related to the client's reserved cultural background may be missing important cues, and the consequences could be dire.

Beta error, or Type II error, is failing to see a difference that exists in reality. This occurs when a therapist neglects the importance of culture—assuming all people are basically the same. This presents problems in cognitive therapy when a therapist presumes that all clients share the same values, assumptions and logical frameworks.

Finding balance is the key. Culture matters, but it is important not to attribute everything to culture. In this way, as in all ways, we should aspire to live like Jesus, who showed respect for different cultures and yet understood truths that are common to all people.

the market economy, greed, materialism, sin, pride and apathy, but they will not mention our lack of rationality. We might all agree that being more rational would be nice and pleasant, but it hardly deserves a central place in our understanding of human health, suffering and folly. This is further complicated when the standards of correct thinking are determined pragmatically—based on what helps a person feel better—rather than on more thoughtful forms of reasoning informed by Scripture, tradition, reason and experience (the Wesleyan quadrilateral, discussed more in chapter six). What is passed off as rationality may actually be contributing to our human problems of pride and self-centeredness.

From a Christian worldview, such as outlined in chapter one, we are created in the image of a rational and moral God. But there is much more to being made in the image of God than logic and thinking capacity. We are also made as relational and functional creatures, and relationships—good and bad—seem to stir souls more deeply than rationality. People are most irrational when close relationships are threatened or broken, which suggests that relational wounds are the primary problem—not irrationality. Two individuals who make their livelihood from thinking clearly—an accountant and an attorney, for example— may come home from work to their troubled marriage and spend the evening immersed in irrational beliefs about one another. Clear-thinking people don't always think clearly when relationships are involved, and this suggests the fundamental problem with the human condition goes deeper than faulty reasoning.

Problem #5: Christian versions of pragmatic rationalism. Various authors have developed religiously based adaptations of cognitive therapy, encouraging people to employ their faith as they fight against faulty and disturbing self-talk (e.g., Backus & Chapian, 2000; Cloud & Townsend, 1995; Johnson & Ridley, 1992; McMinn, 1991; Propst, 1980, 1988; Propst, Ostrom, Watkins, Dean & Mashburn, 1992; Thurman, 2003). Often these authors note the consonance of the cognitive therapy premise with Christian teachings. In many ways this is correct. Christians are taught to think about their thinking. Throughout the Sermon on the Mount (Mt 5–7), Jesus taught his followers to guard their minds and hearts

---

IN THE OFFICE 3.2: Irrationality as an Alarm System

It is often useful to look at faulty thinking as an alarm system for a real or imagined relational problem. When a client seems particularly irrational, it is a good time to probe for interpersonal issues.

Brett: I'm a great employee. I treat people under me well, I'm good with customers, I turn a huge profit for the company every quarter. And then I get a performance review that says I'm doing an average job. This is just outrageous!

Clark: It must have been very upsetting for you.

Brett: Of course. I work way beyond what is expected. I'm usually the first one in the office and the last one to leave. And then I get this. It's like my boss is just shoving me out the door. And I'm tempted to do exactly that, to go somewhere where people appreciate me for the work I do.

Clark: That's a big part of this, isn't it? It's not just the review itself, but what it means about your boss appreciating you and all you do for the company.

Brett: I think that's exactly right. Why do I do all this if I'm only perceived as average at the end of the day?

In this example Brett is nudged toward the interpersonal factors that underlie a mediocre job review. The job review itself would not feel so terrible if it weren't for the interpersonal implication: that Brett's boss does not seem to admire him for how hard he works.

because sloppy minds lead to reckless behavior. It is not just that adultery is a problem, but Jesus taught that adultery begins in the mind with the problem of lust. Similarly, murder begins by entertaining thoughts of anger and revenge. Jesus taught his listeners to monitor their thought lives because thinking has important implications for how people behave. The apostle Paul also instructed his readers to watch their thoughts. In a passage often quoted by Christian cognitive therapists, Paul instructed Christians in Philippi to "fix your thoughts on what is true and honorable and right. Think about things that are pure and lovely and admirable. Think about things that are excellent and worthy of praise" (Phil 4:8). Elsewhere Paul writes:

> Since you have been raised to new life with Christ, set your sights on the realities of heaven, where Christ sits at God's right hand in the place of honor and power. Let *heaven fill your thoughts. Do not think only about things down here on earth.* For you died when Christ died, and your real life is hidden with Christ in God. (Col 3:1-3, emphasis added)

> Don't copy the behavior and customs of this world, but let God transform you into a new person by *changing the way you think.* (Rom 12:2, emphasis added)

> Throw off your old evil nature and your former ways of life, which is rotten through and through, full of lust and deception. Instead, there must be a spiritual *renewal of your thoughts* and attitudes. (Eph 4:22-23, emphasis added)

> Those who are dominated by the sinful nature *think about* sinful things, but those who are controlled by the Holy Spirit *think about* things that please the Spirit. If your sinful nature *controls your mind,* there is death. But if the Holy Spirit *controls your mind,* there is life and peace. (Rom 8:5-6, emphasis added)

Clearly Paul is instructing his readers to fill their lives with particular sorts of thoughts, knowing that those thoughts will shape their daily experiences, giving them hope and meaning and fulfillment. But matching up a few verses of Scripture with the premises of cognitive therapy does not mean that cognitive therapy is completely compatible with Christian teaching. Jesus was not a pragmatic rationalist, and neither was Paul.

Christian adaptations of cognitive therapy have sometimes contained the same errors that characterize the larger cognitive therapy revolution. Sometimes Christian therapists have used Bible verses to support a shallow model of cognitive therapy without considering some of the deep theological problems with pragmatic rationalism. Just because the Bible instructs us to guard our thoughts and to set our minds on noble things, this does not mean Scripture affirms that we should adjust our thoughts in order to feel better.

The Christian narrative is not primarily about correcting sloppy or ineffectual thinking. We are not taught in Scripture that the path to wholeness is found in better thinking. The Bible is a narrative about humans being created for relationship with God and one another, struggling because those relationships are now tainted by the devastating effects of sin, and living with the hope of creation restored. The dominant themes of Scripture are relational. We are the lost sheep, the prodigal children that God is reclaiming, forgiving and gathering. We make this point because we have heard or read well-meaning Christians assert that cognitive therapy is the most compatible psychotherapy with Christian thought. This, it seems to us, is a fallacy that misrepresents both cognitive therapy and Christianity. The techniques of cognitive therapy have a great deal of scientific support for their usefulness, but the underlying premise of pragmatic rationalism is not fully compatible with Christianity.

Summary

Cognitive therapy makes sense, and it works well in relieving symptoms of distress. But despite its strengths, a careful appraisal of cognitive therapy raises concerns. Cognitive therapy seems theoretically adrift, not closely tied to any existing personality theory. Its connection with social learning theory is tenuous at best and its connection with information process theory does not hold up to systematic scrutiny. Much cognitive therapy seems to be based in pragmatic rationalism, meaning that clients are simply taught to think in ways that produce more favorable feelings. Such a philosophical base is utterly shallow and unsatisfying for a Christian approach to therapy, even if a few Bible verses can be plundered to support it.

The bad news is that none of the three theoretical underpinnings described here provide an adequate basis for a Christian form of psychotherapy. The good news is that a Christian view of persons can help inform an integrative approach to psychotherapy that draws some important principles from cognitive therapy, yet without accepting all its underlying assumptions.

References

Augustine (398/1986). *The confessions of St. Augustine* (H. M. Helms, Trans.). Brewster, MA: Paraclete Press.

Backus, W., & Chapian, M. (2000). *Telling yourself the truth: Find your way out of depression, anxiety, fear, anger and other common problems by applying the principles of misbelief therapy*. Minneapolis: Bethany House.

Bandura, A. (1986). *Social foundations of thought and action*. Englewood Cliffs, NJ: Prentice-Hall.

Beck, A. T. (1993). Cognitive therapy: Past, present, and future. *Journal of Consulting and Clinical Psychology, 61,* 194-98.

Beck, A. T., Freeman, A., & Davis, D. D. (2003). *Cognitive therapy of personality disorders* (2nd ed.). New York: Guilford.

Beck, A. T., Rush, A. J., Shaw, B. F., & Emery, G. (1979). *Cognitive therapy of depression.* New York: Guilford.

Bloom, B. L. (1992). Computer-assisted psychological intervention: A review and commentary. *Clinical Psychology Review, 12,* 169-97.

Burns, D. D. (1999). *Feeling good: The new mood therapy* (rev. ed.). New York: Wholecare.

Chambless, D. L., Baker, M. J., Baucom, D. H., Beutler, L. E., Calhoun, K. S., Crits-Christoph, P., Daiuto, A., DeRubeis, R., Detweiler, J., Haaga, D. A. F., Johnson, S. B., McCurry, S., Mueser, K. T., Pope, K. S., Sanderson, W. C., Shoham, V., Stickle, T., Williams, D. A., & Woody, S. R. (1998). Update on empirically validated therapies, II. *The Clinical Psychologist, 51,* 3-16.

Chambless, D. L., & Hollon, S. D. (1998). Defining empirically supported therapies. *Journal of Consulting and Clinical Psychology, 66,* 7-18.

Chambless, D. L., Sanderson, W. C., Shoham, V., Johnson, S. B., Pope, K. S, Crits-Christoph, P., Baker, M., Johnson, B., Woody, S. R., Sue, S., Beutler, L., Williams, D. A., & McCurry, S. (1996). An update on empirically validated therapies. *The Clinical Psychologist, 49,* 5-18.

Cloud, H., & Townsend, J. (1995). *12 Christian beliefs that can drive you crazy: Relief from false assumptions.* Grand Rapids, MI: Zondervan.

Crits-Christoph, P., Chambless, D. L., Frank, E., Brody, D., Karp, J. F. (1995). Training in empirically-validated treatments: What are clinical psychology students learning? *Professional Psychology: Research and Practice, 26,* 514-22.

Ellis, A. (1993). Reflections on rational-emotive therapy. *Journal of Consulting and Clinical Psychology, 61,* 199-201.

Ellis, A., & Harper, R. A. (1997). *A guide to rational living* (3rd ed.). North Hollywood, CA: Wilshire Book Co.

Epley, N., & Dunning, D. (2000). Feeling "holier than thou": Are self-serving assessments produced by errors in self- or social prediction? *Journal of Personality and Social Psychology, 79,* 861-75.

Garfield, S. L. (1996). Some problems associated with "validated" forms of psychotherapy. *Clinical Psychology, 3,* 218-29.

Haaga, D. A. F., & Davison, G. C. (1993). An appraisal of Rational-Emotive Therapy. *Journal of Consulting and Clinical Psychology, 61,* 215-20.

Havik, O. E., & VandenBos, G. R. (1996). Limitations of manualized psychotherapy for everyday clinical practice. *Clinical Psychology, 3,* 264-67.

Johnson, W. B., & Ridley, C. R. (1992). Brief Christian and non-Christian Rational-Emotive Therapy with depressed Christian clients: An exploratory study. *Counseling and Values, 36,* 220-29.

Jones, S. L., & Butman, R. E. (1991). *Modern psychotherapies: A comprehensive Christian appraisal.* Downers Grove, IL: InterVarsity Press.

Jones, E. E., & Pulos, S. M. (1993). Comparing the process in psychodynamic and cognitive-behavioral therapies. *Journal of Consulting and Clinical Psychology, 61,* 306-16.

Kenardy, J., & Adams, C. (1993). Computers in cognitive-behaviour therapy. *Australian Psychologist, 28,* 189-94.

Laird, J. D. (1974). Self-attribution of emotion: The effects of expressive behavior on the quality of emotional experience. *Journal of Personality and Social Psychology, 29,* 475-86.

Lazarus, R. (1984). On the primacy of cognition. *American Psychologist, 39,* 124-29.

Mahoney, M. J. (1993). Introduction to special section: Theoretical developments in the cognitive psychotherapies. *Journal of Consulting and Clinical Psychology, 61,* 187-193.

Mahoney, M. J. (2003). *Constructive psychotherapy: A practical guide.* New York: Guilford.

Martin, J., & Sugarman, J. (1993). The social-cognitive construction of psychotherapeutic change: Bridging social constructionism and cognitive constructivism. *Journal of Consulting and Clinical Psychology, 61,* 375-88.

McMinn, M. R. (1991). *Cognitive therapy techniques in Christian counseling.* Waco, TX: Word Books. This book is out of print and can be downloaded at www.markmcminn.com.

McMinn, M. R. (2004). *Why sin matters.* Wheaton, IL: Tyndale.

Meichenbaum, D. (1993). Changing conceptions of cognitive behavior modification: Retrospect and prospect. *Journal of Consulting and Clinical Psychology, 61,* 202-4.

Messer, S. B. (2004). Evidence-based practice: Beyond empirically supported treatments. *Professional Psychology, 35,* 580-88.

Mischel, W. (1973). Toward a cognitive social learning reconceptualization of personality. *Psychological Review, 80,* 252-85.

Moroney, S. K. (2000). *The noetic effects of sin.* Lanham, MA: Lexington.

Needleman, L. D. (1999). *Cognitive case conceptualization: A guidebook for practitioners.* Mahwah, NJ: Erlbaum.

Neimeyer, R. A. (1993). An appraisal of constructivist psychotherapies. *Journal of Consulting and Clinical Psychology, 61,* 221-34.

Propst, L. R. (1980). The comparative efficacy of religious and nonreligious imagery for the treatment of mild depression in religious individuals. *Cognitive Therapy and Research, 4,* 167-78.

Propst, L. R. (1988). *Psychotherapy in a religious framework.* New York: Human Sciences Press.

Propst, L. R., Ostrom, R., Watkins, P., Dean, T., & Mashburn, D. (1992). Comparative efficacy of religious and nonreligious cognitive-behavioral therapy for the treatment of clinical depression in religious individuals. *Journal of Consulting and Clinical Psychology, 60,* 94-103.

Robins, C. J., & Hayes, A. M. (1993). An appraisal of cognitive therapy. *Journal of Consulting and Clinical Psychology, 61,* 205-14.

Robins, R. W., Gosling, S. D., & Craik, K. H. (1999). An empirical analysis of trends in psychology. *American Psychologist, 54,* 117-28.

Safran, J. D., & Segal, Z. V. (1990). *Interpersonal process in cognitive therapy.* New York: Basic Books.

Silverman, W. H. (1996). Cookbooks, manuals, and paint-by-numbers: Psychotherapy in the 90s. *Psychotherapy, 33,* 207-15.

Strack, F., Martin, L., & Stepper, S. (1988). Inhibiting and facilitating conditions of the human smile: A nonobtrusive test of the facial feedback hypothesis. *Journal of Personality and Social Psychology, 54,* 768-77.

Task Force on Promotion and Dissemination of Psychological Procedures, Division of Clinical Psychology, American Psychological Association (1995). Training in and dissemination of empirically-validated psychological treatments: Report and recommendations. *The Clinical Psychologist, 48,* 3-23.

Thurman, C. (2003). *The lies we believe.* Nashville: Thomas Nelson.

Tversky, A., & Kahneman, D. (1982). Evidential impact of base rates. In D. Kahneman, P. Slovic & A. Tversky (Eds.), *Judgment under uncertainty.* New York: Cambridge University Press.

Wampold, B. E., & Bhati, K. S. (2004). Attending to the omissions: A historical examination of evidence-based practice movements. *Professional Psychology, 35,* 563-70.

Young, J. (1999). *Cognitive therapy for personality disorders: A schema-focused approach* (3rd ed.). Sarasota, FL: Professional Resource Exchange.

Zajonc, R. B. (1984). On the primacy of affect. *American Psychologist, 39,* 117-23.

4

Integrative Psychotherapy and Domains of Intervention

RATHER THAN SETTLING ON THE TENUOUS CONNECTIONS between cognitive therapy and social learning theory, or overlooking the substantial problems with information processing theory, or accepting the superficiality of pragmatic rationalism, we suggest another possibility in this chapter. A Christian view of persons provides a better explanation for the success of cognitive therapy than any of the possibilities described in chapter three, especially when cognitive therapy is blended with other approaches to therapy. After presenting the IP model, we describe a domains-of-intervention approach, where the focus and duration of the therapy is customized in response to the desires and needs of the client.

The IP Model

A complete model of personality would take an entire volume to develop, and it might leave the false impression that we dare present a definitive Christian psychology. We agree with Jones and Butman (1991) that such a grand vision for a Christian psychology is unlikely to be accomplished. They make this argument both because the Bible does not provide a distinct personality theory and because the history of Christianity proves how difficult it is for Christians to agree on fundamental issues of faith.

> We do not have *the* definitive model to propose in place of the many theories we have examined. In fact, we do not believe that a definitive model exists and think it unlikely that it will ever exist. If after two millennia Christians cannot agree about some of the most fundamental points of theology . . . , how can we expect congruence on a "Christian" psychology? (p. 380)

So it seems reasonable to name what follows a barebones model of Christian psychotherapy rather than a comprehensive Christian personality theory. We do so in full awareness that other models of Christian psychotherapy could also be developed. In fact, we encourage it, knowing that multiple perspectives on

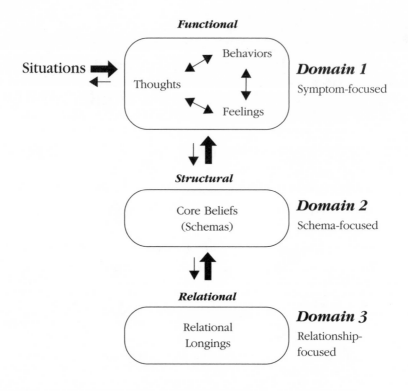

Figure 4.1. A model of integrative psychotherapy

Christian counseling will ultimately improve the services available to those in need of help.

The essence of our IP model is summarized graphically in figure 4.1. There are various similarities between IP and cognitive therapy, but there are also important differences. Perhaps the most important distinction is the different starting points. Rather than beginning with social learning theory, information processing theory or pragmatic rationalism, IP begins with a Christian view of persons.

The **imago Dei** *and three interconnected domains of intervention.* The model begins with the foundations of Christian theology overviewed in chapter one. Theologians have developed three primary approaches to understanding the image of God: functional, structural and relational. Functional views emphasize that humans have the capacity to manage themselves and their environment, to behave in particular ways that reflect God's character. Structural views suggest that the image of God is substantive, an embodied capacity that reflects God's character. Most often, structural views consider rationality and morality as the substance of God's image in humanity. Relational views focus on God's desire to relate as revealed in humanity. Though many theologians have argued that one approach is correct and the other two incorrect, we assume that each of the three approaches is worth considering because each captures some essence of God's nature. And it is fascinating to see how closely the three views correspond to what psychologists emphasize in clinical work: adaptive behavior, cognitive structures (schemas) and effective relationships. Just as it is difficult to argue that one theological paradigm for the image of God is right and the others wrong, it is equally difficult to assert that one emphasis in psychotherapy is always best and the others misguided. As described in chapter two, psychotherapy is effective, but no one therapy is clearly superior to others. Perhaps the entire range of theological and psychological views reflects something of the majesty and complexity of God's character, some of which is revealed in humans.

Notice that the three domains in figure 4.1 are connected by arrows. It is not enough to point out similarities between theological views of the *imago Dei* and major models of psychotherapy; it is also essential in the IP model to recognize that the domains are interconnected. A person engages in functional behavior because of certain structural capacities, and similarly, relationships influence a person's functions and structures. For example, a graduate student, Hasina, is highly motivated to master a particular area of expertise. Hasina reads carefully, she seeks the best supervised training experiences, she goes to class regularly, and so on. All of these behaviors reflect the functional domain—Hasina is mastering a field of study and disciplining herself to do so. But if Hasina's structural capacities are suddenly removed—her intellectual abilities compromised by a sudden car accident, for example—then her functional domain is also affected. Similarly, if Hasina begins the day by arguing with her husband, she may find it difficult to concentrate on her reading and her mind may wander while sitting in class. If enough arguments ensue, she may even lose some ability to concentrate. Both her structural and functional domains are affected by her relational domain. Of course, the connections between function, structure and relationship go the other direction as well, with function affecting structure and relationship.

The first domain of intervention in IP, which is symptom-focused, considers enhancing adaptive behavior. But this is often not enough because behavior is embedded in a life story. These life stories are considered in schema-focused interventions, which comprise the second domain in IP. But this is sometimes not enough because every person's story is shaped by interpersonal relationships. Thus, the third domain of intervention is relationship-focused, based on the belief that relationships are often the source of dysfunction and healing.

Relationships. The top two-thirds of figure 4.1 resembles the model for cognitive therapy described in chapter three (see figure 3.3). Cognitive therapists first focus on specific situations and automatic thoughts (functional domain) and then probe for underlying intermediate and core beliefs (structural domain). Similarly, in IP we suggest beginning with a functional focus in therapy and then moving to a schema-based focused. But IP postulates a third domain that is easily overlooked in cognitive therapy—that of relationships.

Cognitive therapists recognize that dysfunctional automatic thoughts flow from more general core beliefs, and some even acknowledge that faulty core beliefs emerge from dysfunctional childhood relationships, but cognitive interventions are typically limited to functional and structural perspectives. Cognitive therapists may speak of a therapeutic relationship as being important in order to establish trust, rapport and a good working alliance, but rarely do they see the relationship itself as having a curative influence. In IP, we assert that relational wounding is the primary source of human dysfunction and so the therapeutic relationship is of utmost significance.

Hasina was raised in a good-enough home where her basic needs were met, but she never had the sense that her parents delighted in her as a person. For the most part, she stayed out of their way and they left her alone. A young soul crying out for affirmation, Hasina learned to excel in school in order to feel important. She had more gold stars than any of her classmates in elementary school, and her high school and college report cards were always lined with A's. Now newly married and fresh into graduate school, she is facing some unique life circumstances that are stirring up difficulties. She faces certain functional challenges—thoughts that she should be the best in her class, feelings of inadequacy, compulsive studying behaviors that sometimes keep her up until early morning hours. These functional challenges are related to structural struggles— for example, the belief that she is unimportant and must prove her worth with unusual accomplishment. But notice that these structural problems initially emerged in a relational climate as she was raised in a home where she felt unimportant to her parents. So also she now struggles feeling important to her new husband. At times she feels like an utter failure in her marriage because she is not able to make her husband completely happy. Her functional and structural challenges both point to a relational problem, and so effective therapy for Hasina must involve a therapeutic relationship in which she is valued and important. Otherwise therapy will simply be replaying old patterns in her life—Hasina completes all the homework assignments suggested by the therapist, she modifies her thinking as "perfect patients" do, and she reports fewer symptoms of

---

IN THE OFFICE 4.1: Homework and Beyond

Assigning homework can be useful in therapy because it helps the client continue working on the things that are discussed in the sessions. In addition to considering the homework itself, it is also important to keep the nature of the therapeutic relationship in clear focus.

Hasina has always excelled academically, in part because this is where she has found significance and importance. But lurking beneath her hard work ethic, she wonders if she is important to others. This will be important to keep in mind when reviewing her homework.

Hasina: I can't believe this. I was driving to your office today when I remembered that I was supposed to write down some times when I felt unimportant and insignificant this week. Somehow it just slipped my mind. I'm so sorry.

Mark: It's not a problem at all, Hasina. It's good to see you. How have you been?

Hasina: I just feel bad. I value what we're doing here, and I don't want you to think I don't.

Mark: This reminds me of what we have been working on—how you feel important when you get things just right and unimportant when you fall short of perfection.

Hasina: [chuckles] Oh yeah, I see what you mean. So I'm doing it again?

Mark: It seems possible. What do you think?

Hasina: Yeah, probably. I felt pretty terrible when I realized I hadn't remembered. I almost went back home, but then I figured it was too late to cancel the appointment.

Mark: I'm glad you came. You don't have to be perfect to be here.

Hasina: [smiles] Okay. Thanks. I'm glad to be here too.

In this case, forgetting to do her homework may be more therapeutic for Hasina than remembering. It provides an opportunity for Hasina to glimpse the relational issues that drive some of her anxiety and insecurity.

---

anxiety and depression as a result. But none of this addresses the deepest wounds in Hasina's life, so these interventions are not likely to cause deep transformation either. Transformation for Hasina must involve a relational dimension.

Whereas information processing views tend to assume that healthy human are logical and systematic in their thinking, the larger view of IP suggests of us are in a state of dysfunction, more or less. This is related to the Christian doctrine of original sin that suggests we are all broken and all living with the consequences of one another's brokenness. We all have a developmental history of imperfect relationships and therefore are vulnerable to certain core beliefs that cause us to overreact in particular situations or to develop symptoms of distress. And these core beliefs are not easily modified with functional strategies alone. IP postulates a multimodal approach where functional, structural and relational factors are all considered.

Linearity. The linearity of semantic cognitive therapy is not assumed in IP; rather, we emphasize bidirectional connections in ways similar to the constructivist cognitive therapies described in chapter three. IP does not assume a straight-line connection between thoughts and feelings, where thoughts always come before feelings, but postulates more complex interactions between thoughts, feelings and behaviors. Thoughts do indeed shape feelings and behaviors, which is why Scripture is often so clear about the importance of guarding and monitoring our thoughts, but it is also true that feelings and behaviors shape thoughts. Scripture does not merely instruct us to think in certain ways; we are also told to focus on behavior and feelings directly—to walk worthy, to be filled with joy, to put on the armor of God, to be slow to anger, to resist evil, to pray, and so on. Christian cognitive therapists often point to Philippians 4:8 where Paul instructs his readers to "fix your thoughts on what is true and honorable and right." True enough. But it is important to remember the context. Just prior to Philippians 4:8, Paul, writing from prison, provides some counsel for two believers in the midst of a feud. First he instructs the feuding women and the community that surrounds them to focus on feelings: "Always be full of joy in the Lord. I say it again—rejoice!" (Phil 4:4). Then he gives a behavioral admonition by asking them to pray instead of worrying (v. 6). Then Paul makes an explicit connection between the behavior of prayer and the feeling of peace (v. 7). He does all this before even mentioning thoughts in verse 8. Scripture makes no simple linear connection between thoughts and feelings, and neither should we. The scientific data, like the biblical evidence, do not support the assumption that thoughts always come before feelings.

The largest arrows in figure 4.1 reflect the most prominent connections between relationships, schemas and human functioning. Adaptive or maladaptive functioning emerges out of a person's schemas which, in turn, are formed through past and current relationships. But it is also important that every arrow in figure 4.1 has a corresponding arrow going in the opposite direction. IP recognizes the complexity of interconnections between life events and psycholog-

COUNSELING TIP 4.1: Therapy and Motivation

A well-worn riddle poses the question "How many psychologists does it take to change a light bulb?" The answer: only one, but the light bulb has to want to change.

Most clients are intrinsically motivated for therapy or else they would not devote the time and money required. But occasionally a client with very little motivation will end up in a therapist's office.

Most unmotivated clients are participating in psychotherapy unwillingly—perhaps the person is mandated by a court to see a therapist or is an unwilling teenager brought in by frustrated parents. In these cases, establishing therapeutic rapport is an essential starting point. Sometimes it takes several sessions to build a good working relationship, but once rapport is established the client usually becomes motivated to change.

Sometimes clients are simply too depressed to be motivated to change. When this happens, be sure to refer the client for a medical evaluation. Depression and apathy can be related to various medical conditions. Even if the person has no overt medical problems, the physician may choose to prescribe an anti-depressant medication. After several weeks on the medication, the client may gain enough energy to be more motivated in therapy.

ical phenomena, and also among the three domains. Relationships shape schemas, but schemas also shape relationships. Life situations trigger particular functional responses, but those responses eventually influence the kinds of circumstances a person encounters in life.

Any look at human personality or psychotherapy must grapple with determinism and agency. It is beyond the scope of this book to explore these issues in detail, but the arrows go in both directions to reflect the reciprocal nature of determinism. It is not only that life situations, past relationships and cognitive schemas determine how one functions in life; there is also a degree to which one makes personal choices over thoughts, feelings and behaviors, and these choices in turn influence situations, relationships and schemas. As with social learning theory, a Christian view of persons calls us to find a responsible balance between the rigid determinism of behavioral theories and unrealistic views of human freedom found in humanistic theories (Jones & Butman, 1991).

Motivation. Three theoretical underpinnings of cognitive therapy were discussed in chapter three—social learning theory, information processing theory and pragmatic rationalism. Each of these falls short when trying to account for human motivation. Information processing theory assumes that being logical is intrinsically motivating. In social learning theory and pragmatic rationalism, the motivating force is presumed to be a desire to seek reward (e.g., feeling better). These motives seem feasible enough, but they fail to account for the full range of human motivation. In IP, motivation is presumed to come naturally from being made in God's image. That is, there is something intrinsic in the human personality that makes us desire to be more fully human, more as God created us to be.

In the functional domain, we are motivated to be effective stewards of our lives in relation to the rest of creation. The behaviorists, social learning theorists and pragmatic rationalists are partly right—we want to seek rewards and feel as good as possible—but they stop short because we also want to set and achieve goals, to cope well with the difficulties of life, to harness the earth's resources for our benefit, and to do so in a way that honors the goodness and longevity of those resources. In short, we want to function fully.

Humans are also intrinsically motivated in the structural domain. There are certain ontological realities about being human: we think, we use language, we perceive a difference between moral and immoral behavior, and so on. These capacities motivate us regardless of whether they are associated with rewards. In this the information processing theorists are partly right. We value logic and problem solving, even if this does not account for the full array of human motivation. And the humanistic theorists are partly right too. We seem to have an intrinsic desire to grow and become all that we are capable of being. For example, a person may spend an hour each day completing a crossword puzzle. There is no reward at the end of the puzzle—no money, no words of praise, no special attention. But still, the person has some intrinsic motivation to solve puzzles, to figure things out, to honor the ontological realities of what it means to be fully human. Similarly, many moral philosophers argue that humans have a basic moral instinct for right and wrong (e.g., the categorical imperative for Immanuel Kant).

In the relational domain, humans are created to desire relationship. This is part of the image of God, evident from the first chapter of the Bible (Gen 1:27). The psychodynamic and family systems theorists have identified this well: we are intrinsically motivated to have harmonious relationships. Created as relational beings, our hearts yearn for connection from the very first moments of life; this is affirmed both by Christian theology and by the growing psychological interest in attachment theory (Bowlby, 1988). Our yearning is so strong that we will distort logic, repress emotions and rewrite history in order to feel connected. The human desire for connection may be the strongest motive of all.

COUNSELING TIP 4.2: The Kleenex Standard

Psychotherapists are wise to keep a box of facial tissues handy because effective therapy evokes painful emotions. How long the box lasts can be a useful indication of the sort of therapy that is being offered.

Therapists who rarely need to replace their box of Kleenex may want to consider if they are digging beneath the intellectual surface to deal with the deeper conflicts that clients experience. The most effective therapy occurs at both an intellectual and an emotional level, and the emotional work often involves the client reaching for another tissue.

IP's views of motivation correspond with the three main movements of Christian doctrine discussed in chapter one: creation, fall and redemption. Human motives are part of the initial creation, which means that motivation is not typically something that needs to be mustered in therapy; it comes very naturally because humans are created in the image of a functional, structural and relational God. But the realities of living in a fallen world take their toll, and so humans struggle in all three domains. Therapy works because it allows some part of the *imago Dei* to be reclaimed and reawakened in therapy.

Emotions. Pragmatic rationalism and information processing views tend to underemphasize emotions, and many who practice cognitive therapy are guilty of the same. An intellectualized form of therapy may be of some help insofar as it helps people reclaim aspects of the functional and structural image of God, but a more comprehensive view of therapy calls for exploring emotions alongside cognitions and behaviors. In IP we see negative emotions as the alarm system of the human psyche. Painful emotions point to dysfunctional schemas and strained or broken relationships.

In IP, negative emotions are viewed as much more than a post-cognitive nuisance; they point to structural and relational conflicts. For example, a person may experience a moral dilemma—not knowing whether to report a friend who is cheating on an exam. The emotional turmoil is caused by the structural capacity of moral reasoning. The person experiences emotional struggle because of the moral dilemma: is loyalty to a friend more important than disclosing academic dishonesty? This example also points to a relational dilemma: how will this affect my relationships if I report my friend? Virtually every intense negative emotion in life can be traced back to a structural or relational dilemma. While some cognitive therapists may be content dismissing negative emotions through changing thoughts, in IP we also want to look for their deeper significance.

Culture. Information processing minimizes the importance of culture and context and elevates the therapist's views of logic to a place of unhealthy pre-eminence. In IP, looking at deeper cognitive structures requires cultural aware-ness and collaboration between the client and therapist. The therapist must work alongside the client to understand the meanings of particular childhood events and memories, always considering the cultural milieu in the process. Core beliefs can only be fully understood when the structural and relational fab-ric of culture is considered.

The very premise of cognitive therapy—that thoughts precede feelings and that feelings can be altered by changing thoughts—is culturally laden. Cognitive therapy emerged from a modernist framework where a great deal of confidence is placed in rationality, individual autonomy and the personal capacity to control one's life. Many cultures do not share these assumptions, rendering the standard format of cognitive therapy quite useless when working with these clients.

By having three domains, IP allows the therapist and client to customize a therapeutic encounter that works well within a particular cultural context. Some therapeutic encounters will focus quite heavily on the functional domain, some on the structural and others almost exclusively on the relational. Each therapy encounter can be crafted to suit the cultural dimensions at play, and yet the three universal domains (functional, structural and relational) are all being mon-itored by the therapist.

Domain 1: Symptom-Focused Interventions

One of the most remarkable things about human nature is our capacity to eval-uate and regulate our own functioning. Humans are unique in the scheme of creation—we are called to be stewards over life, monitoring the way we manage our lives in order to sustain justice, peace and harmony throughout creation.

Many people who come for psychotherapy are experiencing a lapse of peace and harmony in their lives. Things are out of balance—perhaps a relationship is failing, or their stress is out of control, or they feel overwhelmed with anxiety or depression—so an important part of therapy is to help clients reduce the intensity of their symptoms and function more fully as a result. Those who have spent time around individuals struggling with psychological disorders recognize the degree of suffering that can be involved. Depression is not simply a matter of feeling bad or feeling discouraged about the direction of one's life, but can be a debilitating, even deadly, condition (Young, Weinberger & Beck, 2001). Similarly, those in the midst of severe anxiety disorders may suffer intensely as obsessions intrude into their thoughts and panic grips them without warning (Beck, Emery & Greenberg, 1985). Clients with personality disorders often experience deep and persistent troubles in close relationships and may feel quite frustrated or hopeless as a result (Beck, Freeman, & Associates, 1990). Each of these disorders includes an assortment of functional, structural and relational issues, but the starting point for therapy is almost always to help relieve the symptoms.

It is both wonderful and remarkable that faltering humans have the functional capacity to change in ways that promote greater shalom in their daily experiences. Helping people cope and function better is a noble and high calling that can be done in the name of Jesus, who healed the sick and showed mercy to those in need. For centuries, faithful Christians have followed Jesus in establishing hospitals, medical clinics, orphanages and soup kitchens throughout the world. Using behavioral, cognitive and medical techniques to help people experience comfort and healing is a ministry of common grace, reminding us that God's goodness can be found everywhere.

Skill building. In symptom-focused IP, the therapist teaches the client new skills to help the client function better, as illustrated in figure 4.2. The emphasis here is on confronting and changing thought patterns that lead to unwanted feelings of distress, and teaching new thinking and behavior skills to help the client overcome symptoms of distress.

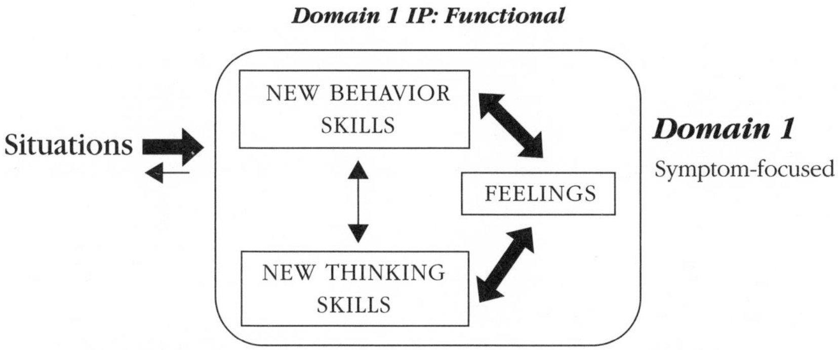

Domain 1 IP: Functional

Figure 4.2. The first domain of IP involves relieving symptoms of distress by teaching behavioral and cognitive skills.

After treatment, the client is able to use new behaviors and thoughts to feel less distressed when faced with the situations that formerly caused turmoil. For example:

Ann suffers with panic disorder. She experiences sudden episodes of terror several times each week. In therapy she learns deep breathing and progressive relaxation skills that help her calm herself when she begins feeling tense. She also learns new ways of thinking to help keep the panic attacks from spiraling out of control when the first symptoms appear.

Robert is experiencing clinical depression. He plods joylessly through each day, wondering if life will ever get any better. Therapy helps Robert learn some new behaviors—he becomes more deliberate about planning his days and adding pleasurable events to his schedule, and he learns to be more direct and expressive in his closest relationships. Robert also learns how to evaluate his thinking and replace the thoughts that make him depressed with more reasonable thoughts.

JoAnn and Robert both improve in therapy, which makes sense both psychologically and theologically. Psychologically speaking, they improve by making healthy changes in their behaviors and by learning to think more systematically and rationally. Theologically speaking, they improve because they are created in God's image; they have the motivation and capacity to exercise some mastery over themselves and their environment.

Objections to symptom-based treatments. Some have objected to symptom-focused treatment on psychological grounds, presuming that if we remove one set of symptoms without resolving underlying problems, then the problem will recur later in some other manifestation. This notion, known as symptom substitution, is a prevalent assumption among many insight-oriented psychotherapists. Although we acknowledge that symptom substitution may occur in some situations—especially among those with personality disorders and some persistent forms of depression—there are other times when current problems do not reflect a deep underlying problem as much as a specific excess or deficit that needs to be diagnosed and treated. Clients with panic attacks, for example, need to learn how to calm themselves in the presence of fear symptoms and to breathe slowly and regularly (Craske & Barlow, 2001). One need not assume that there is any long-term childhood problem or underlying pathology. They simply need a new set of skills to live more satisfying and comfortable lives. Similar arguments could be made for many other anxiety and behavioral health problems.

Others object to symptom-based treatments on spiritual grounds, suggesting that we should not rush to remove symptoms of psychological pain that might ultimately lead a person to search for God. By relieving temporary pain, the reasoning goes, we may be keeping people from a much deeper spiritual healing. There are several problems with this sort of logic. First, if we apply this reasoning consistently, it means that all pain should be viewed as God-given and should not be relieved through human effort. So should we empty our medicine cabinets of prescription and over-the-counter medications and trust that God has

---

COUNSELING TIP 4.3: Y'all Come Back Now

In today's managed care environment, where short-term therapy has become the norm, it is not uncommon for a client to seek help with a particular set of symptoms, stop treatment and then come back at a later time for a different set of symptoms. This may not seem ideal from the therapist's perspective because of symptom substitution. Still, it is important to keep in mind that these repeated interventions help clients function in the midst of various challenges. Perhaps a single long-term intervention would be ideal, but a series of short-term encounters can also be helpful and productive in the client's life.

---

a bigger purpose for our headaches and backaches and inflamed joints? It is difficult to imagine a dentist turning away a patient with severe tooth pain, stating, "I think God can use this pain for good in your life," and yet some people suggest this is what psychologists should be doing. Second, if some pain ought to be relieved by human intervention and others ought not to be relieved, who determines what sort of pain is in which category? Should accountants and attorneys help their clients in crisis, but psychologists not help? Should internists use their allopathic methods, but not psychiatrists? This seems to put human service providers in a position of omniscience, distinguishing the pain God wants us to relieve from the kind that God wants us to leave alone. A third problem is that the entire premise may be false. Do we really know that God is more likely to reach a depressed person than one who is not depressed? When one considers how dark the cloud of depression often is, and how difficult it is for people to hear God's voice from the midst of the cloud, relieving the depression may very well make people *more* open to hearing God's voice than they were during a depressed state.

Our conclusion is that relieving pain is a noble and high calling, and domain 1 IP is an effective means of accomplishing this. Most people come to a psychologist precisely for this reason. Perhaps they want to be able to sleep again at night, recover from irritable bowel syndrome, feel something other than hopelessness when they wake in the morning, or get along better with someone they love. Most people come for symptom relief, and psychologists are prepared to offer it.

Reasons for symptom-focused interventions. Though it may be tempting to think of domain 1 interventions as somewhat superficial because they focus on behavioral and surface-level cognitive changes, it is important to remember that some clients are not interested in looking for the deeper sources of disturbance in their lives. There are several reasons this might happen. First, some disorders are only symptomatic. It would be foolish to assume that every psychotherapy client has some deep relational wound that needs to be unearthed and resolved. Sometimes a panic attack is only a panic attack. Some depressions are simple and situational. Many childhood behavioral disorders can be changed by altering parenting strategies. Some relationships are faltering simply because the couple lacks effective communication skills. Second, changes in health care insurance over the past two decades have pushed both clients and health care providers toward symptom-based treatments. Many insurance companies prefer medication to therapy, and if therapy must be provided, they prefer short-term symptom-relief therapies to longer-term insight-oriented therapies. A third reason is that clients may experience time or money constraints, requiring them to see a therapist for a minimum number of visits. Fourth, one of the strongest motives for seeking psychotherapy is pain. Many people see a therapist only as a last resort and would never enter a psychologist's office if it were not for the intense discomfort in their lives. So when their pain subsides, as it often does over the first few months of therapy, then a client's motivation declines and the person may stop therapy before deeper levels of exploration are possible. Fifth, some clients have a limited capacity for emotional insight, so the gains they make early in therapy are likely to be more significant than changes they might make in the later stages of therapy, which tend to be more relationally and experientially focused. A client with limited emotional insight might try to move to the second or third domain of intervention but may become discouraged because of slow progress. Sixth, some people mistrust psychology and do not want any more psychological care than is absolutely necessary. When their symptoms become manageable, they stop their appointments. Finally, some prefer to look elsewhere for the deepest changes in life. They might look to a psychologist to get through an emergency, but then they turn back to family, friendships or a church community for the deeper changes that require more time to accomplish.

A case example. James comes for therapy with persistent symptoms of stress and anxiety. Referred by his physician, James has a peptic ulcer that has not responded to standard medical treatment. Wisely, his physician recognized that James seems to be a tense person, placing unrealistic expectations and demands on himself, working too many hours each week, and not taking enough time for personal reflection and relaxation. Though a Christian, James's faith does not help him find peace in his life. If anything, it increases his frustration and anxiety by keeping him overly busy with church obligations

---

IN THE OFFICE 4.2: Staying Calm

James needs to learn calmer ways to think in order to ease his physical and psychological problems. He and his therapist might develop a series of note cards that he can keep on his dashboard and review when stuck in traffic.

Clark: That's great. So you were sitting at the stoplight, not making any progress, and you were able to keep from getting upset. What were you saying to yourself?

James: I just realized that it wasn't the end of the world if I got to my meeting a few minutes late. I don't like being late, but you know, life will go on without me.

Clark: Okay, excellent. I'm just writing this down on this note card here. You were saying some reasonable things to yourself: "I don't like being late, but life will go on. It's not the end of the world."

James: Right. It did seem to help.

Clark: Let's fill out another note card too. What else could you say to yourself when stalled in traffic that would help you stay calm and be the person you want to be?

James: Well, I guess just that traffic is unpredictable. If I leave the house on time and then get stuck in a traffic jam or something, I suppose I don't need to get all upset with myself. It's not anyone's fault really. It just happens.

Clark: Okay, let's write that down too. "I left on time this morning. Traffic jams happen. I don't need to blame myself for this."

Once several note cards are completed, James can use them to stay calm. More strategies for changing thinking patterns will be explored in chapters six and seven.

---

and increasing his guilt over not measuring up to God's expectations.

The first task in IP is to help James manage his symptoms of stress and anxiety, with the hope that lowering psychological stress will help his medical condition. The therapist might ask James to describe his usual daily routine, at which point he describes his tense morning commute. At each stoplight his thoughts turn toward the pressures of his day, how annoying it is to be caught in traffic and how terrible things will be if he is late for his morning appointments. Each anxious thought contributes to his eroding stomach lining. A soap opera about James's life could be titled *As the Ulcer Churns*.

Calming James's runaway thoughts and teaching him new behaviors to manage his anxiety will be essential for controlling his symptoms of stress and anxiety. His anxious thinking only serves to make him tense and irritable, and many of his assumptions may not even be true. Perhaps being late for a morning appointment would not be disastrous at all. Maybe his employees would enjoy the chance to have an extra cup of coffee. By calming his thoughts and learning relaxation methods, James will lower his anxiety and improve his health. The primary focus of care is on his adaptive functioning, with the goal of relieving his symptoms.

Still, even at this first domain of intervention that some might caricature as purely functional, structural and relational aspects of therapy are important to consider. The common factors described in chapter two are always at play, even in the earliest stages of therapy, and so it is important to establish a good working relationship with James, to help him tell his story, and to instill hope and positive expectations in the process. In this sense, all effective therapy is relational. The relational emphasis increases as therapy moves toward schemafocused and relationship-focused IP.

Issues of faith are important to consider when providing symptom-focused interventions because religious beliefs often shape the way people perceive events in their lives. Sometimes faith is a tremendous resource for health, but at other times it can be a source of irrationality and can distract from health. James believes that God expects him to be working and productive at all times, and he has even plundered a few out-of-context Scripture verses to support his view. It will be important for his therapist to gently probe these beliefs, always remaining respectful of James's viewpoint, to invite James closer to the abundant life that Jesus offers.

Although symptom-focused interventions can be a helpful way to modify dysfunctional automatic thoughts, at some point both the therapist and the client may wonder about the source of these dysfunctional thoughts. Where do they come from, and why are they so persistent? It is a good goal for James to combat his anxiety-invoking thoughts while commuting to work, and it will help both his emotional state and his ulcer, but he may eventually want to probe deeper to look for the source of his dysfunctional thinking. For this, he and his therapist look to IP's second domain of intervention.

Domain 2: Schema-Focused Interventions

Structural views of the image of God suggest that human beings share something substantive with God, often identified as our rational and moral capacities.

Like theologians, though perhaps with different motives, psychologists have also spent many decades studying how humans organize and find meaning in life events. Psychologists study our stunning human abilities to perceive, store memories, express ourselves through language, order our thoughts, retrieve our memories and exercise control over our cognitive processes. Theologians remind us that these are reflections of God's rational attributes. Psychologists have identified frailties in our thinking—we are overconfident in our opinions and abilities, we tend to seek out evidence that confirms what we already believe rather than evaluating ideas objectively, we often persevere in our beliefs even when the evidence shows we are wrong, and we use mental shortcuts that work well in some situations and not so well in others (McMinn, 2004). Theologians point out that these cognitive frailties are the noetic effects of sin (Moroney, 2000)—thinking the forbidden fruit would open their eyes so they could be as knowledgeable and perceptive as God, the first humans tasted rebellion and found it had the opposite effect. Recently psychologists have been exploring connections between our thinking capacities and interpersonal relationships as they develop social-cognitive theories of human functioning (e.g., Andersen & Chen, 2002). Theologians are pondering connections between structural and relational views of the *imago Dei* (Hoekema, 1986).

Schema-focused interventions go deeper than symptom relief—beyond behavior and thinking skills—to look for the underlying structures that shape one's interpretation of the world (see figure 4.3). Cognitive schemas consist of beliefs and assumptions that help people interpret and find meaning in their lives. These are less conscious than automatic thoughts, more resistant to change and less tied to specific life circumstances.

Intermediate beliefs are considered in both symptom-focused and schema-focused interventions, but the core beliefs underlying the intermediate beliefs become the eventual focus in schema-focused work. Core beliefs are carried in cognitive structures called schemas which, in turn, reside within modes. Modes are composites of cognitive, emotional, physiological and motivational systems. Often an entire mode needs to be activated in order to understand the core beliefs that are causing a client trouble. The relationship between core beliefs, schemas and modes is explored in chapter eight.

Returning to the example of James, he is plagued by anxiety-provoking thoughts because earlier in his life he learned some rules and expectations that do not serve him well in adulthood. For example, "I must meet everyone's expectations in order to be a worthwhile person." This intermediate belief predisposes him to entertain anxiety-provoking thoughts when stuck in traffic: *I'm going to be late for my morning meeting, people will be upset, and that will be*

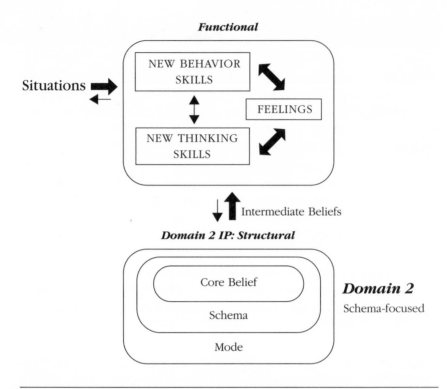

Figure 4.3. The second domain of intervention involves helping clients recognize maladaptive schemas and find meaning in their life stories.

terrible. His intermediate belief about meeting everyone's expectations was, in turn, derived from some deeper core beliefs that have general implications for many areas of life. He probably learned these core beliefs in the context of relationships that were important to him. For example, perhaps James had a disapproving and harsh parent and he ended up believing that there is something fundamentally defective and unlovable about him. This core belief shapes his interpretation of the world, spawns various assumptions and expectations, produces his dysfunctional automatic thoughts, and ultimately predisposes him to having anxiety and ulcer problems. As James begins to explore his schemas, the mode surrounding his cognitions will be activated and he will re-experience some of the pain of childhood—being raised by an alcoholic father who told James he would never amount to anything and a doting mother who tried to protect James from his father. But each time this happens in the therapy office, James will gain a bit more distance from his troubled past. Soon he will be able to experience his story as an observer and not only as a participant. He will be able

COUNSELING TIP 4.4: A Familiar Feeling?

Sometimes it seems more natural to talk about the specific circumstances of daily life than to probe deeper and look for core beliefs. Emotions are often a helpful way to move from a level 1 focus to a level 2 focus. For example, a client may spend twenty minutes discussing how judged and unaccepted he feels by his spouse. After listening for a time, the therapist could ask, "Is that a familiar feeling for you? Have you encountered something like that even before your marriage?" This prompt may help the client explore earlier times in life that have contributed to a general sense (i.e., core belief) of being unacceptable. Emotions can serve as a bridge between present and past experiences.

to decenter himself from his own story and claim a new identity apart from the harsh words of a drunken father. James will also come to see how he replays his psychological history in his spiritual life by perceiving God to be like his harsh and critical father. In terms that the apostle Paul used in Romans 6, James will gain a capacity to view his old self from the vantage point of a new self. This capacity to stand apart and observe his life from an outside perspective will have a curative effect for James psychologically and a sanctifying effect spiritually.

The IP schema-focused approach will seem unfamiliar and foreign to those with a cursory or outdated view of cognitive therapy. Cognitive therapists are often viewed as logic brokers with little interest in the emotional and developmental dimensions of life. To some extent this view has always been false; even early works in cognitive therapy tended to view the organization of thoughts and beliefs as having a historical dimension (e.g., Beck, Rush, Shaw & Emery, 1979). Over time, cognitive therapists have become more and more attuned to deeper cognitive structures (e.g., Needleman, 1999; Safran, 1998; Young, Klosko & Weishaar, 2003). But even with the recent developments that have made cognitive therapy more relational and emotionally focused, the schema-focused domain of IP cannot be considered a pure example of cognitive therapy because level 2 IP shares important similarities with the insight-oriented psychotherapies, such as time-limited dynamic and object-relations therapy. The results of one provocative research study even suggest that the primary reason cognitive therapy works is that it replicates some of the processes used by psychodynamic therapists (Jones & Pulos, 1993). In designing IP, we have attempted to straddle the boundary between standard cognitive therapy and insight-oriented models in various ways (see figure 4.4). Integrative psychotherapy is integrative in two

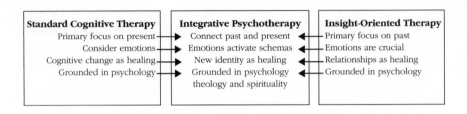

Figure 4.4. Schema-focused interventions in relation to standard cognitive therapy and insight-oriented therapy

regards—by bringing together Christian and psychological views, and by bringing together cognitive and interpersonal approaches to psychotherapy.

Standard cognitive therapists consider clients' early life memories and experiences, but this tends to be a relatively small focus in therapy. The present trumps the past for most cognitive therapists. In contrast, insight-oriented therapists devote a great deal of attention to the memories and mysteries of the past. In IP we attempt to find a balance between these two. Early life is of critical importance to understand the origin and power of a client's maladaptive schemas, and yet it is also important to connect past and present. This is not so much accomplished through insight and interpretation, as might be the case in psychodynamic therapy, but through a process we call recursive schema activation (discussed more in chapters eight and nine).

Emotions are considered in standard cognitive therapy, but they tend to be secondary to cognitions. That is, the typical cognitive therapist will focus on emotions in order to understand the cognitions associated with the feelings being described. In the insight-oriented therapies, emotions are central and crucial to the therapeutic process. In schema-focused IP, the primary focus is on cognitive schemas, but the most effective way to activate schemas is through emotional exploration. Because core beliefs are not accessible on a conscious level, they can only be discovered by activating modes that involve deep emotions. So we place relatively more emphasis on emotions than most cognitive therapists, but perhaps not as much as the typical psychodynamic or object-relations therapist.

What is it that actually promotes healing in psychotherapy? Cognitive therapists answer this by emphasizing changes in cognitive structures. Insight-oriented therapists emphasize the therapeutic relationship. In working with James, a psychodynamic therapist would want to construct a therapeutic relationship that allows James to explore his emotions and interpersonal patterns and to relate these to formative relationships in his life. A cognitive therapist would hope to emerge from discussions of emotions and childhood with a specific core belief that can be written down on paper and examined with evidence. After discussing his past, James might be able to identify his particular belief, "I am defective and unlovable," and perhaps even write it on an index card so that he can be reminded each day to examine the evidence in his current life to see if his belief is true. For example, it may well be that people do love James, which means he can challenge his core belief because it is untenable. In schema-focused IP, we are not so optimistic that maladaptive core beliefs can be eradicated, but still we want to focus on cognitive structures. Rather than utterly eliminating old core beliefs, we believe healing occurs as people grow to recognize the schemas that have been functioning on an unconscious level and then gain some distance from these schemas, enabling them to construct a new identity apart from their old way of thinking. This is both a cognitive and a relational process, but in IP we emphasize the cognitive more in schema-focused interventions and relationship more in relational-focused interventions.

Historically, both standard cognitive therapy and traditional insight-oriented therapies have been grounded in psychology and not in spirituality. This seems to be changing, at least slightly, as spirituality gains attention among the American Psychological Association (Miller, 1999; Miller & Delaney, 2005; Richards & Bergin, 2000, 2004, 2005; Shafranske, 1996; Sperry & Shafranske, 2005). Recently the APA even published a video demonstrating our explicitly Christian approach to IP (McMinn, 2006). But still, even with this more open stance to spirituality, most approaches to therapy avoid the truth claims of particular religious systems. Certainly the theoretical base of both standard cognitive therapy and insight-oriented therapies is psychological rather than theological. In this way IP is unlike either approach because IP's foundation is both theological and psychological. Furthermore, the experiential methods of change draw on both psychology and spirituality (McMinn, 1996). In fact, spirituality and psychology are so closely related within the Christian worldview that they may not always be distinguishable. When Jesus taught people to be wary of lustful and angry thoughts because vile actions emerge from one's thought life (Mt 5:21-30), was he teaching people a new spirituality or a new psychology? When he pronounced the second great commandment, that we should love our neighbors as we love ourselves (Mk 12:31), was he introducing a radical new spiritual paradigm or a psychological paradigm? When the apostle Paul instructed believers at Ephesus to put aside their bitterness and anger so they could be kind and tenderhearted to one another (Eph 4:31-32), was he offering psychological or spiritual advice? The answer, of course, is both. Just as tremendous psychological growth can occur through involvement in a vibrant spiritual community, so also spiritual growth can happen in a psychotherapist's office because psychology and spirituality are closely related when the therapist and client share a Christian worldview. Schema-focused IP with Christian clients provides a psychological methodology for what the apostle Paul described as taking off the old self and putting on the new (Dobbins, 2004; Roberts, 2001).

Faith is an important consideration in schema-focused interventions, especially with clients who share a Christian worldview with the therapist. Good theology will not immediately resolve faulty core beliefs—because they are rooted in deep emotional and relational realities that are not simply dismissed with analysis and reasoning—but nonetheless discussions of faith can help reshape core beliefs. For example, James believes he is defective and unlovable. What does his Christian faith teach him about this? That he is indeed defective, as all of us are, but also that he is wonderfully made and profoundly loved. As this truth sinks deep into James's life, through a caring therapeutic relationship and being part of a community of faith where love is demonstrated in tangible ways, he will gradually come to view himself differently.

Domain 3: Relationship-Focused IP

Relational views of the *imago Dei* emphasize that God's image cannot be contained within a single person but is seen within relationships. Barth noted the importance of an I-Thou connection in understanding the *imago Dei*. Psychotherapists are constantly working with I-Thou relationships, in the client's early life and present relationships, and in the client-therapist relationship. The cognitive schemas considered in schema-focused IP have relational origins, and the resolutions for the problems caused by maladaptive schemas sometimes require an intensive relational focus. Thus, the third domain of IP is relationship-focused, explored more fully in chapters ten and eleven.

From formative relationships, core beliefs emerge. So integrative psychotherapists do not see illogic as the fundamental human problem; rather, they see difficult and broken relationships to be the source of difficulties (the broken relationship with God, creating the condition of sin, is the ultimate source of our difficulties). James's belief that he is defective and unlovable did not simply emerge from his illogic but from a difficult and important relationship. Like every child, he longed to be close to his parents. But he found it difficult because of his father's aloof and critical style and his mother's tendency to try to save James from his father. James created an illogical fantasy that he could become lovable by always meeting everyone's expectations. It began as his way of compensating for his lack of connection with his father, and now it pesters him on the freeway and erodes the lining of his stomach.

Formative relationships. Relationship-focused IP, illustrated in figure 4.5, focuses on understanding deep relational wounds, unresolved conflicts, character issues and questions of ultimate meaning. It shares a good deal in common with contemporary psychodynamic and interpersonal therapies, focusing on crafting a therapeutic relationship that eventually allows a person to gain new insights and grow beyond rigid styles of relating to others.

The process of change in relationship-focused IP is not so much cognitive as it is experiential and relational. Therapeutic change involves the therapist living out a transformative relationship with a client that gradually helps the client develop a new vantage point through which the world can be viewed. With time, a wise and carefully crafted therapeutic relationship can help a client gain a new perspective on life. A client who believes "I must always be strong" may take many months before showing faults and weaknesses to a therapist. But when it happens, and when the therapist responds with compassion, it introduces the possibility of great healing. Clients who split the world and everyone in it into two categories—the good and the bad—may have difficulty tolerating faults and ambiguities in those they love. So the therapist needs to create a relationship with clear boundaries and expectations, while simultaneously pushing the client toward a more nuanced and complex view of the world. The overly dependent client who clings too tightly to relationships and makes unhealthy choices as a result benefits from a therapist who sets good limits and demonstrates that a relationship can be close and caring without being all-consuming. The client who avoids all emotion, fearing that emotion will drive others away, may initially resist the therapist's efforts to explore feelings. As enough safety develops in the therapeutic relationship the client may begin shedding a few tears and expressing some emotions. If the therapist stays calm, accepting the words and the tears

---

COUNSELING TIP 4.5: Read Your Own Feelings

To understand more about how the client relates to others, consider your own feelings as a therapist. How do you feel when interacting with this client? Do you feel empathic and engaged in the client's life? Do you feel annoyed and put off? Are you bored and unenthused about helping the client? Of course some of your feelings may reflect your own struggles and challenges, but keep in mind that others may also react to your client the same way you react. Reading your feelings may help you understand more about the relationships your client experiences outside the office (see also Counseling Tip 11.5).

with kindness and compassion, it opens up a new world of possibilities for the client. In all these examples, the therapist identifies schemas, notices that they are not easily changed, works to understand the relational wounds that caused the core beliefs, and then lives out an intentional therapeutic relationship with the client that ultimately offers the client a new way to view the world.

Crafting a transformative therapeutic relationship requires both theological

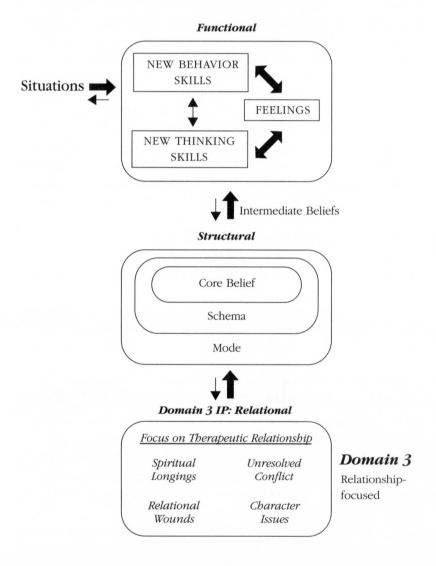

Figure 4.5. The third domain of intervention focuses on healing relational wounds.

and psychological awareness. Relationship-focused IP begins with Christology. Christ, the perfect image of God in human form, engages in relationships that transform people. Every Christian is called to imitate Christ and, in so doing, to demonstrate grace and truth in relation to others. This is the christological core of relationship-focused IP. In addition, we draw on psychological theories to help nuance how this christological core is lived out in therapeutic relationships. In chapter ten we explore the dynamics of interpersonal relationships.

Motivated by the incarnation. The incarnation is a central doctrine of Christianity: God became human and dwelled among us, full of grace and truth (see Jn 1:14 NIV). This doctrine distinguishes Christianity from all other world religions. God, in love, comes to us to understand and empathize with the mess of human brokenness. Born in a barnyard, learning to be a carpenter, getting blisters, sweating to the heat of summer and shivering in the cold of winter, rejected by religious leaders and misunderstood by friends, fighting thirst and hunger and sleeplessness, Jesus understands. The incarnation reveals the depth of God's grace and love: "God showed his great love for us by sending Christ to die for us while we were still sinners" (Rom 5:8). For the Christian, this changes everything. We speak of a having a personal relationship with God because Jesus came to be with us in our squalor, and this relationship with Jesus helps us see our own individual lives differently. We get a bigger picture of the cosmos and find meaning for our finite lives.

Therapy is no metaphor of the incarnation; to suggest this would cast a therapist in the role of the divine. But just as God came to live in our material world as the Wonderful Counselor (Is 9:6), so we also—as those who are being healed by God's grace—are called to be present to one another in the midst of life's difficulties. This is not limited to therapy—all of us are called to accept one another as Christ accepted us (Rom 15:7). Therapy is not salvific, and therapists are not offering anything nearly as important as what Jesus offers. We therapists are broken human creatures—sometimes terribly broken and dysfunctional. Nonetheless, we have a vocation to sit with people in their pain and their questioning, to help them experience a healing relationship, to speak truth even when truth is hard to hear, to offer grace when no one else will. In this, therapy is motivated and shaped by the greatest story of all. Successful therapy is possible because humans are relational, created in the image of God. The perfect image of God is revealed in Jesus.

IP and Cognitive Therapy

In Marilynne Robinson's award-winning novel *Housekeeping,* the main character lives her childhood in an old house built by her grandfather. The house is effective enough—built strong enough and high enough above Fingerbone Lake to remain safe from the harshness of Idaho winters and the perils of flooding. But the house has problems. The bedroom floor slopes so badly that special furniture with lop-sided legs is required to compensate. One has to walk uphill to get to the kitchen from the front door. The sloping house hints at a problem with an underlying foundation, a deeper malignancy metastasizing into several generations. It is a foreboding omen of a bigger problem that lies beneath.

Cognitive therapy is somewhat like that leaning house. It is effective enough—it works well with a variety of disorders—but it is built on a faulty foundation of pragmatic rationalism. Some Christians have responded by blazing the house, assuming it is of no value. IP assumes otherwise: there is much good that can be redeemed from cognitive therapy. Our goal is to rebuild cognitive therapy by replacing a faulty foundation with a solid one, moving beyond pragmatic rationalism to see the larger themes of a Christian view of persons. In addition, we bring in other psychological theories because a Christian worldview demands we attend to various dimensions of human experience.

IP represents an effort to build a foundation consistent with a Christian worldview while holding on to the effective methods of cognitive therapy and simultaneously drawing upon other psychological theories. Symptom-focused interventions in IP have many points of similarity with standard cognitive therapy, though there are important differences in worldview assumptions. These worldview differences become more pronounced as a therapist and client move into the second and third domains of therapy. Table 4.1 summarizes the worldview differences.

With regard to the view of persons (anthropology) employed, standard cognitive therapy is built on the assumptions of pragmatic rationalism—that we are basically functional, rational beings desiring to function more happily by becoming more rational. Relational factors receive minimal attention. In IP the functional, rational and relational are all emphasized because they reflect the image of God that is stamped into every human personality.

What goes wrong to create psychological problems? In the standard cognitive therapy worldview, the problem is a series of cognitive errors. A client has learned faulty ways of understanding and interpreting the world, and these cognitive errors need to be corrected by a competent, rational therapist. To the integrative psychotherapist, the illogic has a deeper source: it comes from the brokenness of our human condition, most profoundly revealed in relational wounds. Because sin entered the world, and all creation now languishes in a

state of brokenness, people are disconnected from and wounded by othe
Sometimes these relational wounds have relatively minor consequences, bu
other times they cause deep pain.

Negative emotions are often treated as a post-cognitive nuisance by cognitive
therapists. Anxiety, fear, depression and other negative emotions are the
byproducts of errant thinking. To the integrative psychotherapist, emotions are
God's gift—a built-in alarm system to alert a person to potential problems. Very
often these are problems in the relational fabric of life. Someone anticipates
abandonment or rejection, so the emotions of insecurity, anxiety and jealousy
erupt. Another person deals with a profound interpersonal loss and feels sad
and depressed in response. Clearly emotional reactions can become misaligned—schemas can be activated without sufficient cause, and all sorts of
emotional havoc may result. But still, the emotions themselves are part of a
good creation and deserve to be honored, understood, and respected in the process of psychotherapy.

Table 4.1. Worldview Differences Between Standard Cognitive Therapy and IP

	Standard CT	**Integrative Psychotherapy**
Anthropology	Functional, rational beings seeking to be even more rational	Functional, structural and relational beings, intrinsically motivated to move toward God's image
Problem	Behavioral and cognitive errors	Sin in all its manifestations—the result of a fallen creation
Negative Emotions	Post-cognitive nuisance	God's gift, often reflecting damage to a good creation and causing us to see our deeper relational longings
Treatment Focus	Moving from illogic to logic	Being with—enlivening God's image in another soul, including functional, structural and relational capacities
Scripture	If used, seen as a text for clear thinking	Narrative for our longing for redemption
Culture	Mostly ignorned	Sets the relational context of cognition and behavior

With regard to treatment focus, standard cognitive therapy corrects cognitive errors in order to give clients more control over their feelings. In other words, clients move from illogical to logical thinking and feel better as a result. This same focus is prominent in IP's symptom-based interventions, but as the integrative psychotherapist moves to schema-focused and relationship-focused IP the attention shifts to understanding the source of the illogic, in terms of both schemas (domain 2) and the deeper relational issues that contribute to those schemas (domain 3). IP assumes that the ultimate source of illogic is relational disconnectedness which, in turn, reflects the alienation of living in a fallen world. This calls a therapist to "be with" a client, to be a sustaining and redemptive presence in a person's life with the hope of enlivening the image of God in the other person.

The fifth row in table 4.1 relates to the use of Scripture in cognitive therapy. Of course most psychotherapists do not use Scripture in therapy because they do not see it as an authoritative guide for living; they see their identity as a clinical scientist rather than a pastoral counselor, or they were discouraged from religious counseling approaches during their training years. Nonetheless, a few Christianized approaches to standard cognitive therapy have been developed, and these approaches tend to view Scripture as a resource for correcting errant thinking. For example, the anxiety-prone client who frets that the future will be dismal can be reminded that God "already knows all your needs, and he will give you all you need from day to day if you live for him and make the Kingdom of God your primary concern" (Mt 6:32-33). Although this can be a useful tool in therapy, it is easy to twist Scripture for therapeutic purposes, which both distorts the intent of Scripture and makes the therapy intervention seem disingenuous to theologically informed clients and therapists. In IP, Scripture is not so much viewed as a logic guide, but as the grand and authoritative narrative describing the story in which we all live. Created by a loving God, and wounded by living in a fallen state, every person is—consciously or not—yearning for redemption. Even for those who have no interest in spiritual matters, still they intuitively know to reach out for reconciliation and inner peace and hope. From the vantage point of IP, this reflects a God-given longing for things to be made right. Scripture tells the story that helps us understand life and cling to hope. Of course there are also many other uses for Scripture in psychotherapy (see Johnson, 1992, for an excellent discussion of this).

Finally, standard cognitive therapy tends to overlook the importance of culture. In IP, culture is viewed as the context in which God's image is lived out. Integrative psychotherapists are students of culture, always wanting to learn from clients about particular assumptions, values and relational patterns. Further, in IP therapists customize a culturally sensitive therapeutic encounter by relying differently on the three domains with various clients.

Conclusion

The model of psychotherapy proposed in this chapter postulates three domains of intervention corresponding with functional, structural and relational views of the *imago Dei*. Though IP relies on some methods of standard cognitive therapy, it also draws on other psychology theories and is rooted in a Christian view of persons rather than the pragmatic rationalist views of standard cognitive therapy. IP begins with the assumption that we were created to be in relationship, both with God and with one another, but our abilities for effective relationships are severely compromised as result of living and participating in a sinful world. Effective therapists probe and investigate emotions, following these emotions and related thoughts to underlying beliefs stemming from previous relationships, and then work to modify those beliefs directly through therapeutic techniques and, perhaps most importantly, through a healthy therapeutic relationship.

IP begins with careful assessment and case conceptualization (chapter five) and then progresses into one or more of the domains of intervention. Most clients find symptom relief with domain 1 interventions (chapter six and seven), many move on to do further work in domains 2 (chapters eight and nine), and 3 (chapters ten and eleven).

References

Andersen, S. M., & Chen, S. (2002). The relational self: An interpersonal social-cognitive theory. *Psychological Review, 109,* 619-45.

Beck, A. T., Emery, G., & Greenberg, R. L. (1985). *Anxiety disorders and phobias: A cognitive perspective.* New York: Basic Books.

Beck, A. T., Freeman, A., & Associates. (1990). *Cognitive therapy of personality disorders.* New York: Guilford.

Beck, A. T., Rush, A. J., Shaw, B. F., & Emery, G. (1979). *Cognitive therapy of depression.* New York: Guilford.

Bowlby, J. (1988). *A secure base: Parent-child attachment and healthy human development.* New York: Basic Books.

Craske, M. G., & Barlow, D. H. (2001). Panic disorder and agoraphobia. In D. H. Barlow (Ed.), *Clinical handbook of psychological disorders* (3rd ed.) (pp. 1-59). New York: Guilford.

Dobbins, R. D. (2004). Spiritual interventions in the treatment of dysthmia and alcoholism. In P. S. Richards & A. E. Bergin (Eds.), *Casebook for a spiritual strategy in counseling in psychotherapy* (pp. 105-17). Washington, DC: American Psychological Association.

Hoekema, A. A. (1986). *Created in God's image.* Grand Rapids, MI: Eerdmans.

Johnson, E. L. (1992). A place for the Bible within psychological science. *Journal of Psychology and Theology, 20,* 346-55.

Jones, S. L., & Butman, R. E. (1991). *Modern psychotherapies: A comprehensive Christian appraisal.* Downers Grove, IL: InterVarsity Press.

Jones, E. E., & Pulos, S. M. (1993). Comparing the process in psychodynamic and cognitive-behavioral therapies. *Journal of Consulting and Clinical Psychology, 61,* 306-16.

McMinn, M. R. (1996). *Psychology, theology, and spirituality in Christian counseling.* Wheaton, IL: Tyndale.

McMinn, M. R. (2004). *Why sin matters: The surprising relationship between our sin and God's grace.* Wheaton, IL: Tyndale.

McMinn, M. R. (2006). *Christian counseling* [video in APA Psychotherapy Series]. Washington, DC: American Psychological Association.

Miller, W. R. (Ed.) (1999). *Integrating spirituality into treatment: Resources for practitioners.* Washington, DC: American Psychological Association.

Miller, W. R., & Delaney, H. D. (Eds.) (2005). *Judeo-Christian perspectives on psychology: Human nature, motivation, and change.* Washington, DC: American Psychological Association.

Moroney, S. K. (2000). *The noetic effects of sin.* Lanham, MA: Lexington Books.

Needleman, L. D. (1999). *Cognitive case conceptualization: A guidebook for practitioners.* Mahwah, NJ: Erlbaum.

Richards, P. S., & Bergin, A. E. (Eds.) (2000). *Handbook of psychotherapy and religious diversity.* Washington, DC: American Psychological Association.

Richards, P. S., & Bergin, A. E. (Eds.) (2004). *Casebook for a spiritual strategy for counseling and psychotherapy.* Washington, DC: American Psychological Association.

Richards, P. S., & Bergin, A. E. (2005). *A spiritual strategy for counseling and psychotherapy* (2nd ed.). Washington, DC: American Psychological Association.

Roberts, R. C. (2001). Outline of Pauline psychotherapy. In M. R. McMinn & T. R. Phillips (Eds.), *Care for the soul: Exploring the interface of psychology & theology* (pp. 134-63). Downers Grove, IL: InterVarsity Press.

Safran, J. D. (1998). *Widening the scope of cognitive therapy: The therapeutic relationship, emotion, and the process of change.* Northvale, NJ: Aronson.

Shafranske, E. P. (1996). Religious beliefs, affiliations, and practices of clinical psychologists. In E. P. Shafranske (Ed.), *Religion and the clinical practice of psychology* (pp. 149-62). Washington, DC: American Psychological Association.

Sperry, L., & Shafranske, E. P. (Eds.) (2005). *Spiritually oriented psychotherapy.* Washington, DC: American Psychological Association.

Young, J. E., Klosko, J. S., & Weishaar, M. E. (2003). *Schema therapy: A practitioner's guide.* New York: Guilford.

Young, J. E., Weinberger, A. D., & Beck, A. T. (2001). Cognitive therapy for depression. In D. H. Barlow (Ed.), *Clinical handbook of psychological disorders* (3rd ed.) (pp. 264-308). New York: Guilford.

5

Assessment and Case Conceptualization

EXCEPT IN EXTREME CASES, PEOPLE KNOW THEY ARE IN PAIN when they seek help from a psychologist or counselor. In fact, the pain and accompanying symptoms are prime motivators for seeking help. But how do we make sense of the pain and the symptoms?

> *When Jan arrives for her appointment she appears nervous and anxious. Her hand-shake reveals moist, clammy hands and her voice quivers as she greets the psychologist. She acknowledges her nervousness, explaining that she gets nervous in most social situations, particularly with people she does not know. As the interview proceeds she talks about her worrying—worrying that at first seemed pretty normal but in the last few years has virtually incapacitated her. She now worries about having diseases and sees her doctor at least twice per month. She worries about losing her family by death, divorce or abandonment because of their frustration with her. She reports that it all began three years ago when she was promoted to a supervisory position at work. The increased responsibility was overwhelming, her coworkers did not seem to respect her new level of authority, and her boss, who arrived shortly after her promotion, constantly criticized her management style. Jan longs for her worry and anxiety to stop so that she can be free to enjoy life again.*

What is going on with Jan? What causes her heightened level of worry? What can be done to help her with these symptoms? A therapist could simply take Jan's worrying at face value, realize that it is a behavior that interferes with her life, and attempt to intervene in strategic ways to reduce it. She seems to be aware of her problems and, based on her healthy and worry-free history, is likely to have the resources to make effective progress. However, this quick analysis and conceptualization could just as easily lead to therapeutic failure without more substantial assessment of Jan and the nature of her struggles.

One of the first steps in working with Jan will be to properly assess her condition so that appropriate interventions can be offered. Assessment and subsequent case conceptualization are extremely important activities for successful therapy.

Assessment, Theory and Case Conceptualization

Assessment is the task of systematically observing what signs and symptoms a client experiences. These signs and symptoms are then understood through a particular theoretical grid, resulting in a case conceptualization (a framework for understanding the symptoms). Case conceptualization is an effort to understand the cause of the symptoms, the role the symptoms play in the person's experience and treatment strategies to help the person improve. The relationship between assessment, theory and case conceptualization is shown in figure 5.1.

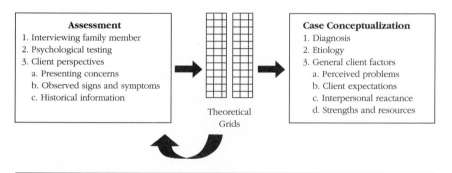

Assessment
1. Interviewing family member
2. Psychological testing
3. Client perspectives
   a. Presenting concerns
   b. Observed signs and symptoms
   c. Historical information

Theoretical
Grids

Case Conceptualization
1. Diagnosis
2. Etiology
3. General client factors
   a. Perceived problems
   b. Client expectations
   c. Interpersonal reactance
   d. Strengths and resources

Figure 5.1. Assessment and case conceptualization

In chapter three we described the linear assumptions of the semantic cognitive therapies and then proceeded to argue that linearity fails to capture the complexity of situations, thoughts and feelings. In the same way, a linear connection between assessment, theory and case conceptualization is somewhat oversimplified because theory not only affects case conceptualization, but it also affects the assessment itself. For example, if a psychologist plans to do psychological testing as part of an assessment, the psychologist will choose particular tests to use and will not choose others. This very act of test selection contains certain theoretical and value assumptions that will then affect the information obtained. Similarly, in a clinical interview, a therapist chooses to ask certain questions and not others. These choices reflect certain theoretical perspectives. At the bottom of figure 5.1, an arrow circles back from the theoretical grids to the assessment processes, indicating that a purely linear relationship between assessment and case conceptualization is never fully achieved.

A Christian Look at Evaluation

Some therapists may be reluctant to embrace assessment and case conceptualization as professional activities, fearing that they are inherently judgmental and therefore place the therapist in a superior role with the client. These are reasonable concerns because Christianity leaves no room for one person to be deemed superior to another (see Phil 2:1-4; Jas 2:1-9). We pose a series of three questions to help articulate the proper role of evaluation for the Christian therapist.

Question #1: Is evaluation acceptable for Christians?
Yes. Scripture recommends evaluation of self and others. In 1 Corinthians 11:28 we are told to examine ourselves when we consider partaking in the Eucharist. We are to evaluate our thoughts, actions, motives and relationships to determine the confession necessary for clear and open communion with God. Similarly, in 2 Corinthians 13:5 Paul recommends self-evaluation to an entire church community: "Examine yourselves to see if your faith is really genuine. Test yourselves. If you cannot tell that Jesus Christ is among you, it means you have failed the test." Self-evaluation is an important part of growing in faith.

Appropriate evaluation of others is encouraged in Scripture as well. Jesus warned against having a condemning, judgmental posture toward others (Mt 7:1) but still called his followers to make well-reasoned judgments of self and others (e.g., Mt 10:5-20; 18:15-20). Similarly, in the apostle Paul's writings the qualifications for elders and deacons in 1 Timothy 3 and Titus 1 are provided so that Christians can evaluate leadership qualities in others. In 1 Thessalonians 5:14 Paul writes, "Brothers and sisters, we urge you to warn those who are lazy. Encourage those who are timid. Take tender care of those who are weak." We are told to differentiate between the lazy, timid and weak so that we can respond appropriately to them. (Unfortunately, we sometimes tend to warn the weak, encourage the lazy and help the timid or in some other way respond inappropriately to the struggles of others.) These passages imply the usefulness of nonjudgmental evaluation of others.

Cooper (2006) makes a useful distinction between making judgments and being judgmental. A judgmental attitude, which Jesus condemns in Scripture, is a quick and harsh response to another based on emotional reasoning, stereotypes and pride. In contrast, judgments are carefully reasoned opinions, reflecting a thoughtful understanding of a situation. One cannot function without judgments. Each of us makes value-based decisions every day, whether it is as simple as slowing down for a yellow traffic light or as complex as making end-of-life decisions for a patient on life support. The Christian faith calls us to make judgments, and yet to do so in ways that are kind and compassionate to others. Judgments need not be judgmental.

Some Christians may be cautious of psychological assessment because it

---

COUNSELING TIP 5.1: Who Is Your Reader?

Psychotherapists are often in a situation of writing reports and treatment summaries about their clients. Therapists need to make thoughtful judgments because their recommendations often have important implications, yet they also want to avoid being judgmental. One helpful standard is to write everything with the thought that the client may someday be reading it. Keeping this in mind helps the therapist avoid abrasive language and a critical tone.

---

seems like a form of judgment. Indeed it is. But again, making judgments is necessary in life. The bigger question is whether assessment can be done without a judgmental spirit. A judgmental assessment may involve belittling or stereotypic perspectives toward another, jumping to conclusions rather than listening well and formulating a careful understanding; a nonjudgmental assessment is marked by compassion, kindness, empathy, attentiveness and thoroughness.

In summary, a Christian view of assessment allows for thoughtful evaluation of self and others. Thoughtful judgments are appropriate, but judgmental attitudes are not.

Question #2: Isn't Christian assessment mostly a matter of identifying sin?
No. Some Christian counselors have resorted to a simplistic understanding of psychological problems, thinking their task is simply to identify sin in a client's life and help the person stop sinning. This view oversimplifies both the doctrine of sin and the cause of psychological problems, and can cause emotional damage to those taking the vulnerable step of seeking help from a therapist. But as we wrote in the introduction of this book, there are two ditches on every road. Many Christian therapists have gone to the other extreme, avoiding the notion of sin altogether (see Monroe, 2001, for a helpful discussion of this). In doing so, many have succumbed to a theoretical grid that bears little resemblance to the Christian faith. And because theory forms the basis of case conceptualization and treatment, many counselors are Christian in name only—their counseling work is not influenced much by the faith they hold to be central to their identity.

Part of the problem is due to a narrow or poorly formulated view of sin and failure to see the myriad ways sin can affect people's lives. Sometimes Christian therapists fail to see the breadth and depth of human brokenness, and in so doing they separate the doctrine of sin from the doctrine of grace. In the Christian narrative, sin and grace must be held together; we can only bear to see the depth of our sin when we experience the possibility of grace, and we can only see the depth of God's grace as we get a glimpse of the enormity of the sin problem (McMinn, in press). When Christian leaders were surveyed and asked what they wished every psychologist knew about the doctrine of sin, they emphasized a comprehensive view of sin, consequences of sin and the grace of God in response to human sin (McMinn, Ruiz, Marx, Wright & Gilbert, 2006).

A comprehensive view of sin (introduced in chapter one) is important because it reminds us that sin is both an act and a state. Sin often involves personal choices, but it is also much more than personal choice. Sin ricochets through all of life, extending through cultures and generations. Sin influences biology just as surely as it influences reasoning, morality and willpower.

The consequences of sin are dire, to both self and others. Virtually all therapists have seen the horrific results of childhood abuse, and even if they choose not to use the word *sin,* they have told their clients that what happened in childhood was wrong, evil or corrupt. It is easier for people to see sins committed against them than to see how their own personal sins have been harmful. Sin has a blinding effect that causes us to deny our sin and our need for God's mercy (Moroney, 2000). Sometimes psychologists and counselors unwittingly contribute to the noetic effects of sin by discouraging clients from exploring areas of personal shortcoming, focusing instead on the shortcomings of others.

A Christian understanding of sin is inextricably linked with the doctrine of grace. Christians can afford to face their sin honestly because of the unconditional nature of God's kindness (McMinn, in press). In Romans 5:7-9, Paul writes:

> Now, no one is likely to die for a good person, though someone might be willing to die for a person who is especially good. But God showed his great love for us by sending Christ to die for us while we were still sinners. And since we have been made right in God's sight by the blood of Christ, he will certainly save us from God's judgment.

Later in the same letter, Paul reflects on the depth and permanence of God's love—a love that transcends all barriers:

> And I am convinced that nothing can ever separate us from his love. Death can't, and life can't. The angels can't, and the demons can't. Our fears for today, our worries about tomorrow, and even the powers of hell can't keep God's love away. Whether we are high above the sky or in the deepest ocean, nothing in all creation will ever be able to separate us from the love of God that is revealed in Christ Jesus our Lord. (Rom 8:38-39)

Though no therapist can love as God loves, all Christians are called to accept one another with the sort of love that Christ demonstrated (Rom 15:7). In the context of a merciful relationship, people are inclined to be honest about their shortcomings and struggles.

For the Christian therapist, understanding sin and the consequences of sin is an important part of psychological assessment, but sin should always be viewed as a comprehensive problem that affects much more than personal choice, and always viewed through the lens of God's grace. This has implications; it means that a simplistic view of sin—a list of dos and don'ts, for example—is simply not sufficient as a theoretical grid for evaluation. Christian therapists need theoretical perspectives that include a comprehensive understanding of sin and also the themes of creation and redemption described in chapter one.

Question #3: How is Christian evaluation unique?
Christian evaluation is unique in two ways—theory and content—but not in process. We argue that the process diagramed in figure 5.1 is appropriate for all therapists, Christian or not. Though assessment processes are similar for all mental health professionals, case conceptualization varies widely based on the theory used to interpret assessment findings and the content of the assessment itself.

Jan, described at the beginning of this chapter, is troubled by worry, anxiety and fear. Any competent therapist will spend time assessing her situation, learning about her job promotion three years ago, her fears about her health, her family situation, and so on. The therapist will then make sense of the information obtained in the assessment using a theoretical formulation of what goes right and what goes wrong with people. One therapist will view Jan's situation, attribute her symptoms to the overactivity of her sympathetic nervous system and recommend an anti-anxiety medication. Another will consider Jan's excessive desire for control over life's circumstances to be idolatrous and will help her release control to God. Another will see the turmoil caused by her job promotion as related to early life conflicts and will recommend insight-oriented therapy. A cognitive therapist may focus on Jan's cognitive errors and recommend cognitive restructuring.

The IP model described in this book provides a theoretical grid—informed by psychological science and Christian doctrine—that helps a clinician translate assessment data into a case conceptualization. IP allows for multiple domains to be considered. All of the previous explanations for Jan's situation may be partly right: she may need to be evaluated for medication, she may have spiritual priorities confused, she may have early life conflicts that ought to be explored, and she may benefit from cognitive restructuring to help with her dysfunctional thoughts. All of these approaches are inherently consistent with a comprehensive Christian view of creation and sin.

In addition to theory, a Christian therapist's evaluation may also be unique with regard to assessment content. All therapists will consider Jan's educational background, prior mental health history, medical history, social relationships, family and job situation, and so on, but many therapists—perhaps most therapists—will neglect to ask anything about her spiritual and religious life. Does she have a religious faith? If so, how does she view God? What sorts of religious practices characterize her life, and how do these practices affect her thoughts and emotions? These are important areas to probe (Hathaway, Scott & Garver, 2004; Richards & Bergin, 2005).

Religious and spiritual assessment is important because religious faith is central to many people's lives, and because religion affects health. The vast majority of people are theistic. In the United States, for example, somewhere between 94 percent and 96 percent of people believe in God (Miller & Thoresen,

---

COUNSELING TIP 5.2: Faith Matters

Many Christian therapists choose to have a paragraph in their initial psychotherapy contract that clients review and sign. This often leads to meaningful conversations about faith, even among clients who hold disparate religious views or have no religious faith. It also provides opportunity for an initial assessment regarding faith values as the client and therapist discuss the contract. Here is an example of such a statement:

My approach to psychotherapy is shaped by my Christian worldview. Though I have no expectation that you share my beliefs, you have a right to know them. Christianity teaches that we are created to be in relationship with God and one another, but because of the brokenness of our world our frustrated longings for relationship often result in various problems. In this sense, psychological problems—like all problems in our world—ultimately stem from our human brokenness. However, we cannot settle for simplistic connections between personal choices and psychological symptoms. Many aspects of our fallen world contribute to psychological problems, including historical, cultural, biological, psychosocial, personal and emotional factors.

Building from a foundation of a Christian worldview, my psychotherapy style involves exploring your personal history and current circumstances to identify feelings, thoughts, behaviors, assumptions and relational patterns that contribute to your current state of distress. Both your personal values and mine will affect the process of therapy. You are free to ask for clarification about my beliefs and assumptions at any point in therapy.

2003; Powell, Shahabi & Thoresen, 2003; Shafranske & Sperry, 2005); of those, most belong to a religious community, believe in a personal God and pray on a regular basis. Furthermore, growing scientific evidence demonstrates that religion and spirituality are associated with some positive health outcomes (Seeman, Dubin & Seeman, 2003). Of course, not all forms of religion and spirituality are associated with better health and recovery from disease, but an emerging body of scientific evidence demonstrates that certain religious beliefs and behaviors are related to some health variables, perhaps in part because of the healthy lifestyle choices related to religious beliefs (Koenig, McCullough & Larson, 2001; Powell, Shahabi & Thoreson, 2003).

Further, assessing religious and spiritual values is important in order to craft a particular approach to therapy that is fitting with a client's faith and personal style. Overall, Christian treatments for depression seem to have about the same efficacy as traditional psychotherapy (Johnson, 1993; McCullough, 1999; Worthington & Sandage, 2001). This is not surprising in light of the scientific findings reported in chapter two—most therapies have about equal success. But outcome studies do not necessarily tell the whole story because a number of different clients and therapists are collapsed into a treatment group and overall averages are compared with control group averages. The particular fit between a client and therapist is easily overlooked in outcome studies, but can be very important for the treatment being provided (Kelly & Strupp, 1992). Spiritual assessment is important in order to craft a particular therapeutic approach with each individual client. For example, clients with a high level of Christian commitment develop a stronger therapeutic alliance and report greater improvement than clients with lower levels of faith commitment when therapists use explicit spiritual interventions in therapy (Wade, Worthington & Vogel, in press).

In summary, a Christian approach to psychotherapy considers religious beliefs and behaviors, which affects both assessment content and the theoretical grid through which assessment information is interpreted. The process itself, however, is similar for Christian and nonreligious approaches. We now turn our attention toward the process of assessment and case conceptualization.

Assessment

One of the principles taught early in graduate school is to use multiple sources and methods when trying to understand anything that is complex, and human behavior is usually complex. What this means in terms of case conceptualization is that the effective therapist will attempt to gather as much information as reasonable in different ways in order to formulate an understanding of a client. One of the signs of a poorly trained therapist, or one with little exposure to many ent disorders, is the tendency to quickly formulate treatment ideas or plans based on little information.

It should be clear from the previous chapters that IP does not settle for simplistic views of human personality or therapy. Humans are wonderfully made, with many different dimensions, so any single approach to assessment or treatment is likely to overlook essential aspects of what it means to be a whole person. Just as IP occurs in various domains, so also assessment needs to be multidimensional. We recommend gaining information from the following sources when possible: a family member, test data and the client. It may not always be possible or prudent to interview a family member or to utilize psychological testing, but when possible and appropriate, these sources can provide useful information.

Family member. Asking the client's permission to speak with a spouse or a parent (if working with a child) can provide corroborating information about the client's situation. For example, a client may report a mild depression, noting that he is having a hard time being motivated and is feeling sad quite often. Talking with his wife, the therapist discovers the client is not able to get out of bed until noon on weekends, has stopped attending church, is talking about suicide, is rude and critical to his children, and is not performing well at work. The additional information gleaned from the spouse helps the therapist see the seriousness of the client's depression.

Beyond assessment, involving a supportive family member can be helpful in treatment as well. The family member can serve as a built-in support system for the client in making therapeutic gains more sustainable. Obviously, there are limitations to this recommendation, and there are times when it is inappropriate to involve a spouse or parent (e.g., in cases of domestic violence or child abuse). Also, it is important to keep confidentiality laws in mind—except when working with young children it is important to get the client's permission prior to speaking with a family member.

Testing. An exploration of psychological testing is beyond the scope of this book, and therefore little will be said about ways in which this substantial form of clinical information can be used in case conceptualization. Testing can be used for a variety of purposes: diagnosis, assessment of strengths and weaknesses, presence of symptoms and therapeutic change. All of these purposes may be useful in a specific case but are not likely to be necessary in every case. Oftentimes psychological testing provides a shortcut to arrive at information that can be obtained through more extensive interviewing.

Testing requires specialized expertise involving coursework and supervised training. Counselors who are not trained in psychometrics and psychological

---

IN THE OFFICE 5.1: The Third Time May Be the Charm

It is important to know the client's perception of the problem, but sometimes a therapist needs to ask this question several times. Initially the client may lack confidence in expressing an opinion, deferring to the therapist's opinion instead. Then the client may be protective or defensive. As trust and rapport are established, and with some persistence on the part of the therapist, the client often becomes more forthcoming.

Early in the Session

Mark: You are describing some serious feelings of dread and sadness. What do you suppose is wrong?

Jenny: I'm not sure. I just know it feels terrible.

Later in the Same Session

Jenny: When Jamie cries at night, it sometimes feels like it's all I can do to take care of his needs without just falling apart. Sometimes after I get him back to sleep, I just sit and sob.

Mark: Those are intense feelings. What do you think is going on with you?

Jenny: That's one of the reasons I wanted to come talk with you. It feels so overwhelming. I was hoping you could tell me what's wrong.

Still Later in the Session

Jenny: I feel so helpless in all this, like I can see myself becoming someone I don't want to be.

Mark: What do you think is causing all these feelings?

Jenny: [pause] Sometimes I worry that I shouldn't have had a child yet. I feel too young for this. I'm not sure I'm ready for the responsibility.

Mark: [noticing tears] I can see that's painful for you to put into words.

Jenny: It seems like such a terrible thing to say. I love Jamie so much, but I just wonder if I can do this without, you know, going crazy or messing him up as an adult.

---

testing can still obtain test results for their clients by referring the client to a licensed psychologist for evaluation. Qualified psychologists offer several kinds of testing: personality, intellectual and neuropsychological evaluations are among the most common.

In addition to the standard forms of psychological testing that have been

it for many years, many psychologists are now considering the importance of religious and spiritual assessment (Hill & Pargament, 2003; Richards &
Bergin, 2005). A variety of instruments are available to measure styles of religious coping (Pargament, 1997), faith-related behaviors and religious beliefs
(Hill & Hood, 1999).

Client. The client will be the primary source of information, and one or more
diagnostic interviews will be the most important way of gaining this information. An initial diagnostic interview should include three parts: exploring complaints or concerns expressed by the patient, observing signs and symptoms in
the client's behavior, and gathering historical information about the client.

Complaints or concerns are simply the statements the client makes about issues that create problems. Typically the concerns are painful enough to have
motivated the client to seek help. The complaints may be about others—"She
doesn't love me like she used to" or "He picks on me all the time." Or the complaints can be about symptoms—"I can't sleep very well" or "I cry all the time"
or "I can't stop thinking about the accident." Paying close attention to the complaints or concerns provides important clues as to how the client sees the problem. Most clients have some idea about the cause of their difficulties. Understanding the client's perception of the problems will be helpful in determining
a treatment approach and goals for the therapy. Some will attribute the causes
of the problem externally, ascribing them to other people. Others will absorb
responsibility for the problem with internal attributions. Most often in this fallen
world problems are caused by both internal and external sources. The client
who tends to attribute causes externally will need a safe therapeutic relationship
and an occasional nudge to begin seeing how personal, internal factors may be
perpetuating or contributing to the problem. Those who naturally make internal
attributions also need a safe therapeutic relationship where they can begin to
release some of the shame that keeps them focused on their personal failures
and inadequacies, and perhaps to explore some ways that external factors and
other relationships have been wounding and difficult. In either case, the therapeutic posture needs to be one of acceptance and mercy, with the goal of
broadening the attributional base that the client brings into therapy.

In addition to hearing the client's concerns, it is important to look and listen
for signs and symptoms from the client. This is where a good grounding in psychopathology is useful, again, something that is beyond the scope of this book.
Signs involve the behaviors the client exhibits during the interview. These are
clinical observations of the client, about which he or she may have little self-
awareness. For example, clients may not be aware of the quality of their speech
(slow, fast, soft, etc.), or they may have little awareness of their agitation level,

clenched fist, rigid posture, and so on. All of these can be signs of various problems and are the kinds of observations therapists make in a diagnostic interview. *Symptoms* are the complaints expressed by the patient that have diagnostic relevance. It is important to distinguish between a complaint that may be troubling a client and a complaint that points to a particular syndrome or disorder. For example, complaints about one's spouse may not have much diagnostic relevance, but complaints about hearing voices will have significant diagnostic relevance. Psychologists and other therapists often use a mental status examination (an interview protocol) to obtain signs and symptoms during a diagnostic interview.

The third part of a diagnostic interview is a review of historical information. The past is important in providing information that will be helpful for a diagnosis, a prognosis and a treatment plan. To evaluate personal strengths and weaknesses, it is important to assess educational and occupational accomplishments. To evaluate interpersonal characteristics, it is important to consider relationships from the family of origin and the current family, as well as dating, friendships and work relationships. Traumatic experiences, such as abuse, injuries (especially head injuries), violence or catastrophes, are important to evaluate in terms of their impact on the client's life. Additionally, substance abuse history and current use is relevant assessment data. A review of medical and psychological conditions in the patient's family of origin will yield helpful information about predisposing causes of current disorders. Finally, understanding the client's past experience with mental health treatment will facilitate a more accurate history of the disorder as well as reveal attitudes about treatment that the client brings to therapy.

Case Conceptualization

The information gleaned in a diagnostic interview and perhaps corroborated with psychological testing or interviews with the client's family will be useful, but it must be interpreted. Just as Bible passages need to be viewed in the larger context of culture, history and the whole of Scripture, so also the information therapists gain about people's lives must be interpreted through a hermeneutical process. Theory provides the frame for this interpretive process. Before turning to the specific theoretical grid of IP, it is important to recognize that mental health professionals also use more generic theoretical tools such as diagnosing, exploring etiology and evaluating general client factors. Though not specific to IP, each of these provides important information.

Diagnosis. An accurate diagnosis is one of the most important aspects of clinical work. In the mental health field, diagnosis has been the traditional turf of psychologists and psychiatrists. Psychologists typically utilize both interviewing and psychological testing to derive an accurate diagnosis, whereas psychiatrists are likely to use interviewing alone. Both psychologists and psychiatrists use the diagnostic system established by the *Diagnostic and Statistical Manual of Mental Disorders,* currently in its fourth edition (*DSM-IV-TR;* American Psychiatric Association, 2000). This manual describes the signs and symptoms necessary to make a psychiatric diagnosis. A complete diagnosis involves assessment of five axes or domains: axis 1 (major syndromes), axis 2 (personality disorders and mental retardation), axis 3 (contributing medical conditions), axis 4 (current stressors) and axis 5 (adaptive functioning). Because mental health problems tend to be complex and determined by multiple factors, a comprehensive diagnostic system involving the five axes yields a helpful understanding of the client.

The comprehensive diagnostic structure provided by *DSM-IV* allows clients with similar complaints or concerns to be understood in a thoughtful, nuanced manner. Thus a person experiencing depression can be described in more detail with the five-axis system than with other systems allowing only a single diagnosis. The depressed person may have substantial or relatively mild symptoms (major depression vs. dysthymia on axis 1), problems relating to others (dependent traits on axis 2), contributing medical conditions (hypothyroidism on axis 3), relatively major or minor situational stressors (described on axis 4), and decreased functioning at work or home (rated on axis 5). In this manner the *DSM-IV* allows mental health practitioners to provide important details on the nature of psychological problems in specific clients.

Another benefit of *DSM-IV* terminology is that it allows practitioners to communicate with one another using a similar language. Describing a client as suffering from generalized anxiety disorder has meaning for mental health professionals. They understand that this diagnosis characterizes the client as having certain symptoms and not having other symptoms. It further allows researchers to categorize clients in meaningful ways to study the nature of these disorders as well as the effectiveness of treatment. The danger, of course, comes in labeling a client, so that the dignity of the client is minimized and reduced to a diagnostic label.

Although the *DSM-IV* is a significant advance over previous diagnostic systems—including the earlier versions of the manual—it is still woefully inadequate in terms of providing sufficient information for case conceptualization and treatment planning. Appropriate diagnosis is helpful in pointing the way to effective treatment strategies but in and of itself does not lead to effective treatment. Many other factors must be considered in formulating a treatment approach for a specific client. For example, a client may be described as having major depression with dependent personality traits and a contributing medical condition, a moderate number of stressors, and significant impairment in daily functioning, but this says little about how to intervene. Other factors such as the client's history of abuse or trauma, previous interpersonal relationships, the personal meaning attached to the symptoms, education level, social support, spiritual resources, and so on all contribute to a better understanding of the client and appropriate treatment approaches. All of these factors warrant consideration when formulating a case conceptualization.

To summarize, diagnosis is helpful but not sufficient. Case conceptualization also involves understanding a person in the context of a theoretical grid that will guide treatment. For some diagnosticians, making an accurate diagnosis is the extent of their assessment, but this typically ends up being a disappointment because effective treatment recommendations require more than categorizing a person.

Etiology. Another conceptualization process involves examining the etiology of the client's complaints and symptoms. Brems (1999) recommends consideration of predisposing, precipitant and perpetuating factors when evaluating the causes of disorders. *Predisposing* causes are those that increase the likelihood of certain disorders. For example, many medical conditions such as diabetes and thyroid disorders serve as predisposing causes of depression, ethnic discrimination is a cultural factor that may raise the likelihood of subsequent problems,

---

COUNSELING TIP 5.3: Remember the Body

There are many possible predisposing causes for psychological problems, some of which cannot be assessed by mental health professionals. Remember to ask the client about any recent medical symptoms or physical trauma (e.g., head injuries, medical conditions) and be sure to refer the client to a physician when indicated. It is also good to ask how long it has been since the client's last physical examination and to refer the person to a physician if it has been more than a year.

Gnostic approaches to faith assume that some secret spiritual knowledge is more important than matters of materiality. In contrast, the Christian faith affirms the importance of materiality. The eternal Word became material and dwelled in our midst (Jn 1:1-14), thus affirming the value of this material world and God's redemptive presence among us. It is good and right to remember that bodies are just as essential as spiritual matters when doing an assessment and case conceptualization.

and having poor role models for effective coping may predispose a person to having similar ineffective coping methods. These historical and background factors must be considered in a comprehensive assessment.

Precipitant causes are those that have a direct link to the psychological condition manifested. Consider why the disorder is manifested at this time. Given the likelihood of predisposing factors, why are the symptoms present now? The death of a family member or the loss of a job could be precipitant causes to depression. These significant stressors may outstrip the person's ability to cope, resulting in a depressive condition.

Perpetuating causes are ongoing conditions that either prevent full recovery or lead to recurrences of the disorder. Perpetuating factors can be forces outside the person's control or generated by the client. Poverty, health problems or an abusive relationship are examples of perpetuating factors for depression that are external and beyond the client's control. Other perpetuating factors are generated by the client, but perhaps on an unconscious level. For example, there may be a hidden benefit for remaining depressed. Perhaps one does not have to participate in as many chores around the house, is allowed to sleep more or has fewer interpersonal expectations as a result of the depression. These behaviors are seen as providing secondary gain for the depression and are a type of perpetuating cause. Another type of self-generated perpetuating causes occurs in ongoing dysfunctional relationships. Teyber (1997) calls these "vicious cycles" because they are repeating interpersonal dynamics that result in dissatisfaction or symptoms for the client. For example, a depressed client may become withdrawn and sullen. As a result he or she is ignored or dismissed by others, which leads to increasing feelings of depression and escalating withdrawal.

Assessing the predisposing, precipitating and perpetuating factors involved in a client's clinical presentation can be helpful in determining the complexity of the case and a treatment plan. These factors are important in conceptualizing the case and planning appropriate intervention.

General client factors. In chapter two we discussed the professional literature related to psychotherapy outcomes. This large body of literature indicates that the strongest predictors of therapeutic success are client factors. In other words, factors such as social support, coping resources and effective interpersonal skills are stronger predictors of success than techniques the therapist utilizes. Because client factors play such an important role in therapy outcome, it is important to assess these at the outset of therapy. One factor discussed previously is the diagnosis, but other factors include the perceived nature of the problem, client expectations, interpersonal reactance, and the client's strengths and resources. Some of these factors are described more fully by Beutler and

Clarkin (1990) in their volume on treatment selection.

Perceived problems. Client problems can be evaluated in terms of insight, severity and complexity. Problem insight refers to the degree to which the client is aware of her or his own problems. Some clients appear to be almost completely unaware of their problems and indicate that the only reason for consulting a psychologist is because a spouse or pastor insisted on it. These individuals do not take appropriate responsibility for interpersonal problems and tend to see their difficulties as caused by others. Interview questions such as "How do other people describe you, particularly those who don't like you or get along with you?" or "What was the most hurtful thing that someone said about you?" may be helpful in probing for some insight in a client who otherwise expresses little.

Conversely, some clients seem to have little insight into their problems because they take too much responsibility for their difficulties. These clients readily assume that any interpersonal distress is caused by themselves and that they should assume responsibility for their own distress and others' feelings as well. Interview probes such as "Tell me about a time when you felt distressed in a relationship and your distress was triggered by someone else" or "If you reversed the roles in this situation and the same things were said to another person, how would that person feel or respond?" may determine the level of insight possible for the client at the present time.

Problem severity can be evaluated by examining the degree to which the problems are pervasive and disruptive. Some problems are circumscribed and are only present under certain conditions. A flying phobia is an example of a circumscribed problem because it pertains only to specific situations. Unless the client is forced to fly to keep a job or get to an essential event, the problem is not seen as severe. In addition to problem pervasiveness, problems can be evaluated in terms of disruptiveness or intrusiveness in life. Although a client may not like eating around others or having difficulty using public restrooms, more than likely the client has found ways to cope with these problems and they may be seen as relatively nondisruptive. A common way to evaluate the severity of problems is to rate the client on axis 5 of the *DSM-IV.* This is the Global Assessment of Functioning scale that rates the level of dysfunction caused by symptoms.

Problem complexity relates to a number of factors regarding the history of the problem. Problems that are seen as complex tend to be enduring ones that have not remitted despite previous attempts at amelioration. Complex problems tend to have several predisposing and perpetuating causes. Relatively noncomplex problems typically have a situational or recent cause with few predisposing or perpetuating causes. Perpetuating causes such as secondary gain and vicious cycles in relationships tend to increase problem complexity because these behaviors "work" for the client to a certain degree. Complex problems tend to recur over time in a repeating pattern, such as when a person has a history of being passive in a variety of relationships. Often there is a symbolic relationship between the current symptoms and the initiating causes. Perhaps a stern father punished self-assertion and, subsequently, passivity became the sole response in the presence of any authority figure. A crude assessment of problem complexity can be made by evaluating the client on axis 4 of the *DSM-IV*. This axis pertains to the stressors the client experiences and can be related to the precipitating causes of the problems.

Client expectations. This is an important area to explore because it relates both to the client's expectations of self as well as the client's expectations of therapy. For example, Jan may come to therapy feeling anxious about whether she will be a "good client." Will she be able to answer the therapist's questions well? Will she follow through on recommendations? Will she be insightful and interesting and motivated? All these questions swirling in her mind reveal that she has high expectations for herself. She wants to be the ideal client. In addition to these self-expectations, she also brings expectations about the therapy and the therapist. She hopes for someone who is well-trained, who will understand and care about her, who will help her figure out ways to better manage her health, career and family life. In chapter two we discussed the psychotherapy outcome literature indicating that 15 percent of the outcome variance is accounted for by client expectations of the therapy and the therapist. When client factors and therapy expectations are combined, they account for a large percentage of change seen in psychotherapy.

Bandura (1977)—a pioneer of social learning theory, discussed in chapter three—describes one form of self-expectation as self-efficacy. He believes that all forms of therapy are successful when they tap into or enhance a client's self-efficacy. Self-efficacy is the expectation that one has what is required to make a change to reach a goal. Obviously increasing self-efficacy is one of the goals or byproducts of effective therapy; most clients enter therapy feeling self-defeated or less than adequate to reach a desired goal. Self-efficacy can be assessed by asking clients about past successes, their current feelings and expectations about making desired changes, and their expectations about the desired outcomes. In other words, a client can agree that a goal for therapy is a good and worthy goal but not believe that it is a goal that can be reached. It is important to determine therapy outcomes or goals that the client believes she or he can reach. Past successes that are based on self-attributions will be helpful in determining self-efficacy.

Expectations of the therapist and the therapy should be evaluated also.

Does the client expect the therapist to do all the talking, to set the agenda for the session, to determine the goals, to indicate when therapy is finished, and so on? Does the client expect to bring dreams to therapy for analysis, to do homework or to be cured in four sessions? Many clients enter therapy with a poor idea of what psychotherapy is and how it works. Much of therapy on television and in the movies is a poor portrayal of the actual therapeutic pro-

---

IN THE OFFICE 5.2: Who Does the Work?

Sometimes beginning therapists confuse a caring, empathic style with taking care of a client. Therapists who are too active and demonstrative may easily take on too much responsibility for their clients, robbing the client of opportunities to grow in self-efficacy. It is important to let the client do the work in therapy.

Trudy: I lost control at the mall and now I don't know what to do. When the credit card bill comes my husband is going to flip. I know I need to tell him about it, but I just wish he didn't have to hear it from me. You've met him. You know how critical he can be.

An inexperienced therapist might offer to break the news to the husband at the next conjoint session. This is not a good idea because it does not allow the client to take responsibility and develop competence in handling tough situations.

Clark: You're feeling stuck. What are your options here?

Trudy: I could just wait until the bill comes and brace myself for what he will say. I could take some of the things back to the mall, but I've already worn these shoes and a couple other things. Or I could just tell him tonight during dinner, but I think that would be really hard. Maybe you could tell him next week when we both come in for our marital session. Or I could just get in my car and drive forever and hope he forgets all about me.

Clark: So you have options. I'm sure some of those sound better than others. Let's explore the first three a bit more—waiting for the credit card bill, taking some things back to the mall or talking with him at dinner tonight. Tell me some of the advantages and disadvantages for each of those options.

This approach allows the client to do the work and ultimately develop a greater sense of efficacy in handling life's problems.

cess. Thus it is important to ask clients about their expectations. Matched expectations between the therapist and the client is an essential factor for good therapy outcome.

Interpersonal reactance. Beutler and Clarkin (1990) described interpersonal reactance as "an individual's likelihood of resisting threatened loss of interpersonal control" (pp. 72-73). In other words, interpersonal reactance involves the likelihood that a client will react against the therapist's attempt to provide conditions for change. It has long been observed that clients come to therapy with a desire to change and a desire to remain the same. The psychoanalytic literature provides lengthy explanations of client resistance to change. The resistance is often connected to a transference relationship with the therapist that is worked through so that changes can be made without resistance. Transference will be discussed in more detail in chapter eleven.

Interpersonal reactance is about the willingness of a client to give up interpersonal control and accept the influence of the therapist. Some people are very reluctant to accept the influence of another, and in response to such influence may withdraw, become argumentative or become passive-aggressive. These interpersonal behaviors are all seen as reactions against giving up interpersonal control and allowing another (in this case the therapist) to have power or influence. Clients with high interpersonal reactance refuse to be influenced by someone else. It is difficult to do therapy with such a client because much of therapy involves incorporating new ideas into thinking and behavior. Many marriages are strained because spouses (often the husbands) are not open to the influence of their spouses (Gottman, 1999).

Interpersonal reactance can be evaluated through questions about past experiences as well as observations during the diagnostic interview. Clients should be asked about past reactions to authority figures, such as "Tell me about how you responded to the work assignments given to you by your boss, your teacher or your parent" or "When you were asked to do something hard or undesirable, how did you respond? Did you complete the task; if so, how did you do it?" These kinds of questions will elicit information about the client's likely response to the therapist's influence in the therapeutic process.

Strengths and resources. Another area of evaluation is that of client strengths and resources. What kinds of support does the client have at this time? Social support is probably the most important resource a client can have when entering therapy. It is important that a client not attempt to change in a vacuum or in the face of interpersonal opposition by a spouse or parent. We have both seen clients who were not supported by their spouses in the therapeutic process. These interpersonal dynamics put significant strain on the therapeutic process and increase the odds that therapy will fail, or if it succeeds, it may do so for unfortunate reasons.

Although one cannot choose when to have psychological struggles, one can choose when to seek help. It is most helpful to pursue therapy when one has support systems and resources such as a spouse, friend, pastor or church group. These supportive people take some of the pressure off both the client and the therapist during the therapeutic process.

Beyond social support, there are many other strengths and resources to consider when evaluating a client. The recent positive psychology movement has emphasized client factors such as hope, gratitude, optimism, positive coping, resilience, forgiveness, love, humility, problem solving, creativity, courage, sense of humor and so on (Synder & Lopez, 2005). For too long counselors and psychotherapists have viewed the problems their clients bring without giving ample attention to the resources they also bring. Lopez and Snyder (2003) recently published a handbook on positive psychological assessment that provides a good resource for evaluating clients' strengths.

Case Conceptualization Within IP's Theoretical Grid

The process of case conceptualization just described is common to most mental health professionals regardless of their faith beliefs. These processes are influenced by theory because all counseling and psychotherapy is theory-laden (Jones, 1994), but the process itself is not shaped by a particular personality theory or psychotherapy model.

In figure 5.1 we picture two theoretical grids because, in addition to the commonly held assumptions about diagnoses, etiology and client factors, each model of personality also has its unique perspectives and influences. Thus a psychodynamic therapist will end up with a different case conceptualization than a cognitive-behavioral therapist. Both will use the same diagnostic system, both will look for various client factors and etiological variables, but ultimately they will come to different conclusions about the best intervention because they have different theoretical grids for understanding the nature of human personality and motivation.

Assessment in IP has some elements that are particular to the IP model. In chapter four we described the three domains of treatment associated with IP. In anticipation of engaging the client in the appropriate domains of intervention, it is important to assess issues associated with each of the three domains. We recommend starting with assessment of maladaptive thoughts and behaviors, and moving on to assessing schemas and interpersonal functioning.

Assessing maladaptive thoughts and behaviors (functional domain).
God's desire for humans to function well, to exert managerial control over themselves and their environment, is easily thwarted in a fallen world. For example, Jan's anxiety and fear interfere with her ability to manage life well. She finds it difficult to communicate well with others, to sleep and eat in healthy ways, and to manage her escalating job responsibilities. Her daily functioning is inhibited in various ways.

Functional domain interventions involve cognitive and behavioral methods designed to alleviate client symptoms, and perhaps recommendations for medical interventions. Within this domain, specific changes in thinking and behavior are necessary to alleviate the symptoms. Thus, the task of assessment is to identify thinking and behavior that needs to be changed or developed.

Though behavioral and cognitive skills are distinct, they are also related. For example, Jan may lack assertive skills, but this behavioral deficit may be related to her thoughts that assertiveness involves being intrusive or inappropriately bold. Her thoughts about assertiveness need to change to allow the appropriate skills to develop. Similarly, a student may have the automatic thought *The professor doesn't like me* when given a lower than expected grade on an assignment. If that thought is allowed to persist, it may lead a student who struggles with self-confidence to be even more inhibited and reticent to initiate discussion with the professor. The automatic thought needs to be addressed to determine its accuracy and adaptability.

Identifying maladaptive thoughts and behaviors and underdeveloped skills is not difficult. Simply asking clients what they think and do in problematic situations usually brings about the problem thoughts and behaviors. Sometimes this requires the therapist to be a bit provocative, pushing clients toward the fears that trouble them. For example, the following dialogue occurs when Jan is asked to be specific about one of her worries.

Jan: What if my husband leaves me and I am all alone?

Clark: What would be so bad about that?

Jan: I would be lonely and I wouldn't have anyone to talk to or to be with me or to help me with the kids.

Since worry can be seen as a form of ineffective behavioral rehearsal, Jan is then asked to change her worry to a fact.

Clark: Jan, I would like you to change that *if* statement to a *fact* statement. Say out loud, "My husband has left me and I am all alone."

After she says this out loud a couple times she is asked what she is going to do now that her husband has left her.

COUNSELING TIP 5.4: Positive Functional Assessment

Though clients come to a therapist because they are not functioning as well as desired, it is also important to assess for positive functioning. The following prompts and questions can be useful:

- You've described several troubles today and how they are making life difficult right now. What are some of the things that are going well for you?

- Tell me about a time when you coped well with a tough situation.

- If someone were writing a letter of recommendation for you, describing your various strengths and abilities, what would they put in the letter?

In the middle stages of therapy, clients typically report success experiences where they begin to feel increasing confidence in their daily functioning. It is important to stop and punctuate these successes with comments such as:

- Wow! That's excellent. How did you do that?

- So you were able to stay calm even as your boss was being critical. Let's figure out how you did that. Talk me through the situation in slow motion—what you thought and what you said.

Jan: Well, I guess I would talk to our CPA about my financial situation and I would probably call my mom to see if she could help me with the kids for a while.

Jan has an idea of what she could do if her husband were to leave, but the idea of abandonment has been so fearful to her that she has not dealt with it as a reality. Once she thinks of it as a reality she is able to formulate a reasonable plan. Of course, the goal is not to make it okay for Jan's husband to leave her; rather, the point is to help Jan see that she can move beyond the stifling confines of her anxiety. In her anxiety-ridden state, she believes she would be a helpless wreck if her husband were to leave, but this new perspective helps her see that she has the behavioral skills to survive, even if her husband leaves.

Sometimes it is best to have a client imagine a bothersome situation, and then try to identify the inappropriate thinking or behavior. A client can be encouraged to describe in detail the problematic situation, and then the therapist can ask, "What went through your mind just then?" or "What did you do next when you were in that situation?" These questions bring forth the specific thoughts and behaviors that are likely to be maladaptive so that they can be evaluated and altered to be more realistic.

Assessment of the functional domain is not just done at the beginning of the therapy relationship; it is done throughout the course of therapy. Effective therapists are constantly looking for thoughts and behaviors that trouble a client and then conceptualizing effective counseling accordingly.

We have introduced only a couple concepts regarding assessment and treatment in the functional domain here, but much more will be described in chapters six and seven.

Assessing schemas (structural domain). As described in the last chapter, schemas are deeper cognitive structures that give meaning to automatic thoughts. Schemas are more difficult to assess because they are less conscious, more removed from specific life circumstances and more resistant to change. We are all quite aware that some thoughts simply pop into our minds. Sometimes we smile at these thoughts, ignore them or feel bothered by them. When we are bothered by automatic thoughts, we can ask what it is about them that feels bothersome. Most likely the thoughts are bothersome because they have certain negative meanings to us.

Schemas act as filters that give personal meaning to our experiences by connecting current situations with previous ones. This process is virtually instantaneous and tacit, occurring outside our awareness. From an adaptive perspective, this process is good in that it helps us understand experiences quickly and respond accordingly. We learn by categorizing our experiences and making them personally meaningful. This process is potentially harmful because it occurs without rational thought. Schemas are adaptive when they help us interpret and respond to our environment and the interpersonal situations we encounter. They are maladaptive when the interpretation is inaccurate and our subsequent response is ineffective in dealing with our environment and interpersonal situations.

Schemas are often equated with core beliefs in cognitive therapy (the more precise connection between core beliefs, schemas and modes is explored in chapter eight). Core beliefs are the fundamental beliefs we have about ourselves, others, the world and the future. These core beliefs develop early in life and help us make sense of our world. Having an idea of self, others, the world in general and the future will help one better anticipate or predict life, and therefore the chances of successful adaptation to the demands of life are enhanced. Unfortunately, these core beliefs are often flawed and actually lead to a poor adaptation to life.

Schemas or core beliefs can be identified by exploring the personal meaning associated with hurtful feelings or ineffective behaviors. Questions such as, "What does that thought or behavior mean about you?" are helpful in promoting exploration of the schema domain. Since this domain of thought processing is not in our awareness, we have to push ourselves and clients to consider this domain. Most clients will attempt to moderate or minimize core beliefs to make them more acceptable to the therapist, but these are not the thoughts that create emotional pain—it is the extreme ways of thinking that create pain. Maladaptive schemas often exist as extreme or unrealistic declarative statements about the self, others and the world in general (Beck, 1995).

An example of meaning created at the schematic domain can be seen in the following scenario. Many young people have experienced both acceptance and rejection when asking someone out on a date. The rejection experience is usually painful and does not have to happen more than once to create caution and hesitancy in asking someone out again. But consider two ways of responding to such a common experience.

Mark: Reflect on what it means that Shanna rejected your date.

Joey: I guess she had other plans or maybe is more interested in someone else.

Mark: But what does this rejection mean *about you?*

Joey: It means that I'm not her type. I probably don't have the qualities she is looking for in a guy at this time.

This is a fairly healthy response, and Joey will not likely feel too upset or lose sleep over the rejection. He may be a little cautious next time but will likely go on to approach others. Now consider another person's response.

Clark: Reflect on what it means that Susan rejected your date.

Brian: She may be interested in someone else, but I don't think she likes me.

Clark: But what does this rejection mean *about you?*

Brian: It means that I'm not going to get very many dates.

Clark: And what does it mean *about you* that you aren't going to get very many dates?

Brian: It means that I'm not very likeable.

Clark: And what does it mean *about you* that you aren't very likeable?

Brian: It means that I'm pretty inadequate.

Clark: *Pretty* inadequate?

Brian: Well, I am inadequate.

Notice that Joey feels bad and realizes that there are some things about himself that Shanna may not like, but he doesn't unnecessarily personalize it or generalize it. Brian's thinking, however, operates on the underlying schema of inadequacy. The rejection is much more painful and will affect his behavior because it taps into a schema. The schema is personal and it generalizes to his being ("I am inadequate"). Notice also how Brian had to be pushed to identify the underlying conclusion. His attempt to say that he was "pretty inadequate" betrayed his stronger feelings and behaviors and indicated a much more pernicious underlying belief about himself.

Schemas are important when understanding a person's experience of faith. The person who feels inadequate in human relations may also be inclined to feel inadequate before God. Rather than experiencing the profound beauty of redemptive grace, this person may end up being stuck in self-focused religious practices, somehow assuming that enough religious zeal may make him or her more acceptable to God. Similarly, the person who has a grandiose, entitled schema may perceive God to be a cosmic vending machine and feel angry whenever God does not deliver a direct answer to prayer. In assessing a person's schemas—especially a person of faith—it is important to probe the client's understanding of God. For example:

Mark: When you describe God seeming so distant from you right now, what does that say to you about God? Or about you?

Erica: I think I need to pray more. I try, but it's just like no one is there.

Mark: Say more about that. What do you make of your thought that God just isn't there for you?

Erica: Well, I guess it's not that surprising. I've been pretty messed up these last few years. I suppose God is disappointed.

Mark: Disappointed because you've messed up?

Erica: Well, yeah. I mean I haven't exactly lived as if God is important to me. So why should I be important to God?

In describing her feelings of distance from God, Erica also reveals a performance-oriented schema that suggests her bad behavior has caused God to seem distant and her good behavior (praying more) is what will cause her to again feel close to God. Her conviction about past sin and her desire to pray more are both good things, but her schema is theologically and psychologically muddled and is likely to cause her to be quite shame-based in her relationship with God and others.

We have only introduced the notion of schema assessment here. Much more detail about schemas will be provided in chapters eight and nine.

Assessing relational functioning (relational domain). The assessment task of the functional domain is to identify the specific thoughts and behaviors that need to change or develop so that the client's suffering can diminish. The assessment task of the structural domain is to identify the schemas that give meaning to the thoughts and behaviors. Whereas clients can typically label thoughts, feelings and behaviors that are problematic in the functional domain, they struggle to identify the schematic thoughts in the structural domain because these thoughts usually operate outside awareness. The assessment task of domain 3 is to describe interpersonal functioning and identify the conditions under which the client may have experienced significant interpersonal wounding. These interpersonal wounds are the source of the schemas that provide meaning to subsequent experiences. Thus, identifying and then providing a mechanism for healing relational wounds and changing interpersonal functioning is the goal of relational domain work. The mechanisms for healing and change will be elaborated in chapters ten and eleven.

In order to identify the conditions that have contributed to interpersonal wounding, the therapist looks at the client's current relationships and the relationships of childhood. The most significant current relationships are those of the client's family and work. We typically spend most of our time at home or work, and the relationships that develop there are significant. We develop the relationships we have for a reason. The nature of our current relationships, the support, alienation, criticism, comfort or hurt that we feel tells us something about the dynamics of our interpersonal functioning. It is very unusual for a client not to mention a relationship within the first minute of psychotherapy. If you are a therapist, try recalling the first couple sentences your client uttered in the first session when asked to describe his or her concerns. With few exceptions, clients describe current relationships as either part of the problem or part of the support system that keeps them from plunging further into emotional pain.

In a diagnostic interview it is important to take note of the description of a client's family and work relationships. The dynamics of current relationships can be identified by asking about them. When working with a client such as Jan, the following questions about her husband (Will) can be very helpful:

- What do you like most about Will?

- What would you like to change about Will?

- In what ways does your relationship with Will fulfill your deepest longings?

- When you get sad, angry or lonely, what do you do, and how does Will respond?

- When do you feel most connected with Will?

- What do you want from Will but rarely get?

These questions help provide information about the dynamics of Jan's significant relationships. This is not about fault-finding. We are not looking for the world's worst husband or trying to find out what's wrong with Will. On the contrary, we are trying to find out what it is that most affects Jan in a supportive or wounding relationship. And what is she doing that is a part of the overall relational dynamic?

In addition to evaluating the current relationships of the client, it is important to look at the relationships of childhood. This means looking in-depth at the family of origin. It is within a family (however that may be constructed) that we are socialized. It is in the family that we learn the rules of relationships, how to express feelings, how to get our needs met, how to get attention and how to be valued. Thus the family of origin is extremely significant in forming our beliefs about ourselves, others, the world in general and the future.

The family of origin is a source of both support and hurt for most people. Virtually everyone has something they wish was different about their childhood experience, which does not imply that there was significant wounding in everyone's background. It simply means that we are imperfect people who raise imperfect children in a sin-stained world. However, many children grow up with various forms of abuse and neglect and do not experience a caring, loving or stable environment. In fact, they may experience a prolonged struggle just to survive. Determining the kinds of relational experience in one's childhood can be ascertained by asking questions such as

- What do you like and dislike about each parent?

- How did you know you were loved as a child?

- What did you always want as a child but never or rarely get?

- What did your parents do to create feelings of safety and security for you?

- What was the main emotion you experienced as a child, and how did each parent respond to your emotional expression?

- What did you do when you didn't get your own way, and how did each parent respond to you?

These questions help elicit information about the dynamics in the client's family of origin. It is important to realize that these recollections may or may not be accurate. They are the memories or perceptions of the client. But accuracy is not what assessment is about; rather, assessment is about eliciting the client's perceptions and the background for those perceptions. These perceptions, whether accurate or not, form the core beliefs one has about self, others, the world and the future.

Spiritual assessment can also be useful in understanding the relational fabric of a client's life. McMinn (1991) recommends three exercises to help assess how people view themselves in relation to God. First, ask clients to describe several words that come to mind when they think of God. The list of adjectives produced reveals something about how they relate to God. For example, the client who views God as merciful, gracious and loving has a different relational experience than the person who describes God as harsh, stern and angry. Second, use guided imagery to assess a Christian client's sense of relationship with Jesus.

COUNSELING TIP 5.5: Not a Sleuth

It is important to keep in mind that a therapist is not a detective. Sometimes therapists feel compelled to discover the "complete truth" about a client's childhood experiences through detailed inquiry, interviewing other family members, hypnosis and so on. Inevitably, one of two errors occurs. Either the therapist inadvertently suggests ideas to the client which then change the client's memories of childhood, or the therapist comes across as not believing the client. In either case, substantial damage can result.

The best strategy is to accept a client's memories as substantial and important, even though no one has perfect recollection of the past. Look for the ways that memories of the past have shaped previous and current relationships. This is ultimately more important than trying to determine the precision and accuracy of every memory.

After going through a brief relaxation exercise, the client is asked to picture what it may be like to meet Jesus after life on earth is finished. How will Jesus respond? What sort of expressions will be on his face? What sort of welcome will occur? Though Scripture does not provide clear answers to these questions, the way clients respond may reveal something important about their perceived relationship with Christ. Third, have clients write out what God thinks of them. Is God disappointed in how little the client has produced? Is God speaking words of joy and delight about the client? These exercises reveal something about how a person relates to God.

One additional domain of relational functioning that is important to consider when evaluating the client's experience of interpersonal wounding is the relationship between the client and the therapist. Transference and countertransference feelings can be significant sources of information in understanding the client's relational dynamics. These may not be seen in the initial sessions with a client, but will almost always be seen when interventions continue into the relational domain described in chapters ten and eleven. Typically these are seen in extreme and unwarranted reactions to the therapist—both positive and negative reactions. Some understanding of the therapist-client relationship also comes through the feelings the therapist has about the client. Again, these are usually extreme or unwarranted feelings such as intense sadness, anger, indifference or sexual feelings. When transference and countertransference feelings are encountered, the therapist should attempt to find how these feelings are connected to the client's interpersonal dynamics. More than likely the client is playing out a significant relationship from the past that involves important and ongoing dynamics.

Pulling the Pieces Together

Formulating an effective case conceptualization involves identifying the appropriate issues related to client distress and describing how the issues are connected. Ideally the case formulation will give direction to interventions and lead to a treatment plan. In IP it is important to assess client factors such as diagnoses, problems, expectations and interpersonal reactance to determine ways in which these factors will relate to interventions and prognosis. It is also important to assess the domains of dysfunction (maladaptive thinking, schemas and interpersonal functioning) to determine the most likely foci for intervention.

The assessment necessary for case conceptualization can occur in a three-step process. First, a *DSM-IV* diagnosis will identify some of the symptoms that the client experiences and facilitate a broader understanding of the client. Also, the diagnosis will provide the language with which to communicate with other professionals about the nature of the client's disorder.

Second, treatment-specific issues must be addressed. These issues are based on the theory of IP and include the maladaptive thoughts, schemas and relational dynamics at the core of IP. The following questions help facilitate a case conceptualization.

- What are the current maladaptive (automatic) thoughts?

- What are the maladaptive schemas (core beliefs about self, others, the world and the future)?

- What does the client anticipate in relationships based on past relational experiences?

- How are the current symptoms related to maladaptive thoughts, schemas and relational experiences?

Third, the case conceptualization should address issues that will inhibit or facilitate therapy. These issues were described as general client factors previously in this chapter. They can be assessed using the chart provided in table 5.2. If the client is rated mostly on the right of the chart, many inhibiting factors may complicate the case and prolong treatment. The thoughtful therapist will consider these factors when formulating a prognosis and treatment plan. If the client is rated mostly on the left of the chart, then there may be fewer inhibiting factors, and instead, factors that facilitate treatment should be evident.

Table 5.2. Therapy Inhibiting and Facilitating Factors

Predisposing causes	few	many
Precipitant causes	clear	vague
Perpetuating causes	few	many
Problem insight	high	low
Problem severity	low	high
Problem complexity	low	high
Self-efficacy	high	low
Outcome expectation	high	low
Interpersonal reactance	low	high
Spiritual well-being	high	low
Social support	high	low
General resources	high	low

Conceptualizing a client's difficulties should provide a clear description of the client's distress (usually their complaints and symptoms), an understanding of how this distress interferes in the client's life, and an awareness of the source of distress, including current relationships and family-of-origin relationships. The source of distress is important in determining the domain of intervention. If the source involves situations that give rise to distressing thoughts and behaviors, then a symptom-focused intervention (functional domain) may be all that is required. If the source involves the meaning given to thoughts and behaviors, then a schema-focused intervention (structural domain) will probably be needed, though it may still be good to begin with symptom-focused strategies. If the source of distress has to do with relational wounding, particularly from past relationships, then a more time-intensive, relationship-focused approach (relational domain) should be considered.

IP should not be viewed as three different treatments for three sets of problems. The different domains of intervention in IP are all interrelated, and most counseling involves working in more than one domain, sometimes simultaneously and sometimes sequentially. Good case conceptualization helps provide an idea of how intensive the intervention will need to be and which domains warrant the most immediate consideration.

References

American Psychiatric Association. (2000). *Diagnostic and statistical manual of mental disorders* (4th ed., text revision). Washington, DC: Author.

Bandura, A. (1977). *Social learning theory.* Englewood Cliffs, NJ: Prentice-Hall.

Beck, J. S. (1995). *Cognitive therapy: Basics and beyond.* New York: Guilford Press.

Brems, C. (1999). *Psychotherapy processes and techniques.* Boston: Allyn & Bacon.

Beutler, L. E., & Clarkin, J. F. (1990). *Systematic treatment selection: Toward targeted therapeutic interventions.* New York: Brunner/Mazel.

Cooper, T. D. (2006). *Making judgments without being judgmental.* Downers Grove, IL: InterVarsity Press.

Gottman, J. M. (1999). *The seven principles for making marriage work.* New York: Crown Publishers.

Hathaway, W. L., Scott, S. Y., & Garver, S. A. (2004). Assessing religious/spiritual functioning: A neglected domain in clinical practice? *Professional Psychology: Research and Practice, 35,* 97-104.

Hill, P. C., & Hood, R. E. (Eds.) (1999). *Measures of religiosity.* Birmingham, AL: Religious Education Press.

Hill, P. C., & Pargament, K. I. (2003). Advances in the conceptualization and measurement of religion and spirituality: Implications for physical and mental health research. *American Psychologist, 58,* 64-74.

Johnson, W. B. (1993). Outcome research and religious psychotherapies: Where are we and where are we going? *Journal of Psychology and Theology, 21,* 297-308.

Jones, S. L. (1994). A constructive relationship for religion within the science and profession of psychology: Perhaps the boldest model yet. *American Psychologist, 49,* 184-99.

Kelly, T. A., & Strupp, H. H. (1992). Patient and therapist values in psychotherapy: Perceived changes, assimilation, similarity and outcome. *Journal of Consulting and Clinical Psychology, 60,* 34-40.

Koenig, H. G., McCullough, M. E., & Larson, D. B. (2001). *Handbook of religion and health.* New York: Oxford.

Lopez, S. J., & Snyder, C. R. (2003). *Positive psychological assessment: A handbook of models and measures.* Washington, DC: American Psychological Association.

McCullough, M. E. (1999). Research on religion-accommodation counseling: Review and meta-analysis. *Journal of Counseling Psychology, 46,* 92-98.

McMinn, M. R. (1991). *Cognitive therapy techniques in Christian counseling.* Waco, TX: Word Books. This book is out of print and can be downloaded at www.markmcminn.com.

McMinn, M. R. (in press). *Sin and grace in Christian counseling.* Downers Grove, IL: IVP Academic.

McMinn, M. R., Ruiz, J. N., Marx, D., Wright, J. B., & Gilbert, N. B. (2006). Professional psychology and the doctrines of sin and grace: Christian leaders' perspectives. *Professional Psychology: Research and Practice, 37,* 295-302.

Miller, W. R., & Thoresen, C. E. (2003). Spirituality, religion and health: An emerging research field. *American Psychologist, 58,* 24-35.

Monroe, P. G. (2001). Exploring clients' personal sin in the therapeutic context: Theological perspectives on a case study of self-deceit. In M. R. McMinn & T. R. Phillips (Eds.), *Care for the soul: Exploring the intersection of psychology & theology* (pp. 202-17). Downers Grove, IL: InterVarsity Press.

Moroney, S. K. (2000). *The noetic effects of sin.* Lanham, MA: Lexington Books.

Pargament, K. I. (1997). The psychology of religion and coping: Theory, research, practice. New York: Guilford Press.

Powell, L. H., Shahabi, L., & Thoresen, C. E. (2003). Religion and spirituality: Linkages to physical health. *American Psychologist, 58,* 36-52.

Richards, P. S., & Bergin, A. E. (2005). *A spiritual strategy for counseling and psychotherapy* (2nd ed.). Washington, DC: American Psychological Association.

Seeman, T. E., Dubin, L. F., & Seeman, M. (2003). Religiosity/spirituality and health: A critical review of the evidence for biological pathways. *American Psychologist, 58,* 53-63.

Shafranske, E. P., & Sperry, L. (2005). Addressing the spiritual dimension in psychotherapy: Introduction and overview. In L. Sperry and E. P. Shafranske (Eds.), *Spiritually oriented psychotherapy* (pp. 11-29). Washington, DC: American Psychological Association.

Snyder, C. R., & Lopez, S. J. (Eds.) (2005). *Handbook of positive psychology.* New York: Oxford.

Teyber, E. (1997). *Interpersonal process in therapy: A relational approach* (4th ed.). Belmont, CA: Wadsworth.

Wade, N. G., Worthington, E. L., Jr., & Vogel, D. L. (in press). Effectiveness of religiously-tailored interventions in Christian therapy. *Psychotherapy Research*.

Worthington, E. L., Jr., & Sandage, S. J. (2001). Religion and spirituality. *Psychotherapy: Theory, Research, Practice, Training, 38,* 473-78.

6

Understanding Symptom-Focused
Interventions

MANY OF OUR GRADUATE STUDENTS SELECT PSYCHOLOGY as a profession after deciding against one of two alternate career paths. Some first consider going to seminary to become ministers. These students are often quite sensitive to the deep spiritual yearnings that are part of being human and living in a fallen world, but they choose to care for souls as professional psychologists rather than becoming ordained ministers. A second group of graduate students choose psychology over medical school. These students are often attuned to relieving suffering and improving health, though they are more interested in psychosocial interventions than traditional allopathic medicine. These medically minded students want to be trained to diagnose problems well and to offer the treatments supported by the latest scientific evidence. Ultimately, both pathways into psychology remind us of important facets of the human condition.

Christian therapists with a minister's heart are likely to concentrate on the human quest for meaning and purpose; they often look deep into a client's developmental history, emotional wounds, spiritual longings and relational joys. This could be called a soul-care paradigm. Those who approach psychotherapy with a physician's sensibilities want to be applied scientists, offering the best possible treatment to help people find relief from their troubles, and as quickly as possible. This approach can be considered a medical-care paradigm, where the therapist focuses more on treating and preventing specific problems than on personality transformation.

Some who read this book will identify more with a minister's perspective and some more with a physician's, but in either case it is important to know something about diagnosing and treating particular symptoms and syndromes. Therapists of both persuasions establish credibility by helping clients through painful symptoms and circumstances that bring them to therapy in the first place. The long-term goals of therapy will be different for the two paradigms, but the beginning point is the same, as illustrated in figure 6.1.

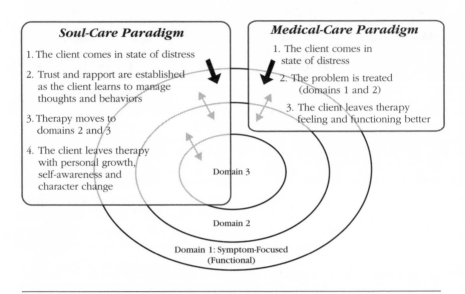

Figure 6.1. IP begins with symptom-focused interventions.

In the medical-care paradigm, clients first come in a state of distress—most often anxiety or depression or some sort of relationship problem—then the therapist conceptualizes the problem and applies a specific treatment. This treatment involves symptom-focused interventions to relieve the distressing symptoms. The medical-care paradigm often involves at least a brief foray into schema-focused interventions (structural domain) to help clients understand underlying assumptions and values that make them particularly vulnerable to dysfunctional thoughts and feelings. Once the symptoms are under control, the therapist and client terminate treatment. Sometime later, if additional troubles are encountered, the client may come back for additional help. This sort of short-term care is preferred by most health insurance companies who reimburse for psychological services.

In the soul-care paradigm, the therapist and client establish bigger goals than symptom management. They decide together to work on deeper character issues, spiritual yearnings, forgiveness, understanding psychological defenses, dealing with past relational wounds and so on. But even here, there must be a starting point to establish credibility and trust. Imagine how frustrating the following dialogue might be to a distressed client.

Client: The strangest thing happened this week. I was driving down the
            road thinking about this complicated mess at work, wondering if I'll

still have a job in a month, and all of a sudden I had a panic attack. I had to pull over to the side of the road. It was terrifying! I've never experienced anything like that before.

Therapist: That sounds difficult. Before we talk about what happened in the car this week, I would like to hear about some of your early life experiences. Tell me about your relationship with your mother.

Client: What?

Not only would this be ineffective therapy, it would also be grossly insensitive to the symptoms frightening the client. The deeper relational issues and traumatic events, if there are any, can be addressed after the initial panic problems are resolved. Symptom-focused interventions come first, and then the therapist and client decide if they want to explore deeper psychological and spiritual issues.

COUNSELING TIP 6.1: Prevention as a Third Alternative

We are describing a medical-care model and a soul-care model, but a third alternative—prevention—deserves mentioning. Just as dentistry has moved toward a preventive model of care, so some community psychologists and psychotherapists have found ways to help prevent problems before they start. *Primary prevention* occurs when mental health resources keep problems from occurring. For example, premarital counseling can help couples learn effective communication and relationship skills, thereby preventing problems they might otherwise face. *Secondary prevention* occurs when help is offered at the earliest sign of risk or trouble. An example of this is a church or community center offering a class for young couples experiencing some adjustment challenges during the first year of marriage. *Tertiary prevention* is aimed at preventing negative outcomes once a problem is identified. A couple with significant marital problems may be referred to a therapist with the hope of preventing divorce and helping the couple improve their marriage.

Most therapy is based on a tertiary prevention model, but other forms of prevention are worth bearing in mind. Community psychologists consider how to garner resources and strengths in communities, using these to help promote healthy functioning. Christians are wise to consider how church communities can function in health-promoting ways. Some of the most encouraging forms of church-psychology collaboration are preventative in focus (M. R. McMinn & Dominguez, 2005).

Two caveats are in order. First, though we are describing three domains of intervention in this book, it is important to note that therapy rarely fits so neatly into categories. The domains of intervention illustrated in figure 6.1 have bi-directional arrows between them to illustrate that these all exist along a continuum of care. Effective therapists move fluidly between different domains of care. Our taxonomy may be helpful in conceptualizing symptom-focused, schema-focused and relationship-focused interventions, but most experienced therapists move skillfully between these at different points in therapy.

Second, we need to distinguish between the sort of soul care that is offered by a professional psychotherapist and the soul care provided by a minister or spiritual director. Someone may come to a spiritual director or minister in order to grow deeper in faith and character, even when there are no troubling symp-

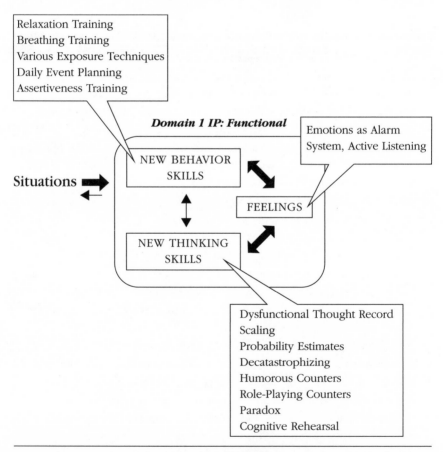

Figure 6.2. Symptom-focused interventions help clients learn new behavioral and cognitive skills.

toms or adjustment concerns. Symptom-focused interventions would not be relevant; the spiritual director and client would move immediately into discussions of character and spiritual formation. But it is exceedingly rare for people to come to a psychotherapist without some symptoms of distress. Those who come to see a psychologist are usually slogging through a difficult time, making it important to give sufficient attention to symptoms of distress.

In IP the methods of symptom-focused interventions are informed by the cognitive-behavioral tradition in psychology, but with some modifications based on a Christian understanding of persons. The primary objective of symptom-focused interventions is to alleviate distress by helping the client explore feelings and learn new behavior and thinking skills (see figure 6.2). Medications may also be considered in consultation with the client's psychiatrist, internist or family physician.

Feelings

Cognitive therapists are sometimes seen as logic brokers who have little interest in emotions. To some extent this is an unfair caricature of cognitive therapy. Most of the leading cognitive therapists have written about the importance of emotions in helping them identify poignant cognitions. They evoke emotions in therapy, help the client identify the associated cognition and then work to modify cognitive errors. There is a place for this approach in integrative psychotherapy, but emotions carry additional significance. Negative emotions are seen as a God-given alarm system—a warning that something is awry in the relational, structural and functional dimensions of life. It is not merely that unpleasant emotions stem from dysfunctional thoughts; they also point toward relational disconnection as a deeper source of pain and struggle. Imagine a beachcomber with a metal detector, looking for hidden treasure beneath layers of sand. As the beach comber approaches a metal object, the detector begins to beep louder and more frequently. Similarly, intense emotions help a client and therapist detect important themes that may be occurring beneath the surface of the conversation, and perhaps beneath the surface of the client's consciousness.

A person may experience intense anxiety over a job situation—perhaps a performance evaluation is coming up in a few days. She wakes early each morning fretting about the possible outcomes and has difficulty concentrating on the routine responsibilities of life. A wise therapist will help her look for the cognitive errors that are driving the anxiety; she may be overestimating the likelihood of a negative evaluation, for example. But in IP it is also important to consider the deeper structural and relational themes in her life. Perhaps she has a schema-domain belief that she must win the approval of others at all times.

Maybe the intensity of her anxiety points back to early relationships in life where she learned that she must appear to be perfect in order to maintain the love and attention of her parents. Her emotions of anxiety are not merely symptoms of a disorder that can be treated with cognitive change; they also help identify the deeper themes that are likely to recur over and over until she better understands her schemas and relational longings. (Emotions, schemas and relationships will be discussed in later chapters.)

Virtually every approach to psychotherapy includes an emphasis on active listening, and IP is no exception. Active listening creates an environment of safety so that clients feel free to explore and express their feelings and experiences. It is beyond the scope of this book to describe the various methods of active listening—genuineness, empathy, positive regard, reflections, interpretations, immediacy, acknowledgments, nonverbal expressiveness and so on—but students of counseling need to learn about these in order to be effective helpers.

Behavior Skills

Though the radical behaviorism of the mid-twentieth century has either died or gone into a lengthy coma, still there are important behavior-change techniques that can be useful in the symptom-focused phase of IP. Relaxation training, breathing training and various exposure methods are useful in treating anxiety disorders, as described in chapter seven. Daily event planning and assertiveness training, described in chapter nine, are useful in treating depression.

Behavioral interventions are rooted in classical, operant and observational learning theory. It is beyond the scope of this book to describe these in detail, but a brief explanation is fitting. Classical conditioning considers emotional responses emerging from situations where a biologically determined stimulus is paired with a neutral stimulus. If the association is strong, the neutral stimulus begins to have the same effect as the biologically determined stimulus. The classic example is seen with Ivan Pavlov's dogs. Pavlov, a Russian physiologist working in St. Petersburg, set out to study salivating behavior in dogs. He wanted to know the amount of salivation associated with various types of food. But the dogs soon made things difficult because they began salivating when they heard the experimenter's footsteps, long before the experimenter presented them with the food of the day. By associating the neutral stimulus (footsteps) with the biologically determined stimulus (dogs naturally salivate in the presence of food), soon the dogs were salivating in response to the footsteps. Pavlov ultimately abandoned his initial research question and studied the phenomenon of classical conditioning.

Classical condition helps explain why some adults fear going to the physician or dentist—they associate the office itself, or the sight of the doctor, with physical pain they experienced in childhood. This also helps explain certain phobias. For example, a child who is startled by a slithering snake may associate the startling visual experience with the sight of a snake, resulting in an inordinate fear of snakes. It also helps explain why a survivor of sexual abuse may have later sexual difficulties, even with a safe and caring spouse.

Behavioral interventions help extinguish the classically conditioned reactions that are causing a person difficulty. For example, a client may be taught how to relax in the presence of a hypodermic needle, lessening the previous conditioning that caused the client to feel anxious and fearful in a physician's office. Most of the behavioral strategies described in chapter seven—including relaxation training, breathing training and exposure treatments—are tools to help people overcome classical conditioning that has caused them problems.

Operant conditioning pertains to emitted, voluntary behavior that is followed by a reinforcing consequence. Often associated with the seminal work of B. F. Skinner, operant conditioning considers how the likelihood of a behavior increases or decreases depending on the consequences that follow. There are two ways to increase the likelihood of a behavior: give a reward or withdraw an unpleasant consequence. The former is known as positive reinforcement and the latter as negative reinforcement. A teenager may learn to take out the garbage because it is followed by getting an allowance (positive reinforcer) or by eliminating a parent's nagging (negative reinforcer).

Clinically, operant conditioning can be both a predisposing and perpetuating factor for various problems. Some problems exist because they were once reinforced—for example, the socially anxious client who was verbally reinforced as a child for avoiding unfamiliar and unpredictable situations. Other problems may have other origins, but they are maintained by operant conditioning. Some problems are inadvertently reinforced by a person's friends or family, a process known as secondary gain. For example, one of us once had a client who ultimately concluded that her snake phobia helped her get sympathy and attention from others. Her problem may have originated from classical conditioning, but operant conditioning perpetuated it. Some of the methods described in chapters seven and nine—such as assertiveness training and daily activity planning—are operant conditioning strategies.

Observational learning accounts for a great deal of what we know. Even before a fifteen-year-old gets behind the steering wheel of a car to learn how to drive, a vast amount of learning has already occurred by watching others drive. Moving the wheel counterclockwise results in a left-hand turn; a clockwise twist

IN THE OFFICE 6.1: Mirroring and Modeling

Observational learning suggests that one way people change in therapy is by observing how the therapist handles life situations. Therapists who model a calm, even-tempered approach to problem solving are helping by setting a good example.

At the same time, active listening in therapy involves a certain amount of mirroring emotion. That is, when the client expresses sorrow, the therapist experiences empathy for those feelings and mirrors it back in words and facial expression. Similarly, if a client is joyful, the therapist mirrors a sense of hope and enthusiasm for life. This is reminiscent of Paul's instructions to rejoice with those who rejoice and weep with those who weep (Rom 12:15).

How does one balance modeling calmness and mirroring emotion at the same time? As important as mirroring is, it is essential that a therapist not be consumed by the client's emotions. Empathy is not sympathy. An empathic therapist feels and expresses concern when a client is distressed, but still maintains a composed demeanor even in the midst of difficult situations. In this sense, the therapist is modeling an unruffled approach to life's challenges. The most effective therapists find a balance between mirroring emotion and modeling calmness.

Carlos: This was a terrible week. I can't believe everything that happened. It started with a car accident over the weekend, and then my teenage daughter was arrested on Tuesday for shop-lifting. Then yesterday I found out that our company is downsizing, and my position is one that may be eliminated.

Mark: Oh my. You have had a lot to deal with.

Carlos: That's for sure. I'm exhausted.

Mark: I imagine you are. It's been quite a week.

Carlos: Yeah, I've been so stressed. I'm not sleeping well. I'm worrying constantly. I try to stay calm about all these things, but I'm not doing well.

Mark: It's tough to be calm in the midst of so much. Let's set an agenda for our time today. You've had several big things happen. What would you like to talk about first?

Carlos: Well, the call from the police station was pretty terrible. That was probably the low point of my week.

Mark: Let's start there, Carlos. Tell me more about what happened.

Here the therapist balances mirroring and empathy with a calm, problem-solving approach to therapy.

results in a right-hand turn. Stepping on one pedal makes the car go
other pedal slows it down. So also psychological problems can somet
from watching how others respond to sad or dangerous situations. Children of
anxious parents may be prone to anxiety problems later in life, not only because
of biological predispositions but also as a result of observing many anxious reactions and behaviors.

Clinically, therapists put observational learning to good use when they model
effective coping responses for clients. For example, after several weeks of relaxation training a therapist may take an airline flight with a client who fears
flying. This intervention not only provides a classical conditioning treatment
(pairing a new relaxation response with flying) but also an opportunity for the
client to observe the therapist model a calm approach to flying.

Despite the importance of classical, operant and observational learning, behavior skills in IP are not merely seen as the sum of these three types of conditioning. In the heyday of behaviorism, some ardent therapists and theorists
believed that virtually all behavior can be explain by laws of learning, but neither Christianity nor contemporary psychology allows for such extreme reductionism in understanding human behavior. Behavior therapists have traditionally been highly deterministic, assuming that past learning contingencies create
unavoidable behavior patterns in the present. Christian doctrine allows for a
certain level of determinism—it is certainly true that human sinfulness determines that we will struggle with selfishness, for example—but does not go as
far as the radical determinism of behaviorism. Christianity assumes a measure
of human agency. Throughout the Old and New Testaments we see various
calls for God's followers to choose a particular way of life that runs counter to
the prevailing cultural forces of the day. We Christians are not only free to
choose, we are called to exert volition in making wise and godly choices. In
IP, human functioning is viewed in the larger context of adaptive behavior; the
powerful influence of past learning and the possibility of human freedom are
both acknowledged. Behavior is also influenced by biological factors, intrinsic
motivations, spiritual awareness, mental processes and various other factors.
Moreover, behavior is viewed as only one dimension of adaptive functioning;
cognition and feelings are also important.

Consistent with Christian theology's functionalist views of the *imago Dei*, in
IP humans are considered to have a unique capacity to manage, even exercise,
dominion over parts of creation. Sometimes these abilities to manage creation
need to be self-directed in order to bring one's own behavior and life situations
under control. The need for self-control, and techniques to accomplish it, are
part of a long and rich tradition both in Christianity and psychology.

Yvette is a forty-two-year-old woman who feels overwhelmed with the responsibilities of life. She works in a demanding job that requires her to travel often, parents three active teenagers and is highly involved in her church. She comes for help because of persistent, free-floating anxiety. Most nights her mind is racing, making sleep elusive. During the day she frets about her job, children, marriage and Christian character.

Yvette is coming for help because she wants to manage her life without being engulfed by anxiety. Rather than simply reducing her behaviors to classical, operant and observational paradigms, it is worth considering the larger theological theme at play. She wants to exercise greater dominion over that small slice of creation that involves her family, work and church life. She wants to function more effectively, and well she should because Yvette is designed by God to exercise stewardship over life. Her therapist can help her reclaim some of her functional capacity by offering behavioral strategies such as relaxation and breathing training to help calm her during stressful times of the day, spiritual meditation exercises to help her focus on issues of ultimate meaning and not just on details of daily life, bedtime routines to reduce insomnia, and assertiveness training to help her set good boundaries at work, home and church. These symptom-focused behavior change methods may provide great benefit to Yvette. It will also be important to consider how she thinks about her situation.

Cognitive Restructuring

Behavior therapy focuses on behavior changes, cognitive therapy on thinking changes, and they both can help a person function more fully. In Yvette's situation, she not only needs to learn new behaviors to manage her life, she also needs to reevaluate the way she views herself in relation to her environment. Cognitive restructuring can be accomplished through various techniques. Perhaps the most commonly used is the dysfunctional thought record, sometimes called the triple-column technique. Here the therapist helps the client tease apart the various components of a bad situation into three separate categories and then probes for more rational ways of evaluating the situation. Learning the dysfunctional thought record requires two sets of skills: sorting an experience into its component parts and gently countering dysfunctional thoughts.

Dysfunctional thought record: Sorting. The first objective in using the dysfunctional thought record is to help a client reorganize a distressing experience into three distinct categories: situation, feelings and thoughts. This is why the dysfunctional thought record is also known as the triple-column tech-

---

COUNSELING TIP 6.2: Not Too Soon

The dysfunctional thought record is a standard cognitive therapy tool, but it should not be used too early in therapy. Because of its structured, detailed approach to problem solving, it can appear reductionistic or even argumentative to clients if it is used before a strong working alliance is built.

The first two or three sessions are typically spent getting to know a client, exploring background issues, setting goals for therapy and so on. This also allows rapport to be established. By the third or fourth session the client and therapist have established goals and a treatment plan. At this point the therapist can begin introducing specific cognitive and behavioral techniques, such as the dysfunctional thought record.

---

nique. It is quite natural to experience distress as a blob of misery; the dysfunctional thought record helps disentangle the blob by sorting it into component parts.

Sorting is a straightforward process where the client tells the story and the therapist maps it out on a piece of paper, using three columns. Often the paper is placed between the client and the therapist so that the client can observe the sorting process as it unfolds. Once clients learn to sort their experiences into three columns, this can be assigned as homework so they can practice between sessions.

Here is an example of how a therapist might implement the dysfunctional thought record.

Cheryl: I've been afraid of having a panic attack while driving. If it ever happened, I'm sure I would have an accident and probably end up in the morgue. I'm scared to death to get behind a steering wheel. I had to call a friend to drive me to your office today. Even so, I'm still all shaky and panicked about having to ride in a car to get here, even as a passenger.

Mark: So just today, as you were driving here with your friend, you were feeling quite anxious.

Cheryl: Absolutely. I'm still shaking.

Mark: Let's take a few moments and try to explore what was going on as carefully as we can. I'm going to draw three columns on this piece of paper. The first we can label "Situation," the second "Feeling," and the third "Thoughts." Let me write the situation here, in the first

column: "Riding in the car with my friend today." Now let's move
to the Feelings column. How would you describe your feelings as
you were riding in the car to my office?

Situation	Feelings	Thoughts
Riding in the car with my friend today		

Cheryl: I was really scared. I just felt like something terrible was going to
           happen on the expressway.

Mark: Okay, let me put "scared" here in the Feelings column. And it
           sounds like you were having the thought that something terrible
           was about to happen, so I'll write that in the Thoughts column.
           Were you having any other feelings, besides being scared?

Situation	Feelings	Thoughts
Riding in the car with my friend today	Scared	Something terrible is going to happen

Cheryl: I felt bad about having my friend drive me. I know he's busy and
           he didn't seem very happy about taking the time off to help me get
           here.

Mark: So you were feeling some guilt.

Cheryl: Yeah.

Mark: Any other feelings?

Cheryl: No, that's about it.

Mark: On a scale of 1 to 10, with 10 being the most intensely scared you
           have ever been, how scared were you on the expressway coming
           here today?

Cheryl: Oh, I was pretty scared. Maybe about an 8.

Mark: That was a strong feeling for you. On that same scale, how guilty
           were you feeling?

Cheryl: Probably about a 6.

Mark: Okay, so here is what the chart looks like now.

Situation	Feelings		Thoughts
Riding in the car with my friend today	Scared Guilty	8 6	Something terrible is going to happen

Mark: Now, a while ago you described a thought you were having: "Something terrible is going to happen." I'm assuming that thought went along with feeling scared.

Cheryl: Definitely. I just kept thinking that I was going to have a panic attack, freak out, my friend wouldn't know what to do, and he would get in some sort of accident.

Mark: And the more you had these thoughts, the more anxious you felt.

Cheryl: That's right. They got pretty intense.

Mark: Yes, I suppose they did. Even to the point where you were shaking and feeling some panic symptoms. Now what thoughts did you have that relate to the guilt you were feeling?

Cheryl: I just kept thinking that he's pretty upset with me for asking. I hate making people upset.

Mark: Okay, so there are two parts to this thought. First, "he's upset with me," and second, "this is really terrible that he's upset." So let's update the chart.

Situation	Feelings	Thoughts
Riding in the car with my friend today	Scared 8	Something terrible is going to happen. I'll have a panic attack and we'll get in an accident.
	Guilty 6	He's upset with me, and it's terrible that he is.

Cheryl: Yeah, that looks right.

In this example, the therapist listens to the client's story and helps sort it into the three columns. There is nothing particularly sophisticated or difficult about the technique—it is simply two collaborators sitting in a room together trying to better understand the experience that one of them has just had.

When beginning therapists have difficulty with this sorting technique, it is usually because they fail to get a specific situation. Vague situations do not work well because the associated thoughts and feelings will also be vague and non-specific. If Cheryl simply expressed that she has been nervous driving lately, it would be difficult for a therapist to understand the precise thoughts and feelings that accompany the nervousness. By specifying a particular time and place (i.e., this morning, on the expressway coming to the therapist's office) the therapist is able to help Cheryl articulate her thoughts and feelings with some precision.

Dysfunctional thought record: Countering. Sorting has therapeutic benefit of its own—helping a client transform an amorphous splotch of discomfort into its component parts and thereby understand it better. But once the client has become adept at sorting, there is another step to the dysfunctional thought record. In this second step, dysfunctional thoughts are countered with the goal of helping the client think more rationally. Here the therapist teaches the client to "fight back" against the upsetting automatic thoughts.

In the animated Walt Disney feature film *Finding Nemo,* Nemo is a fish whose parents, Marlin and Coral, are pondering their litter of eggs that are soon to be hatched. Marlin and Coral agree that one will be named Nemo and most the others will be Marlin Jr. Then Marlin Sr. ponders aloud the question that reverberates in the mind of many new parents: "What if they don't like me?" The thought obviously causes him anxiety about being a parent. Coral, his wife, counters Marlin's thoughts by reminding him that there are more than four hundred eggs and that "one of them is bound to like you." This may not provide all

---

COUNSELING TIP 6.3: Turning the Corner

After situations, thoughts and feelings have been sorted, the therapist wants to help the client generate new thoughts that are more reasoned and less troubling. We sometimes think of this as "turning the corner." The client's automatic thoughts are leading in a particular direction—toward escalating anxiety or depression, for example—and now the goal is to help the client change directions and move toward more calming and rational thinking. One of the effective ways to turn the corner is to ask, "Is there any other way to look at this situation?"

the comfort and reassurance that Marlin is hoping for, but here in the midst of exaggerated Disney humor we see a basic premise of cognitive restructuring: if we can help others alter the way they think, it will help reduce their distress.

We might think of countering as adding a fourth column to the dysfunctional thought record (at which point "the triple-column technique" becomes a bit of a misnomer). This fourth column allows a client to dispute the automatic thoughts that are causing distress. It is typically best for the client, not the therapist, to generate the counter-thoughts; otherwise therapy might feel like an experience in debating or arguing—the client gives the automatic thought, then the therapist gives the rational response, then the client defends the original thought, and so on. Notice the contrast between an approach where the therapist generates the rational thought (example 1, below) and having the client generate the rational thought (example 2).

Example 1: Countering through disputing.

Mark: So you're on the expressway, feeling scared and saying to yourself that you'll have a panic attack, your friend will freak out, and you'll get in an accident.

Cheryl: Yeah, that's right.

Mark: That seems like you're upsetting yourself unnecessarily. First of all, it's not likely that you would have a panic attack. You've had a couple dozen panic attacks over the last few months, but none of them have been in a car. And second, even if you did have a panic attack it is unlikely that your friend would have gotten in an accident. So the thoughts you were having were not very reasonable. How's this as an alternative: "I probably won't have a panic attack, and if I do my friend won't get in an accident"? We can write it here in the Rational Response column.

Situation	Feelings	Automatic Thoughts	Rational Response
Riding in the car with my friend today	Scared 8	Something terrible is going to happen. I'll have a panic attack and we'll get in an accident.	I won't have a panic attack, and even if I do, my friend won't get in an accident.
	Guilty 6	He's upset with me, and it's terrible that he is.	

Cheryl: I suppose, but that's not how I felt at all. And one time I had a panic
             attack just before I got in the car. My friend is a good driver, but not
             a perfect one. You never know how he might drive if someone was
             freaking out beside him.

[Debate ensues]

Example 2: Collaborative countering.

Mark: So you're on the expressway, feeling scared and saying to yourself
             that you'll have a panic attack, your friend will freak out, and you'll
             get in an accident.

Cheryl: Yeah, that's right.

Mark: Let's take a moment to look at the available evidence. How often
             have you had panic attacks in a car over these past several months?

Cheryl: Well, never actually. I had one just before I got in the car once, but
             I was able to go back in the house and get things under control be-
             fore driving.

Mark: Okay, well that's helpful information. As you think about that, is
             there any other way you could have interpreted the situation today
             as you were riding with your friend?

Cheryl: What do you mean?

Mark: Well, you were saying to yourself that a catastrophe was about to oc-
             cur. Is there any other way you could have been talking to yourself?

Cheryl: Well, I guess we didn't have an accident. I could have been saying
             that things are scary, but they will probably turn out okay.

Mark: Yes, I see what you mean. Let's write that down here. I'm going to
             add a fourth column for these more collected, rational thoughts that
             you are coming up with now. Do you notice any change when you
             think this thought, *Things will turn out okay?*

Situation	Feelings	Automatic Thoughts	Rational Response
Riding in the car with my friend today	Scared 8	Something terrible is going to happen. I'll have a panic attack and we'll get in an accident.	This feels scary, but things will probably turn out okay.
	Guilty 6	He's upset with me, and it's terrible that he is.	

Cheryl: It makes me feel calmer I suppose.

Mark: So one of the challenges that you and I have is to help you think more calmly in the midst of a situation like this.

Cheryl: Yes, that would be helpful.

This second example is more likely than the first to be meaningful to the client. Collaborative countering is helped by two strategies: the Socratic method and collaborative empiricism (Beck, 1995). The *Socratic method* involves using questions and reflections to encourage clients to evaluate the validity of their own thoughts rather than the therapist disputing thoughts directly. In the previous collaborative countering example the therapist and client work together to generate a reasonable appraisal of risk, which stands in sharp contrast to example 1 where the therapist is directly refuting the client's thoughts. The Socratic method helps maintain a collaborative relationship between therapist and client. Related to the Socratic method is "guided discovery," which is discussed in chapter nine. *Collaborative empiricism* means that the client and therapist are working together to consider evidence that supports or refutes the thoughts being evaluated. In the preceding collaborative countering example, Cheryl mentions that she made it to the session despite her worries and that she has never actually had a panic attack in a car before. These observations provide empirical evidence for a revised way of looking at the situation and may help her next time she is riding in a car.

The dysfunctional thought record can be used as an overt and explicit method in therapy, but once the client is familiar with the notions of sorting and countering, many conversations in therapy follow the form of the dysfunctional thought record without being as overt or explicit. Notice in the following dialogue that the client and therapist are still using the structure of the dysfunctional thought record to organize their conversation but the dialogue no longer requires the explicit use of a worksheet or four specific columns.

Maggie: It's been a good week. I've felt fairly good most days. There were a couple times I started to get worked up, but I managed to calm myself down.

Clark: That's great. You're making some good progress here. I'd love to hear about one of those times you calmed yourself down.

Maggie: Yeah, well a couple days ago I was in an elevator at work, which happens a lot, but this time it was unusually crowded. There must have been ten or twelve people crowded in this little elevator, and I was stuck in the back corner.

Clark: Wow. How were you feeling about that?

Maggie: It was scary. I kept thinking that I might panic and how weird that would be. I work with these people.

Clark: Yeah, so you felt scared and you were saying some upsetting things to yourself. What were you saying?

Maggie: I guess, you know, "I might have a panic attack, people would notice and they would think I am a crazy person or something."

Clark: Okay, so there you are in the back corner of the elevator, feeling scared, worrying that you'll panic and people will think you're crazy. How does that square with your past experience?

Maggie: It doesn't really. I had a panic attack in an elevator once a couple months ago, and I hated it, but I just went to my office, closed the door and suffered quietly on my own. I don't think anyone even noticed.

Clark: So somehow in that elevator this week you were able to look at the evidence and calm yourself down. How did you do it?

Maggie: Well, I just told myself that I was only going to be in the elevator for thirty seconds or so, that I could keep breathing and stay calm, and that even if I did start sweating or hyperventilating people might not even notice. And, I suppose, even if they did notice it wouldn't be the end of the world.

Clark: So you were able to calm yourself by catching your runaway thoughts and then correcting them.

Maggie: Yeah, it wasn't a great moment, but it turned out okay. I think I handled it fairly well.

Clark: It sounds like you did.

One could think of the dysfunctional thought record as the "bread-and-butter" technique of cognitive therapy, because it is so commonly used. Early in therapy it is used explicitly, using a recording sheet both in the sessions and as homework. As the therapy progresses, the dysfunctional thought record becomes more implicit, as shown in the previous dialogue, guiding and shaping conversations whether or not the actual worksheet is used.

Other cognitive restructuring methods. Many other cognitive restructuring methods can be used in cognitive therapy (see Beck, 1995; Freeman, Pretzer, Fleming & Simon, 1990). Several of these additional strategies are described and illustrated below.

Scaling. When overwhelmed emotionally, people have a natural tendency to respond in an exaggerated fashion, which further escalates the feelings. Depressed clients are prone to exaggerate their misfortunes and anxious clients to overestimate the likelihood of some bad event happening in the future. Scaling entails putting bad outcomes on a continuum, and it helps people avoid the all-or-none conclusions that amplify their negative thinking.

Juanita: This is really terrible. I can't believe my car broke down right now. I can barely afford rent this month, and now I have this to deal with.

Mark: It feels like one more thing to deal with when you're already overwhelmed with other responsibilities.

Juanita: Exactly. I just can't believe this happened on top of everything else.

Mark: Right. It's a big burden for you. Help me understand this in the perspective of the scale we've discussed before, where 10 is the worst thing you can imagine and a 1 is a good day.

Juanita: Right now it feels like a 9.

Mark: Yes, I'm sure it does. It feels almost too big to manage. I think you said last week that a 10 would be something like having your entire family die in a terrorist attack. Having your car break down feels almost that bad today, as you view it through the lens of your stress.

Juanita: Yeah, it feels really overwhelming. But logically I know it's not really nearly as bad as that terrorist thing. It's probably only a 6. It just feels lousy and scary right now.

Here the therapist helps the client move away from all-or-none thinking to put an unfortunate event in perspective. Notice that the therapist does so gently, mixing reflections and empathy with the scaling technique. A gentle and compassionate approach communicates that the client's feelings are being taken seriously, and it prevents the therapist from being critical of the client's exaggerated view of a car problem. The client's final rating of 6 is probably still exaggerated, but rather than challenging the client further, the therapist chooses to accept the revised rating. Moving from a rating of 9 to 6 is good enough—it helps the client moderate the all-or-none thinking, which is the goal of this technique. If it is pushed too far, it may harm the therapeutic relationship by making it seem that the therapist doesn't care about the client's plight.

Probability estimates. Related to scaling, cognitive therapists sometimes encourage anxious clients to estimate the probability of some worrisome event happening. What might initially seem like a certain disaster is typically perceived more reasonably after this technique is used.

COUNSELING TIP 6.4: Scaling as a Way of Life

One of the greatest benefits of scaling is helping people avoid all-or-none thinking. It is common for people to see things as completely one way or another—either my child's little league team is great or they are terrible, my boss is either wonderful or awful, my marriage is fantastic or doomed. Scaling is used often in cognitive therapy because it helps move people away from dichotomous thinking. Almost every little league team, like almost every boss and marriage, exists somewhere on a continuum rather than at one extreme or the other. The more people get used to scaling, the better they are at seeing nuances in life situations rather than resorting to extreme conclusions.

Jo Ann: I've been really worried about my son playing football. He begged me to play, and I eventually gave in and said yes, but what if he gets some sort of injury? Football is a terrible sport. People get injured all the time, and sometimes it cripples them for life.

Clark: So that's been on your mind lately: that Michael may get a serious injury that affects him for the rest of his life.

Jo Ann: Yes. I think about it all the time.

Clark: Let's look at this in a couple ways: first, Michael getting a serious injury, and second, it affecting him for the rest of his life. So first, how likely would you guess it is that Michael will get a significant football injury this year?

Jo Ann: I think it is very likely. Football is a dangerous sport.

Clark: So if there were one hundred seventh-grade boys playing football, how many of them would have a serious injury during the season?

Jo Ann: I'm not sure. Maybe fifty or so.

Clark: So at the end of the season, a team would be down to half its original size?

Jo Ann: [laughs] Well, okay. Maybe only 10 percent.

Clark: And of those 10 percent who get injured, how many will have life-altering injuries from which they will never fully recover?

Jo Ann: Well, that's probably not very likely. Maybe only one out of the ten.

Clark: Okay, so we could quibble about the numbers. I suspect they're lower than you're guessing, but the worst case is a 1-percent chance that Michael will have a life-altering injury this year. What impact does that have on the worries you're describing?

Jo Ann: It helps. I'm sure I'll still worry, but it's true that he's not likely to have a huge life-altering injury.

Of course the numbers used in this example are greatly exaggerated. Probably the likelihood of a seventh-grade football player sustaining a life-changing injury is only a small fraction of a percent, but the point is not actuarial accuracy as much as helping the anxious client to bring escalating fears under control.

Decatastrophizing. People diagnosed with schizophrenia sometimes make up words, known as neologisms. Apparently cognitive therapists share this in common with psychotic patients, because they also make up words! In the grip of depression and anxiety, it is natural for people to perceive misfortune as catastrophe; decatastrophizing is a word invented by cognitive therapists to describe the process of bringing these runaway thoughts back to a place of reason.

Mitchell: I can't stand this any more. She says she loves me, but what does that mean? She says no to sex a hundred times more than she says yes. What kind of marriage is that? Most days I just hate being married to her. The truth is that I hate her too.

Mark: These are intense feelings. They seem pretty overpowering for you.

Mitchell: She's an overpowering person.

Mark: Well, that may be. But I meant your thoughts and feelings. They seem to be very intense for you right now.

Mitchell: Definitely. I've been so upset. I used to ask for sex every night, and she said no every night, so now I just don't ask. I don't think she would care if we never had sex again.

Mark: So that's a source of incredible frustration. How do you get from there—from your frustration over sex—to hating her?

Mitchell: I'm not sure. This has just gone on so long. I'm just so frustrated.

Mark: Yes, I hear that. The frustration is intense. Do you think this is more about frustration than hatred?

Mitchell: Yeah, I suppose it is. We have good times. There are still days when I feel lucky to be married to her, and then there are days like this when I'm just at wits' end.

Mark: Yes, this is a tough situation for you to be in. And the frustration is running high.

Mitchell: It sure is.

Mark: Now a while ago you said you hate being married to her, and you hate her too. What would be a more realistic way to describe what you are feeling?

Mitchell: Just that I'm tired and frustrated, and I don't know what to do. I hate the situation I'm in.

In this example the therapist helps the client identify his extremist thinking and bring it back within the bounds of reason. Notice once again that the therapist works collaboratively with the client. If the therapist were to pronounce, "Oh, it's not as bad as you're saying; you're exaggerating," then it might have a damaging effect, causing the client to become defensive and insist that he really does hate his wife.

Humorous counters. Sometimes people have thoughts that are really quite silly. Creative therapists can help people learn to chuckle at their irrationalities and not always take themselves so seriously.

Scott: I keep thinking that if I don't fill out this dysfunctional thought record just right, that you'll tell me I'm a bad client who doesn't do homework right, and then you'll be mad or won't want to see me any more.

Clark: Hang on. Let me get a red felt pen and mark all over it. Anything below a 99 percent and you're out of here.

Scott: [chuckles] I hope not.

Clark: Of course not. Just do as well as you can and we won't make any judgments here. And remember, the homework is for your benefit, not mine.

Sometimes a brief, light-hearted comment is an effective way to bring some levity into a session while still helping a client restructure a dysfunctional cognition. This needs to be done with caution, of course, so that it is not perceived as sarcastic or poking fun at the client.

Role-playing counters. Learning cognitive restructuring is a bit like learning to argue with oneself: automatic, irrational thoughts are countered with more thoughtful, accurate thoughts. In role-playing counters, this argument is played out in a dialogue. The therapist voices the client's irrational thoughts and then the client counters with more reasoned statements. Through externalizing an otherwise internal dialogue in role play, clients gain insight into their thinking process. They are then more able to dispute their automatic thoughts.

Daleesha: I'm just so worried about this upcoming job performance evaluation. What if they fire me? I really need this job.

Mark: Yes, I can see it's worrisome for you. Let's try a role play. I'll be you. I'll say what you might be thinking, and then you answer the thought and tell me another way to look at it.

Daleesha: Okay, I'll try.

Mark: Okay, here we go. "Oh, I'm just sure this job performance evaluation is going to go badly. They always do go badly."

Daleesha: "No, they don't. Your last four evaluations have gone very well. You even got a raise last time."

Mark: "Yeah, I suppose that's right. But maybe this time it will be bad. Maybe there's something I've done wrong that I don't even know about. Maybe they'll fire me or demote me or something."

Daleesha: "That's not likely. You show up to work on time, your supervisor likes your work, and the company is doing well. You'll probably do just fine on the performance evaluation."

Mark: "Yeah, but still, you never know."

Daleesha: "It's true you can never know for sure, but the chances are high that this evaluation will go well."

Mark: [stepping out of the role play] Okay, nice work. How convincing does that seem when you say these things to yourself?

Daleesha: Fairly convincing. It helps to argue with myself a bit. I think I just worry too much about these things.

This is a relatively advanced skill that first requires the client to understand how to counter dysfunctional thoughts. It should not be tried until after the client is adept with the dysfunctional thought record.

Paradox. With caution and discernment, a therapist can sometimes help a client think more rationally by overstating the client's dysfunctional thought. The therapist's overstatement triggers a desire for the client to correct the exaggerated thought, which is the therapist's goal in the first place.

Maria: Sometimes I think I'm the world's worst wife.

Clark: Okay, so let me get this right. If we lined up all the wives in the world, from best to worst, you would be at the very end of the line—back there with all the women who despise and abuse and cheat on their husbands.

Maria: Well, it might not be that bad.

Clark: Yeah? Why not?

Maria: Well, I mean I don't do those things. He tells me I'm a good wife, and I suppose I am most days, but sometimes I don't think I give him the attention he wants and deserves.

Clark: It sounds like you just moved up to somewhere in the middle of the line. Not the best; not the worst.

Maria: I guess that's right.

This method should be used sparingly and cautiously, and only after rapport is established. If the client takes the overstatement to be the therapist's actual opinion, it can seem mean-spirited and may even add to the client's dysfunctional thinking.

Cognitive rehearsal. If a client has a repetitive automatic thought, the client and therapist can work together to identify the underlying intermediate belief and then develop calming statements to help modify both the belief and the recurrent automatic thoughts. For example, imagine a client who has pressured

---

COUNSELING TIP 6.5: Office Supplies

Therapists who use cognitive therapy techniques will need a few strategic office supplies in addition to the box of facial tissue that every therapist needs to keep handy. A supply of 3 x 5 note cards is particularly helpful for cognitive rehearsal assignments. Other supplies include a package of straws (explained in Counseling Tip 7.3) and an artist's tablet (see Counseling Tip 9.3).

---

thoughts to get more and more done in less and less time: "I have to hurry. I'm behind schedule. I'm not getting enough done." Once an intermediate belief is identified (for example, "My worth depends on how much I get done in life"), then the therapist might suggest cognitive rehearsal as a way to help restructure this belief.

In cognitive rehearsal, several coping statements are developed collaboratively and then written on index cards. For example, one card might read, "Things will work out fine. Even if I don't get everything done today, there is always tomorrow." Another card might read, "There's always plenty to do, but

I can stay calm. I don't have to hurry." Another reads, "My worth is based on my identity in God and not on how much I accomplish." Working together, the client and therapist come up with rehearsal statements on four or five index cards, and then the client keeps the cards and reviews them throughout the week. Clients can be encouraged to store the cards in places where they might be especially useful. The overworked executive might keep the cards on the middle of her work desk. The stressed courier keeps them in the car where he can review them when stuck in traffic.

A variant of cognitive rehearsal is to write out Scripture verses on index cards. This is especially helpful for Christian clients who find comfort in Scripture and accept its authority. The stressed client we have just been discussing might find truth and comfort in the words of Jesus: "Your heavenly Father already knows all your needs, and he will give you all you need from day to day if you live for him and make the Kingdom of God your primary concern" (Mt 6:32-33). Another index card might have Paul's words to the Christians at Philippi: "Don't worry about anything; instead, pray about everything. Tell God what you need, and thank him for all he has done. If you do this, you will experience God's peace, which is far more wonderful than the human mind can understand. His peace will guard your hearts and minds as you live in Christ Jesus" (Phil 4:6-7). When using Scripture in this way, the therapist should be careful not to plunder Bible verses, taking them out of their intended context simply to provide emotional relief for a client. Scripture is not a self-help book. But still, there is great help to be found in Scripture. Many passages of Scripture, understood in their proper literary and cultural context, provide enormous comfort and useful instruction to those facing various emotional struggles.

In time and with practice, cognitive rehearsal helps establish calming self-talk in clients who are otherwise prone to runaway automatic thoughts. It not only brings immediate relief in a moment of stress, it also helps establish long-term patterns that help a person resist exaggerated negative thoughts in the future.

Collaboration, confrontation and power. Each of the cognitive restructuring methods described here can be used in a variety of ways, ranging from a gentle collaborative style to a harsh—even coercive—style of confrontation. IP works best when therapists lean toward the collaborative end of this continuum. If therapists become too confrontive, especially early in the relationship, it can injure the emerging therapeutic relationship. Consider the following example:

Millie: I've been feeling worried that I'm going to lose my job as a result of a mistake I made last week. The store is supposed to open at 6:00 a.m., but I slept through my alarm and didn't even wake up until 6:30. I was an hour late opening the store, and the district manager was really upset with me.

Collaborative Style Confrontive Style

Mark: That must have been a lousy feeling to wake up and realize it was 6:30 already.

Millie: Yeah, I was pretty upset. I raced around and threw some clothes on and drove like a wild woman to the store.

Mark: I bet your thoughts were running wild on that drive to the store.

Millie: Oh yeah. I was sure they would fire me.

Mark: And you're still thinking they might. What evidence do you have that you might be fired?

Millie: Well, the manager was pretty upset.

Mark: Okay, an upset manager is never a good thing. Do you have other evidence too?

Millie: No, not really.

Mark: Let's look at the other side. Do you have any evidence that they may not fire you?

Millie: Yeah, I mean they haven't done it yet, and it's been four days. And I've never been late before in the six months I've worked there.

Mark: You're doing it again.

Millie: What?

Mark: You're upsetting yourself with no good reason.

Millie: Yeah, maybe. But I was an hour late opening the busiest shop in the area.

Mark: How long have you worked there?

Millie: Six months.

Mark: How many times have you been late before?

Millie: This was the first.

Mark: So you're late once in six months and you end up telling yourself that you'll be fired for it. Does that make any sense to you?

Millie: Well, not much, I suppose. But the district manager was really upset with me.

Mark: So let her be upset. Did she fire you?

Millie: No. At least not yet.

Mark: Is she still upset?

Millie: No, I don't think so. She was pretty nice to me by the next day.

Mark: As you weigh these two: having an upset manager on the one hand and having this be the first infraction on the other hand, which seems more convincing to you?

Millie: Well, I'm hoping the first infraction thing is most compelling to my manager, and I think it probably is. I'm a good employee, and she seems to like my work. She was laughing with me about some things by the next day, so I don't think she's still mad.

Mark: So it was an upsetting event for you and for your district manager, but as you think about it, losing your job doesn't seem likely.

Millie: I guess not.

Mark: So let's think about this logically. If she were going to fire you for being late, would she do it the day you were late—when she was really upset—or would she do it several days later when she is being nice to you?

Millie: Probably she would have done it then, the day I came in late.

Mark: Okay, so you see how you're upsetting yourself for no good reason?

Millie: I suppose you're right.

In this example, the collaborative style leads the client to the same conclusion as the confrontive style, but without risking injury to the therapeutic alliance. There are, of course, times when every therapist needs to be direct and confrontive, but it is best to do this sparingly and only after sufficient trust and rapport have been established. The second and third domains of intervention, described in chapters eight and ten respectively, require a safe therapeutic relationship in order to be effective; the safety of the relationship is often established in the early stages of therapy when symptom-focused care is being provided.

There is an ethical matter to consider here also. Therapists are imbued with a good deal of power, simply based on the nature of the work they do. Distressed individuals, couples and families take time out of their busy schedules to come to an expert with a graduate degree who may charge them a good deal of money to listen to their problems and help them get better. This expert helps them evaluate the validity of their thoughts, sorting between rational and irrational. There is enormous power in this role, whether or not the therapist recognizes it, both because of the respect rendered to the therapist and because of the vulnerable state of clients when seeking help. A collaborative style of evaluating thoughts is a more responsible way of handling this power than a confrontive style. Collaboration is partnership, allowing clients the dignity and autonomy to evaluate their thinking and revise it in ways that are consistent with their own culture, values and beliefs. A dogmatic, confrontive style seems to assume that the therapist always knows best and that clients should simply conform to the wisdom of the therapist. This latter approach may be tempting to some Christian therapists who see religious persuasion to be an explicit goal of their work, but this view can easily lead to an ideological arrogance that injures therapeutic relationships and ultimately shuts off the possibility of genuine dialogue about spiritual and psychological matters.

Even for collaborative therapists, unequal power is still an issue. Every time an automatic thought is identified, and each time it is restructured into a more rational thought, the therapist is nudging the client toward a new way of thinking. This gives a therapist substantial influence, and if the influence is not handled well, the client is shaped more into the therapist's image than God's image. It is like going to a barber or hairdresser and saying, "fix it up however you like it," but with much higher consequences because the therapist is tampering with things more important than tresses.

A therapist has great influence in determining what is to be considered rational thinking. This may work out relatively well in those instances when a therapist is godly, wise, mature and culturally sensitive, but not so well when a therapist falls short of these lofty goals (as most of us do). Just as James instructed that "not many of you should become teachers in the church, for we who teach will be judged by God with greater strictness" (Jas 3:1), it is also true that those of us who become therapists should think carefully about our preparation and spiritual maturity because of the influential role we play in other people's lives.

A Christian Appraisal

Managing the power differential in therapy requires therapists to explore and understand the worldview assumptions they bring into their methods of cognitive restructuring. All therapists, whether Christian or not, are guided by basic values which, in turn, shape the way they perceive and relate to therapy clients. One of the most persistent and pernicious values held by cognitive therapists comes directly out of pragmatic rationalism—it is a value we label *functional relativism,* a concept introduced briefly in chapter three. Here the therapist evaluates thoughts based on how they affect the client's symptoms. So if a depressed person thinks, *Nobody likes me,* and is more depressed as a result, then the thought is deemed irrational and must be replaced with something more positive: *I'm good enough, I'm smart enough, and doggone it, people like me.* If an anxious person thinks, *The world is a dangerous and scary place,* then this thought must be changed to something less anxiety-provoking. Functional relativism suggests that thoughts leading to unwanted symptoms are wrong, and thoughts leading to psychological and emotional relief are correct. The problem, of course, is that this can easily devolve into a therapy where clients are taught to view the world through distorted, self-centered lenses simply because it makes them feel better. So the client who feels conflicted for not forgiving her father is encouraged to dismiss her expectations that she should forgive. She feels better as a result. The client who feels guilty around a friend, thinking he shouldn't have slept with her last month, is encouraged to dismiss his arbitrary "should" statement and let bygones be bygones. He feels relief in letting his guilt go. After all, she was a willing participant. The depressed client who has been a loner most of his life and who just lost his wife to divorce is encouraged to replace his automatic thought, *I am alone in the world,* with something more optimistic: *I am a desirable person and will soon find someone else.* In these examples, one wonders if the therapist might be short-circuiting a client's opportunities for personal awareness, understanding others and growth in godliness.

COUNSELING TIP 6.6: Guide Us into Truth

Christian therapists often get into vigorous debates about whether to pray aloud with clients. There are good points to be made on both sides, but perhaps a more important discipline is to learn to pray silently for our clients during therapy sessions. A Christian therapist has a conversation with a client, and a simultaneous conversation with God. One of the most useful silent prayers is simply, "Dear Lord, guide us into truth." With this prayer the therapist is asking for truth to be valued above functional relativism. It helps keep the therapist on track, which in turn helps the client.

In our sinful condition, most of us are already quite skilled at rationalizing and justifying what we want to believe; we don't need a cognitive therapist to conspire with us to make things seem better than they really are.

In describing functional relativism, we want to be fair to our colleagues who do not share our Christian worldview. Keep in mind that relativism is commonplace in our world and may even be considered virtuous among those who do not hold to particular truth claims associated with religious ways of knowing. From a relativist perspective, why wouldn't a therapist want his or her clients to perceive the world in ways that yield optimum freedom and self-acceptance? And Christianity, with its truth claims and moral duties, would then seem oppressive and inhibiting. So we need not be critical of colleagues who do not share a Christian worldview—they are simply practicing cognitive therapy from their worldview assumptions, as we practice cognitive therapy from Christian worldview assumptions. Functional relativism is not a vile plot, and often it is not even a deliberate decision on the part of the therapist. It is the natural consequence of a society that places enormous value on personal happiness and a largely secular profession that rewards therapists for helping their clients feel better as quickly as possible. Inside the consulting office there is a persistent and subtle tug toward functional relativism.

So how does a Christian therapist fight against the subtle pull of functional relativism and maintain a Christian worldview? We suggest three strategies. The first is simply to be aware that therapy is a value-laden enterprise where worldviews are being promoted (Tjeltveit, 1999). Every time a therapist helps a client think more rationally, underlying ethical assumptions are being advocated. It behooves us to know what a Christian worldview looks like to keep us from inadvertently conforming to the prevailing assumptions—such as functional relativism—that surround us.

This leads to a second suggestion: become informed in Christian theology and history in addition to psychology and counseling methods. Almost every therapist is immersed in prominent psychological worldviews through years of study, continuing education, conversations with colleagues and so on. Those committed to a Christian worldview need to complement this exposure to psychology with ample exposure to historical Christian ways of knowing. This involves reading or taking classes in Christian theology, remaining involved in a local church, befriending pastors and theologians, and subscribing to theology journals.

Third, we echo the apostle Paul's parting instructions in his first letter to the church in Thessalonica: "Do not scoff at prophecies, but *test everything* that is said. Hold on to what is good. Keep away from every kind of evil" (1 Thess 5:20-22, emphasis added). Whether inside the church—as Paul intended with these instructions—or outside the church in the domain of the therapy office, the Christian life involves a good deal of filtering. God wants us to evaluate what we hear, think and say in light of Christian views of good and evil.

This notion of testing everything is familiar to cognitive therapists. We are continually testing thoughts and assumptions to see how they fit with reality. But how do we do this in a way that stays true to a Christian worldview, and without slipping into the prevailing paradigms of a field prone to functional relativism?

The Wesleyan quadrilateral—derived from the teachings of John Wesley, the eighteenth-century English evangelist—suggests that Christian views and values be determined by four interweaving sources of information: Scripture, tradition, experience and reason. These "tests of truth" are elaborated below.

Scripture. When determining the validity of one's thoughts, values and assumptions, there is no greater resource for a Christian than Scripture. The Bible—God's authoritative Word—reveals the story of humanity in relation to a just and loving God, and in the process gives instruction for how to live and what to value. In Scripture we learn that humans have dignity and worth by virtue of being created in God's image, that we are prone to self-deception and drifting away from God's love, that God is just and hates oppression and selfish ambition and all other forms of sin, and that God constantly and lovingly calls us back from our rebellion. In Scripture we also have direction as to how Christians should think and behave. We are instructed to be humble, to stand against oppression, to offer mercy instead of revenge and yet to love justice, to be hospitable and generous, to use the gifts God has given us, to care for those who are less privileged than we ourselves are, to be faithful and steadfast. In summary, we learn from Scripture to love God with all our being and to love others as we love our selves (Mk 12:28-31).

Several years ago, one of us had the opportunity to have Dallas Willard—a philosopher and Christian author—speak in a class to clinical psychology students. Near the end of the class, a student asked Dr. Willard what inspires and encourages him in life. Dallas began speaking of his love for the Bible—how he loves to read it, to meditate on its truths, to memorize it, to fill his life with the words of Scripture. Those sitting close enough to the front of the classroom could see the tears welling in his eyes as he spoke of how much he loves God's Word. Dr. Willard is a man of faith and wisdom—a prophet of our time—and his words and feelings about Scripture speak deeply into today's need for truth that transcends the notions of culture and time.

With his words and by the tears that welled in his eyes, Dallas Willard affirmed—along with John Wesley—that the best standard of truth for a Christian is found in the pages of Scripture. The Bible is our greatest resource for determining the validity of our thoughts, beliefs, values and assumptions. But sadly, Christian therapists are notoriously ineffective at interpreting Scripture (Maier & Monroe, 2001; Schultz, 2001). We therapists have often plundered Scripture for our own purposes, beginning with various psychological ideas of dubious origin, finding Bible verses that fit, yanking them out of context and trying to convince the world that the Bible supports our latest psychology. Sometimes we have misinterpreted verses of the Bible by not taking the story of Scripture se-

IN THE OFFICE 6.2: Guided Scriptural Discovery

When Scripture holds an important truth that pertains to a client's situation, the therapist has two options. First, the therapist can simply pronounce the truth of Scripture. For example:

Ruth: I feel guilty about the divorce. I know it was a crazy marriage. He must have slept with twenty other women during our eight years together, but sometimes I wonder if maybe I did something terrible by leaving him.

Clark: Ruth, Scripture is clear on this. In Matthew Jesus allows for divorce in cases of adultery.

A second option—and a better one in our opinion—is to help the client discover the truth of Scripture based on the interpretive methods of her own faith tradition. This involves using the same collaborative approach described throughout this chapter.

Clark: Ruth, what sort of thoughts do you have on Christian teachings about divorce?

Ruth: I think God hates divorce. But I know my pastor has also mentioned that it is allowed under some circumstances.

Clark: How about in your circumstances?

Ruth: I've spent quite a lot of time reading and talking with my pastor about this. Adultery is one of those times when divorce is acceptable. I know that with my head, but in my heart I still wonder if I did the wrong thing.

Clark: Your head and heart are at war over this.

Ruth: At least some days. I think most days I am at peace.

Notice the collaborative nature of this conversation. Rather than pronouncing scriptural truth, it is most beneficial to help the client discover scriptural teachings through collaborative conversation. In this example, Ruth is quite familiar with a scriptural perspective on divorce. If she were not, it might be a good time to suggest she meet with her pastor or another church leader to discuss Christian views on divorce. Sometimes a therapist and client can look at Scripture together in the therapy session, but this approach carries the risk that the therapist interprets Scripture differently than the client's church community. A community of faith provides some accountability for how Scripture is interpreted. Without the accountability of a faith community, clients and therapists might drift toward functional relativism even in how they read the Bible.

riously. The Bible is not so much a text book for accurate thinking as a narrative about how beautifully we are made, how poorly we perceive ourselves and the world around us, how desperately we need God's redemptive presence in our lives and our world, and what great hope and joy we have in Christ.

Consider the problem we have just described. Christian cognitive therapists are in a powerful position of helping others evaluate the validity of their thoughts. Without external moorings, all therapists—including Christians—are prone to drift toward a functional relativism where invalid thoughts are unwisely affirmed because they help a person feel better. Scripture is our greatest resource in determining what is true and right, but even our views of Scripture can be distorted by our self-serving methods of interpretation. So we need additional moorings, beyond Scripture, in order to keep us firmly committed to a Christian appraisal of truth and falsehood. The Wesleyan quadrilateral suggests we turn to tradition, experience and reason.

Tradition. In a time prone to postmodern meanderings, Christian history (tradition) provides an important anchor to hold us steady in our views of truth. Millions of thoughtful, informed and wise people have gone before us, helping us understand the tenets of the Christian faith. Church councils have been assembled to hammer out difficult doctrines, to identify heresies and to affirm orthodoxy. Classic spiritual books—some standing the test of many centuries— can help us find our way. It is the height of arrogance to disregard the people of faith who have come before us and to assume that each generation, or each therapist, must repeat the work of figuring out what is true. This is not to say that Christian understandings of truth can never change. Indeed, history reveals both evolution (slow, gradual change) and revolution (sudden, dramatic change) in our understanding of Christianity. But a thoughtful view of truth calls us back to consider what has been affirmed through the centuries, and to remember how vulnerable we all are to self-deception and misunderstanding. It is a dangerous and vulnerable position for a Christian therapist to stand against an orthodox view of faith, even if the therapist can support the view with verses from Scripture.

Conversely, it is important for a Christian therapist to stand with orthodoxy when clients use Bible verses to support irrational views. An example that is familiar to most experienced Christian therapists is when a client with obsessive-compulsive disorder begins to fret about committing the unpardonable sin. The client may fear having a blasphemous thought and then employ Mark 3:28-29 to justify obsessing about committing an unforgivable sin. In reality, both Scripture and Christian orthodoxy contradict the client's fears, and it is important for the therapist to help the client move beyond a superficial use of Scripture.

Experience. Scripture and tradition alone could be approached in ways that are largely conceptual and ideological, and could result in Christian ministers who are doctrinally correct but relationally inept. One can applaud the importance of orthodox faith and still be quite insensitive and incapable as a Christian therapist. Experience provides a personal encounter with God that serves as a corrective to a rigid, intellectualized approach to faith.

Some people may question whether experience should be set alongside Scripture and church tradition as a basis for discernment. Two explanations are in order. First, neither we nor Wesley would suggest that experience is equally authoritative to Scripture. When experience and Scripture contradict, Scripture trumps experience. Second, we are not referring to experience as whimsy. It's not merely that a person concludes, "I feel strongly that I need to leave my church, so that's what God wants me to do." All sorts of human feelings may be contrary to God's desires for our lives, and so feelings should not be trusted overly much. Rather, we refer to experience as the cautious and wise exploration of God's movement in our lives. It is common for Christians facing difficult decisions to conclude, "I need to pray about that." Indeed, we need prayer for all sorts of reasons, and one of them is to help us discern truth and God's desires for our lives. Centering prayer often prompts a person toward specific decisions or actions, and we affirm this as the good experiential, relational work of God in human lives.

Christians have experienced the riches of God's grace. We have seen the depth of our own sin and our need for God's mercy, and in response God has washed us in forgiveness and grace. This sort of experience changes us—or it ought to. It calls us to be people of compassionate understanding, who can sit with others in their pain as caring companions. It propels cognitive therapy out of the realm of policing logic and into a place of gentle partnership. Experiencing God's grace calls us to Christian community, to accountability, to worship, to joy. For many, it calls them into helping professions where they offer grace and truth to others because God, through Christ, has offered us grace and truth and then called us to accept one another in the same manner (Rom 15:7).

Though science was not part of Wesley's formulation of experience, it is worth noting that science is based on a systematic way of understanding experiences. Scientists refer to their work as empirical, meaning it is based on observation and experience. Cognitive therapy, rooted in science, was developed out of this empirical perspective—helping clients understand their thoughts and test them out in relation to their daily experiences. This is the notion of collaborative empiricism that we discussed previously.

Reason. Finally, reason is our capacity to bring together information from

Scripture, tradition and experience and to make sense of it all. Reason draws us to study, to investigate and explore, to form judgments and opinions. Cognitive therapy involves exploring people's reasoning and helping them reason better.

But reason needs to be grounded. On its own, our capacity to reason can lead us to all sorts of self-deception, rationalization and justification of folly. For the Christian, reason should be grounded in the other three sides of the quadrilateral: Scripture (first of all), tradition and experience.

An example of the Wesleyan quadrilateral in cognitive restructuring. To illustrate the Wesleyan quadrilateral and how it can keep a therapist from drifting toward functional relativism, consider the following dialogue with a hypothetical client, Denise, who was first introduced in chapter three and will be discussed again in later chapters.

Denise: I feel so frustrated in my marriage. It's been a struggle every day for over a year now. I'm not sure I love him. Sometimes I wonder if I ever did. I don't think he's happy either. Sometimes I think we should just admit we made a mistake, and call it quits.

Mark: The ongoing struggle in your marriage is both upsetting and exhausting.

Denise: But I don't think divorce is right either, so that's not really an option. I just don't how I can keep putting up with this. What choices do I really have?

Mark: It must feel rather hopeless to be in this stuck position.

Here the therapist has done a nice job reflecting back the client's feelings and ambivalence about her marriage in an empathic fashion. As the conversation continues, it is inevitable that the therapist's personal values and beliefs about marriage and divorce will influence the client's way of thinking. Consider two possible directions this dialogue can go: the first reflects a functional relativist approach and the second a Christian alternative.

A functional relativistic approach. For the therapist steeped in prevailing mental health ideologies, the decision might be to help Denise explore her thoughts and feelings with the goal of evaluating if she should stay in the marriage. The therapist might view Denise's prohibition of divorce as too rigid and constrictive because these beliefs are contributing to her feeling trapped and unhappy, and so might respond:

Therapist: I've heard you talking like this for several weeks now. Maybe it would be worth us spending some time thinking about your marriage and helping you come to some decisions about the future. Tell me more about what you just said, that divorce isn't an option.

Denise: Well, it's because of my faith. I believe that marriage is a promise, a lifelong commitment, and that divorce isn't an option. But I've been so unhappy lately, and I've been starting to ask myself some questions about all this.

Therapist: The fact that you are unhappy now, and have been unhappy from the beginning of your marriage, is a pretty good indicator that your marriage is not creating fulfillment for you. Perhaps you are staying in your marriage for reasons related to your faith, but is it really in your best interest to stay in such an unhappy place?

Denise: Well, I don't know. I really haven't focused much on my best interest.

From here the therapist and client would work together to evaluate Denise's beliefs about divorce and begin to think about her options for the future.

A Christian alternative. For the Christian therapist committed to avoiding functional relativism, the task is more difficult because there is more than the client's happiness to consider. In this case the therapist might find the Wesleyan quadrilateral quite useful. In Scripture we find that marriage is a covenant relationship, ordained by God. The promise of a lifetime commitment is more than just a contract, it is a sacred oath. Marriage is designed for happiness, and it is tragic when happiness fades, but it is also designed for much more: for character formation, procreation, sexual pleasure and fidelity, and human companionship (L. G. McMinn, 2004). Beyond all this, marriage is a living illustration of God's longstanding commitment to a people who tend to drift away in selfishness. Divorce may be acceptable in some situations, such as adultery, but God hates seeing homes ripped apart. Tradition teaches us that contemporary views of marriage are quite different than historical views. Today we tend to view happiness and lifelong passion as cardinal virtues of marriage, but these views may be shaped more by Hollywood than history. Current expectations for marriage to be a place of continual excitement are higher than ever, and so disappointment often settles in like a dreary fog. Experience reminds the Christian therapist that empathy is the proper response. Marriage is often difficult, and many couples—perhaps most couples—go through seasons of disillusionment and despair. However the therapist responds, it needs to be with a voice of compassion and concern for a client in great distress. Reason helps the therapist evaluate all these factors, balance truth and grace, and respond in a wise and thoughtful way.

Mark: So here you are, convinced divorce is not right and yet feeling so terribly stuck and frustrated in your marriage. The strength of you. values is being pushed to the limit.

Denise: Yeah, that's the way I feel. I mean I believe that marriage is a promise, a lifelong commitment. It's part of my faith, but lately it's just been so tough.

Mark: Yes, I see what you mean. You have these values about marriage. They're part of you and part of your faith community. But right now those values are really costing you some personal happiness.

Denise: Yes, they are. I never knew marriage would be this tough.

Mark: What are you learning about yourself and your ability to manage tough things?

From here the dialogue would likely move toward a redemptive view of Denise's current situation, affirming her beliefs about marriage rather than challenging them. Denise has been focused on how unhappy she is, and this is an important topic to discuss, but there are other important things to consider as well: values, faith and character formation.

Some who do not share our Christian worldview might be concerned with the example we have just discussed because it appears that the therapist is exerting personal values onto the therapy process, nudging the client toward a decision to stay in a difficult marriage. We would agree, but would also argue that every therapist nudges a client toward particular values. The previous example of a therapist steeped in functional relativism demonstrates a therapist nudging a client toward particular values that clash with a Christian worldview. All therapy is value-laden, and this should be acknowledged in advance when the client first gives consent to participate in therapy.

COUNSELING TIP 6.7: Sketching the Quadrilateral

The point of using the Wesleyan quadrilateral is not that the therapist should ponder Scripture, tradition, experience and reason and then pronounce whether or not the client's thinking is proper. Rather, the quadrilateral is used collaboratively—the client and therapist work together to think through each dimension. Sometimes it is even useful to sketch out the quadrilateral on an artist pad and then systematically discuss each quadrant. This provides immediate benefit in helping the client evaluate the belief in question while also modeling a balanced, thoughtful style of decision making for the client.

The Wesleyan quadrilateral helps us understand a Christian perspective on difficult situations in which there is no clear-cut solution. These questions help inform our thinking:

1. What does Scripture say about this situation? (This accounts for a biblical perspective.)

2. How has Christian tradition handled this situation? (This accounts for the community of believers.)

3. What has been my experience with God's leading in this and similar situations? (This accounts for God's leading of the individual.)

4. What is reasonable and logical for all involved? (This accounts for known consequences for self and others.)

Summary

Both behavior change and cognitive restructuring methods are used in symptom-focused therapy. Behavior change skills are based in classical, operant and observational learning, but also in a larger psychological and theological understanding of human functioning. In cognitive restructuring, automatic thoughts are evaluated and replaced with thoughts that are better reasoned. Many techniques are available to help clients restructure their thoughts. From a Christian perspective, this has both positive and negative implications. On the positive side, helping people think more rationally allows us to respond to the redemptive presence of God in a broken world. We function best when we think well and understand our world accurately. Clear, rational thinking helps move us forward to greater self-understanding, awareness of others, and recognition of our need for God. On the negative side, helping others shape their thoughts puts a therapist in a position of great power that is easily misused. Even a well-intentioned Christian therapist who works collaboratively with clients is vulnerable to drift toward functional relativism—where thoughts are deemed true if they make the client feel better and untrue if they make the client feel worse. To prevent this drift, Christian therapists need to remain rooted in Scripture, tradition, experience and reason.

References

Beck, J. S. (1995). *Cognitive therapy: Basics and beyond*. New York: Guilford.

Freeman, A., Pretzer, J., Fleming, B., & Simon, K. M. (1990). *Clinical applications of cognitive therapy*. New York: Plenum.

Maier, B. N., & Monroe, P. G. (2001). Biblical hermeneutics & Christian psychology. In M. R. McMinn & T. R. Phillips (Eds.), *Care for the soul: Exploring the intersection of psychology & theology* (pp. 276-93). Downers Grove, IL: Inter-Varsity Press.

McMinn, L. G. (2004). *Sexuality and holy longing: Embracing intimacy in a broken world.* San Francisco: Jossey-Bass.

McMinn, M. R., & Dominguez, A. D. (Eds.) (2005). *Psychology and the church.* Hauppauge, NY: Nova Science Publishers.

Schultz, R. (2001). Responsible hermeneutics for wisdom literature. In M. R. McMinn & T. R. Phillips (Eds.), *Care for the soul: Exploring the intersection of psychology & theology* (pp. 254-75). Downers Grove, IL: InterVarsity Press.

Tjeltveit, A. C. (1999). *Ethics and values in psychotherapy.* New York: Routledge.

Applying Symptom-Focused
Interventions in Treating Anxiety

ANXIETY LINGERS IN THE SHADOWS OF HOPE AND FAITH AND LOVE, robbing us of the joy of being fully human. Complete humans, last spotted near a fruit grove in Eden, lived naked and free in the presence of the Almighty. Sometimes we excuse our frailty by saying, "I'm only human," as if humanity is some substandard state of life. Oh, to be fully human again, instead of disabled humans hampered by shame and the anxiety that gives it voice. When the apostle Paul instructed Philippian believers to pray instead of worrying (Phil 4:6), he was inviting them to ease a step closer to Eden, to be more fully human, to move toward freedom in Christ Jesus.

It is not surprising, then, that humans have battled anxiety through the centuries. We have teas, pills, bath oils, scented candles, and various sorts of spiritual exercises and psychotherapies to quiet clamoring souls. All these reflect God's common grace—if any grace can be considered common—reaching out to calm troubled humanity. Being part of this common grace, providing therapy to those suffering from anxiety, is a great good.

Though anxiety is a universal human experience, for some it becomes extreme enough to cause serious problems in daily functioning. Social relationships become strained, work performance is hindered, or the uncertainties of living become overwhelming and terrifying. The National Institute of Mental Health considers anxiety disorders to be the most common mental health problem in the United States, affecting approximately 19 million adults each year (National Institute of Mental Health, 2001).

Having explored the nature of behavior change and cognitive restructuring and appraised them from a Christian perspective, we now turn to applying cognitive and behavioral principles to treating anxiety disorders. Though we are discussing anxiety disorders in this chapter on symptom-focused care, it is important to recognize that some anxiety disorders will also require schema-focused and relationship-focused interventions. Nonetheless, we make this choice because anxiety disorders can sometimes be fully treated with symptom-focused interventions. One leading cognitive therapist who specializes in anxiety disorders has even suggested that we should change our terminology to be more consistent with the medical-care model, calling our interventions "psychological treatments" rather than psychotherapy (Barlow, 2004). The term "psychological treatment" clearly connotes a procedure that involves therapeutic technique more than relationship.

Figure 7.1 illustrates our understanding of the three domains of intervention and the various disorders discussed in this book. Some anxiety disorders are treated well with symptom-focused interventions, where therapeutic technique is emphasized above therapeutic relationship (though both still matter). Helping clinically depressed individuals typically requires schema-focused interventions where ample attention is given to both technique and relationship. Those with persistent personality problems and those who are looking for personal insight and self-awareness will often require relationship-focused interventions, where the therapeutic relationship plays a more important role than the techniques being used. Despite the clear categories delineated in figure 7.1, we must emphasize that real-world clinical practice is rarely as tidy as the taxonomy we are offering. For example, sometimes clients with anxiety disorders reveal deep interpersonal wounds in the early stages of therapy, making schema-focused or

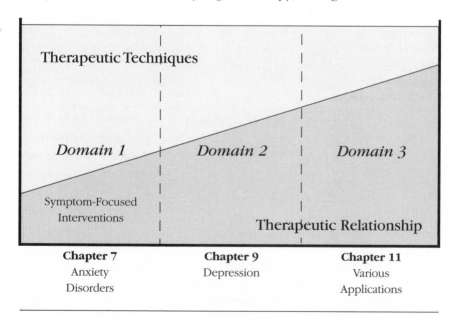

Figure 7.1. Domains of intervention in relation to therapeutic techniques and relationship

relationship-focused interventions necessary. Sometimes depressed clients respond quickly to symptom-focused interventions and therapy is completed within eight to twelve sessions. And, of course, there are many other disorders not covered in this book, such as thought disorders, sexual disorders and dysfunctions, adjustment disorders, impulse control disorders, various developmental disorders, and so on. Our intent is to present a model of integrative psychotherapy and to illustrate the model by considering a few common psychological disorders rather than to provide a comprehensive overview of psychopathologies (see Yarhouse, Butman & McRay, 2005, for an excellent look at psychopathology from a Christian perspective). Many other disclaimers could be offered, but we hope the point of figure 7.1 will not be lost in its oversimplifications. The essential point we are making is that different presenting problems call for different depths of intervention—some can be handled with a primary focus on symptom-focused interventions, some also require attention to underlying schemas, and some require an extensive relational focus.

Each of the five anxiety disorder treatments described in this chapter are symptom-focused treatments combining cognitive restructuring with behavior change techniques. All five include a variant of exposure treatment, which is a technique that involves deliberately exposing a client to the cues that arouse anxiety. The success rates of cognitive-behavioral treatments for anxieties are relatively high, but some clients do not improve. In those situations where a symptom-focused treatment is unsuccessful, then the therapist and client must consider other treatment alternatives. In IP this involves moving toward a schema-focused or relationship-focused intervention.

Panic Disorder

Imagine sitting in a restaurant having a conversation with friends when suddenly you are overwhelmed with fear and dread. Your heart starts pounding and there is tight feeling across your chest. Soon you begin to shake and perspire profusely. You feel nauseated and light-headed, have difficulty breathing, and your thoughts starting running away from you: *I'm going to pass out. I'm having a heart attack. I'm going to die.* You feel both horrified and awful. It's as if your body's alarm system has been inexplicably triggered, like a malfunctioning smoke detector waking you from a peaceful sleep. These are symptoms of a panic attack, where the body's sympathetic nervous system generates a fight-or-flight response without apparent provocation.

Many people experience one or more panic attacks during the course of their life, and because these attacks are so horrifying they may spend a good deal of effort trying to avoid them in the future. When the attacks are recurrent and the person experiencing the attacks is distressed about health implications or worried about getting another attack, then a panic disorder can be diagnosed.

In some cases, people attempt to prevent panic attacks by avoiding unfamiliar places. If a panic attack occurs in a restaurant, a person might conclude that restaurants are unsafe and should be avoided. If the attack occurs while walking in the rain, the person might then avoid being outdoors in inclement weather. Over time, persons with panic attacks may develop long lists of places and events to avoid and be more and more constrained to remain near home. In ex-

---

COUNSELING TIP 7.1: Fear of Fear

Beginning therapists sometimes think of panic attacks as the primary symptom of panic disorder. Although it is true that people who have panic disorder experience panic attacks, it is more helpful to think of this as fear-based disorder. It is not just the attacks themselves that are the problem—it is the fear of having another attack. Clients describe panic attacks as horrific, awful events. One client described it as "what hell must be like." Not surprisingly, people who are prone to these attacks fear having another one. This fear of having another attack often impairs clients more than the attacks themselves.

---

treme cases, they might even become housebound. This is known as agoraphobia. Panic disorder can occur with or without agoraphobia and will affect between 2 percent and 6 percent of the population at some point in their lives (Craske & Barlow, 2001).

A cognitive-behavior conceptualization of panic disorder centers on a person's "fear of fear" (see Craske & Barlow, 2001, for elaboration). All of us experience fear at times, typically triggered by events external to our bodies such as being startled by a car veering into our lane on the expressway or dealing with mounting financial pressures on a limited income. Those with panic disorder are prone to be fearful of internal cues, even cues that may occur beneath the threshold of conscious awareness. So a slight change in blood pressure or heart rate or breathing patterns may elicit fear in an individual prone to panic disorder (Clark et al., 1997). The experience of fear, in turn, produces more physiological symptoms: breathing and heart rate changes, for example. The result is a sort of vicious cycle, where internal physiological events trigger fearful cognitions, the cognitions further exacerbate the internal physiological events, the cognitions

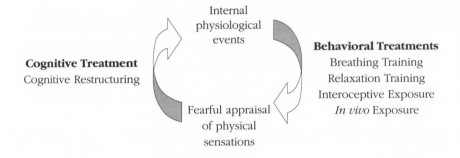

Figure 7.2. A conceptual model for panic disorder

worsen, and so on (as illustrated in figure 7.2). Treatment strategies for panic disorder are aimed at disrupting this vicious cycle.

A Christian view of persons reminds us that every aspect of human nature is tainted in a fallen creation. Human physiology is askew just as surely as our thoughts and behaviors are misaligned. Accordingly, effective interventions are typically multimodal—involving physiology, cognition and behavior.

Many physicians look primarily to medication as a way to alter the physiological symptoms of panic. Some select fast-acting medications, such as the benzodiazepines, while others choose slower acting medications such as imipramine or serotonin specific reuptake inhibitors. Though medications can be useful in treating panic disorder, there is ample evidence that cognitive and behavioral interventions work equally well and perhaps better than medication. Combining medication and cognitive therapy is also an option (Roy-Byrne et al., 2005), but the long-term effects of combined treatment do not appear to be superior to therapy alone. Thus, most psychologists prefer to treat panic disorder with cognitive and behavioral interventions instead of medication (Craske & Barlow, 2001).

Cognitive restructuring, as described in chapter six, is helpful in treating panic disorder. Rather than viewing physiological symptoms as dire and catastrophic, the client is helped to view the symptoms as merely unpleasant and undesirable. Rather than, *I'm going to die,* the client learns to think, *Oh, I'm having some panic symptoms, so I need to sit down, relax and breathe deeply; this will be okay.* Christian clients may also use faith-based self-talk such as, *I can rest safely in the loving arms of God.* Though this may sound straightforward, it usually requires several weeks or months of practice before the client can make these cognitive changes. The ingrained fear response is so automatic that it is not easy to change. To assist in this transition, several behavior therapy techniques are also useful.

Four behavioral techniques for panic disorder provide an important complement to cognitive restructuring. Two of these techniques—breathing training and relaxation training—are designed to help calm the client. Breathing training involves teaching clients to take slow, deep breaths to counteract the tendency to hyperventilate in the presence of physiological changes. Relaxation training entails teaching clients to relax their bodies as thoroughly as possible. This typically involves stretching or tensing one muscle group at a time, and then releasing the tension and allowing the muscle group to become as relaxed as possible. The therapist then progresses through each major mus-

---

COUNSELING TIP 7.2: It's in the Air

Many panic attack symptoms appear to be at least partly related to oxygen and carbon dioxide levels in the bloodstream. When early symptoms cause anticipatory fear, clients may begin breathing rapid, shallow breaths, further worsening the skewed oxygen and carbon dioxide balance in their blood. Slow, deep breaths and calming self-talk can help bring things back to normal.

---

cle group, helping the client concentrate on tensing and relaxing, which is why the technique is sometimes called progressive relaxation. When first learning progressive relaxation, it may take clients twenty to thirty minutes to become relaxed, but with repeated practice most people can learn to relax in just a few minutes. It is not wise to ask a client to do progressive relaxation while in the midst of a panic attack, because this disregards the intensity of terror the client is feeling, but relaxation training can be quite useful as a preventive tool for those prone to panic attacks.

The other two behavioral techniques—interoceptive exposure and *in vivo* (literally, "in life") exposure—deliberately cause arousal in clients, which then provides them opportunity to use their emerging repertoire of cognitive and behavioral skills to calm themselves. These techniques should only be introduced after sufficient rapport is established because, predictably, the idea of deliberately bringing on symptoms of panic is not pleasant. Clients with panic disorder typically find it surprising and distressing when a therapist suggests techniques that elicit the very symptoms they attempt to avoid. With interoceptive exposure, the therapist finds ways in the office to generate slight physiological changes that may resemble panic symptoms and evoke fear in the client. Methods of exposure might include standing on one leg, spinning in a

---

IN THE OFFICE 7.1: Deep Muscle Relaxation

Relaxation methods are used in the treatment of various anxiety disorders. The therapist first has the client sit back (with eyes closed) in a comfortable chair, do some deep diaphragmatic breathing, and then concentrate on tensing and relaxing various muscle groups. The therapist speaks slowly, leaving ample silence between each phrase.

Clark: Now continue to take slow deep breaths . . . You are breathing in relaxation and out the tension . . . in relaxation, out tension . . . Now I would like you to concentrate on your right hand. Form your hand into a fist, hold it, hold it . . . Notice the tension in your right hand . . . now slowly let the tension go. Let your right hand become comfortable and relaxed . . . Notice how warm it feels as your hand becomes completely relaxed . . . You can picture the tension flowing down your right arm and leaving your body through the tips of your fingers . . .

Now once again, form your right hand into a fist. Notice the tension . . . Notice how different it feels than it did just a moment ago . . . Okay, now again, slowly relax your hand . . . Let your hand become completely relaxed, warm and heavy . . . Imagine your finger being so heavy that you could barely lift them even if you wanted to.

After concentrating on the first muscle group, the therapist then continues to move through all the muscle groups in the body. These include

- right forearm (press it down into the armrest on the chair)
- left hand (same as right hand)
- left forearm (same as right forearm)
- shoulders (raise shoulders in a big shrug)
- neck (press head back into headrest of chair)
- forehead (raise eyebrows as if in surprise or bring brows together in a scowl)
- jaw (clinch teeth lightly—note that harsh clinching can cause dental damage!)
- tongue (press up against roof of mouth)
- torso (tense abdominal and chest muscles)
- upper legs (tense thigh muscles)
- lower legs (raise toes up toward knees)
- feet (curl toes downward against soles of shoes to feel tension in arches)

Each muscle group is tensed, then relaxed. Remember to keep the pace slow and easy. The entire process will take twenty to thirty minutes at first, though clients will learn to relax much faster with practice.

It is helpful to audio record the relaxation session (with the client's permission of course) and then send the recording home with the client. This allows the client to practice the relaxation procedure several times between sessions.

chair, stepping up on a stair several times in rapid succession, or hyperventilating with deep, rapid breaths for several minutes. Each of these causes subtle physiological changes that may evoke a fearful appraisal. Then the client is coached through calming self-talk: "I can stay calm. This will be okay. I can breathe slowly and deeply."

In vivo exposure, which is used to treat the agoraphobia that often accompanies panic disorder, requires leaving the therapy office and spending time in a place that is feared. This might mean going to a restaurant where a client once had a panic attack, walking in the rain, riding on the subway together, and so on.

The effectiveness of cognitive-behavioral treatment for panic disorder is quite impressive, either on its own or in combination with medication (Roy-Byrne et

COUNSELING TIP 7.3: Challenge Tests

The procedures used to induce symptoms of panic in the therapy office are known as challenge tests (Smitherman, 2005). Some clinics that specialize in panic disorder treatment use chemical forms of challenge tests—carbon dioxide, caffeine, epinephrine and various other concoctions. These all require specialized training and tailored consent forms. More typically, therapists use nonchemical challenge tests such as hyperventilation, spinning in a swivel chair, mild forms of aerobic exercise and so on. One useful strategy is to have a client breathe rapidly through a straw to simulate the shortness of breath that occurs with panic attacks.

al., 2005). Between half and three-quarters of those who complete psychological treatment for panic are free of panic symptoms at the end of treatment and at a two-year follow up interval (Craske & Barlow, 2001; Westen & Morrison, 2001). Nonetheless, some clients find that other anxiety symptoms remain or experience an occasional panic attack even after therapy is completed, and the treatment is not quite as effective for those who are also diagnosed with agoraphobia.

Phobias

All of us are familiar with fear. For some, standing in an observatory at the top of a skyscraper evokes fear. For others, fear is triggered by speaking in public or driving through a dark tunnel or seeing a mouse. When these fears become persistent and intense and begin to interfere with a person's regular routine, then a phobia is diagnosed. Some may view phobias as a lack of faith, but this is an oversimplified view. Although faith may have some effect on one's experience of fear, so do many other factors, including genetic disposition, past classical, operant and observational learning, medical conditions, and so on. It is important for a Christian therapist to provide a safe, nonjudgmental environment where fears can be expressed and explored.

Other than agoraphobia, which was included in the previous discussion of panic disorder, the most prevalent phobias are considered to be specific phobias and social phobias. Specific phobias are extreme fears focused on a particular object or situation, such as snakes or being confined in a small room or flying, whereas social phobias involve intense fear about how one will perform in a social situation such as speaking or eating in public or meeting a person for the first time.

Social phobia, also known as social anxiety disorder, is of particular concern to mental health professionals both because of its debilitating nature and its prevalence (Turk, Heimberg & Hope, 2001). Perhaps most of us can recall an embarrassing situation where we performed poorly in public and felt humiliated as a result, but these are usually remote memories that do not often bother us. With social phobia, memories and fears of being publicly humiliated are frequent occurrences, with haunting consequences. In order to avoid humiliation associated with feared social situations, people with social phobias often become reclusive, isolated and lonely. A high proportion do not marry, some avoid particular jobs and refuse promotions that might involve supervising others, and most experience a low quality of life. Lifetime prevalence estimates range from 2.4 percent to 13.3 percent (Turk et al., 2001). If the upper ranges of these estimates are correct, then social phobia is the third most prevalent psychiatric disorder, behind depression and alcoholism. Perhaps most alarming is that the prevalence rates seem to be increasing.

Treatment for phobias consists of two elements. The first is cognitive restructuring, with special attention given to thoughts associated with anticipatory anx-

---

COUNSELING TIP 7.4: Trivial Pursuit

Some beginning psychology students assume it is important to memorize all the names for different phobias. Acrophobia is the fear of heights, claustrophobia the fear of closed spaces, and so on. An early edition of the popular board game Trivial Pursuit even had a question about triskaidekaphobia (which, apparently, is the fear of the number 13). Despite the attention given to naming phobias in some introductory textbooks and party games, practicing psychologists rarely concern themselves with such things. No two phobias are exactly alike because no two persons are the same, so it is more important to learn good assessment, case conceptualizing and treatment skills than to memorize a list of esoteric names. We can leave phobia-naming to the folks who publish popular trivia games.

---

iety. Individuals with social phobias tend to anticipate negative outcomes and therefore dread future events. For example, a person might be scheduled to give a presentation at work and spend several weeks prior to the event thinking about all the negative outcomes that might result: *Maybe I'll lose track of my thoughts and I'll freeze up in front of everyone. Maybe my face and neck will get all splotchy and people will think I'm a freak. Maybe the PowerPoint won't work, and I'll just have to rely on my memory. Maybe people will get so bored that they'll leave in the middle of my presentation. Maybe my boss will observe all this and will fire me for being inept.* In all these examples the thoughts are focused forward, anticipating some bad outcome that might result. Cognitive restructuring is used to help control the runaway thoughts and to help clients come to more realistic appraisals about what is likely to happen in the future.

The second treatment approach is guided exposure, where the therapist helps the client confront the feared event or object, either in individual or group therapy. Some early treatments for phobias involved imagining the feared item while in a relaxed state—a procedure known as systematic desensitization—but unfortunately the progress made while sitting in Barcalounger in a therapist's office does not always generalize well to real-world situations. So contemporary approaches also involve *in vivo* exposure, where the client encounters the actual situation that evokes fear (e.g., seeing a spider, eating in a public café). Sometimes this involves gradual exposure to the fearful situation and sometimes it involves sudden all-at-once exposure, known as flooding. Some have also attempted virtual reality exposure for phobias, where a computer simulation is used rather than *in vivo* exposure, but the long-term effectiveness of these treatments is in question (see Maltby, Kirsch, Mayers & Allen, 2002, for an example of virtual reality exposure).

For some specific phobias, exposure alone is often sufficient to treat the problem. In social phobia, both exposure and cognitive restructuring are helpful. Though some have treated social phobia successfully with exposure treatments alone (Turner, Beidel & Jacob, 1994), it appears that combining exposure and cognitive restructuring may lead to better treatment results and produce more stable long-term improvement (Clark et al., 2003; Hofmann, 2004; Mattick & Peters, 1988). Some therapists use group cognitive therapy for social phobias because the therapeutic context itself serves as an exposure to the feared situation, thereby providing both treatment approaches at once: exposure and cognitive restructuring. Turk et al., (2001) conclude that approximately 75 percent of patients show clinically significant change when being treated with group cognitive therapy "or a similar combination of exposure and cognitive restructuring" (p. 120).

Obsessive-Compulsive Disorder

Obsessions are recurrent thoughts that are persistent and anxiety-provoking. For example, a person might fear contamination or have intrusive thoughts of having committed an unpardonable sin. Compulsions are behaviors or mental acts that are done in response to the obsessions. So the person who fears contamination may wash her hands dozens of times each day, and the person who fears committing the unpardonable sin may develop a ritualistic prayer that he says hundreds or thousands of times daily in order to ward off the anxiety caused by his obsession (not to be confused with the well-established practice of repeating the Jesus prayer—"Lord Jesus Christ, Son of God, be merciful to me, a sinner"— for purposes of meditation and spiritual growth).

Though these examples may seem extreme, it is worth noting that none of us are completely free of obsessions and compulsions. For example, have you ever set an alarm clock and then reached over to double-check it before drifting off to sleep? Or have you ever locked your car and then lifted the door handle just to be sure that it is locked? Many people step over sidewalk cracks or count the number of steps between one building and another. The difference between these examples of every-day compulsions and obsessive-compulsive disorder (OCD) is that OCD symptoms have become so distressing or time-consuming that they interfere with daily functioning. Approximately 1 in 40 adults in the United States will experience OCD at some point in life, and it is often concurrent with other mental health problems such as depression and insomnia (Foa & Franklin, 2001).

As with the treatment of social phobia, both exposure and cognitive restructuring have been used to treat OCD. Exposure treatments require the client to encounter the obsessional cue without engaging in the compulsive response. This is known as exposure and ritual prevention (EX/RP) treatment (see Foa & Franklin, 2001, for more detail). Here the therapist first activates the obsession, either through imagery or *in vivo* procedures, and then does not allow the client to escape into the normal ritual behavior. For example, consider the following dialogue in a session where the client fears being contaminated by germs:

Mark: On the way to the office this morning, I found this penny in the parking lot. I would like you to take this penny and just handle it with both hands. [Hands the penny to the client]

Rose: Oh, but it will have germs on it.

Mark: Yes, I'm sure it does. But as we discussed, this is an important part of your treatment. Now just take the penny and rub it in your hands.

Rose: [Takes the penny] Oh, this is so dirty. I'm sure it's going to make me sick. Do I have to do this?

Mark: Yes, you can do it. Just keep moving it and rubbing it in your hands. Remember that many people find and handle pennies every day and don't get sick as a result.

Rose: [Continues rubbing the penny]

Mark: Now I would like you to give me back the penny, then rub your hands on your neck and your face, then on your clothes.

As the session continues, the client experiences significant anxiety and feels compelled to go to the washroom or to flee to the nearest Laundromat where every item of clothing can be shed and washed with extra bleach. Each time, the therapist speaks firmly, clearly and as kindly as possible, reminding the client that escaping into rituals is not an option. Therapy sessions are scheduled each day over several weeks. With time, the client's anxiety begins to subside, which is exactly the point of the treatment. EX/RP helps clients confront their fears and eventually realize they no longer need their rituals in order to manage their anxieties. Of course, informed consent needs to be obtained from the client before engaging in this stressful form of treatment.

EX/RP is not entirely distinct from cognitive restructuring in OCD treatment. The only way for clients to progress through EX/RP is by changing their appraisal of anxiety-provoking situations. Rather than thinking, *I have to wash my hands or I'll get very sick,* a client learns to think, *This penny probably has some germs on it, but people pick up pennies all the time and don't get sick; I suppose*

COUNSELING TIP 7.5: Special Permission

Exposure and ritual prevention (EX/RP) can be exceedingly stressful and challenging because clients are asked to directly encounter their fears, sometimes for a prolonged period of time. Rather than assuming a general psychotherapy consent form is sufficient, it is best to develop a special permission form for EX/RP. Begin preparing the client several weeks in advance. Explain what will happen and give information about the likelihood of success with this particular treatment approach. Be patient in answering the client's questions and addressing concerns. Let the client know that the procedure will only work if he or she continues through to the end, and have the person sign a special consent form that explains the procedure. Ample preparation helps clients persist through the EX/RP procedure, and high success rates make them happy they did.

I'll be fine. In this sense, EX/RP is a combination of exposure treatment and cognitive restructuring (Foa & Kozak, 1986). Some therapists choose to add an explicit cognitive restructuring component to therapy in addition to the EX/RP work. Based on current research, it is not clear whether explicit cognitive restructuring techniques add to the effectiveness of EX/RP. It is relatively clear, however, that cognitive restructuring with EX/RP is more effective than cognitive restructuring without EX/RP (Foa & Franklin, 2001). Thus, EX/RP appears to be the more essential of the two approaches to treating OCD.

Similarly, combining EX/RP with serotonergic medication (i.e., serotonin specific reuptake inhibitors, such as Prozac) provides effective treatment for OCD, but it is not clear that adding the medication helps more than EX/RP alone (Franklin, Abramowitz, Bux, Zoellner & Feeny, 2002). More research is needed to help sort out whether medication adds meaningfully to the effectiveness of EX/RP.

In summary, EX/RP is an effective treatment for OCD. Approximately three-quarters of those undergoing EX/RP are successfully treated and are still doing well two years after treatment (Foa & Franklin, 2001). These effectiveness rates appear to apply to general practice settings as well as the more controlled laboratory environment (Franklin, Abramowitz, Kozak, Levitt & Foa, 2000).

Posttraumatic Stress Disorder

Life in a broken world is punctuated with tragedy, and tragedy damages people. A person diagnosed with posttraumatic stress disorder (PTSD) has encountered an event that involved actual or threatened physical harm and has experienced fear, hopelessness or horror as a result. Examples include rape, childhood abuse, combat and intimate partner abuse. In response to the trauma, the person experiences three sets of reactions. First, the person attempts to avoid memories of the trauma. This could entail staying away from certain people or places, detaching oneself from other people, repressing memories or shutting off emotions. But repressed tragedy typically finds a way back into human consciousness, so the second set of reactions involves reexperiencing the event despite efforts to keep it out of consciousness. Reexperiencing the trauma may occur through distressing dreams, flashbacks, intrusive recollections of the event or excessive reactions to situations that resemble the traumatic event. Third, the person lives in a state of increased arousal, as if a built-in alarm system is sounding to remind the person that some terrible thing has happened. Increased arousal may be marked by difficulty sleeping, irritability, an exaggerated startle response and so on. Like a military unit in a battle-ready state, a person with PTSD lives in a near-constant fight-or-flight state.

As with the treatment of phobias and OCD, most contemporary treatment approaches for PTSD involve both exposure and cognitive restructuring (Resick & Calhoun, 2001). Two forms of exposure therapies show promise. First, prolonged exposure (PE) involves putting clients in situations where they must con-

---

COUNSELING TIP 7.6: Into the Dark Valley

Notice the paradox facing clients with PTSD. On one hand, they have experienced a trauma in life, and their natural tendency is to avoid the unpleasant memories. Not surprisingly, they may prefer not to talk about the trauma in therapy. War veterans may simply proclaim, "I don't talk about that." Survivors of sexual abuse may deny the abuse or change the subject whenever childhood experiences enter into the conversation. On the other hand, the treatment of PTSD requires talking about these traumatic memories. The therapist deliberately leads the client into the dark valley of fear to explore things once deemed too terrible to discuss. A compassionate, safe therapeutic relationship is essential before a client with PTSD will trust a therapist with these most painful memories.

---

front their memories and fears. This is typically done both through imagery, by having the client remember and describe past traumatic events in detail, and *in vivo*, by having the client confront the cues that evoke fear (Foa, Rothbaum,

Riggs & Murdock, 1991). For example, a war veteran would spend several sessions describing traumatic combat events. The therapist audio records the descriptions and then asks the client to listen to the tape each day. For the *in vivo* exposure, the client and therapist might go to a war museum where memorabilia, films and narratives are likely to trigger traumatic memories. Some virtual reality simulations have been developed in recent years and may eventually provide an alternative to *in vivo* exposure (Glanz, Rizzo & Graap, 2003). A second type of exposure is used in cognitive processing therapy (CPT; Resick & Calhoun, 2001). In CPT clients are asked to write a detailed narrative of the traumatic events and then to read the narrative each day. They also read it aloud during two therapy sessions, with the therapist helping clients identify thoughts and feelings associated with the events. Some Christian therapists combine CPT procedures with prayer exercises, encouraging their clients to release the painful events of the past to God.

Both PE and CPT are effective in treating PTSD. In a study of rape victims with chronic PTSD, approximately half of those treated with PE or CPT no longer met criteria for PTSD after participating in nine to twelve treatment sessions. In comparison, 98 percent of the minimal-attention control group still met criteria for PTSD. The effects of PE and CPT held up well over time, with approximately half of each group remaining free of PTSD at three- and nine-month follow-up assessments (Resick, Nishith, Weaver, Astin & Feuer, 2002).

PE can be coupled with cognitive restructuring or not, apparently without compromising effectiveness (Marks, Novell, Noshirvani, Livanou & Thrasher, 1998). In contrast, cognitive restructuring is an integral part of CPT (Resick & Calhoun, 2001). Therapists using CPT employ many of the restructuring techniques that are described in chapter six.

Generalized Anxiety Disorder

Generalized anxiety disorder (GAD) is diagnosed when an individual has excessive, difficult-to-control worry over a prolonged period of time. As a result, the person is often tense, irritable, restless, or tired, or struggles with insomnia and concentration difficulties. It affects between 2 percent and 5 percent of the general population and is more common among women than men (Brown, O'Leary & Barlow, 2001).

Sometimes Christians respond to those who are prone to worry with moral advice and by quoting strategic Scriptures (e.g., Phil 4:6-7). While such advice may come from good intentions, it often has a paradoxical effect. That is, when someone who is prone to fret is told to stop, the person may respond by worrying about worrying. It is more effective to offer a safe relationship where clients can explore what worries them and learn new ways to manage their fears and anxieties.

As with the other anxiety treatments described in this chapter, treatment for GAD includes both exposure and cognitive restructuring. Cognitive restructuring is accomplished by using the dysfunctional thought record and other countering techniques. Exposure treatment for GAD poses a unique challenge because of the varied nature of clients' worries. In treating the other anxiety disorders—panic, phobias, OCD and PTSD—it is relatively easy to identify what cues to target when setting up the exposure treatment. The client diagnosed with panic disorder fears having a panic attack, so symptoms of panic are generated in the session through interoceptive exposure. The person with a phobia has a distinct fear, such as flying or heights or social interactions, so exposure treatment consists of putting the person in a situation where the feared event will occur. In OCD, exposure treatment involves activating a client's obsessions and then preventing the corresponding compulsive response. The person with PTSD is exposed to events and memories that trigger thoughts of an earlier trauma. All of these disorders have a specific focus of anxiety, and the exposure treatment is crafted to fit that particular concern. In contrast, a client with GAD does not focus exclusively on one targeted fear but floats from worry to worry.

So how does a therapist construct an exposure treatment for the client whose worries are, by definition, generalized rather than specific? Craske, Barlow and O'Leary (1992) have suggested an approach they call *worry exposure*, which involves the following procedures:

1. Discuss and write down the top two or three worries that are bothering the client at the present moment. Rank the list from most worrisome to least worrisome.

2. Use imagery to have the client think about the first item on the list. If the client is not already familiar with imagery procedures, the therapist may first need to teach these skills. The initial teaching can be done with pleasant imagery—having the client imagine a serene place, for example. Once the imagery procedure is learned, then the client is instructed to picture the most feared outcome and imagine it coming true. For example, a client concerned about getting cancer might be instructed to imagine sitting in a radiologist's office and being diagnosed with an advanced malignant brain tumor.

3. Keep evoking the negative image, repeating the imagery instructions for approximately thirty minutes. This will be stressful for the client, but the therapist needs to stay on task and keep returning to the disturbing image.

4. After thirty minutes, the client is encouraged to discuss alternatives for how

the situation might turn out. The client worried about chronic headaches, for example, could think of outcomes other than advanced cancer. Perhaps the headaches are due to insomnia or caffeine or dehydration. All these alternatives are written down on a worry exposure worksheet.

5. Once the procedure is completed, then it is repeated for the second worry on the list, following the same steps outlined above.

After clients learn this procedure in session, they are asked to do the same thing at home between sessions. They are instructed to focus on a worry until it no longer evokes much anxiety, and then to move on to the next worry. Various challenges can arise when implementing worry exposure (see Brown et al., 2001, for elaboration), but nonetheless it has become an important component of cognitive-behavioral treatment for GAD.

Brown et al. (2001) also suggest some additional treatment elements to address the multifaceted nature of GAD: relaxation training, worry behavior prevention, problem solving and time management. Relaxation training provides physiological treatment for the effects of generalized anxiety and is conducted as with treating panic disorder, described previously. Worry behavior prevention involves stopping the behaviors that result from worrying. Most people who worry excessively find temporary relief in behaviors associated with the worries, much the same as behaviors follow obsessions in OCD, though without the ritualistic and compulsive nature. The woman who worries that her husband has been in a plane crash may check the Internet over and over or watch *Headline News* each half hour to relieve her fears. The man who fears his college-aged children are making bad decisions may call too often to check up on them. These behaviors provide temporary relief but ultimately end up reinforcing the worry behaviors, as if worrying has prevented something bad from happening. Worry behavior prevention involves helping the client identify these worry behaviors and then stop doing them. Problem-solving interventions help GAD clients find effective ways to manage challenges that cause worry. For example, rather than simply worrying about finances, it might be helpful for a client to see a credit counselor, consolidate bills and develop a monthly budget. Finally, learning time management helps GAD clients, who are overwhelmed with the daily hassles and pressures of life. It is not that GAD clients do more than others, but they are more prone than others to feel anxious about their schedule. With time management, GAD clients learn to create and adhere to agendas, delegate responsibility, and say no to unrealistic demands and expectations.

In addition to these standard approaches to treating GAD, Christian therapists may find meditative prayer exercises useful. In an unpublished doctoral disser-

---

IN THE OFFICE 7.2: Prayer-Based Relaxation

Deep breathing, relaxation and prayer can be combined in a prayer-based relaxation procedure. Begin by having the client do some deep breathing exercises and then lead the person into a time of prayer-based relaxation. The following exercise is based on the time-honored Jesus prayer: "Lord Jesus Christ, son of God, have mercy on me, a sinner."

Mark: As you continue with slow, deep breaths from the diaphragm, now say these words—just to yourself, not out loud—Lord, have mercy . . . Lord, have mercy . . . Each time you breathe in, "Lord" . . . Each time you exhale, "have mercy" . . . Lord, have mercy . . . Lord, have mercy . . . Just let yourself be calm in the presence of God . . . Lord, have mercy.

With practice, this calming prayer-based rhythm can become a regular part of daily life. When the apostle Paul instructed believers in Thessalonica to "pray continually" (1 Thess 5:17), he probably had something like this in mind—that we should find a way to be continually aware of our relationship with God. The Jesus prayer is a way of living, a way of breathing, which continually reminds us that we belong to God and are always in need of God's mercy.

For more about the Jesus prayer, see the classic book by an anonymous author, *The Way of a Pilgrim.* This is a stirring book about a Russian peasant's desire to pray continually. Over time the Jesus prayer became as natural to him as breathing.

For more on using prayer-based relaxation in therapy, Mark demonstrates this in his DVD on Christian counseling, published by the American Psychological Association (McMinn, 2006).

---

tation, Stavros (1998) found that meditating on the Jesus prayer for thirty days reduced anxiety, along with depression, hostility and interpersonal sensitivity. In Philippians 4:6-7, the apostle Paul contrasts worry with prayer, not so much to condemn people who worry but to provide them with an alternative. Worry creates an inner tension; those who learn to turn the inner turmoil over to God in quiet prayer often find some relief from their worry.

The outcome effectiveness of cognitive-behavioral therapy for GAD is mixed. On one hand, cognitive-behavioral treatment for GAD works well in reducing anxiety symptoms. Various researchers have reported success for cognitive and

---

COUNSELING TIP 7.7: How Long Will This Take?

"Doctor, how long will this therapy take?" These are familiar words to most therapists. It is usually wise to answer the question within the first few sessions, once an initial assessment and case conceptualization is formulated. When answering, keep in mind that GAD is not like other anxiety disorders. Some disorders can be readily treated with domain 1 (symptom-focused) interventions and the client will be finished with treatment after a dozen sessions or less. Sometimes clients with GAD improve this fast too, but most often they do not. Troubling interpersonal patterns or other psychological disorders may become evident in the process of treating GAD, and so the longer domain 2 and 3 interventions are pursued.

---

behavioral therapies in treating GAD, whether in individual, group or self-help formats (Borkovec & Costello, 1993; Bowman, Scogin, Floyd, Patton & Gist, 1997; Brown et al., 2001; Dugas et al., 2003; Ladouceur et al., 2000). In a recent study, only 10 percent of clients still met criteria for GAD after fourteen weeks of cognitive therapy, and only 15 percent met GAD criteria at a two-year follow-up assessment. Similar results were reported for a behavioral treatment involving applied relaxation and imagery exposure (Borkovec, Newman, Pincus & Lytle, 2002). It appears that either applied relaxation or cognitive therapy can be effective, and combining the two does not necessarily result in better outcomes than either treatment alone (Borkovec et al., 2002). On the other hand, the positive outcomes for GAD should be viewed cautiously because of the diffuse nature of GAD. Whereas many of the other anxiety disorders are highly focused in their symptom patterns, so that successfully treating the symptoms is tantamount to a medical cure, the manifestations of GAD are more complex. About two-thirds of clients who present with GAD symptoms also meet criteria for another psychological disorder, and 90 percent of those with GAD will have another psychological disorder at some point in their lives—most often another anxiety disorder or a mood disorder (Brown et al., 2001). Also, there is growing evidence that personality style and interpersonal problems may contribute to GAD symptoms. Borkovec et al. (2002) conclude:

> Interpersonal behavior may be a significant element in the interacting response systems involved in GAD. Specifically, worry and anxiety may develop and/or be maintained because of problems in one's relationships with others and/or with failures in having one's interpersonally mediated needs met. Being domineering and

vindictive . . . or intrusive in one's relationships may be particularly associated with maladaptive emotional life. . . . There thus may be potential therapeutic value in adding some form of interpersonal therapy to the [cognitive-behavioral therapy] package. (p. 296)

In their meta-analysis of manualized psychotherapies, Westen and Morrison (2001) found good short-term and long-term effects for treating panic disorder, which is a relatively unidimensional malady, and good short-term but poor long-term results for treating depression and GAD, both more complex disorders than panic disorder. We take these findings as support for a multilevel approach to psychotherapy such as the one we advocate in this book. Some disorders, such as panic disorder, can be treated effectively with symptom-focused interventions, but the more complex disorders often require more nuanced interventions that look at connections between mood and anxiety symptoms, interpersonal relationships, childhood development issues, and spiritual concerns. In IP this is accomplished through schema-focused and relationship-focused interventions.

Christian Spirituality and Fear

In concluding this discussion of anxiety disorders, two seemingly paradoxical observations deserve to be mentioned. First, fear is one of our great spiritual problems. Fear is like a cancer that invades our faith and robs us of joy. Christian author Ben Patterson describes various "joy busters" in his book *He Has Made Me Glad* (Patterson, 2005), and each of them pertain to fear. In our fear, we focus on past wounds and doubts about the future. Fear keeps us focused on the complications of present circumstances, preventing us from seeing the grand and glorious work of God in the scheme of history. We fear losing control, so we put severe limits on the ecstasy we experience in God's love. In all these ways and more, fear is a great enemy of the spiritual life. Henri J. M. Nouwen (1986)— a well-known author and Catholic priest with graduate training in psychology— writes:

> We are fearful people. The more people I come to know and the more I come to know people, the more I am overwhelmed by the negative power of fear. It often seems that fear has invaded every part of our being to such a degree that we no longer know what a life without fear would feel like. (p. 15)

If the spiritual life involves finding a place of peace and security in God's love, then fear stands in sharp distinction, keeping us isolated and self-focused and alienated from the security we long for. In Scripture we see anxiety and prayer contrasted (Phil 4:6)—one pointing us toward our various problems and the other pointing us toward God, who grants incredible peace. We also see fear and love contrasted: "God is love" (1 Jn 4:8) and "perfect love expels all fear" (1 Jn 4:18).

If we still lived in Eden, none of us would have anxiety disorders because we would be surrounded with perfect love and our bodies would be perfectly aligned in a flawless creation. But we do not live in Eden.

So our first observation is that fear is a great spiritual problem, but a related observation—which may seem paradoxical at first glance—is that we should not attribute anxiety problems to spiritual weakness. When a therapist looks at an anxious client with the assumption, "You are anxious because you are not spiritually mature," this creates various interpersonal and theological problems. Interpersonally it detracts from a healthy relationship and inevitably adds to the client's anxiety. Theologically it assumes a direct and immediate correspondence between sin and psychological problems, as if only anxious people live outside of Eden and they choose their own fate by getting involved in sinful thoughts and actions. But Christian theology does not allow such simple associations between sin and struggle. All of us live outside of Eden. Every corner of creation is inflicted with the problem of sin. Our environment and our genes are tainted, our will is compromised, and our relationships are often wounded. Life in a sinful world has different consequences for different people—some get heart disease early in life, some are abused, some are born with Down's Syndrome, some limp along with personality traits that drive others away, some go to bed hungry, some become irritable insomniacs, some work for difficult bosses, some are difficult bosses, some feel excessive anxiety or get panic attacks, some are depressed. To be sure, these maladies may be affected by sinful personal choices or the evil actions of others, but it is damaging and unrealistic to assume direct and immediate connections between a particular problem and spiritual maturity. Many people with great spiritual maturity struggle with all sorts of problems, including psychological disorders.

Our best response is to recognize our own brokenness so that we can, in humility, become people of compassion and understanding, willing to walk alongside others through the difficult passages of life. In the process, we may be privileged to help free others from the anxiety that hinders them and robs them of joy.

References

Barlow, D. H. (2004). Psychological treatments. *American Psychologist, 59,* 869-78.

Borkovec, T. D., & Costello, E. (1993). Efficacy of applied relaxation and cognitive-behavioral therapy in the treatment of generalized anxiety disorder. *Journal of Consulting and Clinical Psychology, 61,* 611-19.

Borkovec, T. D., Newman, M. G., Pincus, A. L., & Lytle, R. (2002). A component analysis of cognitive-behavioral therapy for generalized anxiety disorder and the role of interpersonal problems. *Journal of Consulting and Clinical Psychology, 70,* 288-98.

Bowman, D., Scogin, F., Floyd, M., Patton, E., & Gist, L. (1997). Efficacy of self-examination therapy in the treatment of generalized anxiety disorder. *Journal of Counseling Psychology, 44,* 267-73.

Brown, T. A., O'Leary, T. A., & Barlow, D. H. (2001). Generalized anxiety disorder. In D. H. Barlow (Ed.), *Clinical handbook of psychological disorders* (3rd ed.) (pp. 154-208). New York: Guilford.

Clark, D. M., Ehlers, A., McManus, F., Hackmann, A., Fennell, M., Campbell, H., Flower, T., Davenport, C., & Louis, B. (2003). Cognitive therapy versus fluoxetine in generalized social phobia: A randomized placebo-controlled trial. *Journal of Consulting and Clinical Psychology, 71,* 1058-67.

Clark, D. M., Salkovskis, P. M., Öst, L-G, Breitholtz, E., Koehler, K. A., Westling, B. E., Jeavons, A., & Gelder, M. (1997). Misinterpretation of body sensations in panic disorder. *Journal of Consulting and Clinical Psychology, 65,* 203-13.

Craske, M. G., & Barlow, D. H. (2001). Panic disorder and agoraphobia. In D. H. Barlow (Ed.), *Clinical handbook of psychological disorders* (3rd ed.) (pp. 1-59). New York: Guilford.

Craske, M. G., Barlow, D. H., & O'Leary, T. A. (1992). *Mastery of your anxiety and worry.* San Antonio: Psychological Corporation.

Dugas, M. J., Ladouceur, R., Léger, E., Freeston, E., Langlois, F., Provencher, M. D., & Boisvert, J-M. (2003). Group cognitive-behavioral therapy for generalized anxiety disorder: Treatment outcome and long-term follow-up. *Journal of Consulting and Clinical Psychology, 71,* 821-25.

Foa, E. B., & Franklin, M. (2001). Obsessive-compulsive disorder. In D. H. Barlow (Ed.), *Clinical handbook of psychological disorders* (3rd ed.) (pp. 209-63). New York: Guilford.

Foa, E. B., & Kozak, M. J. (1986). Emotional processing of fear: Exposure to corrective information. *Psychological Bulletin, 99,* 20-35.

Foa, E. B., Rothbaum, B. O., Riggs, D. S., & Murdock, T. B. (1991). Treatment of posttraumatic stress disorder in rape victims: A comparison between cognitive-behavioral procedures and counseling. *Journal of Consulting and Clinical Psychology, 59,* 715-23.

Franklin, M. E., Abramowitz, J. S., Bux, D. A., Zoellner, L. A., & Feeny, N. C. (2002). Cognitive-behavioral therapy with and without medication in the treatment of obsessive-compulsive disorder. *Professional Psychology: Research and Practice, 33,* 162-68.

Franklin, M. E., Abramowitz, J. S., Kozak, M. J., Levitt, J. T., & Foa, E. B. (2000). Effectiveness of exposure and ritual prevention for obsessive compulsive disorder: Randomized versus non-randomized samples. *Journal of Consulting and Clinical Psychology, 68,* 594-602.

Glanz, K., Rizzo, A. S., & Graap, K. (2003). Virtual reality for psychotherapy: Current reality and future possibilities. *Psychotherapy: Theory, Research, Practice, Training, 40,* 55-67.

Hofmann, S. G. (2004). Cognitive mediation of treatment change in social phobia. *Journal of Consulting and Clinical Psychology, 72,* 392-99.

Ladouceur, R., Dugas, M. J., Freeston, M. H., Léger, E., Gagnon, F., & Thibodeau, N. (2000). Efficacy of a cognitive-behavioral treatment for generalized anxiety disorder: Evaluation of a controlled clinical trial. *Journal of Consulting and Clinical Psychology, 68,* 957-64.

Maltby, N., Kirsch, I., Mayers, M., & Allen, G. J. (2002). Virtual exposure therapy for the treatment of fear of flying: A controlled investigation. *Journal of Consulting and Clinical Psychology, 70,* 1112-18.

Marks, I., Lovell, K., Noshirvani, H., Livanou, M., & Thrasher, S. (1998). Treatment of posttraumatic stress disorder by exposure and/or cognitive restructuring: A controlled study. *Archives of General Psychiatry, 55,* 317-25.

Mattick, R. P., & Peters, L. (1988). Treatment of severe social phobia: Effects of guided exposure with and without cognitive restructuring. *Journal of Consulting and Clinical Psychology, 56,* 251-60.

McMinn, M. R. (2006). *Christian counseling* [video in APA Psychotherapy Series]. Washington, DC: American Psychological Association.

National Institute of Mental Health. (2001). Facts about anxiety disorders. Retrieved from http://www.nimh.nih.gov/publicat/adfacts.cfm on May 31, 2005.

Nouwen, H. J. M. (1986). *Lifesigns: Intimacy, fecundity, and ecstasy in Christian perspective.* New York: Image Books.

Patterson, B. (2005). *He has made me glad: Enjoying God's goodness with reckless abandon.* Downers Grove, IL: InterVarsity Press.

Resick, P. A., & Calhoun, K. S. (2001). Posttraumatic stress disorder. In D. H. Barlow (Ed.), *Clinical handbook of psychological disorders* (3rd ed.) (pp. 60-113). New York: Guilford.

Resick, P. A., Nishith, P., Weaver, T. L., Astin, M. C., & Feuer, C. A. (2002). A comparison of cognitive-processing therapy with prolonged exposure and a waiting condition for the treatment of chronic posttraumatic stress disorder in female rape victims. *Journal of Consulting and Clinical Psychology, 70,* 867-79.

Roy-Byrne, P. O., Craske, M. G., Stein, M. B., Sullivan, G., Bystritsky, A., Katon, W., Golinelli, D., Sherbourne, C. D. (2005). A randomized effectiveness trial of cognitive-behavioral therapy and medication for primary care panic disorder. *Archives of General Psychiatry, 62,* 290-98.

Smitherman, T. A. (2005). Challenge tests and panic disorder: Implications for clinical assessment. *Professional Psychology: Research and Practice, 36,* 510-16.

Stavros, G. (1998). *An empirical study of the impact of contemplative prayer on psychological, relational, and spiritual well-being.* Unpublished doctoral dissertation, Boston University.

Turk, C. L., Heimberg, R. G., & Hope, D. A. (2001). Social anxiety disorder. In D. H. Barlow (Ed.), *Clinical handbook of psychological disorders* (3rd ed.) (pp. 114-53). New York: Guilford.

Turner, S. M., Beidel, D. C., & Jacob, R. G. (1994). Social phobia: A comparison of behavior therapy and Atenolol. *Journal of Consulting and Clinical Psychology, 62,* 350-58.

Westen, D., & Morrison, K. (2001). A multidimensional meta-analysis of treatments for depression, panic, and generalized anxiety disorder: An empirical examination of the status of empirically supported therapies. *Journal of Consulting and Clinical Psychology, 69,* 875-99.

Yarhouse, M. A., Butman, R. E., & McRay, B. W. (2005). *Modern psychopathologies: A comprehensive Christian appraisal.* Downers Grove, IL: InterVarsity Press.

8

Understanding Schema-Focused Interventions

OREGON BEACHES ARE STRIKINGLY BEAUTIFUL, AND QUITE DANGEROUS. Every year the ocean claims the lives of several who do not understand the power of an undertow. These powerful currents that exist beneath the water's surface catch swimmers unaware and drag them into salty depths of disaster. In a similar way, it is often the currents beneath the surface of consciousness that have the most power and bring the most troubles in personal adjustment and interpersonal relationships. Most people have wondered why they do the things they do when angry, jealous, sexually aroused, depressed or anxious, or they have wondered why they get so angry, jealous, sexually aroused, depressed or anxious in the first place. We sometimes feel and behave contrary to our wishes as forces deep within our psyche override our conscious desires to live a joyous and good life. Almost every paradigm in psychology and Christian spirituality assumes that human personality and behavior are influenced at least to some extent by deep currents that run beneath the surface of consciousness. The apostle Paul describes these deep currents in spiritual terms, noting that sin has a power over us that is stronger than we might imagine.

> It seems to be a fact of life that when I want to do what is right, I inevitably do what is wrong. I love God's law with all my heart. But there is another law at work within me that is at war with my mind. This law wins the fight and makes me a slave to the sin that is still within me. Oh, what a miserable person I am! Who will free me from this life that is dominated by sin? Thank God! The answer is in Jesus Christ our Lord. So you see how it is: In my mind I really want to obey God's law, but because of my sinful nature I am a slave to sin. (Rom 7:21-25)

When people argue that standard cognitive therapy is highly consistent with a biblical view of persons—most often drawing on other words of Paul found in Philippians 4:8—they seem to neglect that the Bible tells a much deeper story than simply choosing to think right. Paul's words in Romans 7 allude to underlying currents of sin that easily override good intentions. Paul wanted to think and behave in ways that honor God, but these subterraneous forces kept haunting and hindering him. Most of us can relate, and those who cannot may have a problem with denial.

We see the same thing in psychology, though psychologists are much less likely than the apostle Paul to label these underlying forces as sin. Different psychological theorists tell different stories about the subterraneous currents of our lives. Sigmund Freud emphasized conflict in childhood, especially sexual and developmental conflict. Contemporary object-relations theorists have refined Freud's ideas and are likely to emphasize early caregivers as internalized objects. In other words, we learn how to relate to our world because we have observed and internalized how our early caregivers related to their world. Humanistic theorists identify a deep need for acceptance and love. When these needs are unmet by others, we become defensive and incongruent in our relationships with others and may suffer emotional symptoms as a result. Family systems theorists look to roles and relationships within families of origin and present-day families to understand the forces that shape human personalities. Even behavior therapists—whom some would say have no interest in the deeper currents of personality—recognize that past learning shapes the way we behave today whether or not we are consciously aware of it.

Some might argue that we have just articulated a point of departure between Christianity and psychology: Christianity sees the deeper forces of personality to be related to sin, and psychology offers alternative explanations, such as past relationships, families of origin and learning contingencies. But this need not be a dichotomy if one holds to a sound Christian doctrine of sin (McMinn, in press). Sin is not confined to the destructive choices that humans make; it also refers to our general state of brokenness and the consequences of living with other broken people. So a Christian theology of sin tolerates various explanations for psychopathology. Was Sigmund Freud correct that childhood sexuality creates difficult conflicts that spill over into adulthood? Perhaps he was at least partly right, because in our broken state we experience all sorts of sexual challenges and conflicts through life. Are humanists correct that harsh, dehumanizing parenting squashes a child and hinders a sense of self-worth? Probably they are, and this makes sense from a Christian worldview because in our broken world we are often harmed by the consequences of others' sin. Are behaviorists correct in pointing to faulty learning contingencies in the environment? Yes. Our environment can be harsh and punitive in this broken world; sometimes the noblest behaviors get ignored and the worst ones get rewarded. None of the psychological personality systems are based on satisfying metaphysics (Jones & Butman, 1991)—at least not for the Christian practitioner—but each of them makes some sense if viewed from a Christian worldview with an orthodox view of sin and redemption. When therapists segregate Christian explanations for life's problems from psychological explanations, the result is often a simplistic, gnostic approach to helping that undermines growth in character and godliness.

Denise, the twenty-four-year-old unhappily married newlywed whose situation we discussed in chapters three and six, started by going to an elder in her church because she had been depressed—crying often, feeling depleted and tired, and feeling hopeless about her marriage. Denise feared that her marriage was a terrible mistake, that she had stopped loving her husband, Don, and that she and Don were both doomed to misery if they stayed together. The elder listened to her story, then told Denise that she is facing a

---

COUNSELING TIP 8.1: Giving Advice

Denise's experience with the elder at her church was both unpleasant and unhelpful, mostly because he offered her advice without having earned her trust. It is helpful to think about two rules for giving advice:

Rule #1: Never give advice.

Rule #2: Give advice sometimes.

Beginning therapists need to learn the first rule before learning the second. Otherwise, advice-giving comes prematurely, before adequate rapport and trust are established. Experienced therapists offer advice occasionally, but they do so with caution and understanding for how it might affect the therapy relationship.

---

spiritual problem and that she should spend more time praying and filling her mind with the good promises of Scripture. Denise tried to do what she was told, but her depression and marriage problems persisted. Her failed attempt at spiritual guidance provided further evidence to Denise that her life is dismal and her marriage hopeless.

This, of course, is bad psychology. Denise's advisor did not take adequate time to develop a helping relationship and understand Denise's story. And the elder resorted to giving quick advice rather than working collaboratively with Denise to find the deeper currents of pain that make Denise vulnerable to her dismal perspectives on life and marriage. But Denise's advisor is not only guilty of practicing bad psychology; this is also bad theology. The elder seems to be assuming that our human problem with sin can be neatly contained in our immaterial, spiritual essence and resolved through certain spiritual practices. Our human brokenness can never be compartmentalized this way. Sin pervades all of life, tainting our biology, thinking patterns, current relationships and family histories just as surely as our prayer lives. Under the circumstances, referring Denise for psychotherapy or antidepressant medication, or suggesting Don go with her for marital therapy, may be more appropriate than giving her suggestions for enhancing her prayer life. Our healing efforts should consider a wide spectrum of factors that may contribute to psychological and spiritual distress.

Good psychology and orthodox Christianity both affirm that Denise is being affected by underlying currents of pain and struggle in her life. Perhaps the messiness of being raised in a dysfunctional family is catching up with her as she launches into adulthood and a new marriage. It could be that some early marital adjustment problems need to be addressed. Maybe her life is plagued by interpersonal anxiety and now she must face the fear of an intimacy she has never known before. Perhaps she has a biological predisposition to depression. She might be struggling with shameful secrets that make her question her value as a human being. All of these possibilities suggest underlying factors that an effective helper will want to consider.

Medical-Care and Soul-Care Paradigms

The symptom-focused interventions discussed in chapters six and seven are useful in many therapy situations, but there are times when the therapist and client wish to probe more deeply into underlying currents of distress and dysfunction. With Denise, a symptom-focused intervention would help her with her depression, and perhaps this would provide some indirect benefit to her marriage as well, but it seems likely that she is facing deeper pain than can be addressed with cognitive restructuring and behavior management.

Schema-based interventions are useful for therapists inclined toward the medical-care paradigm as well as those who see their work as soul care (see figure 8.1). Those drawn to a medical-model approach might initially be inclined toward symptom-focused interventions for depression and related disorders, but become discouraged by the relatively high relapse rate. By moving into a deeper form of therapy, they are likely to reduce the likelihood of relapse among their clients (Young, Weinberger & Beck, 2001).

Schema-based interventions dig deeper than symptom-based interventions, looking to general core beliefs rather than specific automatic thoughts. These core beliefs often reside beneath the threshold of consciousness and are more resistant to change than automatic thoughts. In the medical-care paradigm, this is the deepest exploration that is likely to occur in psychotherapy.

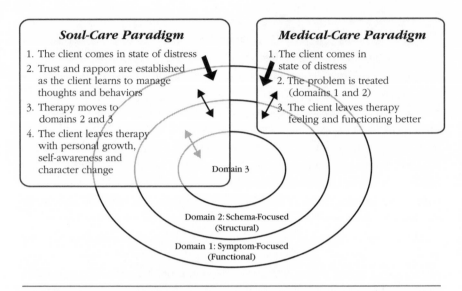

Figure 8.1. Schema-focused interventions probe underlying assumptions.

Like those who practice with a medical-care paradigm, those drawn to a soul-care paradigm of psychotherapy will also find symptom-focused therapy helpful in fostering some initial hope in their clients and in reducing the most distressing symptoms, and they will want to explore deeper schema-based dimensions of personality, development, cognition, emotion, motivation and spirituality with their clients. But unlike those operating from a medical-care paradigm, a soul-care paradigm presumes that schema exploration is a transitional step toward an even deeper level of understanding. Schemas are formed and maintained because of relational patterns, and so it is essential to craft the therapeutic relationship in a way that promotes healing. These relational forms of intervention are discussed more in chapters ten and eleven.

Looking Deeper in Cognitive Therapy

When looking for deeper currents in the human personality, cognitive therapists look beneath automatic thoughts and intermediate beliefs to find maladaptive underlying assumptions, or core beliefs. This, of course, is an oversimplification. In reality, cognitions exist on a continuum from highly specific and conscious to very general and unconscious. In order to simplify this continuum, cognitive therapists have postulated the three categories of thought introduced in chapter three: automatic thoughts, intermediate beliefs and core beliefs.

Just as intermediate beliefs are less accessible to consciousness than automatic thoughts, core beliefs are buried even deeper than intermediate beliefs (see figure 8.2). Most people could stop at any given moment and describe their current thoughts (e.g., "I'm not sure I completely understand what I read in the last paragraph"). Some people could go on to uncover intermediate beliefs (e.g., "I should know everything there is to know about psychotherapy"), but few have direct and immediate access to their core beliefs (e.g., "I am incompetent and bound to fail"). Automatic thoughts are situation-specific (e.g., reading the last paragraph), intermediate beliefs are more general (e.g., understanding counseling in general), and core beliefs are exceedingly pervasive and general (e.g., being incompetent). Automatic thoughts are readily changed through rational analysis whereas core beliefs are highly resistant to change because they are more deeply rooted in experiential and relational phenomena.

In the symptom-focused interventions described in the previous chapters, the therapist and client work together to identify and change automatic thoughts. They also venture into intermediate beliefs, which are implicit rules, if-then

---

COUNSELING TIP 8.2: Know Thyself

It is helpful for therapists to spend time understanding their own developmental backgrounds. Often this involves personal therapy, but self-understanding can also be promoted through reflective journaling. The following questions are helpful in exploring personal schemas.

1. How did you learn to draw close to others (parents, siblings, friends at school) early in your life? Was it through humor? Conforming to their wishes? Seeking approval? Athletic prowess? How has this approach to relationships helped you and hurt you over the years?

2. Describe one organizing rule in your family of origin. For example, some families have rules such as "we don't talk about our problems" or "we are better than other families" or "we get our work done before we play" or "we can do anything if we put our mind to it." How has the rule you listed affected you for good and for ill?

3. Think about the major turning points in your life (moves, deaths, divorce and so on). How did these turning points affect the way you understand yourself in relation to the world around you?

4. What fears, joys, anxieties, rewards and frustrations do you have at this point in your life? How are these related to what you have written in response to the first three questions?

statements, and central goals that are moderately accessible to consciousness, more general and less readily changed than automatic thoughts. In schema-focused interventions, therapists still consider intermediate beliefs, but with the goal of discovering the client's underlying core beliefs. Core beliefs function as the reservoir from which intermediate beliefs and automatic thoughts emerge, and these core beliefs are almost always exacerbated by relationships in the past and present.

Notice the upward direction of the arrows in figure 8.2. Conscious thoughts flow from those that are less conscious; deeper currents affect the surface experiences of life. If Denise has the core belief that people cannot be trusted, then this belief will naturally produce dysfunctional intermediate beliefs and automatic thoughts. Figure 8.2 illustrates how Denise's core belief, which probably stems from an early childhood relational problem, might lead to highly dysfunctional and irrational thoughts in her present-day relationship with Don.

This linear formulation of Denise's problem is both easy to understand and more sophisticated than the simplistic spiritual model used by her first advisor, who told her to pray more fervently and meditate on Scripture. But it is not sophisticated enough. Many have become dissatisfied with the overly simplistic nature of early semantic cognitive therapies and have developed more sophisticated alternatives (e.g., A. T. Beck, 1996). To explore this further, we turn to the construct of *schema*—an important theoretical contribution coming both from

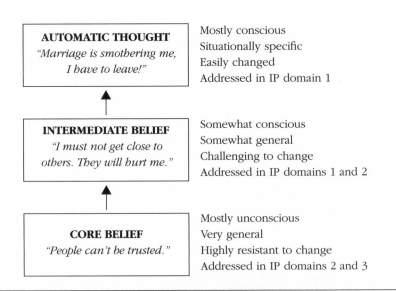

Figure 8.2. Core beliefs affect intermediate beliefs and automatic thoughts.

within cognitive therapy and from other spheres of scientific psychology. Figure 8.3 provides an overview of the IP model for schema-focused interventions.

Schema

Unfortunately, the word *schema* has suffered the fate of many popular terms in psychology—it has been defined and used in many different ways. In some cognitive therapy writings, schema is used interchangeably with core beliefs (e.g., J. S. Beck, 1995). This, however, is too confining for some cognitive therapists, and so various elaborations and refinements of schema have been offered, each tugging the concept in slightly different directions (Needleman, 1999; Safran, 1998; Safran & Segal, 1990; Young, Klosko & Weishaar, 2003). Because the term *schema* has been defined and used in various ways, we will first offer a basic definition that is general enough to be acceptable to most psychologists, and then we will nudge the concept in a distinct direction to elaborate on features of IP.

In its most basic form, a schema is simply a structure that contains a representation of reality. Schemas are comprised of thoughts, assumptions and beliefs that help us maintain a sense of personal identity in the midst of a complex and ambiguous world, allowing us to simplify and understand our environment. Just as the content of a map represents physical geography without being equivalent to the geography itself, so also the content of a schema is a representation of reality but is not reality itself. Schemas, like maps, can contain a more or less precise representation of how things really are.

Schemas affect how we interpret and construct the world. Just as maps reveal approximations of the physical world, so also schemas contain cognitive approximations of how we understand ourselves and relate to others. When a map is grossly incorrect, it may produce substantial misunderstandings of the physical world and send its user in unproductive directions. Many people have had experiences where Internet-generated map services have misled them and sent them far from their intended destinations. Similarly, if a schema contains badly skewed beliefs and assumptions, a person may develop a highly inaccurate self-concept and misperceive social cues in profound ways, sometimes resulting in dire emotional and interpersonal consequences.

IP is based on the assumption that we are active interpreters of our world. Life does not merely happen to us; each of us actively interprets and shapes our life according to our schemas. When Denise got married to Don she entered some new territory of intimacy that she had not known before. How would she find her way in this new territory? She did what any of us would do. She pulled out her map (i.e., she accessed the unconscious dimensions of her schema) to

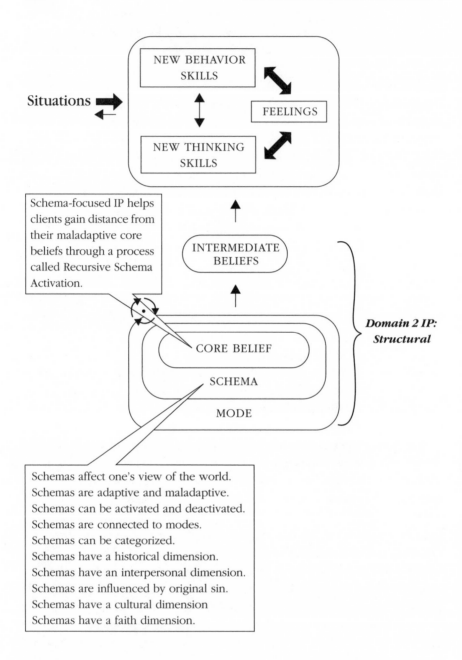

Figure 8.3. Schema-focused interventions involve working with core beliefs in the context of schemas and modes.

see what she knew about intimate relationships. Unfortunately, her map was skewed with the core belief that people cannot be trusted, so now she fears being hurt by Don and is responding by withdrawing from the relationship. She is simply following the map she knows, though it is an unfortunate and inaccurate representation of reality.

Semantic cognitive therapists emphasize that schemas guide the way we interpret our life circumstances, but constructivist cognitive therapists have taken this a step further: we also change life circumstances by how we construct our understanding of reality (Mahoney, 2003). This is illustrated in figure 8.4. The figure above the dotted line illustrates the approach typically taken in semantic cognitive therapy, where schemas alter one's interpretation of the world. Imag-

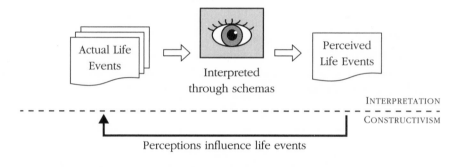

Figure 8.4. Interpretation and constructivism

ine Denise coming home from a long day's work to find Don already cooking her favorite meal. The table is set with tablecloth, candles and a freshly cut rose in the middle. Romantic music is playing in the background. Denise quickly assesses the situation, filters it through her "I can't trust Don" schema, and blurts out, "What is this? Do you think you can make things better by cooking me a nice meal?" She has perceived Don's actions through a schema that results in her being defensive and irritable rather than blessed by Don's kindness.

Constructivist cognitive therapists recognize that perceptions are more than passive interpretations of life circumstances—perceptions actually change life itself. This is illustrated with the arrow below the dotted line in figure 8.4. Consider several examples:

1. The person who fears being rejected becomes detached and withdrawn, and soon her few friends do the same: they withdraw from her because they are put off by her interpersonal aloofness. Her belief has contributed to the rejection she fears.

2. A person who thinks the way to earn love and approval is through unusual accomplishment soon finds that he has neglected relationships in order to accomplish his grandiose goals. His only real contact with others occurs when they congratulate him on his latest accomplishment, thereby affirming his narcissistic schema.

3. A husband fears his wife is keeping secrets from him, so he grills her with questions each evening, looks through her personal files and scrutinizes her credit card bill each month. Given his suspiciousness, his wife finds it easier to keep some things to herself rather than "rocking the boat." His fear that his wife will keep secrets ends up making her more likely to keep secrets.

4. Denise believes others cannot be trusted, so she tends to hold Don at a distance. Eventually Don will become frustrated and may abandon the relationship—either emotionally or physically—thereby confirming Denise's belief that others cannot be trusted.

It is not simply that Denise has interpreted a life situation—Don cooking a special dinner—through her schema of mistrust; she has also affected the life situation itself because of her harsh interpretation. Once she reacts, Don feels criticized and defeated. He sits quietly through dinner. Both Don and Denise have a subdued mood all evening. Imagine how the situation might have turned out differently if Denise had interpreted things differently, and responded differently, when she first walked in the door.

Schemas are adaptive and maladaptive. The example of Denise is a sad example of how damaging a dysfunctional schema can be, but keep in mind that a schema can also be a good thing that yields positive outcomes, just as a good map can be helpful. Properly activated, schemas help us cope with and adapt to our environment. One hopes to have a gregarious, outgoing schema that can be activated at a party or when interviewing for a job as a salesperson. It is good to have a fear schema that is activated in threatening situations so that one doesn't walk alone in a dark alley in a crime-ridden neighborhood. A self-confident, assertive schema helps when returning defective merchandise or bluffing in a card game. Schemas are helpful and good insofar as they help us simplify, interpret and respond in a complex world.

When schemas are maladaptive, it is often because they are self-demeaning or self-destructive, stemming from dysfunctional relationships earlier in life. Young et al. (2003) label these early maladaptive schemas. For example, a person raised in an abusive home may come to see herself as unlovable and worthless. Another person raised in an overachieving home may believe that life is a grand competition and that he must always prove himself superior to others.

IN THE OFFICE 8.1: Schemas Are More Than Filters

A common metaphor for schemas is that they function like filters, as in the top half of figure 8.4. According to this view, people interpret life through their schemas, ignoring certain aspects of the environment and honing in on others.

But schemas are more than filters because one's perceptions of reality also have a reciprocal effect on reality itself. When working with clients, it is often helpful to point out the reciprocal nature of schemas by asking how significant others are affected by the client's perceptions and choices.

Nick: I felt really bad today. My girlfriend and I were hiking, but I didn't plan the timing right and we had to hurry back so that I could get to work on time. Anyway, on the way back we were walking really fast and she tripped on a tree root and fell and hurt her hand.

Clark: And you were feeling responsible for it because you didn't plan out the timing of the hike properly.

Nick: Yeah. I was really upset with myself. After Sara fell I just felt so terrible, like "this is all my fault." It could have been such a nice time, but I really messed up.

Clark: You're on the hike, she falls, and you end up yelling at yourself. This sounds like the schema we've been exploring: "When bad things happen, it's my fault."

Nick: Well, it really was my fault this time. I mean, I planned the hike. My poor planning is the reason we were walking so fast.

Clark: I wonder what that was like for Sara after she fell.

Nick: What do you mean?

Clark: She falls, hurts her hand, and then you become focused on yourself—on your failure. I wonder what that feels like for her.

Nick: You mean instead of thinking about her?

Clark: It's worth thinking about.

Nick: I see what you mean. She needed me to care about her right then, and I was thinking about myself—about how foolish I had been.

Note how Nick's schema keeps him from giving attention to Sara, even when she is hurt and needs his care. The therapist probes the possibility that Nick's schema may further injure Sara by keeping him from focusing on her needs.

And in some strange twist of destiny, the woman who believes she is unlovable and worthless may end up married to the man who thinks he must always prove himself superior, or vice versa. Not surprisingly, early maladaptive schemas often become the focus of domain 2 IP.

Schemas can be activated and deactivated. Most people have a repertoire of different schemas that can be used in various situations. At any given moment, most schemas lie dormant. We access whatever schema we need in order to deal with present-life circumstances, and then when the circumstances change we put that schema back on the shelf and select another one. This process of schema activation and deactivation is good and healthy, but it can lead to problems if a harmful or imprudent schema is activated at the wrong time. The fear schema that keeps one from walking alone in a bad neighborhood is not nearly so helpful if it is activated in the midst of a church service, leading to a panic attack. The self-confidence schema that helps a person do well in a card game may not be helpful for the neophyte air traffic controller who fails to ask for help when an unfamiliar pattern shows up on the radar screen.

Consider the schema involved in falling in love. When Denise was falling in love with Don, she had a hard time concentrating on anything else. Most of her thoughts were devoted to him: *He's perfect, I have to see him again today, I love how he smiles,* and so on. Her thoughts were associated with pleasant emotions—happiness, anticipation, hope and gratitude. She had predictable physiological responses when around Don; her heart raced, her breathing rate increased, sometimes she would tremble when he held her. Don loved Denise too, and the more delight they took in one another the more certain they felt about marriage. The falling-in-love schema accomplished its purpose, drawing together two people who were once strangers. But over time this very pleasant and productive falling-in-love schema began to wane. Most people experience falling in love only occasionally throughout their lives, and this is a good thing— just imagine how troubling it would be to fall in love with someone new every few weeks. As Denise's falling-in-love schema became less active, and as she and Don settled into the full-time intimacy of marriage, some other schema gained prominence—a schema that was previously masked by the powerful emotions of falling in love. Soon her fear of intimacy became a dominant force in her life, she became increasingly anxious and depressed, and eventually she sought the help of someone in her church.

The assumption that schemas can be activated and deactivated has important therapeutic implications in IP. Schemas are deactivated in one of two ways: either life circumstances change or a person learns skills to deliberately deactivate them. Denise's first impulse is to leave her marriage, thereby changing her life circumstances and deactivating this schema that is cloaking her in fear each day. But what if there is another way? If Denise can learn to deliberately deactivate her maladaptive schema, then she can be helped without having to leave her marriage. Perhaps her fear-of-intimacy schema, which probably comes from painful early-life experiences, can be disarmed in the process of therapy.

Before a person can learn to deactivate a maladaptive schema, the schema must be activated in the therapy office. In IP it is not enough simply to talk *about* life; rather we need to evoke the emotions and cognitions that occur outside of the therapy office in order to identify the schemas that ultimately need to be deactivated. Consider the following two interactions with Denise, the first a conversation about her schema and the second a wholehearted engagement with her schema.

Denise: I walked in the door after work yesterday and saw Don cooking dinner. He had put on music, lit some candles and was making my favorite pasta. He's trying so hard. I know I'm not being fair to him.

Mark: We've talked before of how much you fear intimacy. Do you suppose this was playing in the back of your mind as you walked in the door yesterday?

Denise: Yes, I think so. I mean, I love Don, or at least I want to. But then again, I don't really love him. Or at least I am terrified about the thought of loving him. Every time I love someone, they go away or they hurt me or they do something stupid.

Mark: I see. So when you walk in the door you have all this inner conflict. You're feeling drawn to this man who cares so deeply for you, and yet you also have all these instincts to protect yourself so that he can't hurt you.

Denise: Yeah, I think that's right.

In this first example Denise and her therapist are talking *about* her schema, but it is not a conversation where her schema is truly being activated. If Denise is to learn how to deactivate her schema in the therapy office, it must first be activated. This calls for an experiential encounter with her fears, not just a conversation about them. The following example illustrates a more experiential approach:

Denise: I walked in the door after work yesterday and saw Don cooking dinner. He had put on some music, lit some candles and was making my favorite pasta. He's trying so hard. I know I'm not being fair to him.

Mark: What was that like for you when you first walked in the door?

Denise: I was confused. I felt annoyed that he's trying so hard. But then, I guess I want him to try. He's such a dear man. Why can't I love him?

Mark: You felt drawn toward him and yet not drawn. Tell me more about what was stirring deep inside as you walked in that door.

Denise: I don't know. At first I was upset. And then he just seemed so vulnerable there, so afraid of losing me. Things used to be so beautiful. He would cook me dinner, and I would love it. I gave him long backrubs. Sometimes we would dance at midnight on the street in front of his house. Our love was so precious. What happened?

Mark: I see the pain in your eyes even as you ask the question.

Denise: [cries] I feel so confused. I loved him so much once, and maybe I still do, but I just don't feel close.

Mark: What are you feeling right now?

Denise: Sorry for him. Scared. Sad that things turned out this way.

Mark: Scared?

Denise: [still crying] I hate the thought of leaving Don, but the idea of staying is even more terrifying. [Long pause] What will happen to me if I stay? What will I become?

Mark: Tell me what you're afraid might happen.

In this second example, the therapist is working to activate Denise's fear-based schema, using her emotions as a pathway to her underlying cognitions. Only when a schema is activated will she be able to learn new ways of viewing the world to help her consciously deactivate the schema. Notice that the therapist is not trying to fix any faulty schema or misinterpretations. The goal for now is to activate the schema by evoking related emotions and memories. When the schema is activated in the therapy office, the therapist will better understand Denise's core beliefs.

Schemas are connected to modes. Though schemas are cognitive, they are highly interconnected with other human systems such as emotion, motivation, physiological responses and behavior. Denise has particular cognitions about getting close to Don, but these cognitions are interconnected with all sorts of other experiences. She walked in the door last evening embedded in her dismal thoughts and feeling gloomy and sad about her future (cognitions are connected to emotional pain). She felt honored by his efforts to make her dinner and set a romantic atmosphere, but somehow she couldn't find the energy to engage in meaningful conversation over dinner (cognitions are connected to motivational deficits). As she got up from the dinner table she noticed a familiar lump in her throat, slight nausea and tears in her eyes (cognitions are connected with physiological responses). The next day, Don called her at work to say hello, but she was busy and chose not to return his call (cognitions are connected to behaviors). In all these ways we see that Denise's cognitive processes are related to other dimensions of her existence. The schema is cognitive, but the effects of the schema reach far beyond cognition and pervade many aspects of her life.

Though not widely used in the cognitive therapy literature, Aaron Beck (1996) introduced the term *mode* to describe a larger, more complex view of human personality than can be captured with cognitive schemas alone (see also Needleman,

---

COUNSELING TIP 8.3: Pointing Out Emotion

One effective way to activate schemas is to point out emotions as the client experiences them in the session. For example, a therapist notices moisture in a client's eyes, leans forward and points it out: "As you talk about this now, I see the sadness in your eyes." The same can be done with other emotions—anger, frustration, happiness, jealousy and so on. When the emotions are pointed out, it gives permission for the client to explore feelings. In the process, schemas are often activated.

1999). Just as cognitive schemas help orient us to our environment, so also we have affective (emotional), behavioral, motivational and physiological responses to life situations. The novice skier who is afraid of heights will not only be having particular thoughts while standing in the ski-lift line (e.g., "this could be disastrous") but also be experiencing certain emotions (e.g., fear), motivations (e.g., to avoid potential calamity), behavioral inclinations (e.g., to turn and run), and physiological responses (e.g., heart racing, rapid breathing). Each of these systems is functioning according to its own organizing principles, and yet all of the systems are interrelated. Super-ordinate over all these systems is what A. T. Beck (1996) calls a *conscious control system*. The conscious control system allows the skier to make a deliberate choice to stay in the ski-lift line despite all the internal signals to turn and flee. Quite often in life we make rational choices that conflict with primitive instincts. Just as the skier chooses to stay in line and take the ski lift to the top of the mountain, so an athlete continues pushing toward a goal rather than sitting and resting, a married person decides to remain sexually faithful in marriage despite primal impulses to seek a new sexual partner, a woman determines to persist through the pain of natural childbirth rather than accepting the spinal block she has been offered. In all these examples we see the power of conscious control over the various experiences a person may be having at the moment. Cognitive therapists tend to refer to this conscious control as meta-cognition—the ability to think about our thinking and respond accordingly. Similar concepts are found in other psychological and spiritual vocabularies—for example, psychologists sometimes refer to mindfulness skills (Linehan, 1993; Lukoff & Lu, 2005; Segal, Williams & Teasdale, 2002), and philosophers and theologians speak of human agency and volition.

So what is the relationship between core beliefs, cognitive schemas and modes? Think of a core belief as something contained within a cognitive schema, as illustrated in figure 8.5. Needleman (1999) likens a schema to a mosquito and the core belief to the virus carried by the mosquito. When a cognitive schema is activated, the virulent contents do their damage. A cognitive schema is, in turn, a subset of a mode. All of the systems in the mode are interacting with the cognitive schema, so it is not surprising that in a moment of extreme

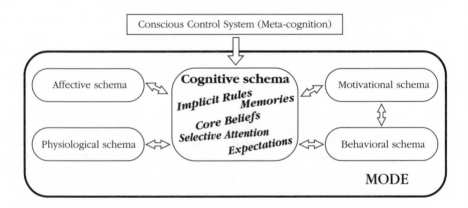

Figure 8.5. Modes, schemas and core beliefs

emotional arousal—hearing news of a sudden death in the family, for example—one's cognitions will not be neatly ordered. We use terms such as "going into shock" on such occasions, which is to say that a particular mode has been engaged including all of the concomitant feelings, motivations, thoughts, physiological reactions and behaviors. All the schemas are vitally important, and all influence one another.

Note that the cognitive schema in figure 8.5 is much less tidy than the view of cognition implied in figure 8.2, where core beliefs flow neatly into intermediate beliefs and then into automatic thoughts. In schema-focused IP we recognize that core beliefs are intermingled with various other cognitive phenomena such as memories, selective attention, expectations, implicit rules and assumptions, and so on. This means that therapy is not simply a linear process of discovering and correcting underlying thoughts; good therapists do more than teach logic. Schema-focused therapists work with whole persons who bring a complex mix of cognitions that are constantly influencing and influenced by emotions, physiological responses, behaviors and motivations.

To further illustrate, a hiker who glances over the edge of a cliff may experience all sorts of things as a particular primal fear mode is activated: trembling, sweating, memories of a story about someone who fell and died while hiking, feelings of dread, and impulses to turn around and head back down the trail. As this happens, this fretful hiker will be having certain cognitive schemas activated, with a range of specific thoughts. Some thoughts will be highly accessible to consciousness: *I could die. This is scary.* Other thoughts—core beliefs—may be functioning beneath the hiker's conscious awareness: *The world is dangerous and unpredictable, and I am bound to be hurt.* In addition, certain memories may come flooding back. The hiker's attention will become restricted—it seems unlikely to notice beautiful ferns on the hillside at a moment such as this. And overriding all of this is a conscious control system that helps orchestrate how the hiker will respond to this flood of experiences.

Notice an important implication for helping relationships: when schemas are activated the person experiences more than just cognition. This hiker has certain thoughts, but the thoughts are accompanied with emotions, motivations, physiological responses and behaviors. If we translate this into the practice of psychotherapy we see that working with a client's schemas is messy. People do not simply talk about their deepest fears and longings and pain. They also feel these experiences. They may shout and behave rudely. They may shake and tremble as they speak. They may avoid certain topics and run away from therapy as soon as they begin venturing into something particularly painful. IP focuses primarily on cognitive structures, but in doing so it must engage the whole person.

Again we are reminded of the Wonderful Counselor and the miracle of the incarnation; Jesus did not merely come to teach correct doctrine and tidy up the sloppiness of human cognition, but rather to live with us in the complexity of humanity. Jesus encountered the confusion, joy and pain of human emotion, experienced the struggle of competing motivations. In his humanity (as in his divinity) he ministered to whole people, healing physical wounds, bringing hope to the discouraged, bringing spiritual life to a broken world. "So the Word became human and lived here on earth among us" (Jn 1:14). Still, despite his incredible mercy and understanding, Jesus also called people to take responsibility for their actions. Jesus is characterized by *both* grace and truth, and so he affirmed the importance of taking conscious control over the challenges of life. IP affirms human agency, and so the conscious control system is an essential and central component of figure 8.5 and schema-based interventions.

Schemas can be categorized. Therapists have a propensity for taxonomies. The fact that most all taxonomies are wrong, or at least overly simplified, doesn't seem to slow us down. Not surprisingly then, people have developed taxonomies for schemas. The three taxonomies we are about to describe all tend to conflate core beliefs and schemas, as if they are identical. This is understandable, both because early cognitive therapists tended to use schema and core be-

---

COUNSELING TIP 8.4: What Are You Going to Do About That?

Therapy involves a compassionate caring for another person, which helps promote trust and rapport. But if the therapist is not aware, therapy relationships can devolve into a "pity party" where the client becomes the sad victim and the therapist the all-wise rescuer. These roles may feel good to both the therapist and the client for a time, but they will not help the client progress toward therapeutic goals. Therapists need to find ways to promote a sense of agency in clients, to encourage them to take responsibility for their lives. This is done by emphasizing the conscious control system shown in figure 8.5. One of the questions that is often useful when a client describes a dilemma or struggle is, "What are you going to do about that?" This should not be asked in a flippant or hostile way, but in a kind, supportive tone. It reminds clients that they have some power and responsibility to make things better in their lives.

---

lief synonymously and because the more recent models of schemas and modes are not yet widely discussed within cognitive therapy circles.

In his early work on depression, Aaron Beck and his colleagues categorized core beliefs around his cognitive triad (Beck, Rush, Shaw & Emery, 1979). The cognitive triad asserts that people with depression have a negative view of self, the world and the future. Accordingly, core beliefs can be understood as focused on the self (e.g., "I'm a failure"), the world (e.g., "People are bound to reject me") and the future (e.g., "I'm doomed and life will never improve"). This taxonomy has some value, but it is based on a formulation for depression that does not always apply well to other treatments. Moreover, it fails to capture the variety and complexities of schemas encountered in therapy.

McMinn (1991) identified three clusters of core beliefs: compulsivity, conformity and control. Compulsivity beliefs relate to a desire to earn love through hard work and achievement. Examples are, "Love must be earned with unusual accomplishment" and "I must be competent at all times." These beliefs often inspire overachieving and desperate efforts to gain love and credibility through personal accomplishment. Conformity beliefs pertain to a need for approval. People with these core beliefs have unrealistic goals to please everyone at all times or to avoid shame by hiding some aspect of their identity. Examples of conformity beliefs include, "I must be approved of by everyone for the things I do" and "If people really knew me, they would think I am a terrible person." Control beliefs have to do with finding security by controlling the events of the world. For example, "If others don't do as I wish, they do not care about me" and "If things do not go as I have planned, I am out of control."

In a more recent taxonomy, Young and his colleagues (2003) have identified eighteen schemas that fit into five clusters, which they call *domains* (not to be confused with the three domains of IP). The domains and schemas are summarized in table 8.1, along with examples of core beliefs that might be contained in each schema. The domain and schema names are theirs, and the examples of core beliefs are our words based on the descriptions Young and his colleagues provide. One of the most helpful aspects of Young's work at the Schema Therapy Institute is his development of an assessment tool that helps identify which schemas are most prevalent for a client (see www.schematherapy.com for more information).

Taxonomies can be helpful in IP because they allow the client and therapist to hone in on particular maladaptive schemas and work to correct them. But it is important to keep in mind that many core beliefs are interrelated, and so the goal is not to isolate and treat a particular belief as one might isolate and destroy a tumor. Rather, the goal is to develop a healing relationship with a human being who struggles with various dysfunctional beliefs and to understand this person's story—how the influences of the past have contributed to present-day struggles and how to help the person disentangle the past from the present and work toward a more hopeful future.

Schemas have a historical dimension. Even highly dysfunctional schemas may have once been functional. To understand how, the therapist takes time to learn something about the client's developmental background. As a therapist learns the client's story, and develops empathy for the situational crises of the client's life, it often becomes clear that today's most troubling and

Table 8.1. Young, Klosko and Weishaar's (2003) Taxonomy of Schemas

Domain	Schema	Example of Core Belief
Disconnection and Rejection	Abandonment/Instability	"People I care about will abandon or reject me."
	Mistrust/Abuse	"I can't trust others. They will mistreat and hurst me."
	Emotional Deprivation	"I cannot count on others to pay attention and care about me."
	Defectiveness/Shame	"I am defective, bad, unlovable or inferior."
	Social Isolation/ Alienation	"I am all alone, isolated from others."
Impaired Autonomy and Performance	Dependence/ Incompetence	Sets the relational context of cognition and behavior
	Vulnerability to Harm	"Something terrible will soon happen to me."
	Enmeshment/ Undeveloped Self	"I can't survive without [parent, spouse, friend]"
	Failure	"I am stupid, untalented and basically a failure in life."
Impaired Limits	Entitlement/Grandiosity	"I am better than others and entitled to special privileges."
	Insufficient Self-Control	"I should do what pleases me at the moment."
Other-Directedness	Subjugation	"I shouldn't rock the boat. I'll do what other people want."
	Self-Sacrifice	"I'll give up my own desires to keep others from feeling pain, or to keep myself from feeling guilty."
	Approval-Seeking	"I must have the approval and recognition of others."
Overvigilance and Inhibition	Negativity/Pessimism	"Life is just one misery after another."
	Emotional Inhibition	"I should not show my emotions; it may cause others to disapprove."
	Unrelenting Standards	"I should be flawless and constantly productive."
	Punitiveness	"People who let me down should be punished."

maladaptive schema was once necessary and adaptive.

Denise was raised in a dozen neighborhoods scattered throughout a large city. Her family lived in a variety of different apartments, usually only for a few months at a time. Her father's alcoholism resulted in long periods of poverty interspersed with an occasional job and paycheck, drunken rages, frequent evictions, and uncertainty for the future. Denise's mother tried to hold it all together, working as a waitress or bartender and caring for four children and a drunken husband, but she had her own struggles with depression. Life was difficult and chaotic. Denise remembers living for several months in a third-floor apartment, twenty feet above crime-infested streets. She fell asleep listening to shouting and occasional gunshots. She often woke to sirens. She and her older brother walked three blocks to school each morning and home each afternoon, always fearful about what might happen. Her brother got the worst of it—he was beat up by local bullies and gang members on two occasions. Meanwhile, Denise was taking it all in and forming conclusions about the world around her. Fortunately for Denise, a high school teacher noticed she was smart and encouraged her to consider college. She was accepted at a state university several hours away. In her first semester at the university a friend invited her to a campus ministry meeting, and Denise became interested in Christianity. In the months that followed, she continued attending the ministry meetings where she met Christ, and Don. A romance followed, and Denise and Don were married after graduating from college. Now they both work entry-level jobs, struggling to pay back college loans while keeping up with living expenses. Both feel frustrated and disappointed with their marriage.

Knowing Denise's history is helpful in understanding her schema that contributes to her fear of intimacy. Her core belief, "people can't be trusted," may not make much sense when looking at her marriage to a kind and loving man, but it makes more sense when looking at her developmental background. In her vulnerable childhood years, as she was observing her life and trying to figure out how to survive, she came to certain conclusions about how the world works. She learned lessons about life while being raised by an alcoholic father and a depressed mother, and while walking to and from school in dangerous neighborhoods. These conclusions stay with a person, even after the environment changes.

Core beliefs can be learned at any point in life, though the childhood years seem to be the most formative. Just as children are born with an innate ability to learn the particular sounds, syntax and grammar of language—without even knowing they are doing so—so it also seems that children acquire particular understandings about how to adapt to their environment. These understandings become implicit beliefs; sometimes they are modified as life's circumstances change, and sometimes they are not. The most resistant core beliefs are often the ones that become the focus of schema-focused and relationship-focused interventions in IP. It is important for the therapist to keep in mind that a client is not intending to be foolish or stubborn by holding on to a maladaptive core belief; rather, the client is clinging to a belief that was functional and adaptive in an earlier life situation.

Young et al. (2003) describe four types of early life experiences that make a child vulnerable to developing maladaptive schemas. First, toxic frustration of needs occurs when a child does not experience enough love and security to feel safe. The child may learn to anticipate abandonment and emotional alienation.

COUNSELING TIP 8.5: The Past Matters

Therapists who function exclusively in the symptom-focused domain tend to think of early life events as mostly irrelevant. They may say, "The past doesn't matter nearly as much as how you choose to live the present." From a symptom-focused perspective this makes some sense, and it is an important affirmation of human agency (see Counseling Tips 3.4 and 8.4), but in the schema-focused domain it can be naive and misleading to dismiss early life experiences. Formative experiences establish the ground rules by which a person lives, and understanding those rules requires an exploration of developmental issues.

Second, traumatization occurs when a child is abused or victimized. A young person in this environment may learn to mistrust others or carry a sense of defectiveness, shame or vulnerability. Third, a child may be pampered or overindulged. This person may grow to be highly dependent on others or to feel entitled to special privileges. Fourth, a child may identify with and internalize the perspectives of a dysfunctional parent. So, for example, a child raised with an abusive father may internalize the father's anger and rage and later grow to have similar problems. This fourth type of life experience becomes especially important when considering domain 3 interventions in IP, described in chapters ten and eleven.

Whereas Young et al. (2003) emphasize childhood events in the development of maladaptive schemas, others have noted that schemas can be developed at any point in the lifespan. Needleman (1999) provides a helpful analysis of schema development in relation to the psychosocial stages postulated by Erik

Table 8.2. Erikson's Psychosocial Stages in Relation to Core Beliefs

Stage	Crisis	Examples of Core Beliefs with Unsuccessful Resolution
Trust vs. Mistrust (age 0-1)	Can I trust others to take care of my needs or not?	"Others can't be trusted." "I can't trust myself."
Autonomy vs. Shame and Doubt (age 1-2)	Am I free and capable to explore my world, or am I too small and weak to do so?	"I am weak and incapable." "I must depend on others."
Initiative vs. Guilt (ages 2-6)	Am I confident in my abilities, or should I feel bad about myself and my desires?	"I am defective." "My desires are bad."
Industry vs. Inferiority (ages 6-12)	Can I be successful in school, or am I inferior to others?	"I am incompetent." "I am stupid."
Identity vs. Role Confusion (ages 12-18)	Will I understand and like myself or sink into confusion and uncertainty about who I am?	"I am worthless." "My life is meaningless."
Intimacy vs. Isolation (ages 19-49)	Am I able to form an intimate and stable relationship with another person?	"I am all alone." "I will be abandoned."
Generativity vs. Stagnation (ages 40-65)	Can I contribute to society and care for others, or am I stuck in self-centeredness?	"I have to look out for myself." "It's a dog-eat-dog world; only the strong survive."
Integrity vs. Despair (ages 65-death)	Has life been satisfying and fulfilling, or simply a series of disappointments and failures?	"You live. You die. Who cares?" "Life is futile."

Erikson (1950). Erikson suggested that individuals experience predictable psychosocial crises throughout their development and that healthy adjustment is, to some extent, contingent upon navigating these crises. His eight stages are listed in table 8.2. Erikson did not ignore childhood; indeed, five of his eight stages occur by the age of eighteen, but his developmental theory continues throughout the lifespan.

Erikson believed the first crisis faced by an infant has to do with the trustworthiness of the world. Some newborns are in environments where their needs are met and the world is basically trustworthy: a parent (or two) provides love, attention, food, dry diapers, housing and so on. These infants are likely to develop in relatively healthy ways during the early stages of life. Other infants find themselves in more chaotic environments. Sometimes their needs for food and love are met, and sometimes they are not. Their world cannot always be trusted, and so they are likely to face problems later in life related to mistrust. The child from this second scenario may—like Denise—emerge from infancy with a core belief "People can't be trusted."

Each of Erikson's eight stages involves a crisis. The crisis is either resolved well, leading to relatively healthy development, or it is resolved poorly, leading to problems in later stages of development. When resolved poorly, the crisis may lead to maladaptive core beliefs such as those listed in table 8.2.

If schemas are formed in the process of psychosocial development, then it follows that schemas are closely connected to interpersonal relationships in their origin, activation and deactivation. And so therapy that addresses schemas must look to relational factors.

Schemas have an interpersonal dimension. Early cognitive therapists seemed content to say that schemas develop somehow early in life, but how this happens was left vague and undefined. In IP, schemas are tied to relationships. This is a theological assertion as much as psychological. In chapter one we made a point of emphasizing that God's image is functional, structural and relational, and that all three of these domains are interconnected. IP is based on these three interrelated dimensions of God's image.

Most semantic cognitive therapies treat schemas as if they are structural phenomenon related to one's rational capacities. This is a step in the right direction, but if God's image is also relational, then a comprehensive approach to Christian therapy looks beyond schemas as cognitive structures to see the importance of human relationships in how schemas are formed, maintained and changed. Schemas are typically formed in order to seek closeness to others or in response to interpersonal pain. Seeing the relational dimensions of schemas is important in schema-focused (domain 2) interventions, and it becomes the central focus as therapy progresses toward relationship-focused (domain 3) interventions.

Denise's schema—that she cannot trust people and dares not get close to them—developed in the context of painful early life relationships and a family context where she learned to be responsible to take care of her own needs at an early age. Living with dysfunctional parents and being surrounded by frightening and dangerous neighborhoods contributed to her ways of viewing the world. She longed to be close to her parents, but it seemed that every time she began feeling safe her father would come home in a drunken rage or her mother would withdraw into another depressive episode. Eventually she came to distrust interpersonal intimacy. In school and in her neighborhood she discovered interpersonal openness made her vulnerable to ridicule, and she ultimately concluded that she could not rely on others to help her. Her college life was more predictable and safer than childhood, and dorm life gave her optimal control over how close she got to other people, so her childhood schemas calmed a bit. But now, several months into a new marriage, it is her marriage to Don that seems to be activating the old intimacy schema that had been relatively dormant for several years.

Schemas are influenced by original sin. Embedded in theories of schema development is the assumption that maladaptive core beliefs come from dysfunctional childhood homes or poor resolution of psychosocial crises earlier in life. This is true in many situations, such as it is for Denise. Difficult childhoods often contribute to difficulties in adulthood. But notice a troubling implicit assumption: if maladaptive core beliefs come from dysfunctional situations earlier in life, then it should follow that those reared in healthy homes do not struggle with maladaptive core beliefs. Why is it, then, that some psychotherapy clients seem to come from relatively stable and healthy homes?

The philosophical foundation of cognitive therapy, described in chapter three, is based on the assumption that faulty thinking comes from our environment. In this, the ideological base of cognitive therapy is closely related to its predecessor, behavior therapy. Both assume environmental causes for life's problems. While environment is undoubtedly one source of faulty thinking, an Augustinian understanding of original sin helps us identify another source of dysfunction: every person is tainted by sin. This means our thoughts, emotions, will and behaviors are all tinged with a hint of sinfulness from the moment of birth. So even if a person were raised in an ideal home, surrounded by loving parents, appropriate discipline and bountiful opportunities, that person would still struggle with some dysfunctional core beliefs throughout life.

Original sin is important for the Christian therapist to consider for several reasons. First, it means that we are in the same basic situation as our clients. All of us—therapists and clients, and everyone else too—are inclined to think in more or less muddled ways. Those of us who are therapists can help our clients learn to deactivate maladaptive schemas and to identify dysfunctional thoughts, but we should avoid the conclusion that we are the absolute arbiter of good thinking by virtue of our training and experience. Training in counseling, spiritual development and personal therapy will certainly help us think better than we would otherwise think, but some measure of humility is always appropriate. Second, the doctrine of original sin frees us from having to pin down a developmental origin for every maladaptive schema we encounter in therapy. Sometimes cognitive therapists slip into the habit of thinking of themselves as detectives: "here is a maladaptive schema, let's figure out what caused it." Sometimes this detective work is useful, and sometimes it is not. In their zeal to make sense of everything, therapists sometimes pile unwarranted blame on a client's parents and relatives. It is wise to be cautious in this regard, because even clients with excellent parents are capable of having maladaptive schemas. Third, the doctrine of original sin reminds us to be realistic with our outcome goals in psychotherapy. We may help a person understand and deactivate some destructive schemas, and to relate better with others as a result, but even after therapy is over our clients will continue to struggle with some dysfunctional thoughts, beliefs and assumptions. We all struggle as we limp along in a broken world.

Schemas have a cultural dimension. Schemas are embedded in communities and cultures. It is important to learn the cultural significance of a client's beliefs and assumptions as early as possible in therapy, keeping in mind that we therapists are also cultural beings. Self-awareness is essential so that therapists do not slip into a mode of cultural imperialism—trying to persuade a client that the therapist's culturally derived view of reality is better than the client's culturally derived view. It is usually unwise to attempt to question or alter clients' culturally normative schemas. People spend many more hours each week in their cultural milieu than they do in the therapist's office, so any efforts to change a person's culture-based schemas are likely to be both culturally insensitive and ineffective. But then again, some core beliefs may be quite destructive to the client or contrary to a Christian understanding of truth and so Christian clinicians may want to gently probe and explore these beliefs with their clients.

In deciding which schemas to accept as culturally normative and which to challenge, therapists need to watch for two errors (see Counseling Tip 3.6). The first, alpha error, is to attribute too much to culture. Perhaps a client has a deeply dysfunctional schema that is not normative for his or her culture, but the therapist who is unfamiliar with the client's culture simply concludes, "Oh, that's a cultural value." For example, a male client may hold belittling and demeaning views of women that are causing him problems in the workplace. Clearly this schema needs to be addressed in therapy, yet the client appeals to culture as the reason for his misogyny. What is the therapist to do? It is often helpful to consult with another professional familiar with the client's culture. Once the therapist is convinced that the client's schema needs to be addressed in therapy, it still needs to be done in a collaborative way. Sometimes it is helpful to encourage the client to check out a belief with a pastor or other professional with a cultural background similar to the client's.

The second error, beta error, is the tendency to ignore culture. For example, a therapist from an individualistic culture may encourage a client from a collectivist culture to discuss painful memories from childhood without realizing the shame this might bring upon the client's family. Another example is seen when a therapist disparages or openly criticizes a cultural value, labeling it a dysfunctional schema. The schema "I should honor all my parents' wishes" might be quite normative for an adult in a collectivist culture, but to the therapist steeped in individualism it might seem unreasonable and irrational.

Navigating cultural issues in therapy is a bit like learning to dance. It needs to be done collaboratively with the client, but it also involves learning the proper steps in advance. Effective therapists need to study various cultures—reading, attending workshops, interacting with others from unfamiliar cultures and so on—and they also need to develop a safe, trusting relationship with clients so that cultural values and assumptions can be discussed in an open, nonthreatening way during therapy sessions.

Schemas have a faith dimension. Christianity provides its own cultural milieu, which means that those in Christian communities will find their schemas influencing and influenced by the doctrines and teaching of the church. A person's view of God, formed in a community of faith, interacts with schemas in two ways. First, theological beliefs shape our schemas about ourselves in relation to God. Good theology can have profound psychological implications by providing an alternative schema through which to view oneself, the world, and God. For example:

> Think for a moment about how Christ-following develops if you assume God looks at you with disgust, disappointment, frustration or anger. The central feature of any spiritual response to such a God will be an effort to earn his approval. Far from daring to relax in his presence, you will be vigilant to perform as well as you possibly can. . . . What a different relationship begins to develop when you realize that God is head-over-heels in love with you. God is simply giddy about you. He just can't help loving you. And he loves you deeply, recklessly and extravagantly—just as you are. God knows you are a sinner, but your sins do not surprise him. Nor do they reduce in the slightest his love for you. (Benner, 2003, pp. 19-18)

Imagine the power of this theology to a person who struggles with impoverished self-esteem or one who has always believed that absolute perfection is the only acceptable standard. Another example of theology shaping our schemas is seen in the distinction that the apostle Paul makes between the old self and the new self. The new self could be called a new schema. Paul describes a new way of viewing oneself in relation to the gift of new life in Christ—a way characterized by hope and love and many other virtues. The idea of a new identity in Christ is often helpful in forming new, adaptive schemas in Christian clients (see Dobbins, 2004; Roberts, 2001), and also in spiritual formation (Willard, 2002). Of course, it is also true that bad theology can have devastating psychological

IN THE OFFICE 8.2: Naming Culture

Therapists need to be comfortable speaking of culture with clients. When cultural differences go unnamed, they can sometimes create a barrier in the therapeutic relationship. In contrast, identifying cultural values and assumptions can help activate the schemas that are being explored in therapy. The following dialogue is abridged from Mark's video in the APA Psychotherapy Series (McMinn, 2006). Here Mark, a European American male, is talking with Celeste, an African American female, about her belief that she needs to hold things together with extraordinary effort and ability. Enough rapport has been established to enter into a discussion of culture.

Mark: There's a certain mythology around being an African American woman that says you're supposed to hold everything together for your family and your world. How have you experienced that?

Celeste: Exactly. Well, you know, you're not supposed to cry. You're not supposed to express pain or anything else because that's not being strong. . . .

Mark: What do you suppose it means in the New Testament when the apostle Paul writes, "when I am weak, then I am strong"?

Celeste: Um hum. Because you have to lean on God and not on yourself. And at your weakest point is when you can be strong. You have no other choice but to call on God to help you. But the way I was raised, and the church I was raised in, it was opposite.

Mark: It's tough when you have cultural messages saying, "Hold it all together."

Celeste: Exactly. "Something must be wrong with your faith if you're acting like that. You know, that's not the way it's done." I went through that too.

Mark: Well, it's one thing for me to come from a different culture and a different gender and say this has got to be a challenge, but you have to live there every day and experience that pressure to be strong. And I just would guess that that's at times a real burden to bear.

Celeste: It is, too much for anyone to bear. And I believe that's why me and maybe many other people who are in African American culture, especially women, in our churches are not experiencing true spirituality because we're too busy trying to hold it all together and be perfect. We're too busy trying to do this; we're so distracted with that, we can't focus on the spiritual parts of our lives. Note that the goal is not to criticize Celeste's culture. Mark points out a cultural message that complicates Celeste's schema, poses a related question from Scripture and then reflects back Celeste's feelings about the pressure she experiences.

consequences. Most Christian psychologists have stories to tell of clients who have been deeply wounded by a faith community, often because of pernicious theology combined with a power-obsessed leader. Still, it is important to keep in mind that most churches are safe communities where people prosper, grow and learn important truths about God's dealings with humankind. Christian psychologists need to know enough about theology to help clients sift through their theological and psychological perspectives and to make wise choices regarding their church involvement.

A second means of theology interacting with schema can be seen when rigid, maladaptive schemas harm one's view of God. We tend to transpose our ways of viewing the world onto our views of God. The person who believes perfection is the only acceptable standard will probably perceive God to be demanding and harsh. The person who believes others cannot be trusted will have difficulty believing God is good. Effective therapy is not only a way to deactivate these maladaptive schemas, it is often a great help in the process of sanctification. As people begin to see themselves more freely and flexibly, they also begin to see God more clearly.

Taken together, these two observations about theology and schemas affirm what John Calvin wrote in the opening to his *Institutes of the Christian Religion:* knowledge of self and knowledge of God are inseparable. The better we know ourselves, the better we know God, and vice versa. Theologian Ellen Charry correctly affirms the importance of both theology and Christian psychology when she asserts that "Christian psychology properly grounds freedom, pleasure, and happiness in God, restoring a link that modernity severed" (Charry, 2001, p. 132).

This calls us to remember that our greatest hope is found in the transforming power of Christ whose unfathomable love helps free us from all sorts of snares and dangers. Therapy can be part of the sanctification process by helping clients

---

COUNSELING TIP 8.6: Theological Roots

In contemporary life, psychology and theology are separate disciplines. But still, it is important to realize that both fields produce metaphysicians— those who develop particular views of truth and then promote those views to others. Christians in psychology need to have at least a basic understanding of Christian theology in order to be responsible in how they influence others. This can be accomplished by taking theology classes at a nearby seminary or Christian college, reading theology books in addition to psychology, subscribing to theology periodicals, and developing friendships with those who are trained in theology.

---

move toward greater awareness of Christ's sustaining love. This is accomplished in various ways—by providing a safe and accepting environment where clients can sort through their spiritual questions, by affirming God's redemptive presence in a broken world, by praying for clients outside of the session (and perhaps in the session), by encouraging involvement in a healthy church, and by demonstrating the love and grace of Christ in the therapeutic relationship. And sometimes we must simply borrow the confidence of the apostle Paul—a man who understood the deep currents of struggle in life—when he wrote to the church at Philippi: "And I am sure that God, who began the good work within you, will continue his work until it is finally finished on that day when Christ Jesus comes back again" (Phil 1:6).

IP and Recursive Schema Activation

IP differs markedly from standard cognitive therapy when it comes to schema-focused interventions. A standard understanding of cognitive therapy is depicted in figure 8.6. In phase one, the symptom-focused phase of therapy, the therapist identifies and corrects dysfunctional automatic thoughts. This is done using collaborative empiricism—evaluating dysfunctional thoughts by having clients test the evidence that supports or disputes the thoughts (collaborative empiricism was described and illustrated in chapter six). In phase two, which is schema-focused, the therapist and client work together to assess and change underlying core beliefs (Young et al., 2001).

The work is more difficult in phase two than in phase one—because core beliefs are more resistant to change and less conscious than automatic thoughts—but the general strategies are similar. In both cases the therapist first helps the client identify faulty beliefs and then the beliefs are systematically changed through treatment techniques, education and the therapeutic relationship (Young et al., 2003). It is the medical-care paradigm: assess first and then correct the problem.

Though some aspects of this model may be useful in therapy, we believe this view of schema-focused change (phase two) is too limited for various reasons. First, we question the assumption that core beliefs are changed through similar mechanisms as automatic thoughts. This seems to minimize the complexity of

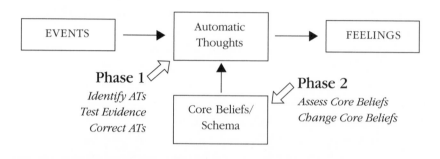

Figure 8.6. A standard cognitive therapy view of treatment

cognitive schemas, which are difficult to change and function mostly on an unconscious level. Therapy is considerably more complex than private lessons in logic. Second, it minimizes the extent to which core beliefs are embedded in a complex array of motivations, behaviors, emotions and physiological responses. Third, it suggests a linear sort of learning where the problem is resolved once the client learns new ways of thinking. In reality, most change is recursive and repetitive—three steps forward, two steps backward. Fourth, this approach seems to minimize the relational forces involved in schemas. Standard cognitive therapists view schemas as substantive constructs contained and resolved within an individual, even if they were initially formed through early childhood relationships. This individualized view of schemas overlooks the reality that humans are constantly relational, always defining themselves in the context of ongoing interactions (Andersen & Chen, 2002). Schemas are dialogical and interactive, and are best understood in the context of human interaction. Finally, this standard understanding of cognitive therapy lends itself to a psychological view of healing that may easily neglect the larger theological narrative that gives hope and meaning to Christians.

The IP model for schema-focused therapy is shown in figure 8.7. Symptom-focused interventions are quite similar to the phase-one interventions involved in standard cognitive therapy. These interventions involve cognitive restructuring, behavioral interventions and perhaps medication. The primary difference between IP and standard cognitive therapy is seen in the second phase of treatment. Rather than using the medical-model metaphor of assessing and changing underlying schemas, in IP we begin with the assumption that core schemas are never fully eradicated. Instead of trying to identify and change maladaptive core beliefs, the strategy in IP is *recursive schema activation*. This means the client's troubling schemas are activated and deactivated in the context of the therapeutic relationship, over and over again, all the time helping to foster the client's ability to stand apart from the core beliefs and reconstruct a new, healthier identity— an outcome known as *decentering*. In decentering the client begins to understand the nature, power and origins of the maladaptive core beliefs while simultaneously developing more conscious control over the schema deactivation process. The relational damage of the past cannot be undone, but it can be understood in the context of today's relationships with God and others. The client gains greater self-understanding and establishes a new identity apart from the maladaptive core beliefs. *The goal, then, is not to eliminate maladaptive schemas but to help clients better understand themselves and become healthier by distancing their true identify from their maladaptive core beliefs.*

Cognitions remain the primary focus of schema-focused IP, but cognitive schemas do not exist in isolation. They are intertwined with emotions, behavioral patterns, physiological responses and motivations, and they are typically activated in the context of relationships or perceived threats to relationships. To activate the schema, the entire mode needs to be activated. This assures that the therapist and client are not merely *talking about* a schema, but are actually *engaging and experiencing* the client's schema.

Recursive schema activation can be supported both psychologically and theologically. Psychologically it seems simplistic to assume that schemas formed through years of childhood dysfunction can be fully reversed by meeting once or twice a week with a therapist for several months. Rather than trying to utterly eradicate schemas that were formed at critical developmental periods in the client's life, the goal in IP is developing enough understanding and insight to grieve past losses and begin forming a hope for the future. Theologically it is important to remember that humans are in an alien state. Our true identity is found in the profound and abiding love of God revealed in Christ, but sin has corrupted every aspect of the world in which we live. Our own sins, the sins of others and the general brokenness of our world blind us from our true identity as God's beloved children. The great hope of the Christian life is not disengagement from living in a broken world but establishing an identity in Christ that gives a new vantage point in understanding ourselves and the world in which we live.

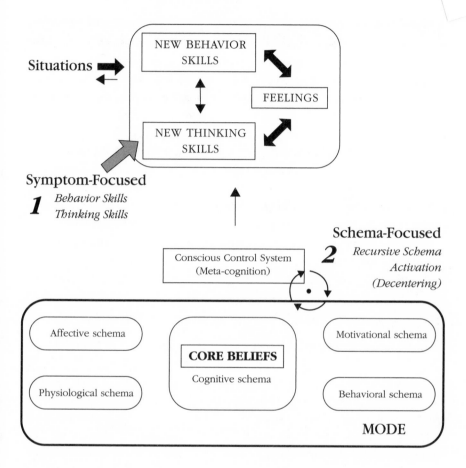

Figure 8.7. The IP view of schema-focused interventions: Therapy progresses by recursive schema activation

This distinction between standard cognitive therapy and IP is crucial. Standard cognitive therapy functions with a parse-and-correct mentality, as if pure cognitions can be extracted from human experience, revised and then infused back into the broader themes of life. In contrast, IP assumes greater complexity and multidimensionality to schemas. Pure cognitions can never be extracted from coexisting emotions, motivations, sensations and relationships. But this is not merely a concession that life is messier than most cognitive therapists imply, it is also a recognition that God created humans with amazing capacities to relate, feel and think and that all these capacities are worth considering in therapy.

COUNSELING TIP 8.7: Embracing the Struggle

Recursive schema activation assumes that changing one's schemas requires more than cognitive techniques. The old and new ways of thinking are repeatedly juxtaposed and compared. Over time the client begins to prefer the new vantage point but still struggles with old patterns, especially in times of stress.

Is this not the way life works for all of us? In our fallen state we rarely find a complete and permanent solution for the struggles of life. Struggle is part of the process of Christian living (Rom 7:21-25). It riddles us repeatedly, even as we grow in character and grace. The mark of Christian maturity is not the absence of struggle but the willingness to bring our struggles into the light of God's healing presence and to live authentically with one another.

Summary

Schemas are like cognitive roadmaps that help us interpret the world, but this metaphor fails to capture the complexity of schemas for a variety of reasons. We do not simply interpret the events of life through schemas like we might read a map to discover our location; we actually change life events based on our interpretations and subsequent actions. In this sense a schema is a dynamic map, constantly being redrawn based on our interactions in life. Schemas are adaptive and maladaptive, moving us closer or further from health, and are highly interrelated with other human systems such as emotion, motivation, physiology and behavior. Schemas are multidimensional: they are influenced by one's developmental history, interpersonal relationships, culture and faith. In all these ways we see the importance and power of schemas in a person's life—much more than can be captured by likening a schema to a map.

Schema-focused therapy involves deliberate activation and deactivation of the client's schemas in the therapy office. Using recursive schema activation, the client learns to make connections between past and present, emotions and cognitions, unconscious and conscious, events and meaning-making, and schema activation and deactivation. This is discussed more in the next chapter.

References

Andersen, S. M., & Chen, S. (2002). The relational self: An interpersonal social-cognitive theory. *Psychological Review, 109,* 619-45.

Beck, A. T. (1996). Beyond belief: A theory of modes, personality, and psycho-pathology. In P. M. Sakovskis (Ed.), *Frontiers of cognitive therapy* (pp. 1-25). New York: Guilford.

Beck, A. T., Rush, A. J., Shaw, B. F., & Emery, G. (1979). *Cognitive therapy of depression.* New York: Guilford, 1979.

Beck, J. S. (1995). *Cognitive therapy: Basics and beyond.* New York: Guilford.

Benner, D. G. (2003). *Surrender to love: Discovering the heart of Christian spirituality.* Downers Grove, IL: InterVarsity Press.

Charry, E. T. (2001). Theology after psychology. In M. R. McMinn & T. R. Phillips (Eds.), *Care for the soul: Exploring the interface of psychology & theology* (pp. 118-33). Downers Grove, IL: InterVarsity Press.

Dobbins, R. D. (2004). Spiritual interventions in the treatment of dysthmia and alcoholism. In P. S. Richards & A. E. Bergin (Eds.), *Casebook for a spiritual strategy in counseling in psychotherapy* (pp. 105-17). Washington, DC: American Psychological Association.

Erikson, E. (1950). *Childhood and society* (2nd ed.). New York: Norton.

Jones, S. L., & Butman, R. E. (1991). *Modern psychotherapies: A comprehensive Christian appraisal.* Downers Grove, IL: InterVarsity Press.

Linehan, M. M. (1993). *Cognitive-behavioral treatment of borderline personality disorder.* New York: Guilford.

Lukoff, D., & Lu, F. (2005). *A transpersonal-integrative approach to spiritually oriented psychotherapy.* In L. Sperry & E. P. Shafranske (Eds.), *Spiritually oriented psychotherapy.* Washington, DC: American Psychological Association.

Mahoney, M. J. (2003). *Constructive psychotherapy: A practical guide.* New York: Guilford.

McMinn, M. R. (1991). *Cognitive therapy techniques in Christian counseling.* Waco, TX: Word Books. This book is out of print, and can be downloaded at www.markmcminn.com.

McMinn, M. R. (2006). *Christian counseling* [video in APA Psychotherapy Series]. Washington, DC: American Psychological Association.

McMinn, M. R. (In press). *Sin and grace in Christian counseling.* Downers Grove, IL: InterVarsity Press.

Needleman, L. D. (1999). *Cognitive case conceptualization: A guidebook for practitioners.* Mahwah, NJ: Erlbaum.

Roberts, R. C. (2001). Outline of Pauline psychotherapy. In M. R. McMinn & T. R. Phillips (Eds.), *Care for the soul: Exploring the interface of psychology & theology* (pp. 134-63). Downers Grove, IL: InterVarsity Press.

Safran, J. D. (1998). *Widening the scope of cognitive therapy: The therapeutic relationship, emotion, and the process of change.* Northvale, NJ: Aronson.

Safran, J. D., & Segal, Z. V. (1990). *Interpersonal process in cognitive therapy.* New York: Basic Books.

Segal, Z. V., Williams, J. M. G., & Teasdale, J. D. (2002). *Mindfulness-based cognitive therapy for depression—a new approach to preventing relapse.* New York: Guilford.

Willard, D. (2002). *Renovation of the heart: Putting on the character of Christ.* Colorado Springs: NavPress.

Young, J. E., Klosko, J. S., & Weishaar, M. E. (2003). *Schema therapy: A practitioner's guide.* New York: Guilford.

Young, J. E., Weinberger, A. D., & Beck, A. T. (2001). Cognitive therapy for depression. In D. H. Barlow (Ed.), *Clinical handbook of psychological disorders* (3rd ed.) (pp. 264-308). New York: Guilford.

9

Applying Schema-Focused Interventions in Treating Depression

A WELL-KNOWN COMEDIAN ONCE BEMOANED THAT DEPRESSION is normal for him because he keeps getting his tongue caught in the roller of his electronic typewriter. It seems a bizarre statement, especially now that typewriters are obsolete, but then again comedians seem to thrive on bizarre statements—juxtaposing the untenable with normal life. The tongue in the typewriter is untenable, but the notion of feeling down or discouraged is quite normal. Almost everyone has experienced feeling "blue" or discouraged from time to time, perhaps related to normal mood fluctuations, disappointments in life or significant losses.

When feelings of sadness persist, or when they are accompanied by appetite and sleep problems, concentration and memory difficulties, hopelessness, or overwhelming feelings of shame and self-hate then some sort of treatment for depression is warranted. Depressive episodes can range in magnitude, from relatively mild adjustment disorders to persistent chronic feelings of low-level depression (dysthymia) to episodes of acute, severe depression (major depression). Related mood disorders—bipolar disorders and cyclothymia—may include a cycling between depressed states and manic or hypo-manic states where a person experiences excessive energy, sleeplessness, impulsive and reckless behavior, and inflated confidence. Cognitive therapy methods have been applied to both unipolar (Beck, Rush, Shaw & Emery, 1979; Greenberger & Padesky, 1995) and bipolar mood disorders (Basco & Rush, 1996; Newman, Leahy, Beck, Reilly-Harrington & Gyulai, 2002).

Depression has sometimes been called the common cold of psychiatry because of its prevalence, with over 300 million people around the world suffering from its grip. But the consequences can be much harsher than those of a common cold, with approximately 800,000 suicides being completed each year by depressed individuals (Koenig, McCullough & Larson, 2001). And the problem of depression seems to be getting worse; epidemiologic studies reveal a striking increase in depression among those in developed countries, especially since World War II (Klerman & Weissman, 1989).

Avoid Point-and-Click Treatments

In this chapter we illustrate schema-focused interventions by discussing the treatment of depression, but we do so with some trepidation. A casual reading might lend itself to a point-and-click mentality for IP: use symptom-focused interventions for anxiety disorders and schema-focused interventions for depression. This is an incorrect and potentially dangerous interpretation for several reasons. First, psychological disorders are imperfect designations. Diagnosing someone with an anxiety or depressive disorder may be helpful in communicating with other professionals and selecting treatment options, but a diagnosis does not capture the complexity of a human being. Many clients have a mix of anxiety and depression symptoms (Kush, 2004). Some have experienced anxiety or depression for many years and in response to many different life circumstances, whereas others' symptoms seem to be limited to particular circumstances or have a sudden onset. Some clients have many supportive relationships and positive life events outside of therapy, and others do not. Many more complexities could be mentioned.

Second, the goals and course of treatment vary from individual to individual, regardless of diagnosis. Some clients with anxiety disorders are not fully treated with symptom-focused interventions, and the client and therapist decide mutually to pursue the greater self-awareness that comes from exploring schemas. Conversely, some clients with simple depressions respond quickly to symptom-focused interventions and do not desire or require more extensive treatment.

Third, there are many human struggles and problems that do not fit in the three categories of disorders that we discuss in chapters seven, nine and eleven. Anxiety, depression and personality disorders are common problems faced in Christian counseling and psychotherapy, but there are many other problems for which IP can also be helpful. Because this is not a book on psychopathology, we have not attempted to cover these disorders exhaustively. Rather, we have selected three categories of disorders in order to illustrate how IP works.

Fourth, in actual practice the distinctions between symptom-focused, schema-focused and relationship-focused interventions are not nearly as distinct as we present in this book; the experienced therapist moves adeptly through different intervention domains, seamlessly integrating symptom-focused, schema-focused and relationally focused methods. The artistic elements and spiritual discernment involved in therapy are oversimplified whenever they are squeezed into words and chapters of a book.

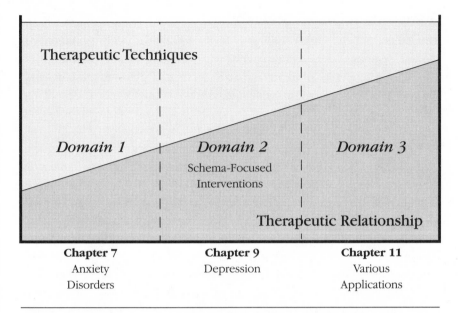

Figure 9.1. Domains of intervention in relation to therapeutic techniques and relationship

For all these reasons, it is important to see the complexities of each therapy relationship and to craft a unique intervention accordingly. We use anxiety disorders to illustrate symptom-focused treatments and depression for schema-focused treatments because there is a general trend for depression to require more intensive treatment than anxiety disorders, as illustrated in figure 9.1, but the variability of different clients, therapists and life situations requires a careful assessment process and collaborative decision making at various points in the treatment process.

Symptom-based cognitive therapy interventions for depression have been researched extensively. In their meta-analysis of twelve studies, Westen and Morrison (2001) conclude that these treatments are useful in the short run, but most clients do not maintain improvement over a follow-up period. Others reviewing the research literature have concurred: "In recent years there has been growing recognition that depression is often a recurrent or chronic disorder and that it is insufficient to simply treat depressed patients until their symptoms have remitted" (Klein et al., 2004, p. 681).

Thus, recent adaptations of cognitive therapy for depression have proposed two levels of treatment that correspond to the first two domains of intervention in IP: symptom reduction and schema-focused treatment for relapse prevention (Young, Weinberger & Beck, 2001).

Symptom-Focused Interventions

Though this is a chapter on schema-focused interventions, it is important to begin with symptom-focused interventions when working with depressed individuals. Easing symptoms of depression early in therapy helps establish a strong therapeutic alliance, provides clients with emotional energy to look deeper into their lives and often helps improve the client's social support network outside of therapy. Several symptom-focused strategies can be useful.

Medication. Antidepressant medications are frequently prescribed, and at an increasing rate (Koenig et al., 2001). Medication can be helpful for depression, especially when combined with therapy. Clients with bipolar disorder almost certainly need to be on medication, and medication compliance often becomes an important part of the psychotherapy work (Newman et al., 2002).

Some clients and therapists will have a negative predisposition toward medication for mood disorders, but this is often based on one of several common misunderstandings. First, some people fear that antidepressant medication is habit-forming or comes with disastrous side effects. Unlike some of the medications used for anxiety disorders, antidepressant medications are not habit-forming. All medications have side effects, but the newer antidepressants (known as serotonin specific reuptake inhibitors, or SSRIs) have minimal side effects compared to the older varieties (tricyclic antidepressants and monoamine oxidase inhibitors). Second, clients may not believe antidepressants are effective. Some cognitive therapists are fond of citing studies that demonstrate cognitive therapy is at least as effective as medication, but this is not a consistent finding, and almost all of these studies were conducted with the older tricyclic antidepressants (TCAs) rather than the newer SSRIs. Perhaps the best conclusion about medication for depression is offered by the National Institute of Mental Health:

> Some people with milder forms may do well with psychotherapy alone. People with moderate to severe depression most often benefit from antidepressants. Most do best with combined treatment: medication to gain relatively quick symptom relief and psychotherapy to learn more effective ways to deal with life's problems, including depression. (National Institute of Mental Health, 2000)

Third, some people may object to medication for spiritual or theological reasons, thinking that if they would simply rely more on God then they would not need biological intervention for their mood. This view, though apparently quite prevalent among contemporary Christians, is based on an inadequate view of human sinfulness. A comprehensive theology of sin reminds us that every part of humanity is broken, including biology. In our fallen world, some are born with

COUNSELING TIP 9.1: Both/And vs. Either-Or

Some physicians argue that depression should be treated with medication alone; they see little or no benefit in psychotherapy. Some psychotherapists suggest just the opposite—that therapy is better than medication.

What does the research suggest? Butler and Beck (2001) reviewed fourteen meta-analyses on the effectiveness of cognitive therapy and concluded that cognitive therapy alone is slightly more effective than medication alone. But the average effect sizes were low (ES = 0.38) and antidepressant medications have improved since the time of the studies Butler and Beck reviewed. More recent research suggests medication alone may be slightly more effective than cognitive therapy alone under some circumstances (DeRubeis et al., 2005), but cognitive therapy appears to have a more enduring effect than antidepressant medications (Hollon et al., 2005).

It seems best to stop asking the either-or question. It is clear from past research that both psychotherapy and medication are helpful with depression. Today most researchers and clinicians conclude that a combination of the two is likely to work better than either alone, especially with treating those with moderate to severe depression. The both/and approach makes more sense than the either-or approach.

a genetic predisposition to high blood pressure, cholesterol problems and heart disease. In the same way, some are predisposed to mood disorders such as depression or bipolar disorder. Certainly it is true that environment and choices play a role also, just as they do with heart disease, but these do not mitigate the biological factors involved. Spiritual factors may play a role in depression, but refusing medication for spiritual reasons is to imply that the cause of and proper solution for depression are exclusively spiritual and immaterial. This verges on gnosticism. Many spiritual giants over the centuries have struggled with depression, and the evidence implicating biological factors in depression is overwhelming. It is unreasonable to attribute depression to spiritual deficits alone.

Behavioral techniques. Depression can have a stifling effect on human freedom. Under the gloomy cloud of depression, people may stay curled in bed or on the couch in front of the television and fail to engage in the more rigorous and pleasant activities of life. Behavioral techniques can be used to help depressed individuals reclaim a sense of engagement and pleasure in life.

Christians believe that God created earth and then pronounced it good. Though earth is now contaminated by the effects of sin, creation is still good.

The physical world is to be celebrated and enjoyed: taking a walk in the woods, having gourmet coffee with friends, enjoying a chocolate chip cookie, going swimming in a lake and so on. Sometimes those who are depressed have difficulty enjoying the pleasures of a good creation because they lack the motivation to do so.

A. T. Beck et al. (1979) describe a weekly activity schedule, where the therapist and client take time in session to develop an hour-by-hour plan in the client's immediate future. This is done collaboratively, with the goal of helping the client become more proactive in scheduling activities in advance. The client then monitors activities throughout the week, filling out a form such as the one shown in figure 9.2. Inside of each cell, the client writes what happened during that hour (e.g., watched television, drove to work, fixed dinner, went bowling), how much pleasure the activity brought (on a 1-5 pleasure scale, with 5 being the highest) and how great a sense of accomplishment resulted from the activity (also rated on a 1-5 scale, known as a mastery scale).

The weekly activity schedule helps clients remember that they can set and accomplish goals. During each session the therapist encourages the client to keep planning every day on an hour-by-hour basis, acknowledging that no one meets all of their goals, and then reviews the client's activities from the previous days—congratulating the client on successes and collaborating with the client to

Table 9.2. Weekly Activity Schedule

	Sunday	Monday	Tuesday	Wednesday	Thursday	Friday	Saturday
8-9 a.m.							
9-10 a.m.							
10-11 a.m.							
11 a.m.-12 p.m.							
12-1 p.m.							
1-2 p.m.							
2-3 p.m.							
3-4 p.m.							
4-5 p.m.							
5-6 p.m.							
6-7 p.m.							
7-8 p.m.							
8 p.m.-12 a.m.							

increase both the pleasure and sense of mastery for activities in the future. Initially the goals need to be small and manageable, but as the client gains momentum, the tasks can be more substantial.

Assertiveness training is another behavioral technique that can be useful in symptom-focused intervention for depression (e.g., Alberti & Emmons, 2001; Koch & Haugk, 1992). Relationships often suffer in the midst of depression, and it is helpful for clients to learn direct and forthright communication skills. Assertiveness training can be accomplished by teaching specific principles of communication, reviewing interpersonal interactions from the recent past, anticipating forthcoming social encounters and role-playing. Properly conceived, assertive communication is a direct expression of thoughts and feelings, though it also is socially appropriate and takes into account the feelings of others while considering their welfare (Rimm & Masters, 1979). Perhaps the best model of assertiveness is found in the Gospels: Jesus struck a perfect balance between honest disclosure and merciful kindness, often shocking people with his directness and yet filled with compassion for humanity.

Cognitive restructuring. All the cognitive restructuring techniques introduced in chapter six are also used in treating depression. The dysfunctional thought record is used in collaborative manner, as are the other countering techniques described in chapter six. There are two fundamental differences when applying cognitive restructuring techniques in a schema-focused intervention rather than a symptom-focused intervention: the complexity of monitoring affects and looking beneath surface thoughts for core beliefs.

First, the affective focus is more complex and central to the conversation. The schema-focused therapist needs to be highly attuned to the interconnections of the various emotions being explored. With anxiety, the client is typically anticipating some future event and feeling fear or dread of what might happen. With depression, the focus is often on losses and guilt in the recent or distant past as well as gloomy interpretations of the present and future. Many clients have both anxiety and depression, which are likely to coincide with depressive regret for the past and anxious apprehension. At times it is important to disentangle the depression and anxiety as much as possible in order to identify dysfunctional beliefs and assumptions. At other times it is important to bring them together and explore how the anxiety and depression are related.

In the following example, carried over from the previous chapter, the client begins with a statement that contains both depressive and anxious elements. The therapist then moves the client toward a specific situation to focus on the depressive thoughts and feelings. Near the end of the dialogue the conversation comes back to how the anxiety and depression may be related.

IN THE OFFICE 9.1: Assertiveness

Assertiveness is found between the extremes of passivity and aggressiveness. It involves helping people express themselves honestly, but within the confines of social appropriateness.

Jared: It just doesn't seem right to me. I realize her work is demanding, but so is mine and I've been feeling so down lately it seems like all I can do just to go to work and come home. I mean, I'm happy to cook sometimes, but I would really like for her to do some of the cooking too. She just seems to assume that I'll cook every night while she catches up on e-mail or talks on her cell phone. I don't think she realizes how depressed I have been feeling and how hard it is to do things.

Clark: I can see how this is a frustration for you. How are you planning to handle it?

Jared: That's just it. I don't know what to do. Sometimes I just sit silently during dinner because I feel so down and so angry. Sometimes I get real upset about it, but she just yells back and tells me how busy she is, how she makes more money than I do, and then we don't talk for a couple days and I feel worse than ever.

Clark: So one option is to say nothing—to sit silently at dinner because you're upset. Another option is to lose your temper, and that leads to tension between you and Sue. Are there any other ways you might be able to communicate your concern and frustration?

Jared: I can't think of any.

Clark: Well, for example, could you ask to have a conversation, maybe at a coffee shop where things won't spiral into an argument?

Jared: Yeah, maybe, but what would I say?

Clark: The goal would be to express your feelings as clearly as possible, without blaming or insulting her, and to stay calm in the process. Maybe something like, "Sue, it seems that I've been doing most of the cooking lately. I'm certainly happy to cook some of the time, but I'm feeling frustrated and uncomfortable with the assumption that I do most or all of cooking."

Jared: Yeah, I could probably do something like that. I'm not sure how she will respond, but it's worth trying. I agree that Sue and I need to talk about this.

Here the therapist helps the client find an assertive voice rather than resorting to quiet passivity or aggressive expressions of anger.

Denise:	I never should have married him. It wasn't fair to him. I didn't realize how bad I would be as a wife. And I can't see how I'll get any better either. I'm afraid I'll just be this distant and prickly person for as long as we're married.
Mark:	Let's work with this. Can you think of a time in the last day or so when you have been saying to yourself that you shouldn't have married Don?
Denise:	Well, last night after that dinner he cooked. I was sitting there during dinner—we didn't talk much—just thinking about how much I've let him down. It was so kind for him to come home early and cook and put on music, and I'm just this loser wife who doesn't even feel that grateful for it.
Mark:	So we have the situation. You're sitting at the table last night, telling yourself you're a loser wife. What emotions are you feeling as you sit there?
Denise:	Mostly regret for marrying him, but then I feel bad for even thinking that way.
Mark:	Okay, let's look at the regret first. On a scale of 1 to 10, with 10 being the most regret you have ever felt, how regretful were you during dinner last night?
Denise:	Probably about an 8.
Mark:	And then you said you were feeling bad for thinking that way too.
Denise:	Yeah, really guilty, like what kind of a wife sits here eating a fabulous dinner her husband makes and thinks about why she shouldn't have married him?
Mark:	Okay, and how would you rate that feeling of guilt?
Denise:	Maybe about a 7.
Mark:	So both of these are strong feelings, regret and guilt. You're probably feeling them a bit even now as you're looking back at last night.
Denise:	Yeah, definitely.
Mark:	You mentioned earlier that you are a loser wife who doesn't feel grateful and that you shouldn't have married Don. What other thoughts were you having?
Denise:	I was thinking about how beautiful things used to be in our relationship and just wondering what happened.

Mark: Were you coming to any conclusions?

Denise: I think it's me. Don's really trying. I think somehow I just don't know how to be a good wife. And it's not much fun for him being around someone who feels depressed a lot.

Mark: "Things used to be so good, and now they aren't because I'm a loser wife."

Denise: Yeah.

Mark: Okay, I've been writing these thoughts and feelings down in the three columns I've shown you before. Does this look about right in terms of what was happening last night?

Situation	Feelings	Automatic Thoughts
Sitting quietly during dinner	Regret 8	I shouldn't have married him.
	Guilty 7	Things used to be so good, but now they aren't because I'm a loser wife.

Denise: Yeah. It looks pretty sick, huh?

Mark: Tell me what you mean. It seems like you're quite upset with yourself.

Denise: [softly crying] Who has these thoughts? What kind of a crazy person am I? I'm just some terrible partner I don't even recognize.

Mark: [Sits silently, validating Denise's tears]

Mark: You're sitting here right now, tears flowing down your cheeks, sort of yelling at yourself. "What kind of person am I? Who has these kinds of thoughts? I'm a loser wife. I'm a terrible partner."

Denise: Uh-huh. [followed by silence]

Mark: Tell me about the tears.

Denise: [still crying] I feel so vulnerable, so scared.

Mark: Because people who get this close can hurt you.

Denise: [nods]

Mark: So maybe this is about fear, about protecting yourself, about staying safe.

From here the therapist and client continue a discussion of how Denise's protective impulses may be causing her to respond to Don in ways that are damaging to their marriage. Ultimately the dysfunctional thought record may look something like this:

Situation	Feelings	Automatic Thoughts	Rational Response
Sitting quietly during dinner	Regret 8	I shouldn't have married him.	Marriage scares me. I am protecting myself in ways I don't fully understand yet.
	Guilty 7	Things used to be so good, but now they aren't because I'm a loser wife.	

Notice in this example that the therapist first teases apart the anxiety and depression by focusing on the depression and then ultimately comes back to connect the two when Denise describes how scared she is feeling about Don's desire to be close.

Second, in schema-focused therapy the therapist is continually looking below the automatic thoughts to find intermediate and core beliefs. In the previous example, some of Denise's cognitions went beneath the surface level of automatic thoughts. She uttered intermediate beliefs such as, "I'm a loser wife" and "I'm a terrible partner." These statements are more general and pervasive—and undoubtedly more damaging—than the situation-specific thoughts pertaining to dinner last night. Even more important are the schema that get activated near the end of the conversation, where she begins to describe how vulnerable and scared she feels. These feelings are based on deep core beliefs that she cannot yet articulate but are essential to understand in helping her move toward healing. It requires discernment and experience on the therapist's part to distinguish between surface-level thoughts and underlying cognitive structures, and then to pursue the underlying beliefs for purposes of deeper therapeutic change.

Schema-Focused Interventions

As described in chapter eight, and illustrated in figures 8.5 and 8.6, the schema-focused phase of treatment is conceptually different in IP than in standard cognitive therapy. The typical model for schema-based treatments involves two steps: diagnosing the underlying schema and correcting it through various techniques. In contrast, the goal in IP involves only a single recursive process—activating and deactivating schemas in the therapy office in order to help the client develop greater self-awareness and begin to develop an identity apart from the depressive maladaptive schemas. We call this process recursive schema activation, with the goal of decentering.

Decentering is a common term in the cognitive therapy literature, so it is worth distinguishing its common use from our slightly nuanced perspective. Most often, decentering is seen as a symptom-based strategy to help a client learn to argue against dysfunctional automatic thoughts. For example, when using the dysfunctional thought record, a therapist might use the following strategy.

Pavel: I just feel like this whole thing is my fault. I mean, if I wouldn't have shown up late for work, then I would have been at that meeting and maybe I could have talked my boss out of firing Sarah. She's been a good employee, and I really think she could have overcome this drug problem with treatment. I don't think he needed to fire her.

Clark: So the way this thought goes is, "I should have been at that meeting, then I could have kept this unfair firing from happening."

Pavel: Right.

Clark: Which then makes you feel guilty, as if it's your responsibility that Sarah got fired.

Pavel: Yeah, more or less.

Clark: Now I'm just wondering, what would someone else who knew the situation have to say about all this? Maybe another one of your co-workers—would they also think that you are responsible?

Pavel: Well no. I mean, they all understand how crazy traffic can be. They understand why I was late. And it was Sarah's third relapse. I don't think anyone else would blame me.

In this example, which is typical of symptom-based therapy, the therapist uses a decentering technique to get the client looking at an automatic thought from another vantage point. Our use of decentering in schema-based interventions is both similar and dissimilar to this example. It is similar insofar as the goal of both symptom-based and schema-based decentering is to help a client gain a new perspective on a life situation. It is dissimilar in that schema-based decentering cannot rely on such a simple logical analysis. Schemas are not changed with logic alone, but by giving clients opportunities to gain insight and practice new ways of viewing their lives. This is the point of recursive schema activation, to give clients many opportunities, session after session, to decenter from the deep, persistent themes of their lives that can never be fully obliterated. Whereas standard cognitive therapists might use decentering as a therapeutic technique to remove irrational thinking, we think of decentering as a life skill that helps people cope with the deep irrationalities of human existence that will never be fully resolved this side of heaven.

Recursive schema activation can be viewed in a Christian theological context, requiring a brief excursion into the work of Abraham Kuyper, a nineteenth-century Dutch Reformed theologian who made a distinction between normalists and abnormalists (Moroney, 2000). Normalists look at the world and assume that what we see is basically normal. From a normalist perspective, the world is not in drastic need of renewal or redemption. The world is simply as good or as bad as we choose to make it. Abnormalists, in contrast, view the world as fundamentally broken, skewed or distorted. Christians believe that we live in an abnormal state—biologically, socially, psychologically, volitionally, emotionally—and yearn for things to be made right. Creation groans for redemption: "All creation anticipates the day when it will join God's children in glorious freedom from death and decay. For we know that all creation has been groaning as in the pains of childhood right up to the present time" (Rom 8:21-22).

Standard models of cognitive therapy are derived from normalist assumptions. The goal of therapy is to identify and correct maladaptive schemas, and from a normalist perspective there is no reason to think it cannot be done. Thus the curative effect of cognitive therapy occurs through correcting faulty schemas. In contrast, IP is built on an abnormalist assumption. The world is fallen and in need of redemption. This means that each of us struggles with personal sin and the consequences of others' sin and that our thinking is not simply misinformed—it is malignant to the core. The goal of correcting our schemas and seeing the world with precision is unrealistic. Rather, the goal should be to gain distance from our maladaptive schemas, to be able to see them as something other than how we want to see the world even as they continue to influence us. It is this distance—this ability to decenter and evaluate our schemas and identify ourselves apart from our greatest struggles—that has a curative effect. This is the psychology of the apostle Paul (see Roberts, 2001) who recognized an ongoing struggle with the old self but still chose to distance himself and identify with a new self in Christ.

By way of analogy, consider the work of a therapist. Therapists actively engage in a genuine relationship with their clients. It is real and immediate and significant. But they also learn to distance themselves from the relationship itself, as if they are standing outside and observing at the same time as being actively engaged in the relationship. They are both relating and meta-relating (i.e., ob-

COUNSELING TIP 9.2: Foreigners and Nomads

Christianity itself involves decentering. The author of Hebrews lists many biblical heroes, noting how they were people of great faith. In describing the commonality among these people of faith, the author writes, "All these faithful ones died without receiving what God had promised them, but they saw it all from a distance and welcomed the promises of God. They agreed that they were no more than foreigners and nomads here on earth. And obviously people who talk like that are looking forward to a country they can call their own . . . a heavenly homeland" (Heb 11:13-16). God has blessed us with a good creation and calls us to enjoy it fully, and yet we are also to decenter from present circumstances in order to see our identity in Christ and to value our heavenly homeland. In a sense, Christians live in two places at once. Remembering this helps us live patiently and gently in the midst of today's travails.

When working with Christian clients, it is often helpful to find subtle reminders that their identity is not limited to the difficult circumstances they currently face. This should not be done in a trite, spiritual-cliché sort of way but by occasionally reflecting on the meaning of Christian faith. For example, a therapist and Christian client might pray briefly during a session, inviting God's grace to be revealed in their conversation. Or a therapist may refer to God's superordinate view: "What do you envision God is thinking and feeling about you right now?" Or a question can be posed in order to bring a faith-based perspective into the process of recursive schema activation. For example, to the client who feels a desperate need to maintain competence and control, a therapist might ponder aloud: "What do you suppose the apostle Paul meant when he wrote that when he is weak, then he is strong?"

serving and relating to the relationship as it develops). In training, therapists audiotape or videotape their sessions in order to develop skills of meta-relating, and even after training many therapists continue in supervision to continue building meta-relating skills. In the same way, each of us is living our lives in the context of certain schemas that help us interpret the world. The goal of schema-focused IP is to help clients learn meta-cognitive skills to stand outside the schemas that influence them every day. So they learn to observe their schemas even as they live them out. This distancing and learning meta-cognition occurs through repeated schema activation and discussions with the therapist. Just as a therapist in training might listen to an audiotape session with a supervisor and discuss its meaning, so a client learns to observe the schemas that influence everyday life and discuss their meaning with the therapist. Eventually the maladaptive schema becomes an object to be observed and critiqued as the client develops a new identity apart from old ways of experiencing the world. This is similar to what McWilliams (1994) calls an "observing ego" (p. 56), which is a client's capacity to both observe and experience the self.

This notion of helping clients distance themselves from their maladaptive schemas has similarities to Segal, Williams and Teasdale's (2002) mindfulness-based cognitive therapy (MBCT). In MBCT, depressed clients learn to gain a moment-by-moment awareness of their feelings, thoughts and bodily sensations. The better they get at mindfulness skills, the more they move away from the vortex of depressogenic thoughts. MBCT helps reduce relapse rates among those prone to recurrent depression (Ma & Teasdale, 2004).

Notice also the similarity between distancing oneself from a troubling schema and the practices of spirituality. Contemplative prayer, for example, is a way to remove oneself from the midst of personal troubles by drawing close to God. Foster (1992) describes this as a shift in one's center of gravity:

> In the beginning we are indeed the subject and the center of our prayers. But in God's time and in God's way a Copernican revolution takes place in our heart. Slowly, almost imperceptibly, there is a shift in our center of gravity. We pass from thinking of God as part of our life to the realization that we are part of his life. Wondrously and mysteriously God moves from the periphery of our prayer experience to the center. A conversion of the heart takes place, a transformation of the spirit. (p. 15)

Of course prayer and therapy are different activities, but they share in common the recursive practice of decentering. In prayer one focuses on gaining God's perspective, which allows some distance from the troubles of daily living (even those who speak of *centering prayer* are presuming that one first decenters from the clutter of life and then centers down into the presence of God). In therapy clients gain a new perspective through a temporary therapeutic relationship, and in so doing they gain distance from the schemas that cause them troubles. Sometimes in Christian therapy both of these are combined as the therapist and client use prayer in combination with standard therapeutic methods to help the client decenter.

There is not a long list of techniques for schema-focused IP for depression. In fact, there is only one primary strategy. The sole focus is on recursive schema activation, helping the client by activating and deactivating maladaptive schemas over and over again. With each recursion the client and therapist discuss the effects of maladaptive schemas, and the client inches toward a new identity that stands opposed to former ways of thinking.

Though recursive schema activation is the overarching strategy for schema-focused interventions in IP, some of the methods suggested by other cognitive therapists can still be useful (e.g., J. S. Beck, 1995; McMinn, 1991; Needleman, 1999; Young, Klosko & Weishaar, 2003). Rather than using these methods to identify and change schemas, we think of these as ways to facilitate recursive schema activation with the goal of promoting decentering.

Life history. Early in the therapy relationship it is important to get a detailed life history. This helps the therapist understand the context for the client's current situation. Almost every therapist will ask about family of origin, childhood relationships with peers, previous psychological problems and treatments, education, occupation, religious values, physical and psychological trauma, legal problems, drug and alcohol use, current relationships, and so on. But the integrative psychotherapist is looking at this information from two sets of lenses: first to understand the client's life context and second to see any recurrent themes that could be identified as maladaptive schemas. Does the client seem to have a history of feeling unworthy and inadequate? Have there been longstanding problems with perceiving rejection from others? Does the client have difficulty trusting others? Have there been control struggles in the client's relationships?

Having a client talk about the past is much more than historical research for the benefit of gathering information. Schemas are often activated in the present moment as clients describe past events. When Denise recounts an angry tirade by her drunken father, she is not simply telling her story, she is also reexperiencing it in the context of the therapeutic relationship. It is important for the therapist to recognize her vulnerability as she tells stories, to observe her emotions and cognitions, and to give her opportunity to revisit the story again in later sessions. Important stories from childhood need to be experienced and reexperienced in therapy because each time the schemas are activated and deactivated it gives the client an opportunity to reevaluate and find meaning in events of the past. And not just the bad stories deserve telling; it is also important to invite the delightful stories of childhood and to consider how these stories relate to the maladaptive schemas the client is battling.

Schema inventories. Some therapists find it useful to give schema inventories early in therapy to help determine which maladaptive schemas affect the client most. One option is the Young Schema Questionnaire (see www .schematherapy.com; Young et al., 2003), which is a self-report inventory to assess schemas.

COUNSELING TIP 9.3: Historical Analysis

It is often helpful to create a diagram of the client's history. A large piece of paper, such as those in an artist's tablet, can be used. First, draw a straight line from one end of the paper to the other, and then place hash marks at regular intervals (one inch or two centimeters works well). Then number each mark from 0 to 18 and use this as a timeline when recording memories the client describes. Add an entry on the diagram each time the client recalls an important memory from childhood—whether pleasant, unpleasant or neutral. The end result will be a visual picture of the client's developmental past. This is particularly helpful for therapists who have many details from many different clients to remember, and also for clients who may have never noticed the ordering of particular formative events in childhood. Furthermore, it gives the client reason to return to formative developmental events over and over in therapy, each time activating an old schema and learning to build an identity as an observer of the schema.

Schema inventories can be useful, but keep in mind that schemas are viewed as relational and dynamic in IP, and not as static and substantive. In other words, one does not have a schema in the same way one has a particular waist size or eye color. Schemas emerge in the context of interpersonal relationships, and they often change from one situation to the next. So though it is sometimes helpful to use schema inventories to help identify particular areas of vulnerability and to get a dialogue about schemas started, it is important that the therapist interpret the results cautiously and flexibly.

The greatest benefit of schema inventories may simply be in their ability to get a client thinking and talking about schemas that may contribute to depression. These conversations then lead to schema activation. As the therapist and client talk about the schemas that are being activated in the session and work together to deactivate them, it helps the client gain capacity for meta-cognitive appraisal.

Discussions of faith. For clients with Christian beliefs, it is often helpful to discuss their views of God. Christian clients who struggle with depression may be prone to view God as harsh, punitive, capricious or disapproving. These views of God can be discussed in therapy, not in a theoretical or academic way, but in the context of daily experiences. Again, this provides opportunity to activate and evaluate maladaptive schemas.

Geri: Sometimes I wonder what God thinks of me.

Mark: That's an interesting thought. What do you think?

Geri: It's probably not good. I mean my life is pretty messed up. Some of
           the things I have done are not pretty.

Mark: So the idea is that God is disappointed with you?

Geri: Yeah, and probably pretty upset.

Mark: Like you're just a big screw-up or something.

Geri: That's about it, I guess.

Mark: Where do you suppose you get your ideas about how God views
           you?

Notice in this example that the therapist is not so much trying to teach proper theology as to explore the psychological dimensions of the client's faith beliefs. As long as psychological debris is cluttering her faith, it is unlikely that this client will be able to understand the depth of God's love for her. At times it is fitting to discuss doctrinal truths in therapy, but often psychotherapy is pre-theology, helping clear the path for a person to see God more clearly. Knowledge of self and knowledge of God are closely related (Calvin, 1559/1997).

Moving from specific to general. Words are the currency of therapy. Clients come each session to exchange words regarding the events and meaning of life. In IP the therapist uses words to move between specific events and more general conclusions about life, and in the moving from specific to general the therapist is trying to identify and activate schemas. The typical pattern involves two steps. First, the therapist encourages discussion of a recent, specific event.

Bill: I've been feeling pretty down this week. It seems like I'm feeling
           worse than ever.

Clark: I'm sorry to hear that. I would really like to get a sense of how this
           looks. Maybe you can think of a time in the last twenty-four hours
           or so when you have been feeling really low, and let's look at it.

Bill: It seems like most of the time lately. [pause] I suppose one of the
           worst times was just driving to your office today.

Clark.   Okay. So you're in the car, driving here, feeling pretty down. Let's
           look at that more closely. What sort of thoughts and feelings were
           you having?

Recent, specific events are much more likely to engage emotions than a general conversation. In this dialogue we see the therapist nudging the client toward specificity. But once the specific anecdote is identified, the second step is to listen for words that reveal general conclusions about life. These general conclusions are the schemas that need to be evaluated in schema-focused therapy.

Bill: I was just feeling so depressed. I don't know, I've been coming here for two months now, and I'm not sure I'm getting any better.

Clark: Okay, I'm getting the picture. You're driving here, thinking about how you're doing in therapy, and you're feeling discouraged about the progress you're making.

Bill: Yeah, I guess so. I mean, it's weird. I usually feel better when I leave, and some days I think I'm improving, but then sometimes I wonder if I'll ever get better. I hope that doesn't sound offensive. I'm not blaming you. I just feel like I'm beyond hope or something.

Clark: It seems important to you that I not feel offended.

Bill: Oh, definitely. I really think you're a good therapist. I just don't know what's wrong with me, why I can't get better.

Clark: So I'm doing okay, but you're a mess. Am I hearing that right?

Bill: [chuckles softly] Yeah, I guess.

Here the therapist moves back to a more general belief, activating a schema about being defective and inadequate. At this point the conversation moves to the schema rather than the specific thoughts about progress in therapy.

Looking for themes. Throughout the symptom-focused phase of treatment, the therapist and client discuss various anecdotes as part of the dysfunctional thought record and other cognitive restructuring methods. In each of these discussions the therapist notices the underlying themes with the goal of understanding and activating the client's most common schemas. Bill, the client who feels he is not getting better in therapy, came a few minutes late to the second session and apologized profusely. In the third session he mentioned being passed over for a promotion at work but reassured the therapist that it is probably for the best. The fifth session involved the dysfunctional thought record. Bill described a lonely evening in a hotel room during a regional sales conference. He sat alone watching television, wishing he could be enjoying dinner with his coworkers yet feeling convinced they didn't want him along because no one called to invite him. The seventh session began with the previous discussion about how he is not getting better in therapy. At this point the therapist notes a theme in Bill's stories—he seems to see himself as defective and unworthy. When Bill blames himself for not getting better in therapy, his therapist uses the opportunity to activate the underlying schema.

Clark: So I'm doing okay, but you're a mess. Am I hearing that right?

Bill: [chuckles softly] Yeah, I guess.

Clark: Do you see that elsewhere in your life? Assuming that you're to blame for things not going right?

Bill: Sometimes I do that.

Clark: I'm just wondering where you learned that.

Bill: Oh, it comes very naturally to me. It was clear in my family that if something went wrong it was my fault.

Clark: Interesting. It seems you still carry that with you.

In this example the therapist moves Bill toward a schema-focused discussion by pointing out a theme that has emerged from previous sessions.

Evoking emotion. When therapists have difficulty activating cognitive schemas, it is often because they are conducting therapy at an intellectual level. Emotions need to be engaged in order to access schemas. This does not mean that every client needs to cry every session, but that conversations are lived experiences more than just dialogues about some other experience. In the following dialogue the therapist makes an effort to engage Bill's emotions by pointing out sadness in his voice.

Bill: Oh, it comes very naturally to me. It was clear in my family that if something went wrong it was my fault.

Clark: Interesting. It seems you still carry that with you.

Bill: Maybe. It's probably better than blaming you for me still being depressed [chuckles].

Clark: Well, thanks for the benefit of the doubt. It's very kind. What would it feel like to be that kind to yourself? To give yourself the benefit of the doubt?

Bill: Hmm. I don't know. I'm not sure I've ever tried it.

Clark: [pause] Bill, when you said that just now, I heard pain in your voice.

Bill: Yeah, it hurts. [pause] It hurts. I feel pretty terrible about myself.

Clark: So your pain is embedded in shame. As if something about you is terribly defective and unlovable.

Bill: [goes on to recount a story of childhood abuse]

Stopping to notice a shaky voice or tears in the client's eyes can be an effective way to evoke emotion, especially once adequate rapport is built. There are various other ways therapists can evoke emotions—leaning forward and soften-

---

COUNSELING TIP 9.4: Disconnected from Feelings

Occasionally a client may seem utterly disconnected from feelings. An adult might describe memories of being sexually molested by a relative and not shed a tear throughout the entire story. Another person might tell of the horrors of combat, complete with images of watching friends being gunned down, and not display any emotion while offering the ghastly details. Still other times, a client may display incongruent emotions—laughing while speaking of a lonely childhood, for example.

Pointing out the incongruity between emotion and the story can be a good way to begin exploring the client's feelings. But also keep in mind that there may be a reason for the person to split off these emotions. Perhaps an abuse survivor learned to deny feelings in order to cope with the trauma. Another client may come from a family where certain emotions were seen as a sign of weakness. Maybe the demands of combat did not allow the luxury of considering feelings.

When a client is disconnected from feelings, it is usually wise to point it out and then to be patient. It may take many weeks or months for the client to feel safe enough in therapy to begin exploring painful emotions.

---

ing one's voice during vulnerable conversations, role-playing, prayer and meditation exercises, to name a few.

Guided discovery. Standard cognitive therapy texts discuss a technique known as guided discovery (e.g., J. S. Beck, 1995). In this the therapist keeps asking for the meaning beneath a thought in order to get to more general core beliefs. This is done collaboratively using Socratic questioning so the client experiences the process of discovering an underlying schema rather than simply having it interpreted by the therapist. This has also been called the downward arrow technique because it helps move the conversation to deeper levels of cognition. The following dialogues show the difference between a therapist who uses guided discovery to help Bill discover the underlying schema on his own and a therapist who simply interprets what the underlying schema is.

Bill: I was feeling pretty down on Tuesday night. Some coworkers and I went to Cincinnati for a regional conference, and after the meeting they ended up going out to dinner and I just stayed in my hotel room and watched television.

Clark: You're feeling down, sitting in front of the television, and what are
            you saying to yourself?

Bill: I was sort of surprised they didn't invite me.

Guided Discovery   ⟵ ⟶   **Therapist Interpretation**

Clark: What did it mean to you, that   Clark: So here again we see this
        they didn't invite you?   shame schema. You're sitting
                                                      alone in the room telling
Bill: Well, you know, that they just   yourself that if people really
        don't care that much about me.   cared then they would have
                                                      invited you. Then I suppose
Clark: And did your thoughts go   the next logical conclusion is
        even further? If you think   that something must be
        they don't care about you,   wrong with you or else they
        what does that mean to you?   would have invited you.

Bill: Just that there is something   Bill: Yeah, I think that's what I
        really wrong with me. I've   was thinking.
        worked with these guys for
        years now. There must be
        some reason they don't want
        to hang out with me.

The more collaborative style of guided discovery is preferred because the client is doing the work of discovering his beliefs, making genuine schema activation much more likely than when the therapist simply interprets what the client may have been thinking and feeling.

Guided discovery can be a useful way to activate schemas, but the amount of questioning it entails can sometimes feel disingenuous or put the client on the defensive. It seems best to balance the questions of guided discover with empathic reflections and affective exploration in order to build rapport while moving toward deeper cognitive structures.

Imagery and meditative prayer. Though most therapy occurs in a verbal context, imagery and meditation techniques can also be used to activate schemas. Sometimes imagery can reach deep into a client's experiential world in ways that are not accessible with words alone. One option is to use an imagery technique early in the therapy relationship in order to help identify the schemas that are most troubling to a depressed client (Young et al., 2003). This involves having the client relax, with eyes closed, imagine being a safe place and allow an image to come to mind. Once the image is present, the client sits calmly and ponders the thoughts and feelings that are being stirred and

---

COUNSELING TIP 9.5: To Pray or Not to Pray

Prayer has been a healing force in people's lives over many centuries. Many Christian counselors and psychotherapists use prayer in their work, noting its power in bringing hope and healing to hurting people.

There is a time and a place for prayer in psychotherapy, but there are also times when prayer should be avoided. If the therapist and client are talking to each other through prayer, rather than to God, then it may be modeling a nonassertive, indirect mode of communication. When a client avoids emotion and personal insight by relying on trite spiritual clichés, then prayer may actually foster greater defensiveness. And sometimes prayer is more self-focused than God-focused; Jesus was particularly offended by those who prayed for personal credibility (see Mt 6:5-18; Lk 18:9-14).

Sometimes clients will ask a therapist to pray, and some may even use the prayer standard to determine if a therapist is providing "Christian counseling"—those therapists who pray with clients are deemed to be Christian counselors and those who do not are considered wolves in sheep's clothing. Praying with a client can be healing, especially when it helps a person experience God's presence and grace. It can also be damaging if it contributes to unhealthy defenses, indirect communication or narcissistically focused views of God.

---

then reports them to the therapist at the conclusion of the imagery exercise. The client can be instructed to invoke an image from the present or from the past, depending on whether the therapist is looking for current situations or developmental events.

Imagery can also be used to deactivate schemas. For example, a client who is experiencing a distressing and painful schema can be taught to relax and imagine going to a safe and beautiful place. Often this can be coupled with spiritual meditation, as in an exercise suggested by Postema (1985) where he has people silently repeat, over and over, "I belong to God," in a reverent and meditative posture.

Though there are many factors to consider in deciding how to use prayer and meditation in psychotherapy (McMinn, 1996), meditative prayer exercises can be quite helpful in moving a person beneath intellectual conversation to see deeper emotional and spiritual currents (see In the Office 7.2). Sometimes prayerful meditation can help clients access their schemas in ways that normal therapeutic dialogue cannot (see McMinn, 2006 for an example of this).

However, this very fact should cause Christian therapists to be cautious with their use of prayer in therapy because spiritual disciplines ought not to be motivated primarily by their psychological benefits. God is undoubtedly pleased that prayer can help therapy clients access experiences and perspectives that words alone cannot access, and the healing power of prayer has been evident for many centuries, but let us be cautious not to do with prayer what many therapists have already done with forgiveness by turning a time-honored spiritual practice into a therapeutic technique designed to make people feel better.

Summary. Getting a life history, using schema inventories, discussions of faith, moving from specific to general, looking for themes, evoking emotions, guided discovery, and using imagery and meditative prayer are various ways to accomplish recursive schema activation. There are many other ways that emerge out of a therapist's own personal style. The important point is not identifying specific techniques as much as finding creative ways to activate and deactivate maladaptive schemas over and over, each time helping the client to make connections between past and present, conscious and unconscious, thoughts and feelings, and to gain some distance so the maladaptive schemas become object rather than subject. This is the essence of meta-cognition—being able to step outside of a schema to evaluate it from a different vantage point and, in the process, to begin telling a new story with one's life.

Recursive Schema Activation as Bridge Building

One can think of the integrative psychotherapist as a bridge-builder, continually helping clients span gaps between cognition and emotion, unconscious and conscious processes, past and present, and so on. The bridge-building nature of IP can be illustrated by looking again at the dialogue between Denise and her therapist as Denise works through feelings of regret and guilt.

Bridging symptom-focused and schema-focused interventions. Near the end of the segment provided earlier in this chapter we saw the therapist moving beyond a symptom-focused intervention to activate a deeper schema. What began as a symptom-focused strategy using the dysfunctional thought record to sort out thoughts and feelings moves into schema activation once the therapist allowed Denise to sit in silence with her emotions.

Mark: You're sitting here right now, tears flowing down your cheeks, sort of yelling at yourself, "What kind of person am I? Who has these kinds of thoughts? I'm a loser wife. I'm a terrible person."

Denise: Uh-huh. [followed by silence]

Mark: Tell me about the tears.

Denise: [still crying] I feel so vulnerable, so scared.

Mark: Because people who get this close can hurt you.

Denise: [nods]

Mark: So maybe this is about fear, about protecting yourself, about staying safe.

This demonstrates moving between a symptom-focused approach, which tends to look at thoughts and feelings in the present moment, and a schema-focused approach, which traces present thoughts and feelings to more pervasive beliefs and emotions.

Bridging cognition and emotion. Notice also the connections being made between cognition and affect. The therapist is calling attention to Denise's tears, highlighting the emotion she is feeling with the hope of encouraging deeper exploration. At the same time, the therapist is reflecting back cognitions, helping Denise see the connections between her thoughts and her feelings.

Mark: You're sitting here right now, tears flowing down your cheeks, sort of yelling at yourself, "What kind of person am I? Who has this kind of thoughts? I'm a loser wife. I'm a terrible person."

In IP the therapist is continually helping a client explore both thoughts and feelings. This is important for both theological and psychological reasons.

Theologically, it is important to keep in mind the breadth of human capacity. God made humans to function in many different ways. We are physical, social, volitional, spiritual, emotional, cognitive and so much more. Thus, a Christian view of persons insists on the multidimensionality of the whole person, placed in a social and spiritual context (Willard, 2002). Whenever an approach to soul care isolates one aspect of human nature and isolates others, it is likely to be narrow and incomplete. Some approaches to psychotherapy have focused almost exclusively on emotions, others almost exclusively on cognitions. Some have ignored spiritual matters; others have focused so much on spiritual matters that they seem to overlook the other dimensions of experience. In IP we attempt to build bridges between the various dimensions of human experience.

Psychologically, Epstein (1994) offers a compelling rationale for cognitive-experiential self theory (CEST). According to CEST, humans have two systems working simultaneously: one cognitive and one experiential. The experiential system is relational, associational and emotional. The cognitive system is logical, analytical, rational and systematic. Both systems are constantly operating. This can be seen throughout normal daily activities, as illustrated by the following example.

	Experiential	**Cognitive**
The alarm clock blares at 6:00 a.m.	Ashley groans in disbelief, her body craving more sleep.	She reminds herself that work starts in 60 minutes, so she needs to get out of bed.
Lunch with coworkers	Ashley enjoys the fun and laughter of being with friends, and the pleasure of good food.	She ponders how many calories and fat grams the club sandwich may contain.
After lunch	She feels a vague sense of guilt for having cheesecake in addition to her club sandwich.	Ashley reminds herself that these group lunches only occur once a month and that most other days she limits what she eats for lunch.
Evening	She enjoys the companionship of her husband as they sit and watch a rented movie together.	She scoffs at the unrealistic plot of the movie.

CEST emphasizes the importance of bridging experiential and rational ways of knowing. Likewise, integrative psychotherapists are wise to consider both cognitive and experiential dimensions of their clients, to help them build bridges between the two, and to do so while maintaining a view of the whole person in social and spiritual context.

Bridging unconscious and conscious processes. Another sort of bridge-building occurs in recursive schema activation as the therapist helps the client connect unconscious and conscious processes. A common adage in psychology is that the things we don't know about ourselves have the most power over us. This is consistent with the theological notion of the noetic effects of sin (Moroney, 2000)—that we have a sort of blindness or intellectual dullness because of our sinful state, and this blindness keeps us from seeing ourselves correctly in relation to God. Psychological growth and sanctification both involve becoming less blind as we gradually gain insight into our vulnerabilities, strengths and weaknesses. This is a relational process; we gain insight as we relate with God and others. Cognitive schemas typically function beneath conscious awareness until there is a relationship that promotes greater self-awareness. By activating

COUNSELING TIP 9.6: Johari Window

The now-famous Johari window was developed in the 1950s by researchers Joe Luft and Harry Ingram (Johari comes from the combination of their first names). It is a simple 2 x 2 grid that has profound implications for how a person relates to others. When relating it to individual therapy, here is how the grid looks:

	What the Client Knows About Self	What the Client Does Not Know About Self
What the Therapist Knows About the Client	Quadrant 1: Open Information	Quadrant 2: Blind Area
What the Therapist Does Not Know About the Client	Quadrant 3: Hidden Area	Quadrant 4: Unknown Information

Some areas are known to both the client and the therapist. Initially this may be limited to basic information—job, marital status, appearance, presenting problem and so on. But over time this open information grows as the therapist gets to know the client better.

Hidden areas are those known to the client but not the therapist. As trust develops, the client feels safe disclosing these hidden experiences and feelings. It is not unusual for a client to disclose some hidden part of life for the first time to a therapist.

Blind areas are evident to the therapist but not the client. This can range from trivial things (e.g., the client doesn't realize he has mustard on his shirt) to important (e.g., the therapist notices how the client makes a joke whenever she begins feeling sad in the therapy sessions). Psychotherapy helps people see some of their blind areas.

Some areas are unknown to the therapist and the client. Perhaps a client eats rudely in public, alienating colleagues and friends. The client does not know because no one has told him, and the therapist does not know because eating is not part of the therapy sessions.

Ideally, therapy fosters an expansion of quadrant 1 as the person becomes more self-aware and disclosing. Quadrants 2 and 3 shrink accordingly. Quadrant 4 may or may not change much early in therapy, but over time the therapist and client are likely to discover new facets of the client's personality and interpersonal style.

schemas in IP, the therapist helps reveal unconscious processes.

In the previous therapy dialogue, activating Denise's emotions helped her gain access to some less conscious schema that seemed to be operating. She shifted suddenly from her guilt-inducing thoughts of being a bad wife to feeling scared and vulnerable. Next, the therapist, who understands something of Denise's childhood from earlier sessions, helps construct a bridge from the current situation to deeper themes that are functioning at a less conscious level. This conversation is not only about Denise's current marriage but also about some deeper belief in life that getting close to someone means she will be hurt, that people cannot be trusted. As the conversation continues, we see the therapist activating Denise's self-protection mode in order to help her gain access to these unconscious cognitive schemas.

Mark: So maybe this is about fear, about protecting yourself, about staying safe.

Denise: I guess so.

Mark: Let's talk more about the tears. What's going on inside?

Denise: I feel scared and ashamed. [pause] I don't know what to do. I just want to get in the car and drive and just keep driving forever.

Mark: You want to escape the fear.

Denise: Yeah. [sobs]

Mark: Denise, is this feeling familiar? Have you ever had it before?

Denise: Sometimes my dad would come home at midnight in a rage, screaming at my mom and anyone else he could find, and I would always feel so terrified. I usually hid under my bed or in the closet, and I felt so helpless.

Mark: Lying in the darkness, wishing you could escape the fear.

Denise: Yeah, and then I felt so bad for Mom, because I knew she could never escape it. She just had to get up the next morning and go to work as if nothing had happened.

Mark: So even if she wanted to escape, she never really could, which meant you couldn't either.

Denise: [sobs]

Mark: "I shouldn't get close to people, because if I do they may hurt me and I won't be able to escape."

Denise: That's what I did with Don last night at dinner.

In this example the therapist helps Denise gain access to a cognitive schema that was birthed long ago but still haunts her. Unconscious forces have moved a step closer toward conscious awareness.

Bridging past and present, constructing a story. Notice also how the therapist bridges past and present using Denise's emotions as the connecting point ("Denise, is this a familiar feeling?"). By activating Denise's self-protection mode and then asking her to connect present and past feelings, the therapist is working alongside Denise to tell her story.

Denise: That's sort of what I did with Don last night at dinner.

Mark: Maybe some old fears were haunting you last night.

Denise: I think that's why I feel so terrible. It's not fair to Don.

Mark: I see what you mean. It's like something in the past is contaminating the present.

This is not merely a passive telling of the past, as might be the case in catharsis-based therapies where the goal is simply to release the pain of some malignant trauma. Rather, the therapist and client co-construct a story to connect past and present.

> One of the most powerful developments of recent years in the field of psychotherapy has been the realization that human beings are embodied stories and creative storytellers. The "narrative turn," as it has been called, has been a central theme of constructivism. We are not simply the bearers or vehicles of our lives; we are also the authors. We write each moment at multiple levels. . . . Among other things, this means that psychotherapy is fundamentally an endeavor in which therapists are attempting to help clients reclaim their *author*-ity and write different and more fulfilling dimensions into their lives. (Mahoney, 2003, p. 100)

Of course Christianity imposes some limits on our story-telling. Truth is not only constructed; it is also revealed. But Christianity also involves a narrative that intersects with our personal stories.

Bridging psychology and Christian spirituality. Throughout the Old Testament we see God telling the people of Israel to build altars, practice rituals and establish ceremonies to help them tell their story. They were called to remember that they were God's chosen people, called out of slavery, blessed with bounty and promised a future. In the New Testament the story is expanded as Gentiles are grafted into the tree of God's favor through the atoning work of Jesus Christ (see Rom 11). And ever since, throughout the history of Christianity, believers have gathered to tell the old, old story through worship and fellowship. It is grand story, a meta-narrative, but it is also a highly personal story that gives each individual Christian a renewed perspective on the past, present and future.

Christian therapists, often highly trained in psychology, sometimes neglect the importance of the Christian narrative as they help their clients tell their stories. In the previous example, Denise has made a connection between past trauma in her childhood home and her unfair treatment of Don in her current marriage. How will the story go from here? Psychologically speaking, it will be important for Denise to gain insight into her past, see the connections between old schemas and current assumptions, and eventually free herself from superimposing past experiences onto her daily experiences with Don. These are good strategies that will help Denise, but there is even more hope to offer from a Christian perspective. A theological vantage point allows us to transcend the specific circumstances of our life stories and simultaneously live in a bigger story. Christians have faced great tragedies throughout the centuries—including great injustice, poverty and persecution as heinous as being rolled up and burned as human candles in the Roman coliseum—and yet they have endured these things by placing themselves in some bigger narrative pertaining to faith. Theologian Ellen Charry (2004) writes elegantly about something she calls "virtual salvation." Just as computerized virtual reality allows us to live in one world and experience another, so a theological perspective allows us to live in one set of circumstances while placing our identity in another. Ultimately, the success of Denise's therapy will not be limited to whatever psychological insight she can gain; she will also be helped by her ability to form her identity in Christ as God's beloved child.

Denise: I think that's why I feel so terrible. It's not fair to Don.

Mark: I see what you mean. It's like something in the past is contaminating the present.

Denise: Yeah.

Mark: It is as if your identity with Don is being defined by your father's drunken rages.

Denise: That's terrible!

Mark: Well, it's understandable given what you have been through. But I agree it's not what you want. How else might you understand your identity, if you were able to define yourself apart from your father?

Denise: I want to see myself as a loving wife and as a follower of Christ. That stuff with my father happened a long time ago, and I just want to be able to grow; to stop giving him that much power over me.

Mark: What would it look like to see yourself as God's child instead of the child of an angry, drunk man?

This, of course, is only the first venture into a spiritual topic that will need to

IN THE OFFICE 9.2: Therapy and Preaching

The Christian story is often associated with the activities of corporate worship, especially with the centerpiece of most church services—the sermon. Sermons are enormously important, providing a weekly reminder of truth in the midst of a society that wants to turn truth upside down and elevate self to the status of God.

As important as sermons are in the spiritual health of Christians, preaching and psychotherapy should not be confused. When the methods of preaching and the methods of psychotherapy get conflated, it makes for ineffective therapy (and probably bad preaching too). Sermons are based on propositional truth and methods of proclamation; psychotherapy is based on dialogue, mutual exploration and personal discovery.

Denise: Sometimes I wonder if this marriage even has a chance. I want it to work, but I feel so mixed up inside that I don't know if we can last for even five years, let alone fifty.

In response to this statement, a proclamation of truth might look something like this:

Mark: It's important to keep your Christian values in mind. The Bible doesn't give you much choice in the matter. Jesus taught that the only legitimate reason for divorce is in situations involving adultery.

Denise: Yeah, I suppose you're right. I need to keep remembering that.

Notice that this proclamation, though true, shuts Denise down and prevents her from exploring her thoughts and feelings. Psychotherapy uses a different methodology, still keeping propositional truth in mind but helping the client explore related thoughts and feelings.

Mark: That must be part of the fear you were talking about earlier.

Denise: Yeah, it is. I stood at the altar and promised before God to stay married to this man, and now I'm not sure if I can keep my promise. That's terrifying to me.

Mark: I see what you mean. You have a lot at stake here: a promise to Don and a promise before God.

Denise: Uh hum. I've got to figure out this fear in me. Why do I want so badly to turn and run from those promises?

In this example the therapist is still able to affirm Christian teachings about divorce but do so in a dialogical way that keeps the client exploring rather than shutting off conversation.

be revisited many times in the course of therapy. Notice that this conversation is not a therapist "preaching at" a client but comes in the context of a holistic psychological engagement with the client's emotions and cognitions. At its best IP helps clients construct life stories that are rooted in a Christian view of redemption.

Bridging events and meaning-making in search of realistic optimism. Consider two ineffective approaches to therapy, both of them caricatures of psychotherapy.

Approach #1: Dr. Bea Dire
The blues are playing in Dr. Dire's waiting room. Her office is decorated in gray, with dim lighting and a faded tapestry lining the ceiling. Each week her clients lie on the couch and tell dismal stories of their past. Dr. Dire pushes for details, always empathizing with the pain and struggle her clients must have faced. Week after week her clients come and tell the events of yesteryear. Week after week Dr. Dire listens, hands tissues to her clients, tells them the time is almost up and receives their personal checks.

Approach #2: Dr. I. M. Bliss
Dr. Bliss plays '70s love songs in the waiting room. His office is painted in pastel colors with wall hangings to promote well-worn clichés. One of his wall hangings reads, "Let bygones be bygones." Another says, "Today is the first day of the rest of your life." Dr. Bliss doesn't talk with clients about their past; he teaches his clients to see the possibilities in life rather than focusing on problems. Think positively, look for the best, don't worry, be happy. He also takes personal checks— both for the therapy he provides and for his latest self-help book on how to overcome depression and love life again.

Neither of these extremes is realistic, but Drs. Dire and Bliss provide anchors for a continuum between event-oriented therapy and meaning-oriented therapy. Dr. Dire is content to help her clients recount the painful events of the past but seems unprepared to help them move forward in life. In reality, past and present events are important to understand because they hold the key to schemas contributing to the client's depression, but it does little good to spend hour after hour recounting past events without moving in a direction that helps the client find greater hope and meaning. Dr. Bliss is at the other extreme, minimizing the significance of past events and encouraging his clients to construct meaning out of sheer willpower. Finding meaning is an important part of therapy, but if the meanings are not embedded in the real stories of the client's life then therapy is little more than the clichés that hang on Dr. Bliss's walls.

Recursive schema activation helps a therapist bridge events and meaning-making without getting stuck in the extremes represented by Drs. Dire and Bliss.

Clients with depression tend to come to therapy with a negative view of themselves, the world around them and the future (A. T. Beck et al., 1979), so an important goal of therapy is to help them gain a more positive, optimistic view of life even as they trudge through difficult and painful thoughts and feelings from the past and present. In IP the client is given repeated opportunities to tell the stories of life while reshaping the meaning assigned to them. Over time, as clients gain some perceptual distance from the schemas that cause them trouble, they often move from despairing interpretations of life events to more hopeful interpretations. It is not that the events themselves are hopeful—it would be damaging to convince a client that a traumatic past is a good thing—but even bad events can lead to hopeful meanings.

An important strategy in IP is to distinguish between events and the meaning assigned to those events. Both are perceived imperfectly, but it is more useful to help clients reshape their interpretation of meaning than rehearsing the events themselves. Schneider (2001) makes an important distinction between fuzzy knowledge and fuzzy meaning, where fuzzy knowledge occurs as a result of being unclear or uncertain about factual reality, and fuzzy meaning occurs when we are uncertain about how to interpret a particular event. For example, a person may not recall exactly what happened to cause an accident on the expressway. "Did the other driver swerve into my lane, or was I the one swerving?" This is fuzzy knowledge. Reality itself is not fuzzy—something objective actually happened on the expressway to cause the accident—but humans are imperfect at perceiving and recalling events, so there is fuzziness to one's knowledge of reality. But then the driver goes on to attribute meaning to the accident. Perhaps the driver concludes, "What a great blessing that my life was spared in that accident; God is good." Or, "I can't believe what idiots we have on this expressway; life is so messed up." Here we see the fuzziness of meaning. The same event can be interpreted in various ways, leading to different meanings.

Recursive schema activation gives opportunity for the client to tell the events of life, and though it is undoubtedly true that some of the client's knowledge is fuzzy, the goal of schema activation is not to linger on the stories themselves or attempt to remove the fuzziness of knowledge. Rather, the goal is to use the fuzziness of meaning as the basis for a more hopeful, optimistic view of reality. With recursive schema activation the client is given repeated opportunities to alter the meaning associated with particular events. Schneider (2001) describes how realism and optimism can coincide as people learn to construct meanings that include a leniency for the past (i.e., giving oneself and others the "benefit of the doubt"), an appreciation of the present moment and opportunities in the future. It is striking to see the similarities between Schneider's psychological

principles for realistic optimism and views of Christian spirituality that emphasize grace and forgiveness for the past, gratitude for the present moment and
hope for the future.

Optimism is complicated. On one hand, if therapists such as Dr. Bliss are trite
or forceful in promoting a naive optimism, it may communicate a lack of understanding and clients may become resistant and increasingly despairing. On the
other hand, when therapists such as Dr. Dire spend all their time empathizing
with clients and validating their painful feelings, they may never help move the
client to a more hopeful place. Recursive schema activation provides opportunities for realistic optimism by allowing the therapist and client to revisit and
reconsider the relationships between life events and the meanings assigned to
those events.

Bridging schema activation and deactivation. In chapter eight we introduced the two ways of deactivating a schema: either life circumstances change
or the client learns specific skills to deactivate it. Sometimes therapy helps a client change life circumstances, but most often clients improve by learning skills
of deactivating maladaptive schemas. One of the benefits of recursive schema
activation in therapy is that each time a schema is activated the client gets to
practice deactivating it. A graph of schema activation and deactivation in IP
would look a bit like a sine wave, with oscillations occurring throughout each
session. Each time the therapist helps the client engage a schema, emotional
arousal increases, and then after several seconds or minutes, the client deactivates the schema and experiences relative calm. Each time this cycle recurs, the
client is gaining practice at schema deactivation.

In Denise's situation, she seems to have old schemas about dangerous relationships emerge whenever she begins to feel close to Don. Rather than trying
to rid her of this persistent schema, which probably will not go away easily, it
is more reasonable to help her develop skills to deactivate the schema when it
emerges and distance herself from it. At the beginning of therapy Denise may
experience this sort of sequence in her experience of Don:

Beginning of Therapy

1. Walks in the door, sees Don preparing a romantic meal.
2. Thinks to herself, *This is too close. I'll get hurt.*
3. Experiences urges to escape, even to leave the marriage.
4. Tense and difficult evening with Don.

Whereas the goal of standard cognitive therapy might be to rid Denise of her
faulty schema (step 2 above), in IP we suspect Denise will always be plagued

COUNSELING TIP 9.7: Finding Meaning and Theodicy

Helping clients find meaning in the midst of difficult life events inevitably brings up the question of theodicy (Hall & Johnson, 2001). How can an all-loving and all-powerful God allow bad things to happen to people? This question is centuries old, challenging even the most articulate philosophers and theologians.

To some extent the problem is irresolvable—a mystery too big for human understanding. But still it is good to ponder the theodicy question and to remember three essential truths of the Christian faith.

First, suffering is a reflection of things being awry in our world more than God's initial design. The world is broken by human sin. This does not mean that suffering is a direct consequence of a person's individual transgressions, but that every part of the world is corrupted by the collective effects of sin. In a skewed, broken existence such as this, some people bear more than their share of suffering.

Second, God is still sovereign, which means that when bad things happen God has allowed them to occur. God could chose to calm every hurricane, quell each terrorist attack, quiet every anguished soul and cure all cancer, but often chooses not to. This has something to do with God's choice to give humans free will to choose right and wrong, though the connections between our immoral choices and human suffering are, at best, complex and oblique.

Third, God suffers too. God is not callous or uncaring about human suffering but experiences anguish over the broken state of this world. God's anguish is so great that the eternal Word chose to become flesh and dwell among us (Jn 1:14) to bring hope and redemption. We have not yet seen the full weight of God's glorious redemption, but we catch glimpses. And by faith we know that the best is yet to come.

> That is why we never give up. Though our bodies are dying, our spirits are being renewed every day. For our present troubles are quite small and won't last very long. Yet they produce for us an immeasurably great glory that will last forever! So we don't look at the troubles we can see right now; rather, we look forward to what we have not yet seen. For the troubles we see will soon be over, but the joys to come will last forever. (2 Cor 4:16-18)

with this schema. Rather than ridding her of it, the goal is for her to learn effective ways to deactivate the schema. By the end of therapy, the sequence might look more like this:

End of Therapy

1. Walks in the door, sees Don preparing a romantic meal.
2. Thinks to herself, *This is too close. I'll get hurt.*
3. Deactivates the schema, remembering she is safe in a loving marriage and that her identity is in Christ.
4. Enjoys the evening with Don.

Denise's success in therapy is partly related to the skills she will develop in deactivating her maladaptive schema, and this will come through repeated practice in the therapy sessions.

Near the beginning of therapy it is often the therapist that helps the client deactivate a schema. The therapist may do this through teaching relaxation skills, collaborative empiricism, discussing the reasons why a schema is faulty and so on. As therapy progresses, the client begins to learn these same skills. At this point the therapist becomes less active in schema deactivation and spends more time observing and affirming how the client deactivates the maladaptive schemas.

One warning is in order. Not every client has the psychological resources to deactivate schemas once they are activated. This is especially important to keep in mind when helping people who meet criteria for borderline personality disorder. Treating individuals with personality disorders will be discussed more in chapters ten and eleven.

   Bridging schema-focused and relationship-focused interventions. Recursive schema activation also has the advantage of enhancing the working alliance between therapist and client. Clients learn that they can express painful feelings and thoughts and that the therapist will respond respectfully and empathically. As schemas are identified and discussed, clients begin to see that the therapeutic relationship is somehow different than previous relationships in which the maladaptive schemas were formed. The deepening therapeutic alliance creates the possibility for relationship-focused treatment, described in chapters ten and eleven.

References

Alberti, R., & Emmons, M. (2001). *Your perfect right* (8th ed.). Atascadero, CA: Impact Publishers.

Basco, M. R., & Rush, A. J. (1996). *Cognitive-behavioral therapy for bipolar disorder.* New York: Guilford.

Beck, A. T., Rush, A. J., Shaw, B. F., & Emery, G. (1979). *Cognitive therapy of depression.* New York: Guilford.

Beck, J. S. (1995). *Cognitive therapy: Basics and beyond.* New York: Guilford.

Butler, A. C., & Beck, J. S. (2001). Cognitive therapy outcomes: A review of meta-analyses. *Tidsskrift for Norsk Psykologforening, 38,* 698-706.

Calvin, J. (1559/1997). *Institutes of the Christian religion* (H. Beveridge, Trans.). Grand Rapids, MI: Eerdmans.

Charry, E. T. (2004). Virtual salvation. *Theology Today, 61,* 334-46.

DeRubeis, R. J., Hollon, S. D., Amsterdam, J. D., Shelton, R. C., Young, P. R., Salomon, R. M., O'Reardon, J. P., Lovett, M. L., Gladis, M. M., Brown, L. L., & Gallop, R. (2005). Cognitive therapy vs. medications in the treatment of moderate to severe depression. *Archives of General Psychiatry, 62,* 409-16.

Epstein, S. (1994). Integration of the cognitive and the psychodynamic unconscious. *American Psychologist, 49,* 709-24.

Foster, R. J. (1992). *Prayer: Finding the heart's true home.* San Francisco: HarperSanFrancisco.

Greenberger, D., & Padesky, C. A. (1995). *Mind over mood: A cognitive therapy treatment manual for clients.* New York: Guilford.

Hall, M. E. L., & Johnson, E. L. (2001). Theodicy and therapy: Theological/philosophical contributions to the problem of suffering. *Journal of Psychology and Christianity, 20,* 5-17.

Hollon, S. D., DeRubeis, R. J., Shelton, R. C., Amsterdam, J. D., Salomon, R. M., O'Reardon, J. P., Lovett, M. L., Young, P. R., Haman, K. L., Freeman, B. B., & Gallop. R. (2005). Prevention of relapse following cognitive therapy vs. medications in moderate to severe depression. *Archives of General Psychiatry, 62,* 417-22.

Klein, D. N., Santiago, N. J., Vivian, D., Blalock, J. A., Kocsis, J. H., Markowitz, J. C., McCullough, J. P., Jr., Rush, A. J., Trivedi, M. H., Borian, F. E., Arnow, B. A., Dunner, D. L., Manber, R., Rothbaum, B., Thase, M. E., Keitner, G. I., Miller, I. W., & Keller, M. B. (2004). Cognitive-behavioral analysis system of psychotherapy as a maintenance treatment for chronic depression. *Journal of Consulting and Clinical Psychology, 72,* 681-88.

Klerman, G. L., & Weissman, M. M. (1989). Increasing rates of depression. *Journal of the American Medical Association, 261,* 2229-35.

Koch, R. N., & Haugk, K. C. (1992). *Speaking the truth in love: How to be an assertive Christian.* St. Louis, MO: Stephen Ministries.

Koenig, H. G., McCullough, M. E., & Larson, D. B. (2001). *Handbook of religion and health*. New York: Oxford University Press.

Kush, F. R. (2004). An operationalized cognitive therapy approach with mixed anxiety and depression. *Psychotherapy: Theory, Research, Practice, Training, 41,* 266-75.

Ma, S. H., & Teasdale, J. D. (2004). Mindfulness-based cognitive therapy for depression: Replication and exploration of differential relapse prevention effects. *Journal of Consulting and Clinical Psychology, 72,* 31-40.

Mahoney, M. J. (2003). *Constructive psychotherapy: A practical guide.* New York: Guilford.

McMinn, M. R. (1991). *Cognitive therapy techniques in Christian counseling.* Waco, TX: Word Books. This book is out of print and can be downloaded at www.markmcminn.com.

McMinn, M. R. (1996). *Psychology, theology, and spirituality in Christian counseling.* Wheaton, IL: Tyndale.

McMinn, M. R. (2006). *Christian counseling* [video in APA Psychotherapy Series]. Washington, DC: American Psychological Association.

McWilliams, N. (1994). *Psychoanalytic diagnosis: Understanding personality structure in the clinical process.* New York: Guilford.

Moroney, S. K. (2000). *The noetic effects of sin.* Lanham, MA: Lexington Books.

National Institute of Mental Health. (2000). Depression. Retrieved from http://www.nimh.nih.gov/publicat/depression.cfm#ptdep5 on May 30, 2005.

Needleman, L. D. (1999). *Cognitive case conceptualization: A guidebook for practitioners.* Mahwah, NJ: Erlbaum.

Newman, C. F., Leahy, R. L., Beck, A. T., Reilly-Harrington, N. A., & Gyulai, L. (2002). *Bipolar disorder: A cognitive therapy approach.* Washington, DC: American Psychological Association.

Postema, D. (1985). *Space for God: study and practice of spirituality and prayer.* Grand Rapids, MI: CRC Publications.

Rimm, D. C., & Masters, J. C. (1979). *Behavior therapy: Techniques and empirical findings.* New York: Academic Press.

Roberts, R. C. (2001). Outline of Pauline psychotherapy. In M. R. McMinn & T. R. Phillips (Eds.), *Care for the soul: Exploring the interface of psychology & theology* (pp. 134-63). Downers Grove, IL: InterVarsity Press.

Schneider, S. L. (2001). In search of realistic optimism: Meaning, knowledge, and warm fuzziness. *American Psychologist, 56,* 250-63.

Segal, Z. V., Williams, J. M. G., & Teasdale, J. D. (2002). *Mindfulness-based cognitive therapy for depression—a new approach to preventing relapse.* New York: Guilford.

Westen, D., & Morrison, K. (2001). A multidimensional meta-analysis of treatments for depression, panic, and generalized anxiety disorder: An empirical examination of the status of empirically supported therapies. *Journal of Consulting and Clinical Psychology, 69,* 875-99.

Willard, D. (2002). *Renovation of the heart: Putting on the character of Christ.* Colorado Springs: NavPress.

Young, J. E., Klosko, J. S., & Weishaar, M. E. (2003). *Schema therapy: A practitioner's guide.* New York: Guilford.

Young, J. E., Weinberger, A. D., & Beck, A. T. (2001). Cognitive therapy for depression. In D. H. Barlow (Ed.), *Clinical handbook of psychological disorders* (3rd ed.) (pp. 264-308). New York: Guilford.

10

Understanding Relationship-Focused Interventions

WE PRESUME THREE METHODS OF TRANSFORMATION IN IP. The first is skill-based. People can learn to function in new ways: an anxious businessperson learns to speak comfortably in public, a depressed person learns how to control runaway thoughts and feels better as a result, or a distressed couple learns to communicate better through skills of active listening. For some clients, these skill-based, functional-domain interventions are sufficient, but others find they need to look deeper for more substantive transformation.

The second domain of intervention looks beneath surface behaviors and thoughts to consider how a person makes meaning of life events. What does it mean when a spouse forgets to wash the dishes as promised? How should a missed lunch appointment be interpreted? Here we must go beneath conscious thought processes to look at schemas—the underlying templates through which one interprets the world. In this second domain, transformation involves helping people gain critical distance from their schemas to become participant-observers of their lives. They form a new identity as they begin to make distinctions between "how I used to be" and "how I am now." But this second domain of intervention is not always sufficient either, because some maladaptive schemas are highly persistent and pervasive and not easily diminished.

Although depression and anxiety can often be treated successfully with the first two domains of intervention, other problems often require a more intensive relational form of treatment. A woman may find herself repeatedly in relationships with men who dominate or control her. A man may find himself isolated and alone and fearful of reaching out to others. This is where the third domain of IP—relationship-focused intervention—is needed. This is the most profound sort of transformation, though it is not recommended for every therapy encounter because it requires a long-term investment in therapy.

The connection between the three domains of intervention can be conceptualized as three sequential questions. In symptom-focused interventions the therapist and client are asking, "What sort of feelings, thoughts and behaviors are causing problems?" Answering this question and making appropriate changes is sometimes all that is needed, usually requiring between eight and twenty one-hour sessions. In schema-focused interventions, the question becomes, "What is the problematic meaning or interpretation of these feelings, thoughts and behaviors?" Attention is turned toward underlying schemas and the relational and developmental issues that cause the schemas to have such power over the client's life. Sometimes gaining critical distance from unhealthy schemas—being able to tell the whole story with a new understanding of how the past connects with the present—is sufficient and therapy can be terminated after fifteen to forty sessions. In relationship-focused interventions, the question is, "How do these feelings, thoughts and behaviors develop in ways that lead to problematic relationships?" Change takes longer at this domain, often requiring one to three years of therapy and sometimes even longer.

Whereas the first two domains of intervention are compatible with either a medical-care or a soul-care paradigm, relationally focused IP fits best with a soul-care paradigm (see figure 10.1). The medical-care paradigm assumes that a problem is diagnosed, treated with a particular sort of intervention, and the outcome assessed by reducing the diagnosed problem. This is well suited for symptom-focused and schema-focused IP, but if the problem is not successfully

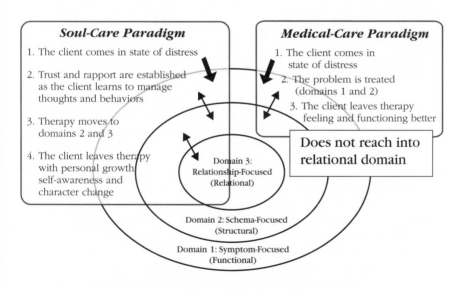

Figure 10.1. Relationship-focused interventions are well-suited for the soul-care paradigm, but not for the medical-care paradigm.

treated within a matter of months, then the medical insurance company stops paying and the treatment is considered unsuccessful. In contrast, depth-oriented psychotherapies have always been about growth and transformation more than symptom-reduction (Strupp, 2001), and they date back many years before medical insurance changed the practice of psychology. If we look back even further we find that other relational forms of soul care existed centuries before the depth-oriented psychotherapies (Yarhouse, Butman & McRay, 2005).

For clients who have desires for deeper transformation, or those who are unable to respond to a traditional medical-care paradigm, relationally focused IP provides continued help within a soul-care paradigm. In these situations the first two domains of treatment are still useful insofar as they help build rapport and relieve distressing symptoms, but the greatest transformation occurs over many months in a long-term therapy relationship. The effects of relationship-focused IP will not always be easily measured with standard psychotherapy outcome measures because transformation in a soul-care model may involve personal growth, self-awareness and character change more than symptom reduction.

Domain 3 interventions can be useful for various reasons, including spiritual longings, relational wounds, unresolved conflicts and personality problems. We focus primarily on personality problems in this chapter and the next, both because they are commonly encountered in clinical work and because failure to recognize them can render interventions in all three domains ineffective.

Personality Styles, Problems and Disorders

One of the miraculous things about God's creation is the diversity and variety of human nature. God was not content to create an earth where the same DNA was shared by every human and passed on to subsequent generations; rather, God built a system with inherent diversity. A strand of DNA gets mixed up with another in the meiotic process, billions of possible permutations result, and each generation amplifies the variety of the generation before. Every person is born unique and special in God's sight, each with distinguishing physical and personality characteristics. It would be a mistake—both theologically and psychologically—to assume that psychotherapy should mold a person into some preconceived notion of a healthy personality style.

There have been many efforts over the centuries at categorizing personality styles, ranging from the four temperaments of Hippocrates and Galen to the Enneagram of ancient spiritual traditions, to various personality theories in contemporary psychology. These are useful to study both because they help organize human diversity and because they naturally set people on a quest to find their authentic self (Benner, 2004; Rohr & Ebert, 2001). Whether talking about introversion or love languages, people seem to have intrinsic interest in how they are different from and similar to others.

Whereas different personality *styles* ought to be celebrated, personality *problems* result when people of different styles attempt to interact without fully understanding their differences. Problems can also result when a person's personality style is inflexible or maladaptive. Personality problems are encountered

---

COUNSELING TIP 10.1: Culture and Personality

There are several factors that form personality, including family history, biological constitution and cultural heritage. When considering personality styles, problems and disorders, it is important to consider the significant role culture plays. Cultural norms are part of what determines the expression of emotions and behaviors. Therefore, a particular behavior in one culture may be considered within the spectrum of normal behavior (a style), while it is considered a problem in another culture. Dramatic expression of emotion may be considered "histrionic" among many American cultural groups but likely considered an appropriate display of thoughtful concern or affection in some southern European cultures. Terms like *avoidant* and *dependent* should be evaluated within a cultural context so that clients are not inappropriately labeled as disordered. It is important to understand the cultural background of clients so that inappropriate personality labels are not inferred.

---

often in the daily routines of life—between teacher and student, employee and boss, parent and child, customer and clerk, wife and husband, and so on. Sometimes these problems are fleeting and temporary and sometimes deeply troubling and persistent.

Problems can be interpersonal or intrapersonal. Interpersonal problems become evident as two or more people relate. We have all known people who were difficult to get along with and challenging to like. For example, some people avoid conflict at all cost, others excessively depend on those who continually hurt them, still others dominate and control people. Intrapersonal problems are experienced within an individual, in the absence of interacting with another person. For example, a person may be especially prone to shame and so avoid others to prevent the possibility of rejection. This is a problem because it leaves the shame-prone individual lonely and longing for companionship.

When a person encounters personality problems frequently over a long period of time, they may be considered to have a personality *disorder*. Personality disorders are defined as consistent patterns of behavior, evident since childhood or adolescence, which impair social functioning and cause significant distress to self or others. Everyone has distinct personality traits, and sometimes these are

---

COUNSELING TIP 10.2: Personality Disorders 'R Us

Some preliminary evidence suggests that professional Christian psychotherapists may see a higher proportion of clients with personality disorders than other clinicians see (McMinn & Wade, 1995). This may be related to the availability of other counseling resources within the church. Christian clients with relatively straightforward problems may seek help from pastoral counselors and lay counselors first and find successful resolution to their problems. The more difficult clients, such as those with personality disorders, are then sent to Christian professionals. Thus, at least for professional therapists who receive referrals from pastors and other church leaders, they may end up with a relatively difficult caseload.

Working with clients who meet criteria for axis 2 disorders can be demanding and difficult work, so it is especially important for Christian clinicians to find ways to bring balance and renewal into their lives. It is also important to be effective with relationally focused therapy, such as that practiced in domain 3 IP.

---

pronounced, but only when they impair social functioning and create distress are they referred to as personality disorders. Personality disorders are at the root of many chronic interpersonal and intrapersonal problems.

These disorders are listed on axis 2 in the *DSM-IV* classification system to distinguish them from the clinical syndromes of axis 1. Unlike the clinical syndromes that tend to remit with treatment or sometimes without treatment, the personality disorders tend to be persistent over time and across various areas of life.

Axis 1 disorders such as depression or anxiety can and often do coexist with axis 2 personality disorders. Millon and Davis (2000) theorize that the axis 1 disorders are often formed by the interaction of environmental stressors with personality traits. Consider the example of Rob, a man referred with adjustment disorder symptoms in the wake of a job loss and criminal charges.

Rob was raised on the gang-infested streets of the Bronx by a single mother who suffered from bouts of severe depression. He learned early that the world is a dangerous place where people get stabbed and shot and molested. Rob learned to deal with his fears by becoming superman. He learned to conquer almost everything and everyone in his world, first through gang involvement, then competitive athletics, then sexual exploits, and later as an entrepreneur and Christian leader. His conquering-hero schema got him out of the ghetto and eventually into the upper-income echelon of his baby boomer generation. But his narcissism made him hard to live with and hard to work for, so in the throes of a devastating job loss and criminal charges he found his way to a therapy office.

Symptom-focused interventions helped calm Rob, and schema-focused interventions helped him glimpse the difference between how he wanted to live and how he had been living. The more he learned about himself, the more he longed for a transformation of character. The first several months of therapy helped create this longing for change and helped Rob and his therapist establish good rapport, but the sort of transformation Rob desired ultimately required two years of intensive relationship-focused therapy. The techniques of therapy were not as instrumental in his change as was the power of a transformative relationship.

Some Schemas Are Not Easily Changed

With schema-focused interventions the goal is to help clients gain distance from a maladaptive core belief so they can learn to see things from a new vantage point. This works well for many clients, but clients like Rob who meet criteria for a personality disorder are often unable to assume a new vantage point. They appear to be rigidly stuck in a particular schema and lack alternative perspectives from which to view their lives. By way of analogy, imagine a person trapped in a large maze. From inside the maze, life seems an endless series of blockades and dead ends. But if the person can assume a super-ordinate vantage point and view the maze from above, then it is relatively easy to figure out how to escape. This is like schema-focused therapy, with the maze being the dysfunctional schema. Clients learn to view life from a new vantage point, to gain a super-ordinate perspective and establish a new identity apart from the harmful core beliefs. As a result, clients learn to disentangle themselves from many of their troubles. But what if a person cannot gain a super-ordinate perspective? What if life within the maze is the only possible vantage point? This is the situation faced by clients who meet criteria for personality disorders. They typically have a rigid set of schemas and are unable to conceptualize what life would be like outside of those particular schemas. This renders schema-based interventions ineffective, making the therapeutic relationship the primary means of growth and change.

Therapy can then go one of two ways. Either the client will successfully pull

---

COUNSELING TIP 10.3: Recursive Schema Activation, Personality Disorders and the Observing Ego

In chapters eight and nine we introduced the idea of recursive schema activation: by encountering a schema over and over, the client begins to gain distance from a dysfunctional way of understanding the world. But this presumes a capacity to stand "outside" of one's experience in order to observe underlying core beliefs and assumptions. That is, recursive schema activation assumes a person can experience and observe reality at the same time. This assumption does not apply equally well to all clients.

Clients with personality disorders have a powerful capacity to experience their life but severe limitations in their ability to observe their life. Observing implies that one can adopt an alternative perspective, at least temporarily, but this is unlikely for those with a rigid and inflexible understanding of the world. As McWilliams (1994) states, "the therapist keeps trying to access an observing ego, and the patient does not have one" (p. 63). Symptom- and schema-focused approaches are unlikely to help personality disordered clients.

Domain 3 IP is built on the belief that some clients must first "borrow" the therapist's observing ego in order to see things clearly. This requires the sort of trusting, confiding relationship that takes time to develop. Thus the therapeutic relationship itself becomes the focus and the active ingredient for change in domain 3 IP.

---

the therapist into the maze so that both of them feel stuck and lost, or the therapist will maintain the super-ordinate vantage point well enough and long enough that the client will eventually be able to see things differently through the eyes of the therapist. This is no easy task, and it requires persistence, discernment and self-awareness on the part of the therapist.

Suzi: I was feeling really terrible Tuesday night, and I couldn't reach you. I didn't know what to do.

Mark: Yes. I wasn't available on Tuesday. Did you remember the alternate plan we discussed, about calling the emergency room if you get feeling desperate?

Suzi: I don't want to call the emergency room. I've been there before, and they are just a bunch of idiots.

Mark: So you were feeling stuck.

Suzi: Yes, absolutely. What do I do if this happens again?

Here the therapist has two options—climbing into the maze with the client, or maintaining a super-ordinate perspective. Clearly the client feels stuck, perhaps because of a rigid schema that splits the world into two categories: the good, which includes the therapist (at least for now), and the bad, which includes the emergency room personnel. The therapist sees a larger view, realizing the client's schema is rigid and exaggerated. The therapist is neither as good as the client imagines nor is the emergency room as bad. An inexperienced therapist might easily be drawn into the client's schema:

Mark: Well, I guess one option is for you to call my cell phone. I tend to keep that with me most of the time.

Suzi: Thank you so much. I knew you would understand. You are such a good person. Thank you! What's that number?

Now we have a confused client and a flattered therapist wandering together in the client's maze. A better alternative is for the therapist to maintain the super-ordinate perspective and to view this as a therapeutic opportunity. The client ultimately needs to develop stronger self-care strategies. Perhaps the client did not fully explore other alternatives, such as taking a long walk or a warm bath or calling a friend.

Mark: I need to stay with the plan we have. You can call the number I have given you, and if I am available I will be happy to talk with you. If I'm not available and you're experiencing a crisis, then you can call the emergency room.

Suzi: Didn't you hear what I just said? I can't stand the emergency room.

Mark: Yes, I heard, and I know you are feeling stuck here.

Suzi: Why won't you help me?

Mark: I very much want to help, even though it may not feel like it at times. Let's go back to Tuesday and think about what led to your feeling stuck. Maybe you and I can brainstorm some other alternatives that didn't come to mind on Tuesday.

Responding in this way may cause frustration in the client, but this is necessary in working toward the best long-term outcome.

Clients with personality disorders often do not relate effectively with others and so have a history of difficult and failed relationships. There are many different sorts of personality disorders, reflecting different interpersonal styles, but in each case the person has a rigid and dysfunctional approach to relationships. One person might be impulsive and manipulative, another could be suspicious and accusing, a third may be incapable of considering others' needs, and so on. This makes the therapeutic relationship both challenging and tremendously im-

---

COUNSELING TIP 10.4: Once Upon a Time

It is important for the therapist to keep in mind that rigid schemas exist because they were once necessary. Clients with personality disorders often come from particularly troubled and difficult childhoods. For example, a person who splits others into primitive categories—identifying some as "good people" and others as "bad people"—may have experienced trauma in childhood, making it difficult to know who could be trusted and who could not. Remembering this helps the therapist maintain a stance of empathy even when a client is being difficult. It also reminds the therapist to keep a dual focus in therapy: on past difficulties and on present relational challenges.

---

portant. Therapy becomes a place where a different sort of relationship is experienced as the therapist models appropriate caring, good boundaries, specific feedback and long-term consistency. In short, the therapist lives out a relationship of truth and grace. With time and the sort of healing that occurs in a long-term stable relationship, the client gains an ability to see life apart from the maze of maladaptive schemas.

Relational Transformation

The working assumption of relationship-focused IP is that relationships change people. Spiritual writers are fond of writing about the transforming power of love, and indeed love is transforming, but it deserves mentioning that hate is also transforming, as are chaotic relationships and abusive ones and overly demanding ones. The point is that relationships continually transform personality and always have from the earliest moments of life. To understand his maladaptive core beliefs, Rob (introduced earlier in this chapter) needed to probe the relational dynamics that gave life to his core beliefs in the first place. He needed to understand and reexperience the fear of being a child on the streets of the Bronx, and ultimately he needed to experience a safe relationship with a therapist where he could feel vulnerable and afraid without the therapist taking advantage of him. Therapy was transforming for Rob because the therapeutic relationship helped create a new vantage point through which he could view his personality and his interactions with others.

Ultimately the Christian faith is about transformation through relationship. Throughout the Old Testament, God is revealed as the Almighty Creator who sought relationship with his chosen people, but God's people turned their back and wandered away, over and over again. With persistence and patience God pursued this wandering people, forgiving and welcoming them back each time they repented. And then on an otherwise ordinary day in an old barn behind an ordinary Bethlehem inn, an extraordinary thing happened. God showed up. The eternal Word became flesh (Jn 1:14), coming to restore relationship with lost humanity. Theologians debate about how the atonement happened—some emphasize the moral influence of Christ, this perfect form of love he demonstrated. Others speak of God's triumph over evil—with the incarnation we see that God is the ultimate victor over all the forces of darkness in our world. Some emphasize that God required a payment for human sin. Still others speak of the first and second Adam, or the restoration of covenant. Perhaps it is best to let the theologians figure out the details of the atonement, but the astonishing thing is to see the extent to which God values a relationship with lost humanity.

The incarnation of Jesus Christ reveals a God who is willing to come live in our squalor and to die, pierced through with human cruelty, in order to establish renewed relationship with us. And this changes everything. It means religion is centered in relationship. It means we have a perfect example of God's relational image, revealed in Jesus. It means we can be transformed by the power of Christ, just as saints through many centuries have been. And if God values relationships this much, it means we also ought to value and attend to them.

Interpersonal Theories

A number of psychologists and psychiatrists have developed theories to help explain the connection between human relationships and personality problems. Sometimes Christian counselors and therapists resist these theories because they lack an explicitly Christian understanding of the world. But we prefer to look at them closely, recognizing that truth and wisdom can be found in all sorts of places. God, who values relationships, created a world where relationships are important, so an astute observer of humanity, whether Christian or not, has the capacity to observe important truths about human relationships.

Interpersonal psychiatry. Two early personality theorists—Karen Horney and Harry Stack Sullivan—devoted their professional lives to understanding and explaining the interpersonal dynamics of our psychological difficulties (see Safran, 1998, for a helpful discussion of Sullivan in relation to cognitive therapy).

Both Horney (1945) and Sullivan (1953) described intense interpersonal anxiety as the root of many psychological symptoms. This "basic anxiety," as Horney labeled it, is the profound feeling of distress that a child internalizes when experiencing a difficult family environment that may include hostility, belittling, domination, unfulfilled promises, neglect, overprotection or other factors that promote insecurity. Interpersonal anxiety is alleviated when one feels secure or a sense of well-being in a relationship with another person. Unlike Freud, both Horney and Sullivan postulated that the anxiety related to interpersonal relationships is as profound as the anxiety related to unmet physical needs.

Sullivan and Horney further promoted the important idea that interpersonal patterns develop as a way to decrease anxiety and to maintain or enhance self-esteem. In other words, people engage in repeated patterns of behavior because these behaviors originally decreased anxiety. The operative word is *originally* because sometimes the same interpersonal behaviors that reduce anxiety in early life end up alienating others later in life. Horney and Sullivan suggested that we all develop strategies to cope with the basic anxiety of our early family experiences. These strategies were successful in early family life in reducing anxiety, soothing our distress and maintaining a sense of self-esteem. Obviously, some individuals have much more anxiety to deal with than others depending on the distressing nature of family interactions. Rob's narcissism developed as a way of coping with his early life experience. His grandiose, over-inflated sense of himself lowered his anxiety and gave him the confidence he needed to be successful early on. Unfortunately, over time his narcissism became unbearable to others, so he was quite isolated and alone by the time he showed up in a therapy office.

Horney (1945) concluded that we have three general ways of responding to others which are designed to lower our anxiety. One interpersonal strategy is to move toward people when we are anxious. We all do this to some extent. When we fly someplace on business, it is not unusual to make a call home when we check in to the hotel. Reconnecting with a familiar voice is reassuring to both parties. After speaking or presenting a paper we seek some affirmation of a job well done. These interpersonal communications are designed to lower our anxiety about stressful events.

Another interpersonal strategy for dealing with anxiety is to move against people. A person who feels time pressure may become very focused, structured and controlling of others. The boss who is trying to meet a deadline may bark at the employees and demand that they step it up. The normal sensitivity of the boss is suspended in order to alleviate the anxiety created by the deadline.

The third strategy Horney described was that of moving away from people

---

IN THE OFFICE 10.1: Moving Toward in the First Few Moments

Often the first few moments of therapy can be useful in seeing a client's way of managing interpersonal anxiety. Using Horney's taxonomy of moving toward, moving against and moving away, consider the following interaction.

Mark: How can I be of help?

Katie: Well, you come highly recommended. One of my friends saw you several years ago, and she just goes on and on about how helpful you were. So you were the first person I contacted when I decided to get some help.

Mark: I'm glad to know your friend was helped. What sort of things led to your decision to seek help at this time?

Katie: I'm really unhappy in my life, in all sorts of ways—my job, my marriage, my children. I've been so unhappy for so many years [tears follow]. I'm so lonely. So I was talking with this friend a few weeks back and she told me that if anyone could help, you could.

Notice the tendency to "move toward" that Katie uses to manage her anxiety. This may simply be a reflection of her initial anxiety, which she manages through flattery and expressions of unhappiness, but if it is a rigid style of interaction it may annoy and alienate others in her life. It is important for the therapist to be aware of what is happening in order to avoid being drawn into ineffective patterns of relating.

Near the End of the Session

Katie: Thank you so much. I can see why my friend speaks so highly of you. You are a very kind man and so easy to talk with. I'm just so unhappy in my life, and I'm really hoping you can help me.

Mark: I'm hopeful that therapy will be helpful for you. I'll see you next week.

Katie: Did I talk about the right sort of things today? I've never really done this before.

Mark: You did just fine. I think you'll find that therapy is very flexible and that soon you won't feel a need to evaluate yourself as to whether you did well or not.

Katie: Oh, okay. Thanks. I'll see you next week.

The client is rather effusive about the therapist's skills and then asks for a similar compliment from the therapist. The therapist responds with a matter-of-fact reply in order to avoid building the therapeutic relationship on the basis of Katie's "moving toward" relational style.

in order to decrease anxiety. We have all heard people say, "I just need to get away from it all and relax." Moving away from others, seeking solace and taking a break is a common way of reducing stress.

Horney observed these strategies as normal ways of decreasing anxiety; however, they become problematic when one strategy is used rigidly in a variety of situations. The person who always moves toward others becomes clinging and dependent. Excessive attempts to get affirmation and reassurance become

---

COUNSELING TIP 10.5: Responding to Conflict

Careful observation of how a client responds to conflict will reveal his or her typical response to coping with anxiety. In addition to the obvious ways of moving away, moving toward and moving against others in response to conflict, an astute observer will notice more subtle ways that these responses are expressed. A client may move away from another by getting quiet or changing the subject. Crying or complaining may be ways of moving toward others and eliciting help. A client may move against another by disagreeing or challenging. These are the more subtle forms of response likely to be seen in the therapist's office.

---

annoying to others and they eventually flee, say hurtful things or ignore the one seeking connection. The person who always moves against others becomes so controlling, demanding and domineering that others don't want to be in a relationship with such a person. The person who always moves away from others becomes aloof, isolated and lonely. A healthy individual may alternate between these interpersonal strategies depending on the situation, while the impaired individual will rigidly employ one strategy over and over thus creating further interpersonal problems.

Object-relations theory. Another interpersonal theory that is useful in understanding the development of personality disorders is object-relations theory. This complex theory is both an extension of and departure from Freud's psychoanalytic formulations. Freud emphasized the internal dynamics of the mind and promoted the idea that most psychopathology was the result of internal conflict between the desires of the id, the unrealistic constraints of the superego and the realistic appraisals of the ego (Jones, 1961). He acknowledged the importance of relationships, but emphasized the internal world of conflict. His psychosexual theory of development had significant relational aspects. For example, he described the Oedipal complex and the Electra conflict as emanating from the emotionally charged relationship between a child and his or her parents. Similarly, his theory of psychotherapy (psychoanalysis) described a special kind of emotionally charged relationship (transference) as being vital to psychological change and growth. Thus, an interpersonal understanding has always been at the core of understanding the dynamics of Freudian psychopathology and psychotherapy.

In contrast to classical psychoanalysis, the emphasis in object-relations theory has been on the internalization of significant interpersonal relationships (Hamilton, 1988). This theory provides a formulation of how early interpersonal experience serves as a prototype for subsequent interpersonal experience. Rather than emphasizing the role of biological drives as Freud did, these theorists emphasize the role of relationship expectations and attachments. In this model, love becomes more salient than sex in motivating behavior.

Through psychological mechanisms of integration and differentiation the developing child incorporates some traits of caregivers and discards some other traits. We form early mental images (templates) of ourselves and others (objects) through which we make sense of our interpersonal worlds and develop relational expectations. Some experience is integrated through mechanisms of incorporation, introjection and identification, while other experience is differentiated (rejected) through projection, splitting and devaluation. We may "take on" the characteristics of parents through these integration processes while discarding other characteristics through mechanisms of differentiation.

Rob's early experience with his mother had a profound impact on his development of narcissism. Rather than identifying with his overwhelmed and depressed mother, he devalued that and projected any sense of personal weakness onto others whom he attempted to control. He was left with a grandiose sense of himself that had all weakness expunged.

Family systems theory. The third interpersonal theory that influences our thinking is family systems theory (Kerr & Bowen, 1988). This formulation of interpersonal dynamics helps us understand how roles and rules within families promote particular behaviors that meet the needs of the family system rather than our own needs. While these behaviors work in the early family system, they rarely work in the subsequent relationships we develop and instead often lead to significant distress.

Every family has rules, but most rules are implicit rather than explicit. Explicit rules are the clearly stated ones such as curfew or expectations around chores. Other rules may be more implicit, such as those around eating—when to eat, who is free to take food from the refrigerator, who prepares the meal, who cleans up, who sits where at a table (if there is one) and so on. The clearest way to find out the rules is to violate one of them. Have you ever noticed how kids never read the rules on the wall at the swimming pool? They just run around, and when the lifeguard blows a whistle they learn that they are not supposed to run. Sometimes family rules are the same way. We find out what they are when they are violated.

Many rules in families tend to get internalized in childhood. A child may learn that a good child is quiet, obedient and never cries. These rules of behav-

---

COUNSELING TIP 10.6: Discussing Implicit Family Rules

One characteristic of implicit rules is that they are not openly discussed. Therefore, clients typically do not think about the rules that may be related to their difficulties. One way to help clients think about family rules is to have them describe ways that birthdays were celebrated in their homes. Was it a big celebration or relatively minor? Were people loud or rather quiet? Were there presents, cards, and cake and ice cream? Was there a formal party with invitations? Was there a special meal prepared? Did relatives call? We all tend to internalize expectations about family celebrations that function as rules. Discussions about family celebrations can generalize to other discussions about family rules.

---

ior are established early and may not be explicit. When the child grows up these rules may or may not be helpful in subsequent relationships. Ned grew up in a Christian family where issues involving strong emotions were not discussed. His parents told him that intense emotion was a sign of weak faith, so the only emotion allowed was a moderate dose of happiness. When Ned got married his new wife admired his emotional strength and referred to him as her "rock." He was just what she needed coming from a chaotic family where emotional upheaval was the norm. Unfortunately, they found that conflicts were difficult to resolve—rocks don't talk much. Over time they had less and less conversation because more topics involved unresolved conflicts.

Families also promote roles for their members. Systemic roles are those that maintain the equilibrium of the family. Families have to deal with a variety of stresses—financial challenges, growing children, involvement with other families, school demands and more. To resist chaos and breakdown, families maintain homeostasis. Just like with the rules, the roles that maintain this balance are often implicit rather than explicit. Some of these systemic roles have been identified as that of the hero, the clown and the mascot. Children adopt these roles unconsciously and fulfill the family needs for stability. Rob fulfilled the role of hero for his family. His mother was single and struggled just to provide the basics for her children. Rob's superman strivings were a source of pride for her that gave her some sense of hope for her existence. Rob didn't realize that his competitive and achieving attributes were subtly reinforced by his mother's need for a hero, which vicariously fulfilled her need for significance.

Summary. The synthesis of these various interpersonal theories suggests that interpersonal patterns are stable and predictable ways of relating to others. These patterns are formed early in life as a means of reducing interpersonal anxiety, maintaining a consistent perception of self in relationship to others, and as a means of stabilizing family life. It is no wonder that interpersonal patterns of behavior are difficult to change. Thankfully, we don't need to change many patterns unless they are rigid and inflexible. It is the inflexibility of interpersonal patterns that creates relationship distress. What worked in childhood and adolescence may no longer work in college or in a new marriage. And it is at these times of transition (leaving home, marriage, new child, new job, retirement) that interpersonal distress is most noticeable.

Questions About the Cognitive Therapy Model

The reader who is familiar with cognitive therapy may wonder why we are not continuing to pursue a cognitive model in the relational domain as we have in the functional and structural domains. There is a growing body of literature on treating personality disorders with cognitive therapy (Beck, Freeman & Associates, 1990; Beck, Freeman & Davis, 2003; Rasmussen, 2005), so why not embrace that aspect of cognitive therapy? It is not so much that we are rejecting the cognitive model of conceptualizing and treating personality disorders as it is that we find it inadequate in its current form to address the deeply entrenched interpersonal patterns that plague many relationships.

As described in chapter three, cognitive therapy is weak in its explanation of motivation. The powerful forces that drive people to relate in repeated self-defeating patterns are not adequately accounted for by dysfunctional schemas. Beck and his colleagues (1990) turn to evolutionary concepts to describe the motivation for interpersonal strategies. Rasmussen (2005) adopts Millon's (1990, Millon & Davis, 2000) personology to describe the "evolutionary imperatives" that drive personality development. Both of these cognitive approaches tie interpersonal behavior to schemas out of evolutionary necessity. Certainly schemas are strong, deeply entrenched, and provide repeated familiar ways for interpreting our experiences, but it is difficult to see why schemas in themselves would motivate an individual to maintain excessive dependence, overtly harm others or seek control over others to the point of relational demise. For a conceptualization of motivation of this magnitude we turn to the interpersonal theories and to our biblical understanding of human nature.

We have other significant questions about the cognitive approach to personality disorders as well. First, we question the assumption that core beliefs are static structures learned early in life. Just as Barth, Brunner, Grenz and other theologians question how God's image could be a structure fully contained within an individual—suggesting instead that God's image is seen in relationships—so we question whether a core belief is merely a structure within an individual. It seems more reasonable to see core beliefs as dynamic and relational, continually being shaped and redefined by current relationships. Consider Rob's belief "I must always be the best." How did Rob develop this core belief, and why is it so resistant to change? If core beliefs are structural in nature, then the answer must be that the schema was taught or modeled to Rob earlier in life. This answer will satisfy some, but relationally focused therapists will ultimately find it shallow. We learn many things in childhood and adolescence—how to tie shoelaces, play baseball, write term papers, drive a car—but simply learning a thing does not give it immense power over us. Yet core beliefs hold incredible power over people, sometimes driving people to desperate emotional states, to impulsive and reckless actions, and even to suicide, homicide or acts of terror. Core beliefs are not merely learned, they are embedded in relationships, and relationships carry enormous emotional significance for a reason that Christian theologians understand better than most psychologists: because we are created to be in relationship.

Second, we challenge the practice of confining intervention to cognitive changes, as if a treatment can be delivered without considering the healing power embedded in the therapeutic relationship. Strupp (2001) critiques the medical-care paradigm because it "assumes that a psychotherapeutic treatment can be conceptualized independent of the human relationship in which it takes place" (p. 605). Cognitive therapists help people feel better by changing their thoughts, but sometimes therapists forget that their clients' thoughts are being revealed and evaluated in the context of a relationship. Rob did not come to therapy in order to be more rational; he came because his life was crumbling and he was once again glimpsing the terror of being helpless in a dangerous world, which he first learned on the streets of the Bronx. The crises of Rob's life had always been relational. It was the relational trauma of childhood that caused him to develop his maladaptive core belief in the first place, the relational response of peers that reinforced his desire to become superman, the relational failure of his schema that led to his job loss, and the relational nature of therapy that helped Rob navigate a difficult time in life and experience some degree of character transformation.

Third, we question the way science is sometimes used to defend cognitive-behavioral treatments. Some have promoted cognitive-behavioral approaches and disparaged relational approaches by arguing that science should be the sole arbiter of which treatments psychotherapists use (e.g., Perez, 1999), as if science is objective and value-free. We bristle at this view, as do others (e.g., Garfield,

---

COUNSELING TIP 10.7: Remember the Methods Section

Psychotherapists try to keep up with the scientific literature on psycho-therapy, or at least they ought to, but it is difficult to find time to read each article word for word. When reviewing an article on the effectiveness of psychotherapy, it is important to scan the abstract, look at the last paragraph of the introduction (where the research question is likely to be found), review the results and scan the discussion to find implications for clinicians. But it is also important to look in the "Methods" section to discover what outcome measures were used for the study. Most often, the outcome measures are based only on symptom reduction. It is important to measure symptoms, but most practitioners are concerned about other issues too—character formation, relationships in the client's life and so on. Christian clinicians are also concerned about spiritual matters, and spirituality is rarely measured in psychotherapy outcome studies.

The researchers may conclude that their approach to psychotherapy "works," but how is *working* defined? The astute clinician will notice and be concerned when symptom reduction is the sole measure of effectiveness.

1996), both because science is far from value-free and because the flaws inherent in psychotherapy research do not permit utter optimism for medical paradigm treatments. Though it is clear that cognitive therapy works well for symptom-focused interventions with specific disorders (Butler & Beck, 2001), it is less clear that a pristine form of cognitive therapy is the treatment of choice for more complex clinical presentations. Research labs are different places than psychotherapy offices. The symptom-focused cognitive therapies are ideally suited for research labs because the treatments are short term and simple enough to be manualized, but relatively few clinicians use treatment manuals in their day-to-day work (Addis & Krasnow, 2000). Researchers often have stringent exclusion criteria for those participating as clients, so the people with the most complex problems are not included in the studies. Many people who come to a therapist's office would not make it through the exclusion criteria being used in most research labs (Safran, 2001). Researchers tend to focus on specific treatments for specific disorders, whereas clinicians tend to think more about therapeutic relationships. Interestingly, the nature of the therapeutic relationship is more closely related to therapy outcome than the particular techniques being used (Lambert & Barley, 2002). Strupp (2001) argues that "every therapeutic dyad is unique, and research that treats therapy as a standardized, disembodied entity will not contribute to our understanding" (p. 605).

The Dynamics of Interpersonal Problems

The interpersonal theories give insight into the development of interpersonal problems, but how are these problems maintained in relationships and how do they develop into rigid patterns characteristic of personality disorders? We turn to three interpersonal models to help us understand the process of internalizing relational dynamics from childhood and reenacting those dynamics in current relationships.

Interpersonal process approach. Teyber's (2006) model involves a three-step internalization of interpersonal anxiety and insecurity. When a child's needs are unmet, or the child is neglected, traumatized or abused, or the innate longings for security and attachment are thwarted in the family of origin, the child experiences a high degree of anxiety. Inevitably the child internalizes these rejecting, judgmental and invalidating experiences and begins to view him- or herself in similar ways. Second, the child begins to treat others in a similar hurtful manner. Third, relationships are maintained with those who continue to respond back in repeatedly hurtful ways. So the three-step process begins early and continues on into adulthood. An individual responds to self and others in hurtful ways that are repetitions of early interpersonal patterns. Although these are painful ways of relating to self and others, they are familiar and provide some level of control over strong feelings of insecurity and anxiety. Painful rejecting and judgmental responses are elicited from others, but again they are familiar responses that are predictable and function to reduce the mounting anxiety of interpersonal conflict.

Repeated painful interpersonal patterns continue because they (1) provide a sense of familiarity, (2) provide a sense of control over potentially threatening situations and (3) decrease escalating tension in relationships. These factors promote the inflexible rigid quality seen in personality disorders. Rather than relating in a variety of ways to solve problems and reduce anxiety, these individuals resort to familiar patterns. From the outside these patterns are obviously self-defeating, but from the inside they make sense. An interesting phenomenon develops that allows these patterns to make sense to the personality disordered individual; that is, they interpret their interpersonal patterns as special or unique. The excessively dependent person who seeks reassurance and continues in abusive relationships sees her behavior as loving or selfless sacrifice. The person who constantly moves against others sees his behavior as necessary to get the job done or as necessary to the mission of the organization (even when the organization is a church or other religious organization!). The person who is aloof and moving away from others sees his behavior as providing him with the space to "think the big thoughts" or "to feel more deeply" about his concerns.

The feeling of specialness, necessity or uniqueness that accompanies the self-perception of people with personality disorders is one of the truly interesting aspects that helps us understand how people can maintain such obviously self-defeating behavior. Rather than focusing on the impact of their behavior, they focus on the intent of their behavior which is interpreted in a positive manner that maintains self-esteem. In this sense all personality disorders involve narcissism. They are all self-serving in that they maintain a sense of attachment, belonging, specialness or importance. This narcissism is not the same as narcissistic personality disorder, which is the obvious and extreme manifestation of narcissism. Rather, this narcissism simply accounts for the self-justification of people who engage in repeated hurtful or self-defeating interpersonal behaviors. If a therapist punctures that belief too early in the therapy process, a client will experience a narcissistic wound. Thus the timing and manner of responding to such persons therapeutically is a significant issue that is discussed more fully in the next chapter.

Cyclical maladaptive patterns. Contemporary psychodynamic theorists have introduced the concept of cyclical maladaptive patterns (CMPs) which can be useful in understanding and crafting a healing therapeutic relationship (see Levenson, 1995). A CMP is a vicious cycle where the client recreates a similar problem over and over in different relationships. Of course the client is not doing this intentionally—almost no one has the intentional goal of causing difficulties in relationships—but these patterns function on a subconscious level. Typically they are reenactments of earlier life situations.

Levenson (1995) suggests that CMPs can be organized in four categories: acts of the self, expectations of others' reactions, acts of others toward the self, and acts of the self toward the self. These four categories can be seen in the following interaction between Rob and his therapist. First, Rob expresses himself aggressively toward the therapist.

Rob: That prosecutor was just staring at me, like "I'm going to get you." I wanted to march over and lay him out right there. What a self-righteous prig, with his starched white shirt and his wire-framed glasses and his $400 briefcase. It's just him against me, and I am going to show him a thing or two.

Clark: It's like you were back on the streets of the Bronx for a moment.

Rob: What are you talking about? You're always bringing up the Bronx, like I'm still in a gang or something. Can't you get this straight? We're not in the Bronx. I'm not fourteen any more. I was in court this morning, I may be going to prison, and you're talking about the Bronx.

Without knowing it, Rob is proving the therapist right. He is reenacting the same pattern he learned in his combative childhood environment. Now the therapist, feeling angry, has a choice to make: to defend the interpretation and move into the CMP that Rob anticipates, or to give up the desire to be understood in order to connect with Rob and disrupt the CMP.

Clark: [pause] This is a frightening time for you.

Rob: Of course it is. Wouldn't you be frightened?

Clark: [silence]

Rob: I feel alone here, like I'm up against some pretty big forces that want to bring me down.

Clark: And when I bring up the Bronx it feels like I'm not really getting it. I'm not understanding how big and scary this is today, right now.

Rob: That's right.

The confrontation with the prosecutor and now the confrontation with the therapist are reenactments of patterns learned early in life. Rob perceives the world as hostile and then acts out aggressively, as he learned to do in a dangerous Bronx neighborhood.

Second, once Rob acts he then anticipates how others will react. He notices the prosecutor staring at him, which shows that he is expecting a combative, hostile response from others. It may very well be true that the courtroom will be combative and hostile, so his expectations will likely be proved correct. In therapy, Rob also expects his therapist to react in a hostile and combative way. Therapists are often drawn into a client's CMP, either in terms of their emotional reaction or behavioral or both. In this example, the therapist is naturally drawn in to Rob's CMP emotionally and experiences anger. But will the therapist also be drawn in behaviorally? Notice how easy it would have been to do so.

Rob: What are you talking about? You're always bringing up the Bronx,
         like I'm still in a gang or something. Can't you get this straight?
         We're not in the Bronx. I'm not fourteen any more. I was in court
         this morning, I may be going to prison, and you're talking about the
         Bronx.

The therapist is drawn into the CMP emotionally, and feels angry

Drawn in to CMP Behaviorally

Clark: Listen. We can argue this if
you want, but even the way
you responded to me right
here is combative and competitive, like you're in one
gang and I'm in another.

Argument ensues.

Avoids CMP Behaviorally

Clark: [pause] This is a frightening
time for you.

*Rob tries again to draw the therapist
into the CMP.*

Rob: Of course it is. Wouldn't you
be frightened?

Therapist still avoids it.

Clark: [silence]

The third part of the CMP is how others act toward the self. When the other
acts as expected, illustrated by the example on the left, then the cycle is perpetuated. When the therapist responds in a way that is unexpected, then the
cycle is broken. Rob tries again to engage the CMP with a second aggressive
comment, but still the therapist avoids it. If the therapist is aware of the CMP
and avoids falling into it, then Rob will eventually need to reevaluate his view
of how the world works.

Finally, the fourth part of the CMP is how the self responds to the self. How
does Rob explain and respond to the CMP reenactments that he creates? In
court he reenacted the CMP by having a stare-down with the prosecutor, and
his ultimate conclusion was, "It's just him against me, and I am going to show
him a thing or two." Here we see that the CMP is reinforced by his narcissistic,
competitive impulses. These narcissistic impulses will make him more inclined
to act aggressively in the future, which then perpetuates the CMP by taking
him back to the first category (acts of the self). In contrast, when the therapist
does not engage behaviorally in the CMP, Rob has to react differently to himself. He tries twice to engage the therapist in the CMP, and when both efforts
fail then he moves beyond his narcissistic defense and reveals something
about his feelings:

Rob: I feel alone here, like I'm up against some pretty big forces that want to bring me down.

Clark: And when I bring up the Bronx it feels like I'm not really getting it. I'm not understanding how big and scary this is today, right now.

Rob: That's right.

In this example we see the therapist helping Rob to take a step away from his CMP so that he can see the feelings beneath his narcissistic defense style.

Rather than responding in a defensive and angry way when provoked by a client, effective therapists learn to step outside of the client's CMP and respond in an unexpected way. This requires both self-awareness and virtue on the part of the therapist. In chapter eleven we discuss two of the virtues displayed by Christ—truth and grace—and show how these are related to the relational domain of IP.

Reciprocal role procedures. In developing cognitive-analytic therapy, Ryle (1990) postulated something he called reciprocal role procedures (RRPs). Though Ryle did not articulate a religious or theological basis for his model, it is fascinating to see the overlap between his ideas and the relational view of the *imago Dei* postulated by Barth (1945/1958). Barth suggested that "I-Thou" relationships are central to understanding the image of God. The individual self is created to be in connection with the other; one cannot fully understand the essence of being human without seeing the self in relation to the other. Ryle discusses this from a developmental perspective, drawing on Bowlby's attachment theory (1988) and other object-relations ideas.

Every child learns to experience self in relation to others. At first this may be quite rudimentary as infants learn to distinguish those features and abilities that reside within their own bodies from things that reside elsewhere. This may lead to a primitive and fragmented view of the other. For example, infants learn that breast milk comes from outside their own resources, from someone they later come to know as mother, but they lack a nuanced view of what a mother is. At first mother may only be a breast to provide food and a set of eyes to view while feeding, but as infants grow so also their views of mother grow. Over time a person begins to develop more sophisticated ideas of where self ends and other begins. The growing child learns ways of relating with the other so as to maintain attachment between the I and the Thou. Accordingly, the child learns certain roles that will allow for some balance of autonomy and connectedness. But each of these roles is reciprocal; that is, they are met with a response on the part of the other. Both the initial response and the reciprocal response are internalized in the developing child.

For example, imagine that Susan is a child in a healthy home environment who learns that expressing a desire for comfort is met with her parents providing for her need. Here we see both Susan's role (crying out for help) and the reciprocal role on the part of her parents (providing comfort). An operant behaviorist might be concerned that Susan's crying is being reinforced and that she will never learn to take care of her own needs. But the object-relations view is different. Over time, Susan internalizes both her help-seeking role and her par-

---

COUNSELING TIP 10.8: I Would *Never* Do That

Many children and adolescents have the experience of being annoyed by a parent and saying to themselves, *I will never behave like that when I grow up*. But to their surprise, when they get older they find themselves doing the exact things they vowed never to do. This illustrates a reciprocal role procedure. Even the annoying roles of the other person are internalized and often get played out later in life.

---

ent's comforting role, and she becomes capable of both expressing needs and providing self-care for the needs she experiences. Her parents' gracious, kind responses allow Susan to be gracious to herself when faced with challenging situations later in life.

Unfortunately, many homes are not as benevolent as Susan's, so harsher RRPs are internalized. Rob learned that cries for comfort were met with ridicule, and so he suppressed his needs in order to maintain some semblance of attachment with his mother. Rob also learned and internalized the reciprocal role—that ridicule is the appropriate response to weakness. These reciprocal roles then became self-perpetuating; a person naturally chooses friends and lovers according to their views of relationships.

Ryle (1990) uses this concept of RRPs for a relatively short-term form of psychotherapy, but we find the idea more helpful in the context of lengthier relationship-focused therapy. The original set of I-Thou rules, which may have been badly distorted in the client's formative relationships, are slowly relearned in the context of a long-term relationship with a therapist. Some therapists refer to this as reparenting (e.g., Young, Klosko & Weishaar, 2003)—a term that seems unfortunately paternalistic—but they are, in essence, referring to same idea. The therapist lives out a new set of role procedures in relation to the client.

Returning to the example of Rob, he expects expressions of pain to be met with ridicule. Therapy may cause him to reevaluate this expectation if the therapist is able to create a safe environment where Rob feels he can express his pain and then the therapist responds with compassion rather than ridicule.

Rob: I feel alone here, like I'm up against some pretty big forces that want to bring me down.

Clark: And when I bring up the Bronx it feels like I'm not really getting it. I'm not understanding how big and scary this is today, right now.

Rob: That's right.

Clark: This must be a lonely place for you, facing these legal problems, losing your job. And just a minute ago you felt like I was working against you too.

Rob: Welcome to my life. It's always been me against the world pretty much.

Clark: How does it feel to be in therapy and to be talking with someone who really wants to be working with you instead of against you?

Rob: [pause] I'm not always sure how to respond. It seems different. But I like it too. It would be hard to be facing this ordeal without talking with you about things.

There is no dramatic breakthrough in this dialogue, and it may not even seem like much progress is made, but it is important to keep in mind that a healing relationship with Rob will not be accomplished quickly. It will evolve through many conversations over a long period of time.

Summary. These three models show that interpersonal problems start early in life, usually in the family of origin, and are maintained in current significant relationships. In IP it is important to evaluate the family of origin for experiences of trauma, neglect or relational wounding that led to inflexible relationship patterns. Linehan (1993) describes this kind of family environment broadly as an invalidating environment. Similarly, it is important to evaluate current relationships to see how these patterns are maintained and perhaps entrenched into personality disorders. The four primary relationships relevant to IP are family of origin, current significant relationships (often marital or employment relationships), the therapeutic relationship and relationship with God.

A Christian Perspective on Personality Problems

A Christian therapist can learn from various theories of human nature and personality, but these are best viewed in reference to a Christian view of persons. In IP we attempt to build our understanding of human nature on a biblical and theological foundation that keeps it within a historical Christian context. In chapter one we described three broad Christian themes that form the core of our understanding of human nature: creation, fall and redemption. We return to these themes here as we consider the development of personality problems.

Creation. We are made in the image of God, and three perspectives of the *imago Dei* were described in chapter one. The functional perspective indicates that we have God-given abilities that no other creature has to function, operate, and manage ourselves and the world around us. When we function in this way to care for God's creation we bring honor to our Creator. The structural perspective describes our capacity to think and decide like no other creature. When we use these capacities for the glory of God, we image God in this world. Finally, the relational perspective states that we are relational creatures like none other. Our desires and longings are for relationship with each other and ultimately with God. When we relate in communion with each other we honor God's creation of humanity.

The relational perspective of the *imago Dei* is most relevant to the third domain of IP and to this discussion of interpersonal patterns of behavior. We are born with a natural drive to attach or connect with others. What theologians and Christian writers have described for centuries has been observed and described by psychologists more recently (Bowlby, 1988). Our natural, God-given inclination to connect with others leads us to loving human relationships, friendships, sexual relationships and parenting. These longings also lead us to God; to seek a transcendent yet personal relationship with the only one who can both fully know us and fully love us. It is these longings that provide the motivational component that is inadequately conceptualized in cognitive theories of interpersonal patterns. Relationships are intrinsically motivating. Fulfilling our interpersonal longings motivates us to seek intimacy and to develop virtuous traits such as altruism and empathy.

Unfortunately, as a result of sin and its distorting effects on our desires, we seek relationships for the wrong reasons—because they repeat the familiar hurtful patterns of the past. As a result of sin we may sacrifice noble behavior for that which is secure. As a result of sin we hurt those who are closest to us. Our longings for relationship are distorted through the sin of others, our own sin and the brokenness of the world so that disastrous consequences ensue. Instead of personality patterns developing that show love and care repeatedly, we have a tendency to repeat patterns that inflict harm on others and ultimately defeat ourselves.

Fall. The Fall resulted in the sinful condition of our world (original sin) and our propensity toward sinful acts. We are broken people who live in a broken world. The consequence of our brokenness is that we hurt others. We say and

---

IN THE OFFICE 10.2: Noetic Effects and Personality Disorders

The theological notion of noetic effects of sin has psychological implications. Sin blinds us so that we are often unaware of our weaknesses and transgressions. This is what makes sin so pernicious—sin keeps us from seeing our sin. Psychologically this means we are prone to blame others for our problems rather than accepting responsibility. This tendency is especially pronounced among those with personality disorders.

All of us face troubles in life. Sometimes these troubles are due to circumstances beyond our control, and sometimes we cause our own problems. Most often it is a combination of both. Clients with personality disorders avoid taking responsibility for their problems, preferring instead to blame others or life situations. It is often helpful to ask questions early in treatment to assess the degree of responsibility clients are willing to take.

Rex: We were really happy together at first, but lately everything just seems ugly and painful and difficult. Hardly a day goes by when we aren't yelling at each other about something.

Clark: It sounds like you and Sandy are experiencing a lot of conflict.

Rex: Yeah, she's all worked up about me not being home enough, and always harping on me to come straight home after work. She thinks she's my mother.

Clark: You're feeling like she's watching you too close.

Rex: Yeah, I mean I'm a grown man and I'm going to make my own decisions about what I do and when I do it.

Clark: What sort of role do you play in the conflict?

Rex: What do you mean?

Clark: Well, you're describing what Sandy does: watching you too closely, asking you to come home right after work and so on. I'm wondering what part you play in the conflict.

Rex: I just want her to leave me alone.

Clark: Are there things that you are doing or saying that are making things more difficult for Sandy?

Rex: I'm just doing what every man does—trying to get some freedom from a controlling woman. She changed. This isn't the woman I married.

Rex has difficulty seeing his part of the problem. It is premature to diagnose him with a personality disorder, but the therapist will want to keep this possibility in mind.

do things that are harmful and, alarmingly, we justify it. Some of the most difficult work therapists do involves therapy with personality disordered clients. It is not difficult to develop a caring and empathic relationship with clients who exhibit axis 1 disorders. Though their distress is often palpable and the dysfunction in their lives can be significant, they typically take responsibility for their mistakes and work to grow in the midst of their pain and struggle. In contrast, clients who meet criteria for personality disorders rarely display personal responsibility for their symptoms when they come for therapy. They can and do feel pain, but frequently as a result of the behavior they elicit from others. More often they create pain in the lives of other people, and the typical referral for help comes at the insistence of a distressed spouse or employer.

Both of us have seen our share of clients who exhibit personality disorders, and one of the most profound aspects of this work is the entrenched nature of their interpersonal patterns accompanied by the self-serving interpretation of their behavior. For example:

> *A mother left her nine-year-old daughter home for the weekend with the mother's live-in boyfriend while she attended a seminar at the coast. Her explanation was, "I thought the two of them would have a chance to get to know each other better. I never thought that he would molest her." However, upon further discussion it became quite clear that the mother was aware of his previous arrest for sexual abuse.*

> *A husband who is having an affair but is unwilling to tell his wife of the affair or to stop the extramarital relationship just happens to arrange a meeting between his wife and a single friend of his. Although he left them alone for the evening and didn't plan to come home that night, he was "hurt and shocked" when he found out that she slept with his friend. "I can't believe she was unfaithful to me. I was just trying to have her meet someone so that she could talk."*

> *A pastor has been released from four consecutive churches, each time after his inability to manage conflict in the congregation. Rather than seeing his role in the problem, he insists that key people in each of the congregations have deliberately sabotaged his ministry.*

As described earlier, clients with personality disorders tend to interpret their own behavior in a positive manner. They present themselves as hurt and victimized by the behavior of others even though they have elicited such behavior. It is the blinded self-serving quality of these clients that further makes therapy difficult and long term. This narcissism is a direct result of the Fall and its many relational consequences.

Scott Peck, in his book *People of the Lie* (1983), describes human evil as a "particular variety of narcissism" (p. 77). His description of narcissism helps us understand the common ways in which people do evil to others and yet do not see it as evil. Narcissism is "a kind of pride that unrealistically denies our inherent sinfulness and imperfection—a kind of overweening pride or arrogance that prompts people to reject and even attack the judgment implied by the day-to-day evidence of their own inadequacy" (p. 80). In its most blatant form, narcissistic personality disorder, people are so absorbed with themselves that they cannot see the impact of their actions on others or experience others' feelings. So filled with themselves, there is no room inside for the perspective of another. A somewhat related personality disorder, antisocial personality disorder, is characteristic of someone who can harm others with no feelings of remorse or empathy.

Isaiah 5:20-21 warns a nation about the self-deception that comes from a lack of honesty and insight: "Destruction is certain for those who say that evil is good and good is evil; that dark is light and light is dark; that bitter is sweet and sweet is bitter. Destruction is certain for those who think they are wise and consider themselves to be clever." The narcissistic lack of insight into the impact of one's behavior and the self-serving rationalization of hurtful behavior is evidence of the damage of sin in our world.

Redemption. The source of interpersonal problems and more extreme personality disorders stems from early life experiences in our sin-stained world, most notably in the family of origin. As described previously, interpersonal problems are born in an invalidating environment of high anxiety and low security. When the child's needs are not met in this context, the child will seek ways to obtain security and decrease anxiety. These behavioral patterns are then repeated in subsequent significant relationships as the familiar dynamics are reenacted.

What would prevent such behavioral dynamics from developing? The answer is a loving home filled with grace and support. This answer is both true and oversimplified. It is true that a loving, grace-filled home would decrease the likelihood of one developing interpersonal problems, but it is oversimplified to think that the right environment would permanently protect a child from such dynamics. One cannot fully protect a child from the brokenness of the world, and so sooner or later the harsh realities of trauma, conflict, wounding and evil will be experienced. Additionally, since parents and children have a sin nature they will sooner or later inflict wounding even in the best home environment. We cannot escape the messiness that sin brings into our lives. However, redemption gives us the opportunity to experience hope and security.

It is not just that early relationships form faulty interpersonal patterns and current relationships sustain these behaviors; healthy relationships also help reform faulty interpersonal patterns. Christianity, a relationally based faith, posits that people experience a real relationship with God through Jesus Christ. This is not merely an idealized projection of one's wish for a father figure, as some psychoanalytic therapists might suggest, but a real relationship with a living God. Christians have been involved with spiritual direction and formation for centuries, which reflects a deep conviction that relating to God transforms people and helps them recover from previous relational damage. Of course relating to other humans is also important; a healthy human relationship is sometimes necessary before people can grasp the notion of relating to a loving, benevolent God. Redemptive human relationships are found in a variety of places—in coffee shops, pastors' studies, psychotherapy offices, houses of worship, small groups, prayer chapels and workplaces all over the world. Whenever one person helps another grow into healthier relational patterns, it can be considered a type of soul care. The Christian faith has a long tradition of soul care, and psychotherapy is one of several available methods. Accordingly, we turn our attention toward the healing role of the psychotherapy relationship in chapter eleven. A strong therapeutic relationship provides the safety, security and lowered anxiety necessary for a client to experience a validating relational environment. This kind of relationship mirrors the redemptive qualities found in a relationship with Christ, not because the therapist is a Christ-figure but because all of us are called to treat one another as Christ treated us.

References

Addis, M. E., & Krasnow, A. D. (2000). A national survey of practicing psychologists' attitudes toward psychotherapy treatment manuals. *Journal of Consulting and Clinical Psychology, 68,* 331-39.

Barth, K. (1945/1958). *Church dogmatics* (Vol. 3, Part 1) (J. W. Edwards, O. Bussey, & H. Knight, Trans.). Edinburgh: T & T Clark.

Beck, A. T., Freeman, A., & Associates. (1990). *Cognitive therapy of personality disorders.* New York: Guilford.

Beck, A. T., Freeman, A., & Davis, D. D. (2003). *Cognitive therapy of personality disorders* (2nd ed.). New York: Guilford.

Benner, D. G. (2004). *The gift of being yourself: The sacred call to self-discovery.* Downers Grove, IL: InterVarsity Press.

Bowlby, J. (1988). *A secure base: Parent-child attachment and healthy human development.* New York: Basic Books.

Butler, A. C., & Beck, J. S. (2001). Cognitive therapy outcomes: A review of meta-analyses. *Tidsskrift for Norsk Psykologforening, 38,* 698-706.

Garfield, S. L. (1996). Some problems associated with "validated" forms of psychotherapy. *Clinical Psychology, 3,* 218-29.

Hamilton, N. G. (1988). *Self and others: Object relations theory in practice.* Northvale, NJ: Aronson.

Horney, K. (1945). *Our inner conflicts: A constructive theory of neurosis.* New York: W. W. Norton.

Jones, E. (1961). *The life and work of Sigmund Freud.* New York: Basic Books.

Kerr, M. E., & Bowen, M. (1988). *Family evaluation.* NewYork: W. W. Norton.

Lambert, M. J., & Barley, D. E. (2002). Research summary on the therapeutic relationship and psychotherapy outcome. In John C. Norcross (Ed.), *Psychotherapy relationships that work* (pp. 17-32). New York: Oxford.

Levenson, H. (1995). *Time-limited dynamic psychotherapy: A guide to clinical practice.* New York: Basic Books.

Linehan, M. M. (1993). *Cognitive-behavioral treatment of borderline personality disorder.* New York: Guilford.

McMinn, M. R., & Wade, N. G. (1995). Beliefs about the prevalence of Dissociative Identity Disorder, sexual abuse, and ritual abuse among religious and non-religious therapists. *Professional Psychology: Research and Practice, 26,* 257-61.

McWilliams, N. (1994). *Psychoanalytic diagnosis: Understanding personality structure in the clinical process.* New York: Guilford.

Millon, T. (1990). *Toward a new personology: An evolutionary model.* New York: Wiley.

Millon, T., & Davis, R. D. (2000). *Personality disorders in modern life.* New York: Wiley.

Peck, M. S. (1983). *People of the lie: The hope for healing human evil.* New York: Simon & Schuster.

Perez, J. E. (1999). Clients deserve empirically supported treatments, not romanticism [comment]. *American Psychologist, 54,* 205-7.

Rasmussen, P. R. (2005). *Personality-guided cognitive-behavioral therapy.* Washington, DC: American Psychological Association.

Rohr, R., & Ebert, A. (2001). *The Enneagram: A Christian perspective.* New York: Crossroad Publishing.

Ryle, A. (1990). *Cognitive-analytic therapy: Active participation in change.* New York: Wiley.

Safran, J. D. (1998). *Widening the scope of cognitive therapy: The therapeutic relationship, emotion, and the process of change.* Northvale, NJ: Aronson.

Safran, J. D. (2001). When worlds collide: Psychoanalysis and the empirically supported treatment movement. *Psychoanalytic Dialogues, 11,* 659-81.

Strupp, H. H. (2001). Implications of the empirically supported treatment movement for psychoanalysis. *Psychoanalytic Dialogues, 11,* 605-19.

Sullivan, H. S. (1953). *The interpersonal theory of psychiatry.* New York: W. W. Norton.

Teyber, E. (2006). *Interpersonal process in therapy: An integrative model.* Belmont, CA: Brooks/Cole.

Yarhouse, M. A., Butman, R. E., & McRay, B. W. (2005). *Modern psychopathologies: A comprehensive Christian appraisal.* Downers Grove, IL: InterVarsity Press.

Young, J. E., Klosko, J. S., & Weishaar, M. E. (2003). *Schema therapy: A practitioner's guide.* New York: Guilford.

11

Applying Relationship-Focused Interventions

PEOPLE TODAY WANT MEASURABLE RESULTS. Business investors look for profitability and growth, educators assess competencies and outcomes, and health care providers promote empirically supported treatment procedures. Not surprisingly, the practice of psychotherapy has become increasingly results-oriented also. Mental health insurers want to see their dollars being spent wisely, so they insist on short-term interventions that provide rapid symptom reduction. Consumers of mental health services often want the same, and isn't it interesting that we call them consumers? Presumably we do so because it completes the measurability cycle: the therapist provides measurable results in exchange for measurable financial resources.

Measurability is a good thing from within the medical-care paradigm. It makes therapists accountable, spurs on important research and helps keep health care reimbursement systems cost effective. We both have clinical practices that are partially rooted in this medical-care paradigm, and we find symptom-focused and schema-focused IP quite useful in this regard. But some clients do not respond quickly to psychotherapy, or they are looking for a deeper sort of transformation than symptom checklists can measure, so we have also come to value long-term relationship-focused interventions for these more complex clinical situations. Hans Strupp (2001), a psychodynamic researcher and therapist, writes:

> There is a basic difference between contemporary forms of psychotherapy—particularly the time-limited or "brief" variety—and the psychoanalytically oriented, time-unlimited treatment. The former typically follows the "medical model," whereas the latter, which usually calls for a considerable investment of time and effort, embraces an educational one. . . .
>
> It is important to recognize that the medical model and the educational model subscribe to divergent goals. The former is primarily geared to symptom relief, whereas the latter has as its basic objective personality growth. . . . This, I believe,

is one of the reasons why symptom relief requires a yardstick very different from that used for personality change. Failure to recognize this difference has contributed markedly to the reigning confusion in the field. (pp. 610-11)

Relationship-focused IP is not based on the psychoanalytic model that Strupp holds, but both share in common the assumption that inner transformation may require a good deal of time and cannot be measured with simple outcome criteria.

The distinction Strupp makes between a medical model and an educational model is generally consistent with relationship-focused IP, but two differences are worth noting. First, Strupp implies a clear bifurcation between two types of therapy, as if therapists trained in one tradition offer a particular kind of therapy and those trained in another tradition offer something entirely different. In IP we see long-term therapy as an amalgam of the two approaches. Therapy generally begins with symptom resolution and then progresses to deeper forms of transformation if the client and therapist deem it necessary and appropriate. We acknowledge that some therapists have greater interests in a medical-care paradigm and others in a soul-care paradigm, but we see value in all therapy beginning with symptom-focused and schema-focused work even if the ultimate goals are bigger than this. Second, Strupp refers to relationally oriented therapies as based on an educational model, but we prefer calling it a soul-care paradigm. Though education is certainly involved in relationship-focused IP, we wish to connote something more than education.

Relationship-Focused IP as Soul Care

Some people think of the soul as if it is less than a whole person, implying a person has a soul that is separate from one's body. This was the view of French philosopher René Descartes, who saw the body as material and the soul as immaterial and even suggested a particular gland in the body where the soul and body interact. Most philosophers and theologians now reject this stark dualism for its reductionism and limited view of the soul.

It is better to view the soul as a person. One does not *have* a soul, but *is* a soul. Soul care involves caring for a whole person who has both spiritual significance and physical substance. But we need to take this a step further because a soul is more than a self. A soul integrates the various dimensions of a person—thoughts, feelings, choices, body and relationships—into a life that has significance and meaning in a spiritual sense (Willard, 2002). So *soul* is not simply synonymous with *person,* but implies that the whole is bigger than the sum of its parts. The soul organizes and makes meaning of the whole person. It is what Willard calls "the deepest part of the self" (2002, p. 37). Similarly, Benner

(1998) writes, "Caring for souls is caring for people in ways that not only acknowledge them as persons but also engage and address them in the deepest and most profoundly human aspects of their lives" (p. 23).

The medical-care paradigm tends to parse out one dimension of a person and provide some corrective treatment. Surgeons, for example, focus on the biological. So do most psychiatrists. Cognitive therapists focus on the cognitive. All of these can be crucially important, but none of them works with a whole person. The educational model that Strupp (2001) describes is more comprehensive than a medical model because education may involve thoughts, feelings, choices, body and relationships. Still, education seems to neglect a larger spiritual perspective that organizes and gives meaning to all of these. Soul-care encompasses all the various dimensions of a person while also recognizing that each person has significance in God's creation. Clebsch and Jaekle (1964) define the cure of souls (they prefer "cure" to "care") as helping acts by Christians "directed toward the healing, sustaining, guiding, and reconciling of troubled persons whose troubles arise in the context of ultimate meanings and concerns" (p. 4). Here we see the notion of a soul as a whole person with spiritual strivings (see Emmons, 1999).

Our choice to describe relationship-focused IP as soul care may seem awkward because for much of the twentieth century modern psychology supplanted the language of the soul with a secularized vocabulary of personality and behavior change. But the shifting winds of time brought revitalized interest in spirituality and psychology near the end of last century, and now we live in a time when psychotherapists publish books such as *Care of the Soul* (Moore, 1992), *Care of Souls* (Benner, 1998), *Care for the Soul* (McMinn & Phillips, 2001), and *Spiritual Direction and the Care of Souls* (Moon & Benner, 2004). We see this as a positive movement, allowing spiritually oriented psychologists to reclaim the notion that psychotherapy can be soul care, but it is also important to be discriminating, because not all forms of soul care are psychotherapy.

The Christological Core of Soul Care

Psychotherapy is only one of several forms of soul care. Benner (1998) identifies eight forms in the Christian community alone: care within one's family, mutual relationships, pastoral care, lay counseling, Christian counseling, pastoral counseling, spiritual direction and Christian psychotherapy. We will distinguish between psychotherapy and other forms of soul care later in this chapter, but it is important to first look for an essential commonality: all forms of Christian soul care share in common some sort of life-promoting relationship.

How should we view the essence of a soul-care relationship? We suggest that the starting point be found in the life and work of Christ. We come to this conclusion based on several interrelated Christian perspectives.

1. A relational view of the *imago Dei* asserts that the fullness of God's image is not revealed in an individual, but in a relationship between two or more persons (Grenz, 2000). Neither Adam nor Eve was a sole owner of the image, but together they were: "So God created people in his own image; God patterned them after himself; male and female he created them" (Gen 1:27).

2. Sin tainted the image, so human relationships no longer provide a proper reflection of God's character. Now relationships are contaminated with sinful desires and self-serving perceptions that cloud God's image. But there is one exception.

3. Jesus was the one sinless human, "the visible image of the invisible God" (Col 1:15), a second Adam (1 Cor 15:45-47) who reflected the full glory of God's image.

4. Therefore, if we want to know what is good and right about human relationships, our beginning point should be the person and work of Christ, who is the "very center of Christian theology" (Erickson, 1985, p. 661).

Jesus transformed the world, and he did it without military rank or a political office or a transnational corporation. He transformed the world through the power of relationship. He gathered twelve followers around him, spent three years with them in itinerant ministry, and influenced eleven of these apostles so profoundly that they went on to change the world by establishing the church. These apostles were so completely transformed that they died martyrs' deaths for the sake of Jesus. For centuries after Jesus lived on earth the credibility of Christian doctrine was established by how closely an idea was linked to the teaching of Jesus' apostles, because the apostles were in relationship with Jesus himself.

Some might object to choosing a man who lived two thousand years ago as the exemplar of a healing relationship in twenty-first-century psychotherapy, reasoning that contemporary science has surely identified more relevant qualities for psychotherapy training programs to instill in their students. We affirm the importance of psychotherapy training, and later in this chapter we turn to specific strategies for crafting a therapy relationship, but it is also important to acknowledge a common relational core to all forms of soul care. Consider the classic Vanderbilt I study, where Strupp and Hadley (1979) assigned troubled college students to talk with either professional therapists or college professors who were known to be warm and empathic but who had no formal training in psychotherapy. Both groups improved when compared with control groups, but the group seeing professional therapists did not fare any better than the group the college professors. Strupp (1993) is careful in interpreting these results, noting several reasons to avoid the rash conclusion that professional training makes no difference. Nonetheless, the study speaks clearly to the importance of so-called nonspecific factors (similar to the common factors described in chapter two). The primary ingredients of change in Strupp and Hadley's study had to do with the relationships shared between two human beings—one needing help and the other providing compassionate care—and not the specific re-

---

COUNSELING TIP 11.1: Don't Just Sit There, Do Something

In our technological world it seems like there is a gadget for everything that is supposed to make our lives easier or more efficient. But for some problems, technology is not the answer. We hear students say, "I'm not doing anything for this client, I'm just listening and trying to form a relationship." We underestimate the value of relationships in our culture. Christ transformed the world without technology, a bestselling book or a stand-up comedy routine. Relationships are powerful. Listening, being attentive, engaged and genuine are human qualities that technology cannot provide.

---

lational or therapeutic skills taught in graduate school. Since the Vanderbilt I study, many more studies have been reported that affirm the importance of relational factors in psychotherapy (Norcross, 2002). The best resource Christians have in identifying healthy relational patterns is by looking at the life of Jesus, the one who was not marred by sin.

Christology scholars distinguish between a *view from below* and a *view from above*. The former looks at the life of the historical Jesus without making any theological assumptions about his nature. From this vantage point we can see a man who related to others with humility, kindness, assertiveness and love. In contrast, the view from above begins with the theological assumptions about Jesus that were established by the church in the first several centuries following his life, death and resurrection. By drawing on a view from above we not only see a good man with effective relational skills when we look at Jesus, but the flawless image of God revealed in human form. We see one who related to others exactly as God would, because indeed Jesus was fully God and fully human. There is plenty to learn in a view from below, but by faith we choose the view from above in looking at Jesus. Drawing on a view from above, Brunner (1932/1947) suggests that we look especially to the Gospel of John and the writings of the apostle Paul when building christological arguments, because these are the writings with theological interpretations of the life and work of Christ. There is no better place to begin than John 1:14: "The Word became flesh and made his dwelling among us. We have seen his glory, the glory of the One and Only, who came from the Father, *full of grace and truth*" (NIV, italics added).

Grace. Grace is extending kindness to one who can do nothing to deserve it. Jesus, full of grace, offered bounteous and undeserved kindness to those who had been living under the law of Moses. None of us can reach God, even with our noblest efforts, but Jesus graciously restores us to God, not because any of us deserves it but because of the grace of God, revealed fully in Jesus. The apostle Paul writes that Jesus "has brought you into the very presence of God, and you are holy and blameless as you stand before him without a single fault" (Col 1:22). John also describes it beautifully: "We have all benefited from the rich blessings he brought to us—one gracious blessing after another" (Jn 1:16). Paul and John see in Jesus one of the most important qualities of healing relationships: grace. Just as Jesus was full of grace, so also we are called to be gracious to one another, generous with our compassion and understanding, forgiving, blessing others with our words and behavior.

The heart of grace is love. Throughout his Gospel account John refers to himself as the one whom Jesus loved. John's life was transformed by the love of Christ, and when he later wrote his first epistle he made love the centerpiece of his theology:

> Dear friends, let us continue to love one another, for love comes from God. Anyone who loves is born of God and knows God. But anyone who does not love does not know God—for God is love.
>
> God showed how much he loved us by sending his only Son into the world so that we might have eternal life through him. This is real love. It is not that we loved God, but that he loved us and sent his Son as a sacrifice to take away our sins.
>
> Dear friends, since God loved us that much, we surely ought to love each other. No one has ever seen God. But if we love each other, God lives in us, and his love has been brought to full expression through us. (1 Jn 4:7-12)

John experienced the full image of God, revealed in Christ, as a fierce and faithful love. Perhaps he encountered Jesus' love in conversations by the Sea of Galilee, in glimpses of compassion on a dusty path from one village to another or in the Upper Room where Jesus washed his follower's feet and then taught them a new commandment: "Just as I have loved you, you should love each other" (Jn 13:34). However it happened, John was changed, and he knew to instruct others about the importance of love.

also emphasizes the love of Jesus. In his letter to Ephesus, he gives an
ible, paradoxical instruction:

> And may you have the power to understand, as all God's people should, how
> wide, how long, how high, and how deep his love really is. May you experience
> the love of Christ, though it is so great you will never fully understand it. Then you
> will be filled with the fullness of life and power that comes from God. (Eph 3:18-
> 19)

If we want to experience the most abundant life and the healing power of
relationship that comes from it, we must first experience the love of Christ. But
here is the paradox, because Paul reminds us that the love of Christ is too vast
to grasp. We can move toward it, try to understand it, but in our finitude and
our brokenness we fail to grasp the full magnitude of divine love. We are a fearful people, stooping under the weight of sin, making it difficult to experience
this love that "expels all fear" (1 Jn 4:18).

It is so easy, so seemingly natural, to exchange the possibility of grace, rooted
in the love of Christ, for the shame and fear that epitomizes contemporary life.
Soul care offers hope of a better way, experienced through a caring human relationship based in the love and grace of God. Tjeltveit (2004) concludes his
thoughtful article on grace and psychology by reminding us: "We stand, always,
in need of grace. Through the cross, grace is available to us, always. In our efforts to understand human beings, that may be the most profound fact of all"
(pp. 116-17). Jesus demonstrated how humans were intended to treat one another—with grace, rooted in the love of God. He reached out to touch lepers,
healed the sick, fed the hungry, sacrificed sleep and fought through fatigue to

---

COUNSELING TIP 11.2: There but For the Grace of God Go I

Counselors work with the ugly side of life. We see illness, twisted thinking,
corrupt motives and evil desires on a daily basis. As a result of this daily exposure it is easy for a counselor to develop detrimental attitudes. We can
become cynical and pessimistic in our view of others, and we can become
superior and arrogant in our view of ourselves. These are potential negative side effects of our vocation. A daily reminder of God's grace is helpful
in combating these attitudes. God's grace is sufficient for the redemption
of the most heinous sin, and if it were not for God's grace, we would all be
hopeless.

help the needy, and even gave up his life as the ultimate expression of love (see Rom 5:6-8). But notice that this loving, gracious, fearless Jesus was far from passive. He stood up against injustice. He handcrafted a whip to drive marketers out of the temple. He knew to take care of himself by getting away to pray and be alone. Jesus had a comprehensive understanding of love that caused him both to care tenderly for people and to be fearless in his quest for justice. His love was full of grace and truth.

Truth. Jesus was not only filled with grace but also with truth. He was direct and clear with others, even when he disagreed with them. If truth is measured by healthy assertiveness, then Jesus is surely the exemplar—he was honest and forthright in his communication yet motivated by love rather than self-interest. But the Greek word that John used for "truth" means much more than assertive and honest expression. Jesus was true in the sense that a plumb wall is true. He was perfectly aligned with the will of God, completely faithful and right in his perspectives, a person of total integrity, uncompromised by the tarnishing effects of sin. Paul used the same word for truth in writing to the Ephesians:

> Since you have heard all about [Christ] and have learned the *truth* that is in Jesus, throw off your old evil nature and your former way of life, which is rotten through and through, full of lust and deception. Instead, there must be a spiritual renewal of your thoughts and attitudes. You must display a new nature because you are a new person, created in God's likeness—righteous, holy, and *true.* (Eph 4:21-24, italics added)

The heart of truth is faithful obedience. John records Jesus' words to his followers: "You are truly my disciples if you keep obeying my teachings. And you will know the truth, and the truth will set you free" (Jn 8:31-32). Some have taken these words of Jesus and turned them upside down, as if Jesus is teaching us to look inside, find our most compelling desires and then be true to ourselves by honoring those desires. To the contrary, Jesus was referring to a bigger truth found in faithful obedience to God's desires. Jesus calls his followers to live pure lives of integrity.

In our therapeutic culture, it is tempting to view grace as the only virtue relevant to help a struggling soul achieve balance and hope. Mercy and kindness and love are thought to be the sole pathway to healing. This is partly right— grace is indeed a balm that leads to hope and healing. But truth matters too. Christians are called to grow toward faithful obedience to God, and so soul care helps orient a person to a life of holiness and right living.

Healing relationships are found in that place where grace and truth meet. In addition to writing this book together, the two of us are friends and have been for many years. One measure of our friendship is that we are gracious to one another. When one of us is discouraged or uncertain, the other offers kindness and hope. But an equally important aspect of our friendship is truth. We have helped one another to live truer lives than we might have otherwise lived, encouraging one another by example and timely counsel. Of course neither of us has attained complete truth in our lifestyle—integrity is an aspiration more than a reality in this broken world—but our mutual friendship has helped us move toward truth.

Mutual friendship is one form of soul care in Christian communities; psychotherapy is another. But in all cases, Christian soul care helps move people toward the truth that was revealed fully in Christ. This means that Christian psychotherapists working from a soul-care paradigm are interested in character formation as well as symptom relief. If Christ is at the center of Christianity, then Christ is also at the center of transformative Christian relationships. In relationship-focused IP, the therapist is continually striving to reflect the grace and truth of Christ and to help clients move toward grace and truth.

Diverse Expressions of Soul Care

Christ is central to all soul care, but the specific nature of healing relationships varies according to the sort of soul care being offered. Likewise, throughout his New Testament letters the apostle Paul gives both general directives for how to treat one another and specific instructions for particular types of relationships. In a general sense we are to be humble and gentle (Eph 4:2), to avoid selfishness (Phil 2:3), to love others (1 Cor 14:1), to live industrious lives (1 Thess 4:11) and so on. Paul also offers more specific guidance for how husbands and wives are to relate to one another (Eph 5:21-33), how children and parents should interact (Eph 6:1-4), how older and younger women can relate (Tit 2:5-6), how church leaders behave (1 Tim 3:1-13) and so on. All of these specific instructions emerge out of the general themes of how Christians relate to one another—with kindness, humility, gentleness and love. Analogously, the grace and truth of Christ serve as the general directives for how soul care ought to happen, but various forms of soul care may call for different relational emphases and skills. Christian psychotherapy—one form of soul care—involves different relational styles and priorities than other forms of soul care, such as spiritual direction.

We are skeptical of the current movement to conflate psychotherapy and spiritual direction. Benner (2005) recommends intensive soul care as a combination of psychotherapy and spiritual direction—a combination that he once thought untenable.

Anyone who dares to put ideas in print must be prepared for the experience of enforced humility that comes when one changes publicly presented positions. In *Psychotherapy and the Spiritual Quest* (Benner, 1988), I argued that psychotherapy and spiritual direction were different enough in focus and goals that practitioners should not attempt to integrate them. In the 10 years between that book and *Care of Souls* (Benner, 1998), I became convinced that it was both possible and, in some circumstances, desirable to integrate these two forms of soul care. (Benner, 2005, pp. 287-88)

Benner's creative means of integrating spiritual direction and psychotherapy are laudable, and we have tremendous respect for him and his work. Nonetheless, we are not optimistic about blending these two types of soul care, at least not in an activity that is publicly promoted as therapeutic and offered by a licensed mental health professional.

Psychotherapy has a unique focus which sets it apart from spiritual direction. Sperry (2004) identifies various differences between psychotherapy and spiritual direction. In spiritual direction, the initial assessment focuses on spiritual functioning while psychological functioning is the focus of a psychotherapist's initial assessment. Whereas spiritual directors consider transformation to be a lifelong process of finding one's true self in God, psychotherapists tend to have a narrower view of transformation—one that is limited to a particular relationship pattern or personality style. Spiritual directors often use advising as a way of helping others learn new methods of drawing close to God. In contrast, psychotherapists rarely advise their clients. They are much more likely to use methods such as guided discovery, restatement, interpretation and so on. Spiritual directors help others discern God's leading whereas psychotherapy is more about mutual collaboration between the therapist and client. Benner (2002) also identifies differences between spiritual direction and psychotherapy, noting that therapy is problem-centered whereas spiritual direction is Spirit-centered, therapists focus their empathy on the client while spiritual directors focus on the Spirit, and therapists keep records and notes whereas spiritual directors find this detracts from a focus on God. After articulating these differences between spiritual direction and psychotherapy, both Sperry (2004) and Benner (2005) show openness toward rapprochement. In contrast, we do not see IP as a blend of psychotherapy and spiritual direction. IP is an integrated model of psychotherapy that relies on spiritual practices and Christian metaphysics, but the goals and procedures fit squarely in the realm of psychotherapy and not spiritual direction.

Numerous ethical challenges arise when trying to combine psychotherapy and spiritual direction, and though most of these can be worked out (see Tan, 2004) there is a looming problem that cannot be resolved—the problem of

COUNSELING TIP 11.3: Spiritual Direction and Psychotherapy

Though we do not favor conflating psychotherapy and spiritual direction, we are favorably inclined toward both. Spiritual directors help their directees experience a closer relationship with God. This can be tremendously meaningful and helpful to people trying to find their way in a world where they feel suffocated by unrealistic achievement goals, consumerism gone amuck and unrealistic standards for approval.

Just as spiritual directors are careful to distinguish what they do from psychotherapy, and to refer those have stumbled into the wrong office to a psychotherapist, so also Christian psychotherapists ought to make a similar distinction and refer some clients to pastors, priests or spiritual directors. A client whose primary concern pertains to his or her experience with God and who shows no overt symptoms of psychological disturbance should be referred to a spiritual leader working under the auspices of the client's faith tradition.

church authority. Spiritual direction has historically been offered under the authority of the church. Both the director and directee are accountable to particular theological perspectives and ecclesiological practices that help keep the spiritual direction from drifting into an experiential whimsy. Historically directors were not so much trained as they were recognized for their gifts of wisdom and discernment by a group to which they remained accountable. In contrast, psychotherapists are under the authority of state regulating bodies that grant licenses, establish ethical standards and regulate compliance. The implications of removing spiritual direction from its authoritative moorings and putting it in the hands of psychotherapists who are accountable to a different sort of authority are troubling. Psychotherapists who offer spiritual direction tend to keep their spiritual direction work hidden from their regulating bodies, or perhaps they conceive of spiritual direction meetings as distinct from psychotherapy and so they practice without accountability to any authority. The immediate questions of insurance billing, multiple-role relationships and content of treatment notes are troubling enough, but the bigger question of accountability seems larger than whatever benefits may come from integrating psychotherapy and spiritual direction. Thus, we are quite insistent that IP is psychotherapy and not a form of spiritual direction.

To summarize, soul care is the broad category of caring for whole persons,

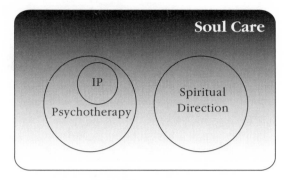

Characterized by Grace and Truth

Figure 11.1. Soul care, psychotherapy and spiritual direction

which includes various helping activities (see figure 11.1). Effective Christian soul care is modeled after the virtues of Jesus, who was full of grace and truth. Both psychotherapy and spiritual direction are forms of soul care, but in our opinion they are to remain nonoverlapping activities. IP fits within the psychotherapy paradigm. Of course there are other forms of soul care that, for sake of simplicity, we have not listed in figure 11.1. These would include pastoral counseling, lay counseling, support groups and so on.

Therapeutic Considerations in Soul Care

Thus far we have argued that a soul-care paradigm is appropriate for understanding relationally focused IP and that a christological core provides an ideal basis for all soul-care activities. This has been premised on a Christian understanding of persons, and unapologetically so. To a large extent we concur with Charry (2001), who concludes that "Christian spiritual health is based not in the skills one cultivates but in the deeper theological foundation from which they are cultivated" (p. 132). But if one accepts our premise that psychotherapy is a unique activity, distinct from other forms of soul care in various ways, then it also is reasonable to assume that psychotherapists have discovered some important dimensions of how change occurs. This may be so regardless of the psychotherapists' religious convictions.

In chapter one we mentioned the phrase "All truth is God's truth" and made the point that this phrase has caused a good deal of mischief. Although it is true that we should look to both general and special revelation whenever possible, it does not follow that both sources of truth are equally reliable or authoritative in all situations. Some things are addressed directly in one source of revelation but not in the other. Special revelation is trump when it comes to discussing the morality of greed or standards of sexual morality, for example, because these are so clearly addressed in Scripture. General revelation is more authoritative when understanding photosynthesis in plants or serotonin reuptake mechanisms in the central nervous system. These distinctions between sources of authority can be helpful, but some areas of inquiry are addressed in both special and general revelation and so both sources should be considered.

An understanding of healing relationships is rooted in both general and special revelation, and so we ought to look to both in order to understand effective psychotherapy relationships. The Bible is filled with practical guidance for effective relationships, and a Christian psychotherapist is wise to study and understand Scripture well. In addition, psychotherapists have contributed considerable wisdom to how healing relationships work. This is also a source of valuable information—one to which we now turn our attention.

The essence of soul care is that transformation involves a healing relationship. Relationships change people, and the power of a strong relationship can bring about profound interpersonal changes. In psychotherapy the transformative relationship can be described in terms of the therapeutic alliance, therapeutic frame and relational dynamics.

Therapeutic alliance. The therapeutic alliance is essential to any form of psychotherapy. It describes the strength of the bond that exists between the therapist and the client. In IP the therapeutic alliance exists in each of the three domains but is most important in domain 3 because the relationship itself becomes the primary instrument of change. Figure 11.2 shows that explicit techniques become less important and the relationship becomes more important as therapy moves from domain 1 to 3.

A therapeutic alliance involves a safe and trusting relationship in which the client feels understood. Safety and trust allow clients to explore their inner thoughts and feelings in a nonthreatening relationship. Accurate empathy (Rogers, 1957) allows a client to feel understood. Bowlby (1988) described this kind of relationship as a holding environment that provides security. When a person feels "held" in the therapist's attention (not literally held), the client experiences safety and trust.

Beck, Rush, Shaw and Emery (1979) emphasized collaboration as essential to a strong therapeutic alliance. Collaboration between therapist and client implies a partnership that is different than the hierarchical relationship conceptualized by early psychologists. A collaborative relationship facilitates active participation by the client rather than a passive stance in which the therapist does something to a client. A collaborative relationship may reduce the client's defensiveness

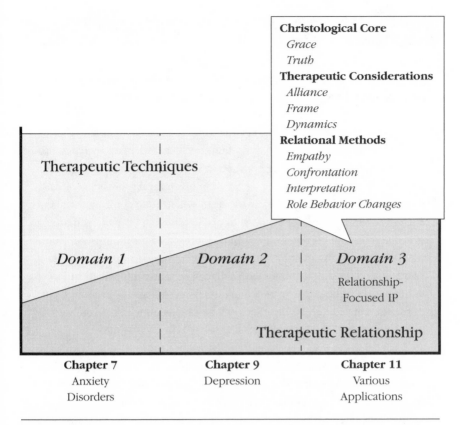

Figure 11.2. Domains of intervention in relation to therapeutic techniques and relationship

and instill a belief that the client's observations and interpretations are of significant value. It is important that the therapist establish a collaborative therapeutic alliance early in therapy so that the client is an active partner in treatment. This will entail agreement between the therapist and client regarding the nature of the relationship (bond), goals to be accomplished and the tasks that will facilitate the goals (Bordin, 1979).

Therapeutic frame. A therapeutic frame implies a setting that is conducive to therapy. This setting involves the actual therapeutic environment and much more. The frame has to do with the general boundaries that define the therapeutic relationship—the time, place and fees for services provided. Expectations involving confidentiality and the roles of the therapist and client are part of the frame as well. Seasoned therapists recognize that consistency in practice is very important. When the therapist maintains consistent expectations of the therapy

COUNSELING TIP 11.4: SETTING LIMITS

Maintaining a therapeutic frame often involves establishing clear expectations and setting limits with clients, especially those who meet criteria for personality disorders (discussed in chapter ten). When a client brings up an emotionally volatile topic a few minutes before the session is to end, the therapist may choose to end the session on time rather than extend the session for an additional fifteen to thirty minutes. The therapist may have clear guidelines about when, if ever, home telephone calls will be accepted from clients. Or perhaps the therapist will charge for calls outside regularly scheduled office hours. Maybe the therapist will need to confront the client about showing up late for sessions or about showing up early and asking invasive questions to other clients in the waiting room. All of these examples illustrate a consistent frame in which therapy occurs. Though the therapist's choice to set clear boundaries may upset the client, it can still have a therapeutic benefit insofar as it models self-respect and limits on the part of the therapist and treats the client as a capable adult who can tolerate disappointment and frustration (McWilliams, 1994).

With some clients, it may seem that enormous time and energy is being spent on boundary-setting. Rather than seeing this as a hindrance to therapy, it is better to realize that this is an important part of the therapy. As the frame is being established, the client gains self-awareness and learns effective problem solving by watching how the therapist responds with grace and truth.

process—that the therapy will occur in the same place at the same general time for a consistent fee—then interruptions to the frame can be interpreted in a meaningful manner.

Bion (1962) initially described the therapeutic relationship as a container. By this metaphor he meant that the framework of good therapy provides a secure context in which the client feels safe enough to reveal any troubling thoughts, feelings or memories. A common initial experience for clients is to be frightened by their own thoughts and feelings. A significant experience of guilt may inhibit a client from describing his struggle with sin. An overwhelming feeling of sadness may lead another client to fear that if she starts crying she will never stop. When the therapeutic frame involves an effective container, these thoughts and feelings can be contained and the client can feel secure in knowing that the therapist can effectively handle overwhelming experiences.

The therapeutic alliance and frame are similar concepts that play a significant role in establishing effective therapy. The alliance implies a strong bond with a collaborative partnership. The frame implies consistent expectations of the therapy sessions and of the professional behavior of the therapist. A strong alliance and frame help prevent therapeutic ruptures, which are incidents in therapy when the client pulls away from the therapist, feels insecure and becomes self-protective. A rupture may result from a poorly established alliance or frame, a misunderstanding between the therapist and client, or fear of the intensity of emerging thoughts and feelings by either the client or therapist. When these ruptures can be identified and addressed quickly by the therapist, the therapy is likely to be more successful (Safran, 1998).

Relational dynamics. Once a therapeutic alliance and frame are established, the inevitable interpersonal dynamics involved in IP can become meaningful. These dynamics are crucial to effective therapy in the interpersonal domain. It is difficult to accurately interpret any statement or behavior from a client prior to the establishment of the alliance and frame because the ground rules of the relationship are ill-defined. It is similar to knowing how to play baseball in your own sand lot. You know the field, the potholes, the broken glass, the odd dimensions, and as long as the lot doesn't change you have the opportunity to play consistently well. When others come over to play they need to play within the confines of your sand lot. Knowing the ground rules of your field allows you to practice and perform well. (Whether or not you are truly a great baseball player remains undetermined until you play on a regulation field under standardized conditions. This, of course, is the focus of research in psychotherapy—to see the outcomes of therapy when the rules of the field are standardized or controlled.) The therapeutic alliance and frame provide a consistent therapy field upon which one can make more accurate interpretations of behavior.

Relational dynamics refer to the interpersonal "dance" that occurs in any close relationship. Psychotherapy involves a series of interpersonal exchanges that are designed to improve the functioning of the client. These exchanges (behaviors and communications) portray an overt and a covert message. Watzlawick, Beavin and Jackson (1967) described two levels of communication that occur simultaneously—a report and a command function of communication. The report level consists of the words that are used, while the command function describes the meaning or the response the words are intended to elicit. A parent may say to a child, "the trash is full" (report function), which really means "you should take out the trash" (command function). When people develop relationships they tend to communicate in this fashion over time, which obviously leads to misunderstanding and feelings of manipulation. The command messages become most important and actually define the relationship. Some couples come to therapy, make a few seemingly innocuous comments and begin fighting. Although the comments may seem neutral to the therapist, the comments carry

---

IN THE OFFICE 11.1: Listening on Two Levels

Skilled therapists are always listening to their clients on two levels—what is said (report) and how it is to be taken (command). The command level is referred to as metacommunication because it is a form of communication that does not rely on the words themselves. Metacommunication always trumps the actual words used in the communication, and metacommunication always indicates who has the power in a relationship as well.

Holly consulted a psychologist because of increasing concerns about her fifteen-year-old son's depression. She brought her son (Aaron) to the consultation. Mark met Aaron and his mother in the waiting room and invited them into the therapy office.

Mark: It's nice to meet you. Please have a seat wherever you would like.

Holly: Wouldn't you like to sit there, Aaron?

Aaron: [No comment. Sits down where mom pointed.]

Mark: Holly, I understand that you have some concerns about Aaron. What's been on your mind?

Holly: I think Aaron can respond best to that. [Looks at Aaron and pauses]

Aaron: [Silence]

Holly: Aaron, you should feel free to say whatever you want.

Aaron: Well, my friends don't want to come over to the house . . .

Holly: [Interrupting] Aaron, we're not here to talk about your friends.

Aaron: [Silence]

Holly: Aaron, I know you're feeling depressed and you have trouble talking, but we're really here to talk about your problems. What are you so worried about?

In this scenario Holly uses a question to imply that Aaron should sit in a certain chair. Further, she tells her son that he can speak about anything, but as soon as he does she interrupts and cuts him off. While the words state that Aaron has freedom, the metacommunication is that he should be quiet and do what mom wants. Holly maintains interpersonal control over her son through this subtle manipulation.

meaning that functions at this deeper level.

When a solid therapeutic alliance and frame exist it is possible to interpret these communications in a meaningful manner. The client who says, "I tried what you recommended and it didn't work as well as I hoped" may mean "I don't think you are a very good therapist" or "I'm hopeless." The interchange can go back and forth between therapist and client while never addressing the command functions of the exchanges (how the words are to be interpreted). The astute therapist attends to the relational dynamics of these communications because they involve important comments designed to control the relationship. The reason the dynamics are important is that relationship control is a significant aspect of interpersonal problems. Clients may be trying to reenact issues from their past in their current relationships or in the therapeutic relationship.

We described three interpersonal models in chapter ten: interpersonal process approach, cyclical maladaptive patterns and reciprocal role procedures. These models have various similarities and differences, but an essential commonality is that all three consider how people reenact former patterns in current relationships, including the therapy relationship. These reenactments are important to understand in domain 3 IP so that the therapist can be intentional and prudent about how to relate to clients.

Teyber (2006) described three ways in which clients re-create their early relationship patterns within a therapeutic relationship. One way clients relive their past interpersonal problems is through eliciting maneuvers. "An eliciting maneuver is an interpersonal strategy that wards off anxiety and brings about certain desired, safe responses" (Teyber, 2006, p. 280). In other words, a client may exhibit behaviors that are designed to elicit particular responses from a therapist. The client who moves away from others to decrease anxiety may cancel an appointment, desire to terminate therapy prematurely or become quiet during a session. These behaviors could be attempts to elicit caring but distant responses from the therapist, such as hoping the therapist will invite the client to participate but not really engage in the therapy. Similarly, a client who moves toward others may elicit kind and approving responses from a therapist by describing wounded feelings or by being a star patient. The client who moves against others may criticize the therapist to elicit submissive or argumentative behaviors in a therapist.

If a therapist engages the client by colluding in this reenactment of the interpersonal problems, the therapist will become ineffective. In longer-term therapy clients will attempt to elicit these old behavior patterns, and therapists need to be astute observers so that they do not simply give the elicited response. Thus, it would be easy and perhaps natural to argue with some clients, praise some and pursue others. This "dance" would reenact the original interpersonal patterns and lead to the same outcome. A therapeutic response that could lead to problem resolution rather than reenactment would be one that simply describes the eliciting behavior or the therapist's felt response in a nonthreatening manner. Below, the same therapeutic dynamic is presented with two possible outcomes.

Jim: I got the impression from our last session that I should go ahead and ask my boss for two weeks off. So I did, and he gave it to me.

Clark: Sounds like you made a decision to be assertive.

Jim: I also made an appointment to talk to my doctor about antidepressant medication because it sounded like that may be helpful as well.

Clark: It looks like you're working really hard to get better by following through on the things we talk about.

Jim: I'm trying to. I really want to feel better and make good use of our time.

Clark: That's important. Not all clients follow through like that.

Jim: Well, I came here to get better and I believe you can help me, so I want to follow through.

Clark: You certainly are motivated. I believe that will help you get better more quickly.

By showing approval the therapist is simply re-creating the interpersonal dynamics for Jim. When he is distressed he moves toward people, seeks to engage them and elicit their approval. When he is approved his distress subsides temporarily. He is a "good" client, and the therapist (who likes to work with clients who follow through and also wants to think of himself as making good suggestions) readily gives his approval. Both client and therapist can feel good, but little interpersonal change has occurred.

Consider the same interaction with different feedback from the therapist after the first few exchanges.

Jim: I got the impression from our last session that I should go ahead and ask my boss for two weeks off. So I did, and he gave it to me.

Clark: Sounds like you made a decision to be assertive.

Jim: I also made an appointment to talk to my doctor about antidepressant medication because it sounded like that may be helpful as well.

Clark: It looks like you're working really hard to get better by following through on the things we talk about.

Jim:	I'm trying to. I really want to feel better and make good use of our time.
Clark:	Your motivation to get better will be helpful in this process, and it seems like you are working hard outside the office.
Jim:	Well, I came here to get better and I believe you can help me, so I want to follow through.
Clark:	Following through on recommendations is helpful, yet there is a sense in which you're working hard to do what you think I want you to do.
Jim:	Oh, I don't think so.
Clark:	Well, it may be useful to consider multiple desires—some to get better and some to do what you think I may want you to do.

In the second interaction the therapist acknowledges Jim's follow-through and motivation but also comments on his desire for approval. While this poses some risk to raising Jim's defenses, it also provides an avenue for further exploration about how Jim seeks to alleviate his own distress through eliciting approval from others. Therapeutic gain is a possibility in this interaction.

A second way clients re-create their interpersonal struggles in therapy is through testing behavior (Teyber, 2006). Eliciting strategies are client-initiated attempts to avoid interpersonal anxiety by eliciting responses from the therapist that reenact patterns of behavior. Testing behavior involves strategies to approach their anxiety by facing into the interpersonal dilemmas. At times clients see therapy as a good place to try something new, to try and develop alternate coping strategies. Unfortunately, they don't announce their attempts at this but instead just enact testing behavior. These tests are designed to assess safety in the therapeutic relationship and frequently occur toward the beginning of therapy.

A therapist can fail a test by unwittingly invalidating the client's attempt to change. In this case, both the client and the therapist lose. The client loses because the attempt at new interpersonal behavior was not successful in leading to new interpersonal responses. The therapist loses because the client temporarily feels unsafe in the relationship and may be less likely to initiate subsequent new behaviors. Conversely, a therapist can pass a test and promote growth in the client, in which case both client and therapist are "winners." Consider the testing behavior in a session with Jim (described above), who has an interpersonal pattern of alleviating anxiety by moving toward others and being compliant, which, in turn, typically elicits approval and appreciation from others.

Clark: How have things gone for you this week, Jim?

Jim: They went okay, but I thought more about your suggestion to make
            an appointment with my doctor and decided not to do it at this
            time.

Clark: You know there is a lot of evidence indicating that antidepressant
            medication can be very helpful in treating the symptoms of depres-
            sion.

Jim: I know, but I thought I would keep trying to work through this for
            a while.

Clark: You really should talk to your doctor about your symptoms.

Jim: Well, maybe I can do that next week.

Clark: It's really at the top of the list of what you should be doing outside
            of our sessions. I'll ask you about your doctor's appointment again
            next time.

The testing behavior in this scenario involved Jim not following through on
a suggestion by the therapist. Rather than being compliant and doing what was
asked, he was testing the therapist to see what would happen if he didn't comply. His response "maybe I can do that next week" is quite noncommittal and
indicates the old desire to please the therapist by doing what he asks, but also
reveals his feeble attempt to be noncompliant and to assert his own ideas. The
therapist's response is harsh and stern, likely reenacting the similar responses
from earlier authority figures. Both Jim and his therapist lose. An alternative interaction may have proceeded in the following manner.

Clark: How have things gone for you this week, Jim?

Jim: They went okay, but I thought more about your suggestion to make
            an appointment with my doctor and decided not to do it at this
            time.

Clark: It sounds like you gave that suggestion some serious thought and
            decided not to follow through now.

Jim: Yeah, I think I'll continue to work on the therapy for awhile.

Clark: That's your decision Jim, but let's keep an eye on your symptoms
            and talk about alternatives if the symptoms continue to persist.

Jim: Okay.

The same testing behavior occurs, but this time the therapist validates the client's autonomy and desire to attempt noncompliance. The therapist passes the

test by not insisting that the client follow his suggestion, and the client obtains a different response than anticipated from the therapist. The likelihood of attempting other new responses with the security of the therapist's support is heightened.

This scenario is particularly delicate. It is not typical for therapists to affirm a client for not following through on a suggestion. It seems counterintuitive (if you didn't want him to do it, then don't recommend it in the first place). But in this case, knowing that the client's default style is to comply and please others calls for the therapist to respond differently when the client attempts a new response. Also, this is a delicate example because it deals with medication in the treatment of depression. Obviously if the symptoms of depression are profound there comes a time when a therapist should insist on a medication evaluation regardless of the client's testing behavior. In that situation the therapist runs the risk of promoting the best symptomatic treatment (medication) but potentially reenacting an interpersonal pattern from the patient's past whereby the client is passive and compliant while others insist on action.

A third way in which interpersonal dynamics are re-created in psychotherapy is through transference and countertransference. There is a long history to the concept of transference in psychotherapy. In the late 1800s Freud began treating hysterical patients with what became known as psychoanalysis. He discovered that many of his patients developed unrealistic feelings for him, both positive and negative. Some fell in love with him and some seemed to hate him. These feelings, he believed, stemmed from strong feelings these patients had toward parental figures, and they were transferred onto him in the midst of a close relationship. He found that if he could remain detached and analyze the transference he could make interpretations to the patients that helped them get better. The interpretations helped the patients redirect their strong feelings to the appropriate source (the parent), and thus the symptoms—which developed as a partial and ineffective way of managing the feelings—were no longer necessary. Countertransference described the unrealistic feelings the psychoanalyst had for the patient.

We are not suggesting that IP therapists remain detached as Freud insisted, but we do recommend a careful consideration of transference in understanding interpersonal dynamics. The detachment of psychoanalysts contributed to their perspective that all reactions, feelings and perceptions of the client were distortions of previous significant relationships. A contemporary view is that many client reactions and feelings are reality-based, and although there may be distortions there is likely a kernel of truth to the transference (Teyber, 2006). Transference is common in everyday life. Both of us have taught numerous

---

COUNSELING TIP 11.5: Understanding
Countertransference

Beginning therapists often think of countertransference as a bad thing that always should be eliminated. More experienced therapists learn to value their countertransference feelings as helpful in the therapy process. What does it mean if a client continually evokes feelings of anger or frustration in a therapist? What if a therapist is repeatedly sleepy when working with a particular client? Some clients may evoke in the therapist a desire to rescue or save the person. All of these can provide helpful information about the therapeutic relationship, especially for therapists with a good sense of self-understanding. Countertransference can help the therapist understand how the client is experienced by others and how the therapeutic dynamics may be reenacting previous patterns in the client's life. Rather than disregarding or attempting to eliminate countertransference feelings, it is better to accept the feelings and attempt to understand them in a way that helps move the therapy forward.

---

graduate and undergraduate courses and have had experiences with students in which some of their reactions were partial distortions. We did not fulfill the students' expectations in a lecture, on a test or in an interaction. Sometimes we have been unrealistically glorified and at other times unrealistically vilified. The same phenomenon is experienced in many realms. Pastors in particular are the recipients of parishioners' distorted perceptions.

Transference is recognized by most therapists when a client makes a strong comment or has an extreme reaction to something that seems relatively routine to the therapist. A client may respond to a change in the appointment time or to the way the fees are charged. More specifically, a client may share a story from the past week and feel hurt or elated by the therapist's response to the story. The client's exaggerated reaction is the sign that transference may be operating. Remember that there is often a kernel of truth in the client's reaction, so it is important to explore the reality components as well as the distorted components to these reactions.

To fully understand a transference reaction, it is helpful to have knowledge about a client's history. Who were the significant authority figures from the past? What kind of relationship did the client have with these figures? What feelings may have been internalized from these relationships? What kinds of schemas were created in these relationships? All of this information provides a means of understanding the expectations a client brings to a therapist's office.

In responding to transference it is important not to take the client's reaction personally and not to respond defensively (countertransference). If the therapist responds personally or defensively, the interpersonal dance continues and the old patterns of relating are maintained. The client likely leaves the therapist's office feeling wounded once again by an authority figure or at best misunderstood. The therapist likely finishes the session feeling somewhat inept and certainly misunderstood. The best response is one that opens the door to exploration by the client. Thus, saying something like, "That was a strong reaction" or "You have some strong feelings about that" may provide an opening for further processing. Of course, the therapist has to be open to the kernel of truth in the transference and willing to own part of the client's frustration.

The interpersonal dynamics covered here include eliciting behavior, testing behavior and transference reactions. (There are other interpersonal dynamics, such as projective identification, but a discussion of those dynamics exceeds the purpose of this book.) The dynamics initiated by the client in these ways will re-create old interpersonal patterns. Some of the patterns will be somewhat flexible but familiar ways of responding, while other patterns will be deeply entrenched coping styles that can best be described as personality disorders. The therapeutic response to these dynamics will lead to therapeutic progress or to a therapeutic cul-de-sac (Greenberg & Safran, 1987). Various relational methods have been described to facilitate therapeutic responses, and we now turn to these.

Relational Methods

Figures 7.1, 9.1 and 11.2 all imply a relatively stark distinction between technique-focused interventions and relationship-focused interventions. To some extent this is an oversimplified and artificial distinction because some methods in therapy are simultaneously technique-focused and relationally focused. We refer to these as relational methods.

Christians are no strangers to relational methods. The Bible includes various concepts that have the power to transform relationships. These include forgiveness (Eph 4:32), admonishment (Col 3:16), conflict management (Mt 18:15-17), exhortation (1 Tim 5:1), encouragement (1 Thess 4:18; 5:11) and blessing (Rom 12:14). Christ responded in a variety of ways to hurting people. He had a rational discussion with Nicodemus (Jn 3:1-21), curious open-ended questioning to the disciples on the road to Emmaus (Lk 24:13-35), confrontation with the Pharisees (Mt 12:22-37), compassion with the woman at the well (Jn 4:1-26) and the woman caught in adultery (Jn 8:1-11), and he initially ignored the Canaanite woman whose daughter was afflicted with an evil spirit (Mt 15:21-28). The variety of his responses acknowledges a diversity of needs and situations that call for various redemptive responses.

Additionally, spiritual disciplines such as prayer, meditation and fasting have been endorsed by spiritual directors and clergy for centuries. The point of these disciplines is not merely to encourage pious or ascetic behavior, but to transform one's understanding and experience of God. In other words, they are relational methods that help a person grow in grace and truth.

Broadly speaking, relational methods in psychotherapy can be conceptualized as strategies to provide simultaneous support and confrontation (grace and truth) that are designed to promote psychological growth. Without support a client will not feel valued and instead is likely to withdraw in fear. Without confrontation a client will not be challenged in ways that yield change in thoughts, feelings and behavior. More will be said about the meaning of confrontation below.

Interestingly, the apostle Paul describes a simple yet profound mechanism for growth and maturity that includes the concepts of support and confrontation. Ephesians 4:14-15 states: "Then we will no longer be infants, tossed back and forth by the waves, and blown here and there by every wind of teaching and by the cunning and craftiness of men in their deceitful scheming. Instead, *speaking the truth in love,* we will in all things grow up into him who is the Head, that is, Christ" (NIV, italics added). Paul recommends speaking the truth in love as a way of promoting maturity in the church. It is so easy to speak truth without love and in so doing offend and hurt others. It is unfortunate that people have been abused with "the truth" by well-intentioned people. On the other hand, some speak love without truth; that is, they do not want to hurt others or say anything that could be construed as intolerant. The challenge is to speak the truth in love—to honestly convey ourselves in a loving manner, to be filled with both grace and truth. Paul says that this type of speech, characterized by support and confrontation, produces growth in relationships in the church. We believe this principle is likely to produce growth in many relationships outside the church as well.

Acknowledging that there is no precise formula or set of responses that the Bible teaches, we describe four relational methods from the professional literature that are particularly salient to soul care and relational intervention in IP. The methods can be thought of as ways to speak the truth in love, or to provide support and confrontation. The first three methods are widely acknowledged within a broad spectrum of theoretical orientations, while the fourth has its origins in family systems theory.

Empathy. Empathy is the ability to communicate an accurate understanding of the client's experience to the client. It involves seeing the world through the

IN THE OFFICE 11.2: The Additive Quality of Empathy

Researchers who explore the components of psychotherapy indicate that effective empathy adds something to the client's experience. Beginning therapists have a tendency to erroneously believe that empathy is just paraphrasing the client's statements. Effective empathy is much more than parroting or paraphrasing; it adds to the client's understanding of the problem.

Steve: My mom was really out of line in the way she treated my wife. We had the whole family over for Thanksgiving dinner, and my mom kept interfering with what my wife was planning for the meal. My wife had everything planned for the dinner and we don't have a big house, so it was upsetting to her when my mom stepped in.

Clark: She was intruding into your wife's domain and taking charge.

Steve: Yeah, she acted like it was her own kitchen and just took over.

Clark: Your wife must have felt frustrated that what she had planned wasn't working out the way she thought it should.

Steve: She finally stopped trying to compete with my mom in the kitchen and just let my mom take over.

Clark: Wow, it sounds like she was hurt and probably angry by the way the day unfolded.

Steve: Yeah, she cried after they left. She said she didn't want to try that again next year.

Clark: It was a defeat to her. Perhaps she was looking at this as an opportunity to make a good impression on your family as well as a chance to prepare a good-tasting meal.

Steve: I think you're right. She has so much wanted to please my family, especially my mom . . . you know . . . to kind of be the daughter they never had.

Clark: So in addition to being hurt, frustrated and angry about the way the dinner went, she felt disappointed that she couldn't please them with her efforts. It's like she wasn't good enough for them.

The additive quality of empathy expands Steve's understanding of the situation. Simply paraphrasing may not have led to Steve's grasp of the magnitude of his wife's hurt and disappointment.

client's eyes and communicating that view back to the client. When this is accomplished clients feel understood and no longer need to convince the therapist of their experiences. Rogers (1957) wrote that empathy is "to sense the client's private world as if it were your own, but without ever losing the 'as if' quality—this is empathy, and this seems essential to therapy. To sense the client's anger, fear, or confusion as if it were your own, yet without your own anger, fear, or confusion getting bound up in it, is the condition we are endeavoring to describe" (p. 99).

Empathy provides support to the client. With empathy a client can feel heard and understood. A client can also feel safe because there is a sense that the therapist retains the "as if" quality. The therapist is not lost in a morass of feelings with the client but maintains an external perspective simultaneous with a client's perspective. Though we resist any metaphor that makes therapists seem Godlike, it is worth noting that empathy is similar to how God holds us in love. God is personal, knows our private world and can understand our pain. Yet God is transcendent and retains an external, superordinate perspective. In therapy, empathy facilitates a therapeutic alliance and provides the safety necessary to keep the client's defenses down. The net result is that empathy provides a context for relational growth and transformational change in IP.

Confrontation. Confrontation in the context of psychotherapy does not carry the same meaning as it does in most contexts. It does not mean pinning a person down and forcing him or her to "see the light." Nor does it mean pointing out a client's problems with sufficient evidence that the person cannot continue to deny the problems. Confrontation in psychotherapy means gently pointing out inconsistencies or discrepancies to the client. Inconsistencies may occur in what is said: "Joan, you said that you wanted to leave him, but now I hear you saying that you want to stay with him." Or an inconsistency may be in the way something is said: "Fred, you say that you care about your wife, but the expression on your face looks contemptuous." Or the discrepancy may be between what a person says and what he or she does, or between seemingly mutually exclusive thoughts or feelings. The fact of the matter is that all of us sometimes think, act and feel in inconsistent ways, and when we gain clarity on these aspects of our experience we have the potential for personal integration and growth.

The discrepancy that is perhaps the most relevant to working with clients who have personality disorders is the inconsistency between intent and impact of behavior. As described in the previous chapter, clients with personality disorders seem to be unaware of the inflexibility of their behavior, and as a result, the intent of their behavior does not match the impact of their behavior. The histrionic person may intend to be friendly but does not see her behavior as flirtatious. The paranoid person may intend to be cautious and vigilant but not realize that his behavior is seen as odd by others. The dependent person may intend to be caring but not realize that his behavior is clingy and obnoxious. In a self-serving manner, the intent is viewed positively through various defense mechanisms. A relationally focused intervention in IP involves confronting the discrepancy between the intent and impact of the behavior.

It is important to determine what is being confronted in a relationally focused intervention. It is unhelpful when the client feels confronted as a whole person. That leads to feelings of invalidation and a reenactment of early trauma or conflicted relationships. What is helpful is a two-step confrontation process. First, the impact of the client's actions is confronted to elevate the client's awareness of his/her behavior. It is helpful to have the client ask others how their specific behaviors are perceived. This is particularly useful in marital therapy when a spouse can ask the partner how his or her behavior impacts the relationship. This can be a sobering insight for the client who has focused on the intent of the behavior rather than the impact. It is similar to coming to grips with the reality of one's sinfulness to see that what had been perceived as appropriate behavior really has a hurtful impact on others.

This confrontation is similar to what is recorded about Christ's confrontation with the Pharisees. Christ seemed to confront their behavior and its impact on others rather than to pursue their intentions. The Pharisees had many justifications for their behavior, and pursuing their intentions would likely lead to defensiveness and further self-justification while confronting their behavior and the consequences of it seemed to yield more possibility of change.

Once the impact of the client's behavior is confronted, it is quite natural for the person to slip into self-justification by focusing on the intent.

Mark: Jon, how did you respond to Mandy looking through your e-mail files without being invited to do so?

Jon: I felt pretty terrible about it—like she doesn't trust me. No, it was more than that. It's like she doesn't respect me either. I felt like I wanted to turn and run from this relationship.

Mandy: That's not what I meant at all. I just needed to know that our relationship is still good—you know, that I'm still enough for Jon. I wanted to be sure I wasn't competing with another woman.

It is natural, almost automatic, for a person to focus on intent when confronted with impact. The second step in the confrontation process is to help the client resist this tendency and to stay focused on the impact of the behavior.

This forces the client to view the behavior from the perspective of the partner in the relationship and thus facilitates empathy. For example:

Mark: Mandy, before we think more about what you intended, it would be good to linger here a bit with how Jon experienced it. Try saying back to Jon the impact this had on him.

Mandy: Well, I guess you felt I had crossed a boundary, Jon. I didn't mean it that way, but you felt that way, huh?

Jon: Yeah, I really did. You were trying to see if our relationship is still good, but it made me think it isn't.

Cognitive therapy techniques can be useful at this point in the relational confrontation. For example, clients could be instructed to write down the impact of their behavior on others and to record their feelings while focusing on the impact statements. Additionally, cognitive techniques can be useful in confronting the self-serving dysfunctional intentions. For example, a person who has abused others could be asked to confront the statement "she really did want it; she liked it." The dependent person could be instructed to confront the statement "I'm being helpful when I take care of all of the needs of others." The histrionic person could confront the statement "people really think I'm cute when I wear revealing clothes." The specificity of cognitive therapy in pinpointing dysfunctional ideas can be very useful in this aspect of relationship-focused IP.

Interpretation. An interpretation involves connecting current behavior, feelings and images to previous ones in the client's life. In its original use, interpretation connoted making something conscious that was unconscious. This is not the meaning of interpretation here. The idea of interpretation in IP is akin to what Hamilton (1990) calls "parallels." A therapist draws parallels between current reactions and past reactions. The past reactions typically come from experiences in the client's family of origin, so current relational dynamics parallel the previous relational issues.

When clients re-create their interpersonal problems in therapy through reenactment, testing or transference, they are not aware usually of the connection between their current reactions and the coping strategies learned in childhood. An interpretation makes the connection for the client. In the sense that clients are not aware of these connections, there is an unconscious aspect to it. But clients usually acknowledge the previous coping strategies, and when interpretations are timely clients see the connection. So, rather than revealing the unconscious, an interpretation simply raises awareness.

The key to making a therapeutic interpretation is the timing of it. Ideally an interpretation is not provided by the therapist but rather is made by the client.

IN THE OFFICE 11.3: Parallels Between the Past and the Present

An interpretation connects the client's current experience with past experiences so that the client can make sense of the situation or relationship. Drawing a parallel and allowing the client to make the interpretation leads to insight and the potential for new interpersonal behavior.

Kim: I was really hurt by Dr. Corning's comments on my paper. He could have just said that my paper wasn't well written, but he actually said that I didn't work very hard on the paper. I'm angry about his comment.

Clark: It sounds like his comment really offended you.

Kim: Yeah, it did. It was unnecessary and it isn't true. I worked hard on that paper. I guess it doesn't make any difference, though; I decided to drop the class. I don't have to put up with him.

Clark: That's a strong response. Are you sure it wouldn't be worth it to talk to him about the comment on your paper before you decide to drop the class?

Kim: I could, but I just don't want to have any more contact with him. Honestly, I don't know if I feel very safe around him.

Clark: I wonder if there is a parallel between your feeling unsafe now and some of your experiences from the past.

Kim: What do you mean?

Clark: Sometimes strong reactions, no matter how well founded, indicate hurtful experiences from the past. I know that you had some significant struggles with your dad, and so I wonder if there are some parallels to your situation with Dr. Corning.

Kim: I know that my dad was difficult to get along with and I felt like I was never close to him.

Clark: You mentioned in one of our previous sessions that you felt judged by your dad, like you couldn't meet his expectations and that you weren't good enough for him.

Kim: Yeah, and that's what I'm feeling now with Dr. Corning. He's judging me unfairly.

In a well-timed interpretation a therapist draws the parallel and suggests a connection, but encourages the client to verbalize the actual similarities.

The effective therapist leads a client to the connection between the present and the past but allows the client to put the connection into his or her own words. In psychoanalytic terms, an interpretation works because it reveals an unconscious conflict, and insight into the conflict releases the cathected psychic energy that had been bound in the conflict and makes the energy available for other psychic activities. In IP terms, an interpretation works because it helps a client realize that conflicts from the past still operate in the present, and the conflicts tend to be relational in nature. People unwittingly engage others in conflicts and fail to see that the conflicts in current relationships are often related to those from their past. Insight into the connection provides the client with the opportunity to take responsibility for the current relationship conflicts.

As mentioned at the beginning of this section, empathy, confrontation and interpretation are methods common to several models of psychotherapy, so one may wonder what is truly relational about these methods. The relational function of these methods pertains to their purpose, which is to affect the relational dynamics of the client-therapist relationship. If the methods facilitate insight and further processing of the relational dynamics that culminates in growth, then the methods have served their purpose. But this relational purpose in IP is different than the purpose of these methods in other systems. In some psychotherapy models empathy is used only to promote a therapeutic alliance so that the "real" work of therapy can occur. Confrontation may serve merely as the refutation of irrational beliefs, and interpretation may serve resolution of intrapsychic conflicts in other systems of psychotherapy. In IP these methods serve to bring the relational dynamics between the therapist and the client into sharper focus so that interpersonal transformation can occur.

Role behavior changes. The concept of role behavior change comes from the family systems literature. People get stuck in interpersonal conflict because they are confined by their determined relational roles. As described in the previous chapter, we learn behavioral patterns early in life that serve to stabilize significant relationships. Consider the boy who is described as a risk-taking adventurer in a family that is otherwise safety- and security-conscious. This boy fulfills a systemic function for adventure in the family that balances an otherwise rather stale existence. The family subtly encourages the risk-taking by pointing it out, describing it to others and smiling about it. The boy internalizes this role and feels good when acting in an adventuresome manner. In short, part of his identity involves seeing himself as impetuous.

It would not be unusual for such a boy to continue living out this role in college and enjoy pranks and other behavior "on the edge." It would feel normal and familiar to the young adult. This "fun" behavior may actually attract the attention of young women and the man may eventually marry a woman who is a little cautious. He appreciates the caution and careful attitude she brings to the relationship, and she appreciates the fun and spontaneity he brings. These roles may work well through the early years of marriage but will likely run amok when a child is born. Such a major change in the relationship will call for different role behaviors from the young father. His risk-taking, adventuresome behavior may now be interpreted as self-indulgent. His joy of spontaneity is now seen as immature. His wife may tell him he needs to be home more to help out with the needs of the child and to do things that the three of them can enjoy, not just activities for his own interest. The early role behavior is no longer working, and conflicts are evident in the relationship.

Duvall (1977) proposed a model of the family life cycle, contending that couples move through stages of development over the span of their relationship. The eight commonly accepted stages are: married couple, childbearing family, preschool children, school children, teenagers, launching children, middle-aged parents, aging family members. Each stage requires a transition for the couple to negotiate in order to successfully move to the next stage of development. For example, the couple must accept the child's independent adult role to successfully transition from the launching stage to the middle-aged parent stage. When transitions are not negotiated successfully, relational problems are inevitable (Goldenberg & Goldenberg, 2000.) The family life cycle model has been elaborated and expanded over the years to include various family structures (Carter and McGoldrick, 1999).

Clients seek therapy because of relationship struggles ("We are constantly fighting"; "I can't get him to do anything around the house;" "She is always complaining about something"). Often these struggles are related to the transitions that couples go through in the family life cycle. Relationships are hard work; they require patience, good communication and negotiating skills. A person who rigidly adheres to a pattern of relating developed early in life is likely to face many relationship struggles later in life.

Each transition to the next stage of family life involves negotiation between spouses. For example, "developing parent roles" implies a negotiation of what it means for each spouse to be a parent. This requires an examination of who does the chores and who provides for the child's needs (especially in the middle of the night). Family therapists describe this examination, which may occur in a more covert than overt manner, as a re-negotiation of the rules and roles in the relationship. The rules of the relationship have to change to successfully manage the next stage of development.

Maggie came to therapy with significant symptoms of depression. She wasn't

COUNSELING TIP 11.6: Second-Order Change

Family systems theory refers to the changes necessary to successfully move through the developmental stages as second-order changes or positive feedback. These changes involve alterations in the rules that govern a relationship, and therefore they are more significant and long-lasting than first-order changes. It is called positive feedback because the relationship itself changes after the issue is resolved. First-order changes are more superficial and temporary, and they are the result of negative feedback. This is not negative in the sense that something negative has been said, but negative in the sense that the relationship remains the same even after the issue is resolved. First-order changes may lead to good feelings, but they don't lead to substantial changes in the way the relationship operates.

For example, a husband got into an argument with his wife about the chores around the house, and the next day he felt bad, apologized for the things he said and bought her some flowers. His wife may feel good and appreciate his kindness, but his response is likely a reflection of negative feedback. The immediate problem is resolved, but nothing fundamental has changed about the relationship. The issue at hand is addressed, but not the rules in the relationship regarding chores that led to the argument. If the husband initiated a conversation that led to a new way of negotiating chores around the house, that would be positive feedback. The rules that govern this area of the relationship would have changed.

In therapy we seek second-order changes in clients. We want them to discuss and change the rules of their behavior in relationships, not simply to seek a superficial détente.

sleeping well, didn't have an appetite and couldn't muster the energy to do much more than shower and get dressed. She described the intense guilt she felt about not providing for her husband and two-year-old daughter in the way she expected. She derided herself for feeling exhausted and withdrawing from others. She indicated that her relationship with her husband was strained; they were fighting often and had little intimacy. When her husband threatened to leave if she didn't get help, she came to therapy.

Working in domain 1 a therapist could address automatic thoughts that spring into Maggie's mind whenever she sleeps in, doesn't cook a meal or fails to do the shopping ("A good mother would always cook and shop without fail"). Work in domain 2 would help Maggie understand the negative meanings she assigns to these thoughts. She would be encouraged to look at where these schemas come from, what she learned from her family of origin about being a good mother, the way her mother functioned in the family, and the kinds of subtle messages given to her about being a wife and mother. Domain 3 work would look at Maggie's tendencies to reenact roles learned earlier in life and at the current transition in her family life—moving from couplehood to parenthood and the kinds of rule negotiations necessary for this successful transition. She would be encouraged to explore the relational rules in her marriage and whether changes in these rules would be helpful in alleviating the depression. Typically her husband would be asked to join the therapy to participate in the examination and renegotiation of the rules to facilitate her adjustment to motherhood.

In addition to the natural stages of change in families described by Duvall (1977), there are other major life transitions that require changes in the rules and expectations of relationships. Retirement, major illnesses, caring for a chronically ill family member or learning to deal with a drug-abusing family member are examples of life issues that require new ways of relating to others. When people adapt to these situations, they demonstrate new ways of getting their needs met and meeting the needs of others. When people cannot relate in new ways, they get stuck and their emotional growth is stunted.

In IP the therapist recognizes these natural changes in family life and realizes that new role behaviors are needed to promote relational growth. The method of role changes requires an open discussion of the demands on a couple's current relationship and the ways each partner contributes to the relational conflicts. By relating in persistent patterns with each other the couple's problem-solving ability stagnates. By attempting new ways of relating they open fresh avenues to problem resolution.

Conclusion

While the targets of change in domain 1 are automatic thoughts related to symptoms and the targets of change in domain 2 are the schemas related to personal meanings, the targets of change in domain 3 are the relationships of the client. In order to bring about relational change, the therapeutic relationship becomes extremely important. Transformation within the therapeutic relationship becomes possible as the therapist assesses and responds differently than significant others from the client's past. Changes in the client's relational expectations and behaviors set the groundwork for transformational change in other current relationships.

Domain 3 work is associated with relational views of the *imago Dei*. All persons are created to be in relationship, and so we function most fully when we treat one another in ways that honor the God-image in each of us. Jesus—the visible image of the invisible God—provides the clearest picture of how we can relate to one another. In Jesus we see grace and truth revealed in human form. Jesus is the goal—we should set our gaze on him as the author of Hebrews reminds us (Heb 12:2). The various theories and findings of psychology can be useful as we translate the relational capacities of Christ into this specific sort of soul care known as psychotherapy.

References

Beck, A. T., Rush, A. J., Shaw, B. F., & Emery, G. (1979). *Cognitive therapy of depression*. New York: Guilford.

Benner, D. G. (1988). *Psychotherapy and the spiritual quest*. Grand Rapids, MI: Baker Books.

Benner, D. G. (1998). *Care of souls: Revisioning Christian nurture and counsel*. Grand Rapids, MI: Baker Books.

Benner, D. G. (2002). *Sacred companions: The gift of spiritual friendship & direction*. Downers Grove, IL: InterVarsity Press.

Benner, D. G. (2005). Intensive soul care: Integrating psychotherapy and spiritual direction. In L. Sperry & E. P. Shafranske (Eds.), *Spiritually oriented psychotherapy* (pp. 287-306). Washington, DC: American Psychological Association.

Bion, W. R. (1962). *Learning from experience*. London: Heinemann.

Bordin, E. S. (1979). The generalizability of the psychoanalytic concept of the working alliance. *Psychotherapy: Theory, Research & Practice, 16*, 252-60.

Bowlby, J. (1988). *A secure base: Parent-child attachment and healthy human development*. New York: Basic Books.

Brunner, E. (1932/1947). *The mediator: A study of the central doctrine of the Christian faith* (O. Wyon, Trans.). Philadelphia: Westminster Press.

Carter, B., & McGoldrick, M. (1999). *The expanded family life cycle: Individual, family, and social perspectives* (3rd ed.). Boston: Allyn & Bacon.

Charry, E. T. (2001). Theology after psychology. In M. R. McMinn & T. R. Phillips (Eds.), *Care for the soul: Exploring the interface of psychology & theology* (pp. 118-33). Downers Grove, IL: InterVarsity Press.

Clebsch, W. A., & Jaekle, C. R. (1964). *Pastoral care in historical perspective: An essay with exhibits*. Englewood Cliffs, NJ: Prentice-Hall.

Duvall, E. M. (1977). *Marriage and family development* (5th ed.). New York: Lippincott.

Emmons, R. A. (1999). *The psychology of ultimate concerns: Motivation and spirituality in personality*. New York: Guilford.

Erickson, M. J. (1985). *Christian theology*. Grand Rapids, MI: Baker Book House.

Goldenberg, I., & Goldenberg, H. (2000). *Family therapy: An overview* (5th ed.). Belmont, CA: Brooks/Cole.

Greenberg, L. S., & Safran, J. D. (1987). *Emotion in psychotherapy: Affect, cognition and the process of change*. New York: Guilford.

Grenz, S. J. (2000). *Renewing the center: Evangelical theology in a post-theological era*. Grand Rapids, MI: Baker Academic.

Hamilton, N. G. (1990). *Self and others: Object relations theory in practice*. Northvale, NJ: Aronson.

McMinn, M. R., & Phillips, T. R. (Eds.) (2001). *Care for the soul: Exploring the intersection of psychology & theology*. Downers Grove, IL: InterVarsity Press.

McWilliams, N. (1994). *Psychoanalytic diagnosis: Understanding personality structure in the clinical process*. New York: Guilford.

Moon, G. W., & Benner, D. G. (Eds.). (2004). *Spiritual direction and the care of souls: A guide to Christian approaches and practices*. Downers Grove, IL: InterVarsity Press.

Moore, T. (1992). *Care of the soul: A guide for cultivating depth and sacredness in everyday life*. New York: HarperCollins.

Norcross, J. C. (Ed.) (2002). *Psychotherapy relationships that work: Therapist contributions and responsiveness to patients*. New York: Oxford University Press.

Rogers, C. R. (1957). The necessary and sufficient conditions of therapeutic personality change. *Journal of Consulting Psychology, 21*, 95-103.

Safran, J. D. (1998). *Widening the scope of cognitive therapy: The therapeutic relationship, emotion, and the process of change*. Northvale, NJ: Aronson.

Sperry, L. (2004). Spiritual direction and psychotherapy. In G. W. Moon & D. G. Benner (Eds.), *Spiritual direction and the care of souls: A guide to Christian approaches and practices* (pp. 171-86). Downers Grove, IL: InterVarsity Press.

Strupp, H. H. (1993). The Vanderbilt psychotherapy studies: Synopsis. *Journal of Consulting and Clinical Psychology, 61*, 431-33.

Strupp, H. H. (2001). Implications of the empirically supported treatment movement for psychoanalysis. *Psychoanalytic Dialogues, 11*, 605-19.

Strupp, H. H., & Hadley, S. W. (1979). Specific versus nonspecific factors in psychotherapy: A controlled study of outcome. *Archives of General Psychiatry, 36*, 1125-36.

Tan, S-Y. (2004). Spiritual direction and psychotherapy: Ethical issues. In G. W. Moon & D. G. Benner (Eds.), *Spiritual direction and the care of souls: A guide to Christian approaches and practices* (pp. 187-204). Downers Grove, IL: InterVarsity Press.

Teyber, E. (2006). *Interpersonal process in therapy: An integrative model.* Belmont, CA: Brooks/Cole.

Tjeltveit, A. C. (2004). Understanding human beings in the light of grace: The possibility and promise of theology-informed psychologies. *Consensus: A Canadian Lutheran Journal of Theology, 29*(2), 99-122.

Watzlawick, P., Beavin, J. H., & Jackson, D. D. (1967). *Pragmatics of human communication.* New York: Norton.

Willard, D. (2002). Renovation of the heart: Putting on the character of Christ. Colorado Springs: NavPress.

12

Concluding Thoughts

IN THE PRECEDING CHAPTERS, WE HAVE ARTICULATED an integrative Christian approach to psychotherapy. It is an ambitious endeavor, and one that has much importance in a time when, unfortunately, the influence of psychotherapy seems to be growing more rapidly than the influence of the church in much of the developed world. We conclude by considering three key concepts embedded in this book's title: integrative, psychotherapy and "toward a comprehensive Christian approach." Each of these three terms or phrases denotes an essential part of IP while also implying limitations to the approach we have presented.

Integrative

IP is integrative in two dimensions: theoretical and theological. It brings together various theories in psychology, and it integrates a Christian view of persons with psychological theory and practice. Both dimensions are crucial in understanding the theory and practice of IP.

Regarding theoretical integration, Jones and Butman (1991) describe various ways of combining different approaches to counseling and psychotherapy. With *chaotic eclecticism*, therapists draw from an assortment of therapeutic methods without much thought about their theoretical assumptions, how the various methods fit together or even what is in the client's best interests. The choice seems to rest on the therapist's whims more than anything. Perhaps a counselor has just attended a workshop on a new therapy technique, and so the therapist then uses the new technique with every client for the next month without thinking through the relational, theoretical and theological implications. *Pragmatic eclecticism* is when therapists select methods from various theoretical systems based on what seems to help clients the most. This is a very common form of eclecticism among practicing clinicians, and the rationale is quite compelling. They choose methods that effectively help clients feel and function better. But there are various problems with pragmatic eclecticism: it lacks a theoretical core that helps make sense of the various methods being employed in counseling, it presumes that clinicians stay abreast of the scientific outcome literature and that the clients seen in the scientific laboratory setting are similar to clients in more diverse practice settings, and it is based on the optimistic belief that therapists are capable of mastering many different approaches to therapy. In *transtheoretical eclecticism,* the therapist identifies a common thread that runs through virtually all approaches to psychotherapy. A transtheoretical approach is seen in the work of Carl Rogers (1957), who attempted to identify necessary and sufficient conditions for change in psychotherapy; Jerome Frank (1973), who described nonspecific factors that are common to all therapies; and Prochaska and his colleagues, who described processes of change (Prochaska & DiClemente, 1983, 1984, 1985; Prochaska & Norcross, 1994). *Theoretical integrationism* occurs when a person begins with a particular theoretical starting point and then extends the theoretical base by incorporating one or more additional theories (see Norcross & Goldfried, 2005). For example, Ryle (1990) has expanded a cognitive therapy framework in order to incorporate psychodynamic ideas, Pinsof (1995) has integrated several theoretical models into a comprehensive approach, and various psychodynamic therapists have incorporated the cognitive-behavioral idea of treatment goals into time-limited dynamic therapy (e.g., Levenson, 1995; Strupp and Binder, 1984).

After describing these various forms of eclecticism, Jones and Butman (1991) conclude that theoretical integrationism is the "approach of choice for the Christian counselor" (p. 395). They assert that the Christian faith offers a cohesive core which allows us to critique the various psychotherapeutic systems and to build an integrated model for therapy. We agree.

IP is an example of theoretical integrationism, but with a twist made possible by having coauthors trained in different theoretical orientations. One of us was trained in behavioral and cognitive therapy and has, over time, grown to appreciate more relational approaches to therapy. The other was trained in interpersonal and family therapy and has gained interest and specialized training in cognitive therapy over time. Thus, our starting points were disparate and complementary. IP represents the expanded and overlapping theoretical base that both of us have developed over years of practice.

IP is also integrative in a theological dimension, reflecting something parallel to what Jones and Butman call transtheoretical eclecticism, but from a theological rather than a psychological vantage point. Whereas most transtheoretical psychologists tend to look for common psychological elements of the various psychotherapies, we have attempted to look for a common theological theme that helps explain the effectiveness of various counseling and therapy models. The doctrine of creation—being made in the image of God—serves the core of

IP, though it is also important to understand the Christian themes of sin and re-demption. Three views of the *imago Dei*—functional, structural and relational—form the bases for the three domains of IP.

Herein lays both strength and limitation in our approach to integrative psy-chotherapy. The strengths of basing our model on a Christian view of persons are outlined throughout this book, especially in chapters one and four. The lim-itation is that we have presented a narrow view of the *imago Dei* by confining its application to psychotherapy. This can be seen in each of the three views. We have appropriated functional views of the *imago Dei* to personal matters of self-control and self-management, but the concept in Genesis 1:28 is much larger: "God blessed them and told them, 'Multiply and fill the earth and subdue it. Be masters over the fish and birds and all the animals.'" Mastering one's anxiety, de-pression and relational patterns is part of managing God's creation, but only a small part. A larger view would take us well beyond the work of psychotherapy, outside our areas of expertise and beyond the page limits for a book such as this. A comprehensive discussion of managing creation would also involve zoologists, environmental scientists, economists, demographers, geologists, botanists and so on. Similarly, we have limited our discussion of the structural image of God to schemas—a concept of great importance in psychotherapy, but one that pales in comparison to the larger conversations about human ontology. A thorough en-gagement with structural views of the *imago Dei* would involve philosophers, mathematicians, theologians, artists and others. Finally, we have limited our dis-cussion of the relational image of God to the sort of relationships encountered in psychotherapy. This is also quite limited when one considers the breadth and depth of various relationships, all of which are made possible because the rela-tional *imago Dei* is woven into the fabric of human nature.

Psychotherapy

At the crux of every life is the question of transformation. What causes a person to move from point A to point B? How does a cantankerous, difficult person evolve into a person with solid friendships and new social graces? How does a problem drinker reduce alcohol consumption, or a smoker stop smoking? Why does depression give way to hope, and anxiety to peace? How does a person learn to draw close to God in prayer? How can people learn to handle anger better, or lust or greed or contempt? These questions are for psychotherapists and spiritual leaders, but they are for everyone else too because each of us wants to change and grow in various ways.

Transformation occurs in many ways. Good sermons, kind words of affirma-tion, suffering, prayer, medication, meditation, encouraging smiles, criticism,

solitude, effective parenting, ineffective parenting, charitable giving and comforting hugs are all means by which change occurs. And, of course, the list could
go on page after page. Psychotherapy is only one means of transformation, but
in today's society it has become an important and ubiquitous one. Even within
the church there appears to be a strong and growing interest in counseling and
psychotherapeutic ministries, though suspicions about psychology persist in
many congregations and denominations. Church-based counseling ministries
are now commonplace, most pastors and church leaders have a referral network
of therapists in their community, seminaries offer courses and degrees in counseling, and support groups and peer-counseling ministries are being established
in many churches. This trend is encouraging insofar as it helps the church care
for whole persons as Jesus ministered to the spiritual, physical, relational and
emotional needs he saw in others.

But there is also a potential for confusion and harm by conflating psychotherapy and the church. Given the popularity of psychological topics, some
have neglected the church's historical testimony of transcendent truth in favor
of a more popular self-oriented perspective. The Gospel (capital G, related to
the life and work of Jesus Christ) is easily replaced with a gospel (lower-case g,
related to one's own life and work) of self-help and self-actualization. We offer
IP as a model of psychotherapy, with the hope and expectation that it *not* transform sermons or ministry practices. The church needs to maintain its distinction
as an institution that proclaims truth and shines the light of God's love in a dark-
ened world. Psychotherapy may be an important part of a church's caring ministry, but it is a peripheral ministry and should not be perceived as central.

Conflating psychotherapy and ecclesiology can also harm those seeking
counseling help within church settings. Good-hearted, ministry-minded individuals without adequate psychological training can do great good, but they can
also do great harm. Dare we suggest that a sizeable portion of the burgeoning
Christian counseling movement is populated with those who are not adequately
trained to provide psychotherapy? Psychotherapy is a unique sort of helping relationship, both conceptually and historically. It comes with a particular set of
regulations established by state and local jurisdictions, certain ethical standards,
training and supervision guidelines, and clinical suitability requirements.

As the title implies, IP is meant for a particular kind of transforming ministry,
and not for others. Specifically, we offer this book for those who are studying
or practicing psychotherapy. Though we welcome the idea of IP being practiced
in ministry settings, it should be limited to those who are qualified and creden-
tialed as pastoral counselors or psychotherapists. We hope this book finds its
way into training programs at seminaries, Christian colleges and universities,

and other places where Christian counselors and psychotherapists receive their training. We also hope it makes it into the hands of practicing psychotherapists who desire to think integratively and Christianly about the work they do.

Toward a Comprehensive Christian Approach

Our subtitle implies movement *toward* a comprehensive Christian approach, though much remains unfinished. Some may question whether we have met the lofty standard of a comprehensive approach. We also have questions about this, described later, though first we point to six ways that IP is more or less comprehensive.

First, IP is comprehensive insofar as both Christianity and psychology are considered when viewing a person. We have made this point throughout the book and will not belabor it here.

Second, IP provides three different domains to consider. Each client is viewed through three lenses—functional, structural and relational—which renders a more complete picture than any of these perspectives alone. The linearity of pages and chapters in a book has required us to present these three domains sequentially, as if functional perspectives dominate the early stages of therapy, structural come next, and then relational. To some extent this is true; functional considerations come early as clients seek to overcome the troubling symptoms that are causing distress, structural perspectives come into focus as therapy moves into the schema-focused work, and relational methods of change are required for long-term therapy. But rather than following a scripted linear approach, skilled therapists are continually moving back and forth between all three domains. Relational considerations are evident from the first moments of the intake session, functional matters are revisited throughout the entire therapy process, and structural perspectives are continually addressed. If each domain was represented by a set of glasses, a beginning therapist might wear functional lenses for the first six sessions, then structural lenses for the next eight, then relational lenses until the therapy is complete. In contrast, an experienced therapist would constantly be switching glasses throughout each session, sometimes wearing two or three pairs at once.

Third, IP is comprehensive in its efforts to bridge multiple dimensions in psychotherapy. Some psychotherapies are primarily oriented in the present, others in the past; IP attempts to bridge this span by considering both. Some psychotherapies focus on emotions, some on cognitions and some on behaviors; in IP we attempt to bring all three into focus. Some therapies see the therapeutic relationship as essential for change, other approaches view therapeutic techniques as central; in IP it is both.

Fourth, IP takes a serious view of science, but without discounting the relational approaches to psychotherapy. An unfortunate split has occurred among clinical psychologists, and we have attempted to position IP in the middle of this split. Some psychologists emphasize the centrality of science and gravitate toward short-term therapies with measurable outcomes. These psychologists are often employed in academia or in research laboratories. Others work in professional practice settings and tend to emphasize therapeutic relationships more than scientific rigor. Unlike the scientists in the research lab, professional practitioners cannot exclude clients who fail to meet particular criteria. For example, a person with an anxiety disorder and a personality disorder might be excluded from a laboratory study because the personality disorder is likely to complicate research results. In contrast, the professional practitioner will choose to work with the client. Pristine research conditions are not necessary or even desired in a practice setting. As a result, clients seen in professional practice settings tend to be more complex than those participating in the research studies. Over time, a not-so-subtle divide has occurred between clinical psychologists. One group values empirical outcome studies for short-term therapies, and the other is less concerned about laboratory science and more interested in relational interventions that work for clients with complex personalities and symptom patterns. IP attempts to bridge this gap by providing both short-term and long-term treatment strategies. Some simple problems can be solved with straightforward therapeutic techniques in a dozen sessions or less. Other problems are more complex and require a relationally focused intervention over a long period of time.

Fifth, any Christian model for soul care is only comprehensive if it is christocentric. Because IP is based on the *imago Dei,* which is perfectly revealed in Christ, IP emphasizes Christology in various ways. Jesus, the Great Physician, cared for whole persons, body and soul, which lends credence to the functional domain interventions offered early in IP and to engaging more than intellect in structural-domain interventions. And in the relational domain we have emphasized a christological core to soul care, described in chapter eleven. Jesus, full of grace and truth, serves as the one perfect exemplar of how we are to treat one another. IP is not merely spiritually sensitive therapy; it is rooted firmly in Christ. Our greatest freedom is discovered by identifying ourselves as beloved children of God, those who are being re-formed into the *imago Dei* that is revealed perfectly in Jesus Christ. "And now, just as you accepted Christ Jesus as your Lord, you must continue to live in obedience to him. Let your roots grow down into him and draw up nourishment from him, so you will grow in faith, strong and vigorous in the truth you were taught. Let your lives overflow with thanksgiving for all he has done" (Col 2:6-7).

Sixth, IP is comprehensive in that it can be used with both Christian and non-Christian clients. This may seem surprising at first glance, but consider the alternative—that a Christian therapist would use one theoretical grid to understand Christian clients and a different theory to understand non-Christian clients. Having two theoretical grids is unnecessary because IP provides a theologically and theoretically informed worldview for Christian psychotherapists regardless of whether this worldview becomes an explicit topic of conversation in therapy. All clients come with functional, structural or relational matters to consider in therapy, and IP helps them understand and address their troubles. Whereas IP is fitting with clients of various faith persuasions, it should not be used by non-Christian therapists because the underlying worldview is thoroughly steeped in Christian doctrine. This is summarized in table 12.1.

Table 12.1. Using IP with Christian and Non-Christian Clients

	Christian Therapist	Non-Christian Therapist
Christian Client	IP is appropriate. Explicit discussions of faith are common and useful.	IP is not appropriate.
Non-Christian Client	IP is appropriate. Initial consent is obtained. Therapist is noncoercive and respects faith differences.	IP is not appropriate.

The upper left quadrant of table 12.1 is the ideal scenario for IP. Both the client and therapist share a Christian worldview, making it natural and comfortable to speak of faith-related issues and concerns in therapy. At times the therapist might use spiritual interventions, such as prayer and Scripture. These should be used prudently, keeping in mind that some clients protect themselves from psychological pain by using spiritual defenses and rituals (McMinn, 1996), but spiritual interventions can be profound if applied properly.

Christian clients are likely to value the doctrinal underpinnings of IP, but the principles of intervention can be used with a wide variety of individuals regardless of their religious and spiritual values. The lower left quadrant of table 12.2 occurs when a Christian therapist is providing help for a non-Christian client. We suggest that IP is still an appropriate intervention under these circumstances because theory guides the therapist more than the client. Many therapists and clients have widely differing worldviews and yet they are able to work together well as long as two conditions are met. The first is consent. Every therapist—religious or not—has a worldview, and every client has a right to know what it is. The IP worldview is unapologetically Christian, and clients ought to be informed of this (see Counseling Tip 5.2). The second condition is respect. Therapists of all faiths need to respect their clients' freedom to hold differing values. Psychotherapy is a particular sort of helping relationship that is easily disrupted and can cause damage if it gets confused with coercion or friendship evangelism. When faith is discussed with non-Christian clients, the therapist bears responsibility to be respectful and noncoercive. If a client expresses interest in learning about or converting to Christianity, it is best to introduce a new relationship in the client's life—with a pastor or priest, for example—rather than changing the nature of the psychotherapeutic relationship to involve religious education.

The upper and lower right quadrants of table 12.1 suggest that IP is not a good choice for non-Christian therapists. A therapist must have confidence in a theory for it to be effective, just as an athlete must have confidence to perform well. It makes no sense for non-Christian therapists to use IP as a theoretical model, because they do not accept the underlying presuppositions regarding creation, fall and redemption.

We have outlined six ways that IP is comprehensive, but in other regards it is not yet comprehensive. For example, most of what we have discussed pertains to individual psychotherapy with adults facing anxiety, mood and personality disorders. Much of our own clinical work focuses in these areas. But other sorts of applications may also be fitting for IP, and these are left relatively unexplored in this book. For example, we have not addressed working with children and adolescents, and have only alluded to marriage and family therapy without describing any detailed strategies. We have opted to present the basic model of IP in this volume by focusing on individual therapy with adults, though we may address more complex variations in subsequent writing.

Further, our discussion of relationally focused interventions in chapters ten and eleven is heavily weighted toward treating those with interpersonal problems and personality disorders. These are fitting applications for domain 3 IP, but there are other uses for domain 3 interventions as well. Some clients have good interpersonal adjustment and no evidence of personality disorder but choose to linger in relationally oriented therapy in order to come to a deeper understanding of their life stories, relational and spiritual yearnings, prolonged grief, addictions, unresolved conflicts and so on. Many difficulties in life do not lend themselves to either diagnosis or healing. In these situations a troubled person often needs a companion to walk alongside rather than an expert to diagnose and treat a problem. These other forms of relationally focused intervention deserve more careful attention than we were able to provide in this introductory text.

A comprehensive psychotherapy should have substantial research support demonstrating its effectiveness. Facets of IP enjoy this sort of support. As described in chapter seven, much of the symptom-focus domain is backed with solid empirical support. These interventions are much easier to research than the more time-intensive domain 2 and 3 interventions. Schema-focused and relationship-focused interventions have some preliminary research support demonstrating their effectiveness, but more is needed.

Finally, no psychotherapy model can be comprehensive until other scholars and clinicians have critiqued it and offered improvements. We publish this book with the hope and expectation that it will generate useful conversation. These conversations may occur in undergraduate and graduate classrooms, at professional conferences, and in the pages of scholarly journals. We welcome review, critique and reappraisal, knowing that every conversation has the potential to improve the IP model and thus serve the cause of Christ. "As iron sharpens iron, a friend sharpens a friend" (Prov 27:17).

References

Frank, J. (1973). *Persuasion and Healing* (rev. ed.). Baltimore: Johns Hopkins University Press.

Jones, S. L., & Butman, R. E. (1991). *Modern psychotherapies: A comprehensive Christian appraisal.* Downers Grove, IL: InterVarsity Press.

Levenson, H. (1995). *Time-limited dynamic psychotherapy: A guide to clinical practice.* New York: Basic Books.

McMinn, M. R. (1996). *Psychology, theology, and spirituality in Christian counseling.* Wheaton, IL: Tyndale House.

Norcross, J. C., & Goldfried, M. R. (2005). *Handbook of psychotherapy integration* (2nd ed.). New York: Oxford University Press.

Pinsof, W. M. (1995). *Integrative problem-centered therapy: A synthesis of family, individual, and biological therapies.* New York: Basic Books.

Prochaska, J. H., & DiClemente, C. C. (1983). Stages and process of self-change of smoking: Toward an integrative model of change. *Journal of Consulting and Clinical Psychology, 51,* 390-95.

Prochaska, J. H., & DiClemente, C. C. (1984). *The transtheoretical approach: Crossing traditional boundaries of change.* Homewood, IL: DowJones/Irwin.

Prochaska, J. H., & DiClemente, C. C. (1985). Common processes of change in smoking, weight control, and psychological distress. In S. Shiffman & T. Wills (Eds.), *Coping and substance abuse.* New York: Academic Press.

Prochaska, J. H., & Norcross, J. C. (1994). *Systems of psychotherapy: A transtheoretical analysis* (3rd ed.). Pacific Grove, CA: Brooks/Cole.

Rogers, C. R. (1957). The necessary and sufficient conditions of therapeutic personality change. *Journal of Consulting Psychology, 21*, 95-103.

Ryle, A. (1990). *Cognitive-analytic therapy: Active participation in change.* New York: Wiley.

Strupp, H. H., & Binder, J. L. (1984). *Psychotherapy in a new key: A guide to time-limited dynamic psychotherapy.* New York: Basic Books.

Name Index

Subject Index

Scripture Index

CAPS
INTERNATIONAL

An Association for Christian Psychologists,
Therapists, Counselors and Academicians

CAPS is a vibrant Christian organization with a rich tradition. Founded in 1956 by a small group of Christian mental health professionals, chaplains and pastors, CAPS has grown to more than 2,100 members in the U.S., Canada and more than 25 other countries.

CAPS encourages in-depth consideration of therapeutic, research, theoretical and theological issues. The association is a forum for creative new ideas. In fact, their publications and conferences are the birthplace for many of the formative concepts in our field today.

CAPS members represent a variety of denominations, professional groups and theoretical orientations; yet all are united in their commitment to Christ and to professional excellence.

CAPS is a non-profit, member-supported organization. It is led by a fully functioning board of directors, and the membership has a voice in the direction of CAPS.

CAPS is more than a professional association. It is a fellowship, and in addition to national and international activities, the organization strongly encourages regional, local and area activities which provide networking and fellowship opportunities as well as professional enrichment.

To learn more about CAPS, visit www.caps.net.

CAPS Books
from IVP Academic

The joint publishing venture between IVP Academic and CAPS aims to promote the understanding of the relationship between Christianity and the behavioral sciences at both the clinical/counseling and the theoretical/research levels. These books will be of particular value for students and practitioners, teachers and researchers.

For more information, visit InterVarsity Press's website at www.ivpress.com, type in *Integrative Psychology,* and follow the links provided there to CAPS books.